FROZEN TOMBS OF SIBERIA

the Pazyryk Burials of Iron Age Horsemen

FROZEN TOMBS OF SIBERIA

the Pazyryk Burials of Iron Age Horsemen

by SERGEI I. RUDENKO

translated and with a preface by M. W. Thompson

with 33 plates in colour, 147 in black-and-white and 146 figures in the text

UNIVERSITY OF CALIFORNIA PRESS

Berkeley and Los Angeles · 1970

Printed in Great Britain
University of California Press
Berkeley and Los Angeles, California

© Translator's Preface, M. W. Thompson, 1970
© Translation, J. M. Dent & Sons Ltd, 1970

Library of Congress Catalog Card Number: 69: 20480

SBN: 520 01395 6

First published in Russian, *Kultura Naseleniya Gornogo Altaya v Skifskoe Vremya*,
Academy of Sciences of the U.S.S.R., Moscow/Leningrad, 1953

First English edition (with author's revisions), 1970

CONTENTS

v

CONTENTS

vi

TEXT FIGURES

ILLUSTRATIONS

PLATES

x

weave; D, woollen cloth of linen weave; E, woollen cloth of lace weave from inner cover of pigtail; F, woollen cloth of lace weave from outer cover of pigtail

134 Examples of cloth: A, piece of patterned silk from barrow 3; B, silk pouch from barrow 3; C, piece of woollen cloth with whole pile loops, from barrow 2

135 Saddle from second riding outfit in barrow 1: A, extended view of top; B, side view

136 Articles sculptured or carved in low relief: A, lion's-head runner of antler from small Katanda barrow; B, bronze open-work belt buckle, deer seized by winged lion-griffin, from barrow near Biysk; C, wooden feline heads on terminals of bag handle from barrow 2; D, tiger's head of antler, runner from barrow at Biysk; E, F, saddle rods with feline head terminals, E from barrow 3, F from fifth riding outfit in barrow 5; G, wooden elk head with leather antlers, pendant from barrow 2; H, I, wooden griffin heads, H with leather ears; pendants from barrow 2; J, as G, without antlers

137 Wood and leather articles sculptured or carved in low relief: A, B, wooden griffins from barrow 2, B with attached leather ears and wings; C, D, sculptured leather mountain goats' heads from barrow 1; E, cut-out leather elk from barrow 2; F, cut-out leather blackcock from barrow 2; G, H, carved wooden deer with attached leather antlers, from barrow 2

138 Various saddlery adornments: A, feline head cut in a wooden medallion from the Frolov collection; B, wolf head from the same collection; C, wolf head from the Pogodin collection; D, E, feline heads from the Frolov collection; F, G, cut-out leather human heads from barrow 1

139 Various saddlery adornments: A, horn bow of saddle arch from Shibe barrow; B–D, horn saddle adornments from Shibe barrow; E, part of a horn saddle arch facing from the Frolov collection; F, carved wooden head of feline from the Frolov collection; G, wooden tassel from

Shibe barrow; H, I, saddle pendants from the Frolov collection; J, carved wooden medallion with cat's head from Shibe barrow; K, wooden facing of saddle arch from the Frolov collection; L, fragments of a leather cut-out composition from Pazyryk barrow 2

140 Miscellaneous decoration: A, horn saddle bow from the Uvarov collection; B, excised wooden belt-plate from Katanda barrow; C, carved wooden wolf's head from Katanda barrow; D, carved wooden goose from the Pogodin collection; E, excised wooden belt-plate from Katanda barrow; F, carved wooden monster from Katanda barrow; G, hemispherical wooden adornment from Katanda barrow; H, wooden disk with excised swans from the Pogodin collection

141 A–D, carved wooden crest from barrow 2

142 Work in sculpture and low relief: A, leather head of griffin with large ears and antlers, from barrow 4; B, carved wooden roebuck's head from Berel barrow; C, carved wooden deer's head from Berel barrow; D, a carved wooden composition showing head of deer in beak of griffin, from barrow 2

143 A, excised horn facing for saddle arch from the Pogodin collection; B, antler arrow-heads from barrow 2; C, nocks on arrow-shafts from barrow 3; D, cast copper griffin from Berel barrow; E, griffins on a frontal plate from Tuekta, barrow 1

144 Shields from barrow 1

145 Amulets from barrow 2: A, a rectangular piece of leather with human hairs sewn into it; B, piece of felt with human hairs sewn into it; C, triangular piece of leather into which was sewn a purse containing human finger-nails; D, leather purse in which human finger-nails were found; E, the same prior to restoration

146 Musical instrument from barrow 2: a kind of harp

147 Large felt carpet or wall-hanging from barrow 5

ACKNOWLEDGMENTS

S. I. RUDENKO: Plates 1–8, 10, 12, 13, 15–21, 23–6, 28

A. A. GAVRILOVOI: Plates 9, 11, 14, 22, 27, 29, 30–2

V. M. SUNTSEVOI: Plates 148, A, C, 149–51,

152, A, B, 153, 155, A, C, D, 156–8, 160–3, 165A, 166, 167, 169–73, 178–80

N. M. RUDENKO: Plates 148A, 152C, 154, 155B, 159, 164, 165B, 168

S. G. GASILOVA: Plates 174, 175, 177

xvi

IT MAY at first seem surprising that an account of the excavations of a group of burial mounds near the Russian frontiers with Mongolia and China should deserve translation into English and lavish publication in the form of the present volume. Unfortunately it is a reflection of the rarity of a reading know-ledge of Russian that the original should not be accessible to most English readers. While this is to be regretted, the translator's first concern must be to justify the labour and cost involved in producing the translation.

The condition of survival of the recovered objects, in a permanently frozen state, is remarkable enough, but even more remarkable are the refrigerated objects themselves. They not only throw a flood of light on aspects of the life of the people who used them which have normally left no trace, but also throw some light on the civilized areas with which these people were in contact; the Persian and Chinese textiles at Pazyryk are older than any surviving examples in Persia or China. In western Europe we have had no experience of those incursions by nomadic herdsmen and their far-flung empires that have played so important a part in the history of eastern Europe and Asia. The herdsmen were illiterate, and any attempt to reconstruct their early, or even their later, history must perforce be largely based on the material remains they have left us, of which those described in this book are amongst the most noteworthy. Although the tombs in these barrows had been ransacked, the horses which had been buried adjoining them in the same shaft, together with their saddlery,[1] were in all cases undisturbed, and thus constitute far and away the richest archaeological remains throwing light on the early history of horse-riding. Finally, from a more philosophical point of view, study of the early history of Siberia has a special interest of its own. Because we live in a temperate climate we are hardly aware of the extent to which we are influenced by our environment; in the savage seasonal extremes of the Siberian climate the influences are only too

[1] Here and in the translation saddlery is the word used to describe both bridle and saddle with their straps, except in the case of draught animals where 'harness' is used.

xvii

apparent and obvious. By studying the peoples of that area, as it were indirectly, we learn a little more about ourselves.

Sergei Ivanovich Rudenko was born in 1885. If we cite some of the titles of his earlier published works from the British Museum Reading Room catalogue we shall understand something of his range of interests: *Anthropological Researches on the Aborigines of North West Siberia* (1914), *The Bashkiry* (1916), *The Kazakhs, Anthropological Sketches* (editor, 1927), *Materials on the Anthropology of the Kazakhs* (1927). The author is then primarily an anthropologist, although in Siberia the archaeology of an area is normally regarded as an extension of its anthropology. A very good example of this combination is Rudenko's own monograph on the Eskimos which has been translated into English.[1] Frozen barrows had first been very summarily excavated in the Altai in 1865 by W. Radloff, and two more were dug by Gryaznov during the Hermitage expedition of 1925–9 to the Altai, Shibe (1927) and Pazyryk, No. 1 (1929). No further work was carried out until 1947–9, when the other four large barrows at Pazyryk were excavated by Rudenko. It is the work at Pazyryk in 1929 and 1947–9 that forms the subject of this volume, published in its Russian edition in 1953. The results of excavations since 1949 in other Altaian barrows, where the finds were a good deal less spectacular, were published by the author in 1960, together with some revised judgments on his earlier work.[2]

When Rudenko restarted work at Pazyryk in 1947 he had had the inestimable advantage of a lifetime's first-hand experience of living 'nomads' before turning to dead ones. It may also be remarked that as travelling in Siberia until the last war was done largely on horseback, he had had a lifetime's experience of horse-riding, an important matter when the subject of study is mounted herdsmen. The author frequently draws upon his personal experience of the primitive peoples of Siberia and central Asia to illustrate points in the discussion, while his anthropologist's training is very evident in the chapter on the bone measurements. In fact the whole layout of this book bears the impress of an anthropologist's mind. The chapters deal with aspects of the life of the people buried in the tombs rather as if they were still alive. This has a good deal to commend it, since it gives the book a coherent framework; it has certain weaknesses, however, if not treated with caution, by suggesting the remains are able to present a fuller picture of the life of the people than may in fact be the case. The main snag from the reader's point of view is the burden of description within the text and the difficulty of finding the description of a particular object. The Inventory at the end and the Index and extended Contents List in this English edition may help to obviate the

---

[1] S. I. Rudenko, *The Ancient Culture of the Bering Sea and the Eskimo Problem*, trans. P. Tolstoy, Arctic Institute of North America (Toronto, 1961).

[2] Rudenko, A, 1960.

latter difficulty. I do not wish to decry Rudenko's treatment, which may well provide the archaeologist with food for thought, but I have doubts as to its application on sites where the finds were more prosaic and much less numerous than at Pazyryk.

The present English translation (with altered title) has been made from a copy of the 1953 edition corrected in the author's hand. Three substantial typescript alterations consist of a rewritten Introduction, and new sections describing the carved tree-trunk coffin from Bash-Adar and a reconstruction of the carriage in barrow 5 at Pazyryk. There are some alterations in text, figures and plates. It is only fair to recall the author's age when he made the alterations; they are possibly not so thorough-going as would have been the case had he been younger. (In order to give better reproduction the photographic text figures have been put amongst the plates, so that both figures and plates have had to be renumbered.)

It may be convenient to approach the site of the barrows by means of an imaginary aeroplane flight from London Airport, flying eastward roughly along the 50th Parallel, ignoring modern frontiers and towns.

As we enter Russia, keeping the Carpathian Mountains on our right, the two most marked features are the absence of mountains or hills, the 'land that looks like the sea', the steppe, and the dwindling number of trees. The dwindling of the trees is due to the lower annual rainfall as we move east, and the same factor affects agriculture.[1] The famous black earth of the Ukraine is as rich a wheat-growing area as any in Europe, but agriculture becomes increasingly difficult as one approaches the Caspian. The great rivers that pass by underneath flow into the Black Sea: Dniester, Bug, Dnieper, Don.

An English traveller of *c.* 1800 calculated that his heavily laden droshky covered seventy miles a day over the open Kuban steppe, but that a light vehicle would cover 130 miles.[2] This was simply running over the turf of the steppe without a road; the absence of trees and obstacles due to cultivation, combined with an arid climate that kept the ground hard, made roads unnecessary. It is possible that the traveller was confusing versts and miles, and he was of course using posting stations to change horses. He was also impressed by the volume of carts moving over the steppe; as there were no obstacles the drivers continued day and night and merely stopped to sleep when they were tired. This description vividly brings out the incentive to speedy travelling, whether on wheels or on horseback, that such a landscape offered from the earliest prehistoric times. Its influence can certainly be detected in the Bronze Age, if indeed

---

[1] Cf. pp. 26–7, 30–1, 34–5, 38–9 in *The U.S.S.R. and Eastern Europe*, Oxford Regional Economic Atlas (Oxford, 1956).

[2] E. D. Clarke, *Travels in Various Countries of Europe, Asia and Africa* (4th edition, London, 1816), II, 14.

the close similarity of the Neolithic painted pottery found in the Ukraine to that of China does not point to even earlier movements along the Eurasian steppe.

The aeroplane now passes over the mighty Volga and the smaller River Ural, both of which flow south into the Caspian Sea. The River Ural is frequently taken to be the boundary between Europe and Asia, and does at all events mark a change in the direction of the drainage. East of it the rivers flow northwards instead of southwards, rising in the great tableland of Asia and flowing either into inland seas or, like the huge Siberian rivers, winding through great marshes into the Arctic Ocean. There are, furthermore, appreciable ranges of hills east of the Caspian which become mountains as we pass out of central Asia into Siberia. Most of the area below is very arid steppe or semi-desert. It differs from tropical deserts mainly in the very sharp seasonal fluctuations, being snow-covered in the winter but very hot in the summer.

These regions were colonized by the Russians in the eighteenth and nineteenth centuries. In the whole area from the Caspian Sea to the Altai Mountains the Russian colonists found people living who spoke various Turkish dialects and had a very similar means of livelihood. They were pastoralists who practised little cultivation, but kept herds of horses and cattle, sheep and goats. Their herding was done on horseback, and the horse held a peculiar position in their society. It was regarded as a unit of wealth, and a rich owner might possess several thousand. Geldings were ridden, and the main herds of horses were kept more or less wild under a stallion, control being exercised through the mares, which were milked and kept hobbled near the tents.[1] This is not the place to describe this specialized form of pastoralism, but as the builders of the Pazyryk barrows and the Scythians of Herodotus led a similar sort of life we must pause to consider one aspect of it.

Rudenko has claimed that he was familiar with every Kazakh tribe by 1914,[2] and from his remarks and the descriptions of Radloff it can be seen that between the Caspian Sea and the Altai Mountains there was a decreasing mobility among the herdsmen. The key factor was the depth of winter snow cover, since thoroughbred horses, and the finer cattle and sheep, cannot feed themselves in the open when the snow reaches any depth, and have to be stalled. The region between the Caspian and Aral seas was inhabited by Aida Kazakhs and Turcomans living in small groups. As the winter snow cover is slight, and they kept no cattle, they lived almost literally 'nomadically' with no fixed winter quarters. The vast majority of Kazakhs lived east of the Aral Sea in larger groups, sometimes with herds running into thousands of animals. Each family had its own winter grazing area which was privately owned. Although the head of the family might spend eight months of the year taking the herds northwards or up

[1] The classic descriptions are in Radloff, C, 1883, vol. i, pp. 249 ff., pp. 409 ff.   [2] Rudenko, A, 1952, pp. 22–4.

into mountains, he was not strictly 'nomadic', since he had a permanent winter home to which he returned. The Altaians or Mountain Kalmyks who inhabited the Alpine pastures of the Altai Mountains lived in felt tents like the Kazakhs but were, according to Radloff, quite static, only moving at intervals of a few years when the accumulation of filth made it necessary.[1] The snow cover is light, the pasture good and there are few noxious insects in the mountains to harry the animals, so seasonal movements were unnecessary.

The point is important since Rudenko has argued, not unreasonably, that the builders of the barrows at Pazyryk who lived in the same area as the modern Altaians had also achieved a static way of life. He believes that the massive larch-log burial chambers in the shafts point to a similar type of log dwelling, which hardly suggests a 'nomadic' way of life. The earthenware bottles again point to a settled life. Rudenko considers that the builders of the barrows were living a more or less settled life not far from them, and this assumption underlies much of his discussion.

Greeks, Chinese and Russians, being agricultural peoples, were mainly impressed by the nomadic aspect of pastoral life, and had very little understanding of the need for seasonal movements that it demanded. Nearly all people who do not till the soil have to wander in search of food for themselves (like Eskimo, Bushmen and so on) or pastures for their flocks (like Masai, Bedouin and so on). To a great extent the herdsman has to adapt his own life to that of the principal animal he rears. In this case it was the horse, but there are many analogies with nomadic camel-rearing among the Bedouin of Arabia.[2] 'Nomadism' is an extreme form of pastoralism in which not merely the head of the family but the whole family moves about and requires portable dwellings (tents) and household utensils.

The flight across Kazakhstan can be resumed east of the Aral Sea where there are quite marked mountains, the Kazakh Uplands. The area is still largely steppe and desert, but there are forest areas in the Uplands. Ahead lie the great Altai Mountains at the point where the eastern tip of the Kazakh S.S.R. and southward projection of the R.S.F.S.R. meet the western point of Outer Mongolia and the northern tip of the Sinkiang province of China. The ranges run deep into Mongolia. On the Russian side the place-names are, as one might expect, Turkish. The etymology of the word Altai itself is obscure, but Radloff suggested possible alternatives: *Al-taiga* (high rocky hills) or *Altyn-tau* (gold mountains), or *Ala-tau* (coloured mountains). All seem equally appropriate.

At Semipalatinsk we turn north and follow the edge of the mountains round to the River Ob', following this south to Biysk and then taking the left stream and pursuing it into the mountains. The trees have become more and more

---

[1] Radloff, C, 1883, vol. i, p. 286.

[2] P. K. Hitti, *History of the Arabs* (9th edition, New York, 1967), ch. iii.

numerous until the lower mountains are clothed in dense pine forest. The forest gives way to the open alpine meadows interspersed with larch trees, the larch *taiga*. At Pazyryk the burial chambers were constructed of, and the shafts filled with, larch logs, and it is clear that at that time the vegetation was very similar to that of today. By the time Lake Teletskoye is reached the landscape is entirely alpine, great cliffs, gorges and moraines. At the southern end of the lake we follow the right-hand gorge as far as the settlement of Ust'-Ulagan, where the valley of the Great Ulagan enters from the east. About nine miles up the Ulagan valley on the left is a flat, dry valley, quite deserted but known to the local people under the name of Pazyryk, in which the barrows are situated at about five thousand feet above sea level.

It will be convenient at this point to dispense with the imaginary aeroplane.

The barrows lie in the High Altai Autonomous Oblast about 120 miles north of the Chinese frontier and ninety miles west of the Mongolian frontier.[1] During Radloff's journeys in the Altai in the last century the inhabitants fell into three categories: Russian colonists, largely working in the state-owned gold-mines; the aboriginal Turkish horse-breeders, living in encampments in the mountain pastures; and, during the summer, a mixed group of traders carrying on a lively trade between Mongolia and China on the one hand and Siberia on the other. The presence of Chinese objects in the Pazyryk barrows suggests that such trade has had a very long history.

Including the first two frozen Altai barrows opened by Radloff in 1865 perhaps a dozen or so are now known. Although areas of permanently frozen ground occur in the region, they would have been too hard for primitive people to dig, and it is clear that the burial shafts were dug in unfrozen ground; the refrigeration took place afterwards. Freezing does not occur beneath small barrows, and it is evident that the size of the cairn and depth of the shaft were the crucial factors in insulating the tombs from the short summer thaw.[2] As with the flooded Bronze Age barrows of Denmark the builders had no intention of creating such peculiar conditions of preservation, which arose quite accidentally.

When the barrow was composed of gravel which became set in the ice it was like concrete and more difficult to deal with than sand in ice. Radloff had adopted the very drastic method of lighting a fire on top of the ice, but a much more satisfactory method, employed by Gryaznov and subsequently, is the liberal application of buckets of hot water. It means the whole excavation has to to carried out in slush and shoring is necessary for the sides of the trenches.

[1] The largest scale map of this area at 1: 1,000,000 is sheet NM 45, series 1301, published by the U.S. Army Map Service, Washington, D.C., whence it may be obtained. As it is almost certainly an enlargement from smaller scale maps it has to be used with caution.

[2] The last snow falls in mid June and the first frosts occur in mid August. Rudenko, A, 1952, p. 12.

The Altai Mountains are rich in gold and no doubt, with the Ural and Caucasus deposits, furnished the enormous quantity of gold that found its way into Eurasian barrows in the last six centuries B.C. The collections of gold in the Hermitage in Leningrad were partly brought to Peter the Great from west Siberian barrows, but mainly originate from burials in the Black Sea area excavated in 1850–1920. If one remembers that these barrows, like those at Pazyryk, had been already looted in antiquity, some idea of the prodigious amount of gold buried in the Iron Age can be grasped. The robbers at Pazyryk as they lowered themselves through the trap cut in the tomb roof must have been confronted by glistening heaps of gold. Alas, the thorough and systematic robbing left merely scraps, and only the gold facings of the intact horse-trappings give some inkling of what has been lost. The main practical effect of the robbing was to allow rain water to penetrate the tombs, which filled with ice.

Before leaving the contemporary conditions around the barrows three features of the modern Altaians that have been described by Radloff, which may help us to understand the ancient herdsmen, deserve mention.

The modern Altaian lives in a large felt tent inside which, opposite the doorway on the left, are stacked the leather bags containing the household's wealth, mainly carpets, mats, saddlery and so on,[1] recalling those found in the barrows of two thousand years before. The point is that these bags were carried on pack-horses, since the terrain is quite unsuitable for carts. Primitive trolleys were used in constructing the barrows at Pazyryk, and in barrow 5 there was an elaborate carriage. The latter could hardly have been used on the stony ground of this area, and it has been suggested that it was brought there dismantled. The inference seems to be that the barrow builders had not long since, perhaps only a generation or two back, left the steppe where wheeled vehicles were in their element.

Unlike the Kazakh, who led a busy life moving his herds around, the Altaian man spent the winter trapping and the summer more or less in idleness. He was normally either getting drunk or being drunk. Both men and women smoked tobacco pipes almost continuously. The barrow builders had no tobacco but they found relief from boredom in a narcotic, Indian hemp, the smoke of which was inhaled. Another alternative form of relief stood on four feet outside the tent, the horse. It is perhaps not an accident that in the historic period the large nomad upheavals often had their origin among the mountain, not the steppe, herdsmen.

In the nineteenth century, while the Kazakhs had become Muslim and the Mongols Buddhist, the Altaians retained their primitive Shamanistic beliefs, which Radloff took considerable pains to study.[2] An interesting point was the extent to which Shamanism borrowed ideas from adjoining religions. When we

[1] Radloff, C, 1883, vol. i, pp. 265 ff. and Pl. VI.   [2] Radloff, C, 1883, vol. ii, ch. i.

study the animal art of the people buried in the barrows we recognize the borrowings from the Middle East, particularly Achaemenid Persia, but it must be remembered that the people of the time had little notion of art as such and were almost certainly thinking in terms of borrowed religious beliefs, albeit no doubt imperfectly understood. A dualism, recalling that of Thomas Hardy, in which the scales were tipped slightly in favour of the force of evil, was a persistent feature of Persian Zoroastrianism, as it was of later Shamanism in the Altai, and Rudenko no doubt is right to interpret the constant motif at Pazyryk of the carnivore leaping on herbivore, predator on victim, as dualistic in origin.

As we have just seen, the aridity of the climate in the Eurasian steppe discouraged agriculture and favoured stock-breeding, while the severity of the winter encouraged the rearing of animals that were by nature capable of withstanding the rigours of the season and, most important, were able to hoof aside the snow to reach their food. The horse, which is native to this region, is preeminently adapted to this way of life, and one way of men ensuring their own winter survival in this area was to possess an animal which knew how to maintain itself. The use of the horse for meat and milk by the steppe peoples is a fair indication that that was the original motive for its domestication. Cattle, sheep and goats can be fairly easily herded on foot, but to breed horses on any scale the herdsman cannot exercise the necessary control unless he is himself mounted. From herding on foot to herding on horseback is a very big change for primitive people to make, and it seems likely that it was produced in the steppe by outside stimuli from the early civilizations of the Middle and Far East.

In the last few decades much information has been vouchsafed us about the early history of Siberia and central Asia.[1] We need not describe this in detail. As might be expected in Siberia agriculture was very retarded and slow in coming, the word 'Neolithic' being applied to people who had neither agriculture nor domestic animals. During the Bronze Age both of these were known to the people of this area, although it is evident that in most areas there was a pastoral bias. The Bronze Age monuments are chiefly barrows which reveal that already there was some degree of uniformity of way of life across the steppe, while the actual rites show a measure of continuity extending into the Iron Age. The main change at the end of the Bronze Age is the burial of horses in the tomb, a practice that is assumed to mark the abandonment of a settled, and the adoption of a 'nomadic', way of life. All scholars agree that a sharp change in the manner of life took place over most of the area. Agriculture has never been entirely extinguished among the herdsmen, many of whom cultivate areas

---

[1] S. V. Kiselev, *Ancient History of Southern Siberia* (2nd edition, Moscow, 1951); relevant sections of *Outline History of the U.S.S.R.*, I (Moscow, 1956).

varying from garden plots to irrigated fields (among the Kazakhs[1]). When one is trying to assess the extent of the change that took place at the end of the Bronze Age it is a sobering reflection that the archaeologist who excavated a nineteenth-century Kazakh winter settlement might be quite misled as to the real way of life of its inhabitants by the traces of agriculture he found there!

Among animals that are ridden today—reindeer, oxen, camels—the ropes used for their control are of a very simple nature, and it is Rudenko's view that, making use of some simple kind of halter, casual riding of horses probably took place from their initial domestication. Such riding would have left no material evidence for the archaeologist. In the second millennium B.C. horses were extensively used in the Middle and Far East for drawing war chariots. During the course of the first half of the last millennium B.C. evidence for regular riding in the form of metal bits and antler cheek-pieces appears over much of Europe and Asia. It is thought that the two antler cheek-pieces were originally linked by a solid wooden, or perhaps leather, bit,[2] bits of such material being used in Swedish folk culture until the eighteenth century.[3] (Rudenko regards the large cheek-pieces at Pazyryk not as survivals but as a deliberate introduction from the Middle East, p. 126.) The evidence normally occurs in settlements or hoards, except in Eurasia, where the objects accompanied the horses in the graves of their owners, indicating the introduction not merely of a new method of locomotion but of a new kind of life.

Rudenko [4] has criticized some of the theories put forward as to the origins of this way of life, and as in many respects his own theory goes furthest to explain the known facts we may briefly follow it. He starts from the assumption that the widespread adoption of riding in Eurasia was not due to spontaneous discovery of how to ride. Riding was essential for large-scale horse-breeding, and this was made profitable and worth while by an increasing demand for horses from the urbanized areas to the south. Rudenko is thinking of Chinese sources of the end of the last millennium B.C., with their references to the gifts of large numbers of horses to the Chinese emperors, horse fairs and so on. In the Middle East the sources are less explicit, but a record of the dues from satrapies of the Achaemenid Empire in the fifth century B.C. shows again the massive breeding of horses expected from two northern satrapies.[5] The change from chariot to cavalry warfare, that can be followed on the bas-reliefs in the Assyrian gallery at the British Museum, indicates one reason for the increasing demand for horses in the ancient civilizations. If the evidence of the latter end of the last

[1] Radloff, C, 1883, vol. i, 463 ff.
[2] See M. Ebert: *Reallexikon der Vorgeschichte*, XIII, 424–30.

[3] *Prähistorischer Zeitschrift*, II (1910), 280. According to Montelius.
[4] Rudenko, A, 1960, pp. 95–201, 223.
[5] Olmstead, C, p. 291.

millennium held good for its beginning then we can see that there was a very strong motive for abandoning the uphill struggle with agriculture and taking to the life of a mounted horse-breeder. Rudenko does not envisage this as a catastrophic process with whole tribes changing over at once, but rather as a trickle of the wealthier members of the tribe making off into the wilderness with their herds. Immense herds of animals such as the written sources imply could only be fed, when grown foodstuff was not available, by constantly moving them over large tracts of natural grassland. This willy-nilly required the herds-man to be mounted and to live a more or less nomadic life.

Rudenko's explanation of the origins of this specialized form of pastoral life may encounter some snags, but it has the virtue of providing answers to two of its most puzzling aspects. Most European travellers among these horse herds-men have been surprised by the size of the herds. It was not unknown for one Kazakh to own several thousand horses. The horse was a unit of value, a man's wealth being assessed in the number of horses he owned, so that an individual would keep far more horses than he could possibly need. The animal was of course essential to his livelihood, but its peculiar position was due partly to the value set upon it by people of the neighbouring civilized areas. The second point is that, as this form of life in large measure owed its existence to the economic demands of the areas of higher civilization, there was a powerful reverse current of objects and influences from the civilized area. In a Bronze Age barrow in Siberia it is unlikely that there will be even the slightest indication of connections with the ancient civilizations, but in the Pazyryk barrows there are actual Persian and Chinese imports, while the influences of Achaemenid Persia permeate the decorative motifs employed on other objects.

As references to intrusive mounted raiders appear in written sources from the seventh century B.C., and Rudenko regards the process of creation of this way of life as slow, it presumably started not very long after 1000 B.C. The Pazyryk barrows as we shall see can be dated to about 400 B.C., and so belong to an early, although not to the initial, stage of this way of life.

As one might expect with a spirited animal like the horse, the equipment for controlling it was perfected at a much earlier date than that necessary for the comfort of the rider. The bridles from the Pazyryk barrows differ only in relatively minor respects from modern bridles (absence of brow band, large cheek-piece and bifurcation of cheek-straps and the lead-rein), but the very rudimentary saddles are quite different from those of today. Instead of sitting astride a wooden tree made to the right shape, padded and covered with leather, the rider at Pazyryk had only two leather cushions to protect the inside of his thighs, and as there were no stirrups he had to grip the horse with his knees. The saddle was held not only by a girth but also at front and back by breast-strap and crupper. These no doubt were necessary on the steep mountain gradients to prevent the saddle slipping, and for the same cause, but to prevent the rider slipping, the front and back arches were stiffened and bridged by a wooden bow. Although primitive, such representations as we have from Persia and Classical Greece indicate that the Altai examples were more developed than those known in the former areas. As with some modern herdsmen the horses were ridden unshod.

Modern Kazakh and Altaian herdsmen ride exclusively on geldings, each possessing a small number used for this purpose. On the owner's death these animals are not ridden again. The animals in the Pazyryk barrows were geldings and few in number, so Rudenko has reasonably inferred that they were the riding-horses of the deceased buried in the tomb. Indeed he assumes that all the objects buried in the barrows were in each case the property of the deceased, an assumption that the reader should appreciate if he wants fully to understand the author's line of thought.

The objects, particularly in the ice of barrow 2, that escaped the tomb robbers are sufficient, quite apart from horse burials in the shafts, to leave little doubt that the deceased spent much of their time on horseback. I have in mind the costume and wide range of bags and pouches.

Finally, we may turn to consider the date of the barrows and the identity of the people who built and were buried in them. It is unfortunate that barrow 1 was excavated nearly twenty years before the others, since far the best dating evidence came from barrow 5. Most leading authorities had committed themselves on the first barrow to a date 250 years or so later than that given them by Rudenko. Indeed when this book first appeared in 1953 the phrase 'in the Scythian period' in the title was something of a challenge to the leading authorities, one of whom, Kiselev, as late as 1951, had attributed the barrows to the 'Hunnish' period. It is instructive to trace the reasons for this change, or rather correction, for it is certainly right.

In the 1920's two barrows were dug in the Altai, at Shibe and Pazyryk 1, and a group of several barrows seven hundred miles to the east in Mongolia, at Noin-Ula about a hundred miles north of Ulan Bator. One of the latter contained a lacquer cup bearing an inscription in Chinese giving the name of its maker and the date of manufacture, A.D. 2. In some respects the contents of the two Altaian barrows resembled those of Noin-Ula: double-lined chamber, carpets and drapes in the tomb, little tables, the clothes, the embroidered motif of the predator leaping on herbivore and so on. Understandably there was a tendency to regard the Altaian barrows as not much earlier than the Noin-Ula ones, and the matter appeared to be clinched by the claim of a Japanese archaeologist that a Chinese lacquer datable to the mid first century B.C. had turned up at Shibe. This was an error, for lacquer is extensively used in the Altaian barrows, and the object in question was almost certainly native work. No article found in any Altaian barrow is as closely datable, or as recent as that object would have been, but the false identification tended to fit in with ideas current about the dating in the 1930's and 1940's.

The numbering of the barrows at Pazyryk not only records the sequence in which they were excavated, but also, according to Rudenko, relying on the saddlery, the sequence in which they were erected. Barrows 1 and 2 are similar and contained no Chinese objects, which did, however, occur in barrows 3, 5 and 6. They appear to be casual imports, and there is not the slightest influence in the motifs of the decoration. Now that Rudenko has published the Noin-Ula barrows more fully [1] we are far more conscious of the differences between the monuments in the two areas. The Noin-Ula barrow shafts are deeper, oriented north/south, have a sort of access ramp and there are no horse burials (horse burials were *de rigueur* in all Altaian burials). There were no superincumbent cairns at Noin-Ula. The objects in these latter barrows, as one would expect, show a high degree of sinicization. They are reasonably considered to be the graves of Hsiung-Nu chieftains; the Hsiung-Nu, according to Chinese sources, formed a confederacy under the Shan-yu Mao-Tun at the end of the third century B.C. and advanced west where they overcame the Yue-Chi. The Noin-Ula barrows seem to be strong negative evidence for dating the Pazyryk barrows to before 200 B.C., since had they been later than the events referred to a much higher degree of sinicization would have been expected than was found.

The Chinese imports at Pazyryk, the embroidered silk and mirror, cannot be dated precisely, but sinologists would probably agree that they would fit well into the third quarter of the last millennium B.C. The Persian imports in barrow 5, the carpet and pieces of damask, point more definitely to fifth-century Achaemenid Persia. The great majority of the intrusive motifs in the art again are unequivocally Persian. Of course this type of motif can linger on for a long time; we have already referred to the carnivore-seizing-herbivore motif at Noin-Ula, while Rudenko believes some of the motifs at Pazyryk, notably the sphinxes, are of Assyrian and earlier origin. Nevertheless the cumulative evidence is impressive and negative evidence, I believe, decisive. After Alexander the Great destroyed the Achaemenid Empire he planted new towns at various points. One of these, at Ai-Khamoun, situated on the River Oxus on the Afghan-Soviet border, which has recently been excavated,[2] proved to be an entirely Greek city. The Hellenistic influences emanating from cities such as these must surely have affected the whole of central Asia and even the Altai by 300 B.C.; the complete absence of traces of any such Greek influences in the

[1] Rudenko, A, 1962a.

[2] Lecture to the British Academy on 15th February 1967 by M. Paul Bertrand.

Pazyryk barrows is a cogent argument for dating them earlier than that date.

Two kinds of evidence derived from the laboratory have thrown some light on the chronology of the Pazyryk barrows. The first, dendrochronology, depends on the synchronization of years of poor growth in trees that produced thin rings. The details need not concern us. The logs of the chambers and shaft fillings provided ample material for such work at Pazyryk. The method of course only gives a relative date unless it can be tied to the present or to an ancient exact date, as at Novgorod. At Pazyryk it indicated that barrows 1 and 2 were constructed in the same year; barrow 4 was constructed next after an interval of seven years, barrow 3 next after thirty years and barrow 5 after eleven years. In other words the erection of the five barrows spanned a period of forty-eight years.

A number of readings of radiocarbon content have been made on objects from Altai barrows. A minute but constant quantity of an isotope of carbon exists in the carbon dioxide of the atmosphere, C14, which becomes incorporated into the organic matter of all living things. As the rate of decomposition is known by measuring the surviving amount of isotope in the material, the period since it ceased to live can be calculated. Although very widely used in the West, it is only in the last few years that it has been employed in the Soviet Union. With an error of ± 130 years, dates of 2,480, 2,400 and 2,350 years before the present are given by Rudenko for Bash-Adar 2 and Tuekta 1 together, Katanda and Pazyryk 2 respectively.[1] The first three are barrows excavated subsequently by Rudenko. Pazyryk 2 was built in the same year as Pazyryk 1, while Pazyryk 5 was built forty-eight years later, so the maximum and minimum ages are 520 and 260 B.C. for the first two barrows and 472 and 212 B.C. for No. 5. The actual reading for barrow 2 was 390 B.C. However these figures are interpreted they clearly support Rudenko's dates, rather than the later ones advocated by earlier workers.

It is pointless to discuss the matter further: the barrows cannot be exactly dated, but it is reasonably assumed that their erection spanned a period of about fifty years, three generations that is, and the date 400 B.C. probably lies somewhere within, or near, that fifty years.

From the time of the construction of the barrows there are substantial surviving written sources from Classical Greece and ancient China. The Altai Mountains, as one might expect, were really beyond the ken of writers from both areas. China is nearer and, as we have seen, Rudenko tentatively identifies the people as Yue-Chi, relatives perhaps of the people who invaded India in about 100 B.C. to form the Kushan Empire.

[1] Rudenko, A, 1960, p. 335. However, although the six published readings from Altaian barrows are consistently 5th century B.C. in date (*Radiocarbon*, vii, 1965, p. 223) the date for Pazyryk 5 of 490 B.C. ± 50 cannot be reconciled with Rudenko's sequence; for this reason in this edition he gives a mean date of 430 B.C. between the two, for the whole group (p. xxxvi).

Although much more distant, the Classical Greek sources are in many ways more interesting because Herodotus, who is virtually a contemporary writer, went to Scythia and gathered a great deal of first-hand information about the Scythians. The excavations of the barrows in the Black Sea area in the second half of the last century and the beginning of this one did much to confirm the accounts of Herodotus and, of course, added much new information. Some of the discoveries at Pazyryk, the censers for burning hemp, the shaven heads, the scalping, the joint burial of man and woman and so on, are further vindication of Herodotus' authority. The student of this period is indeed lucky to have this description to assist him.

In many respects the most interesting discovery about the Scythians of a purely archaeological kind, not hinted at in the written sources, is the well-known animal style of decoration. It has been discussed many times in the literature and only needs very few words here. Some kind of animal art existed in Siberia and central Asia in the Bronze Age, but the two principal factors that led to its rapid development were probably the exuberance of the early horse-riders and the contact with Mesopotamian art, the two being connected as we have seen. No doubt people entirely concerned with the rearing of animals were particularly attracted by the range of animals and monsters portrayed in Assyrian art; by contrast in the west the Celts selected mainly plant motifs from the parent Greek art. The distortions that the figures underwent were partly taken over from Assyria, but partly due to having to fit the shapes and attitudes of the animals into the limits of the various bridle and saddle fittings. As might be expected, although the art of Pazyryk presents close affinities with that of the Black Sea barrows, the Greek influences of the latter are quite absent and a number of idiosyncrasies of the one area do not occur in the other. The Altai seems to form the eastern limit of the extent of Scythian art, since where Scythic motifs occur to the east as at Noin-Ula or in the Ordos bronzes they appear to be intrusive rather than native. This again hints at some marked ethnic or linguistic boundary to the east of the Altai, which it is tempting to assume with Rudenko corresponded to a change from Iranic to Turkish dialects.[1]

Unassisted by written sources, as we are at Pazyryk, archaeology can give us no certain answer on questions of race and language. All we can say is that the people inhabiting the Altai at this period had a manner of life resembling the contemporary tribes occupying the steppes of central Asia and west of the

---

[1] Rudenko takes the traditional view that the Hsiung-Nu were Huns and Turkish-speaking, while the Pazyryk folk would have been presumably Iranic or at all events Aryan in speech. The identification of the Hsiung-Nu with the Huns has recently been again challenged (Altheim, C, pp. 16–17, 369), but even if we accept this, and we need not, that does not mean that the Hsiung-Nu were not Turkish or indeed affect Rudenko's argument.

Caspian Sea as far as the Ukraine, and that the decorative art of both the latter and former was similar and had drawn the same inspiration from Mesopotamia and Persia. Rudenko's suggestion that the builders of the barrows were Yue-Chi of the Chinese sources seems feasible.

It only remains for the translator to express the hope that the reader will derive as much pleasure from reading the book as he has had in translating it. Thanks are due to William Watson, Professor of Chinese Art and Archaeology in the University of London, for the fresh transliteration and translation from the original Chinese of the stanza on p. 306.

Claygate, August 1967   M. W. THOMPSON

ACCORDING to Classical traditions a substantial portion of eastern Europe and western Asia was inhabited in the middle of the last millennium B.C. by tribes who, by the testimony of Herodotus, were called Scyths by the Greeks and *Saka* by the Persians.

In the eighteenth–nineteenth centuries archaeologists were principally concerned with the European Scyths, although the Siberian collection of Peter the Great, the collection of 'Scytho-Siberian gold', was of course well known. It was also realized that the collection derived from seventeenth- and eighteenth-century excavations on barrows between the Ural and Altai mountain ranges.

A hundred years ago, in 1865, Academician V. V. Radloff, the well-known authority on Turkish studies, excavated two large barrows at Berel and Katanda in Altai Mountain province, and found objects, in particular artistic ones, with characteristic Scythian decoration. It was not until 1927, however, that the Russian Museum at Leningrad excavated a barrow at Shibe in the central Altai of just the same type as that dug by Radloff.

The Pazyryk group of barrows was discovered in 1924 when the author did some trial trenching on them. Their great altitude above sea level, the climatic conditions and composition of the soil indicated conditions favourable to the formation of barrow congelation, which causes excellent preservation of structures and objects. An excavation was organized in 1929, when the first barrow was investigated.

Subsequent excavation took place in 1947 under the auspices of the Institute of the History of Material Culture of the Academy of Sciences of the U.S.S.R., with the participation (from 1948) of the Hermitage Museum, where all the material from Pazyryk has been deposited. In 1947–8 the second, third and fourth, and in 1949 the fifth, of the large cairn-covered barrows were excavated.

The yield of the four seasons' work at Pazyryk, in spite of the fact that all the barrows had been robbed in antiquity, was quite unparalleled in quantity, variety and scientific value. This was due to the fact that a combination of circumstances—climatic conditions and the method of construction of the great barrow-cairns—had caused permanent refrigeration (barrow congelation) soon after the interments took place. So there were finely preserved articles not only of metal and horn but also of wood, leather and fur, as well as textiles of different kinds; not only skeletons but the actual bodies of interred men and horses survived. Detailed examination was carried out of five tombs, four embalmed human bodies and three skeletons, twenty horse bodies and thirty-four skeletons. Thorough study was made of articles of dress and adornment, a variety of textiles, domestic utensils, objects of art and cult and numerous sets of saddlery. Besides a huge quantity of material testifying to an individual and sharply defined local culture, the barrows produced the first finds of very ancient textiles and carpets from China and Hither Asia of remarkably great historical and aesthetic value.

The Pazyryk excavations form part of the studies in the Altai region and neighbouring provinces of southern Siberia and central Asia, which have built up our understanding of both the remains themselves and the life of the inhabitants of the Altai Mountains in the middle of the last millennium B.C. The study of these remains is therefore a basic contribution to historical science, and has revealed to the investigator an ancient and hitherto unrecorded cultural sphere of antiquity.

A whole series of publications have already been devoted to the Pazyryk finds, and in the future they will undoubtedly attract the attention of scholars, revealing new facts and unforeseen aspects of this ancient culture. But already the main point is clear: the excavations in the Altai area have fully demonstrated that in the last millennium B.C. there already existed an independent and obviously native culture, which shared much in common with the cultures of neighbouring and more distant stock-rearing tribes.

Surveying the Pazyryk finds and those akin to them we can see that in the steppe and foothill area of southern Siberia and central Asia, as well as eastern Europe, there lived in the middle of the last millennium B.C. numerous tribes, distinct in origin and language, but sharing one material culture and to some extent at the same social level, and with similar customs. Such a uniform way of life arose not only from a similar livelihood but also as a result of varied, but often close, inter-tribal connections. Not only the archaeological finds but written sources, Chinese and Greek (including the works of the 'Father of history', Herodotus), testify to this.

One cannot fail to see the remarkable coincidence between the Pazyryk finds on the one hand and the accounts by Herodotus on the other about the life of the steppe tribes of eastern Europe and Asia. It is true that his reports even in Classical times had given rise to doubts, for Herodotus, recording information about the people of the time, was not always himself able to verify his facts. Furthermore he did record legendary matter, although he commented on its improbability, and even Aristotle regarded him as a 'fable-monger'. The majority of eighteenth- and nineteenth-century scholars were prejudiced against Herodotus, in spite of numerous archaeological discoveries showing that as a witness he was conscientious and trustworthy. It is therefore the more interesting and noteworthy that a number of his statements about the life and customs of the steppe tribes of eastern Europe and Asia have been unexpectedly borne out by the results of the Altai excavations.

Apart from the way of life, occupation, dress, weapons and other aspects of material culture, such customs as embalmment of corpses of the Scythian chieftains, burial with a concubine, purifying after burial, scalping of slain enemies, and much else, are confirmed, which could not have been established by excavation in the Black Sea Scythian area. The Altai finds therefore not only confirm the reliability of Herodotus' description of the steppe tribes of his time, but reveal in an unexpectedly clear light the ancient cultural ties between the western and eastern pastoral tribes.

It is not merely a case of connections between the steppe tribes themselves, but of links between them and the peoples of the then advanced countries, the world cultural centres of that period. Thus the Black Sea finds clearly demonstrate links between the natives and Greece and, more especially, Iran. Even in Outer Mongolia, where the influence of China showed itself very deeply in the culture of nomadic tribes in its normal form, materials have come to light testifying to the acquaintance of the ancient Huns with the products of Graeco-Bactrian craftsmen. In High Altai province links have been established with central and Hither Asia, and to some extent with China. Especial importance attaches to the Pazyryk finds of articles of high technical and aesthetic quality produced by Persian and Chinese craftsmen, which throw new light on the level of culture in those countries at this remote time. It is not surprising therefore that the Altai tribes had so much in common with other pastoral peoples developing in contact with the cultures of the Classical East and China.

I have had the task of recording on a historical-cultural basis the information yielded by the Pazyryk barrows: first, that which sheds light on the life of the ancient population of the Altai Mountains at the threshold of history, and, secondly, the additions of world significance that the finds have contributed to the treasure-house of history.

The book falls basically into three sections. In the first the details of the natural environment prevailing in the eastern part of Altai province are given, especially the conditions that gave rise to the refrigeration. Then follow accounts of the Pazyryk group of barrows and of the physical type of people buried in them. In the second part material revealing the economy and way of life is described, and in the third that throwing light on the social structure, art and religious beliefs.

It goes without saying that this material, even when relatively fully described, still only partially answers a number of questions that confront the student. This applies in particular to such crucial matters as the form of society. Nevertheless it does entirely broaden our field of vision of the ancient history of the tribes of southern Siberia and adjacent regions, and allows us a general picture of the life of the Altai tribes in the relevant period, notably of their individual and sharply defined culture.

On the problem of dating of the Pazyryk barrows there has been no consensus of opinion; some referred them to the Scythian period, some to Hunnish-Sarmatian times. For my part the latter dating seemed quite baseless, as I have discussed in detail in the final chapter. I would only repeat that besides typical Achaemenian objects, and native products just as characteristic of that style found in the barrows, there are other dating factors. Thus Graeco-Bactrian or Han dynasty Chinese articles are absent. In the last centuries B.C. mirrors of the Han period reached far to the west, as far even as the Volga, and consequently would no doubt have been found in the Pazyryk barrows if they had belonged to the Han period. However, in spite of normal finds in the Altai barrows of Chinese textiles, no Han mirror was found.

Since the first edition of this book a radiocarbon dating of the Pazyryk barrows has been made, which gave an average age of 2,395 years before the present, or 430 B.C. Thanks to the beautiful survival of the logs in all the barrows it has been possible to define their relative age with precision down to a year by means of tree-ring dating. It was shown that the first two Pazyryk barrows were thrown up in the same year; then the third and fourth, and last of all the fifth, forty-eight years after the first two.

In 1950 in the central Altai I dug two large barrows with superincumbent cairns at Bash-Adar near the River Karakol, tributary of the Ursul, and in 1954 two similar ones at the village of Tuekta. The average age of these barrows was 2,480 years before present, that is 520 B.C., or almost a hundred years older than the Pazyryk barrows. The difference in age between the earliest barrow at Tuekta and barrow 5 at Pazyryk was 178 years.

The rich material from the central Altai has been the subject of a special study, where it was shown that these tombs, like the Shibe barrow, belonged to just the same culture as the Pazyryk ones, sharing certain peculiarities in the representational art, discussed in the study, and with the first reflections of the art of Hither Asia revealed in representations of griffins.

Special importance being attached to the fullest possible record of the objects being published, we arranged to have the majority of them drawn in colour on the site, directly after their removal from the barrow.

The artists responsible for the coloured plates are named in the Acknowledgments. The text figures are the work of the artists N. M. Rudenko and V. M. Suntsevoi.

1. THE VALLEY OF PAZYRYK
AND BARROW CONGELATION

BARROWS with a cairn over a small earthen mound occur everywhere on the open steppe areas of the valleys of the Altai rivers. A particularly large number is known in the valley of the River Ursul, a left-hand tributary of the River Katun', on the alluvial terraces of the Katun' itself and in its tributaries from the right, the Argut and Chuya. There are many similar barrows in the valley of the River Bashkaus and its right-hand tributary, the Great Ulagan; they occur less frequently in the Chulyshman valley. The eastward distribution of these barrows extends over the Tuva A.S.S.R. and into part of the Mongolian Altai.

Mountainous country with exposures of rock and heaps of scree with frequent moraines everywhere furnished the ancient population with the necessary material for constructing such barrow-cairns.

An exceptional peculiarity in the great barrow-cairns, not yet known outside the High Altai, is the presence of barrow congelation outside the limit of permanently frozen soil. The significance of this for the archaeologist cannot be overestimated, as the study of the Pazyryk group of barrows in the valley of the Great Ulagan has strikingly demonstrated. This circumstance obliges me to give a detailed description of the physico-geographical peculiarities of Pazyryk valley and an explanation of the factors that produce barrow congelation.

The place called Pazyryk lies on the southern slopes of the Chulyshman range, in the eastern part of High Altai oblast bordering on the Tuva A.S.S.R. The range runs from north-west to south-east, between the River Chulyshman, flowing from the south into Lake Teletskoye, and its tributary, the River Bashkaus. Pazyryk, which is situated at 50° 44′ N. and 88° 03′ E. of Greenwich, is a dry hanging valley in the valley of the Great Ulagan. One kilometre to the south of Pazyryk lies the U-shaped valley of the Great Ulagan; the River Balyktyul flows into the Great Ulagan south-west of Pazyryk (fig. 1).

The right-hand slope of the Great Ulagan valley, which at the relevant point faces south-east, bears typical steppe vegetation with slight clumps of larch in the narrow hollows transecting the hillside. The left (north-facing) slope of the

1

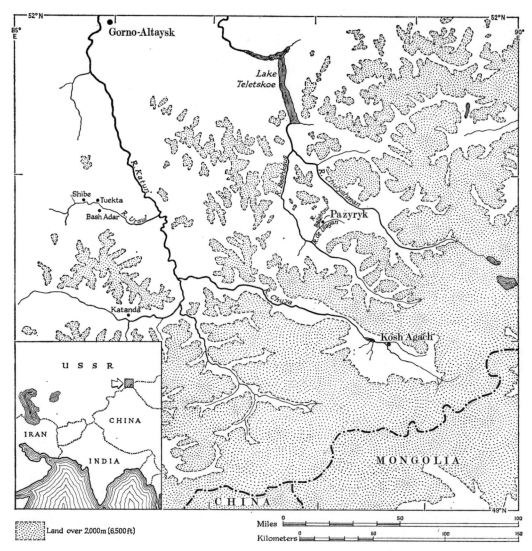

1.Altai Mountain Province showing position of Pazyryk (drawn by Translator).

valley bears a thick growth of larch-fir taiga. The River Balyktyul, flowing west from Pazyryk, is separated from it by quite a high spur.

Pazyryk valley itself, running southward, is short and deeply eroded, and intersects the right slope of the Great Ulagan valley which is covered by fluvio-glacial and lake deposits. I. Y. Baranov refers the origin of the valley to a pluvial period preceding the first regular glaciation of this part of the Altai, and considers that the shape of the valley has not been determined by contemporary physico-geographical conditions. In spite of a large catchment area and the long

2

period of its existence, permanent or temporary streams do not occur in it, nor do traces of their action.

The upper part of the valley where the first four large barrows are situated rises up above the bed of the Great Ulagan, and its higher points are marked by precipitate slopes. Everywhere on the slopes are exposures of browny-red metamorphic slates and erratic boulders of porphyritic and biotitic granites and granite-gneisses. On the relatively gentler slopes transected by hollows there is a growth of larch, with some fir and shrubs. The bottom of the valley has a slightly hollowed form with a depression in the middle. Under a thinnish layer of chestnut-coloured (humus) soil the bottom of the valley is filled by laminated, fine-grained white quartz sands, below which there are gravel and clay.

In 1924, when I made the first reconnaissance, these sands were identified as of lacustrine origin. I. Y. Baranov inferred that in the interglacial period succeeding the first glacial ice-sheet a barrage was formed in the Bashkaus valley below its confluence with the Great Ulagan that produced a lake of great dimensions.

In the subsequent second glaciation glaciers of alpine valley type pressed forward into the eroded valleys and gave this valley its typical U-shape. As it moved the glacier carved itself a flat bed, mostly in the lacustrine deposits. At the outlet of Pazyryk valley, where the fifth barrow lies, the earlier deposits were torn out by the edge of the glacier moving down the Great Ulagan valley and only partially survive. A lateral moraine separates this barrow from the upper part of the valley where the first four lie.

During research on the ground close to the valley outlet springs of underground water have never been found. The fine permeable deposits filling the valley allow soakage of the slight precipitation. In contemporary climatic conditions the natural humidity of the sands is very low, and only in the area influenced by the barrow-cairns is there a marked rise of ground humidity.

The northern barrows (nos. 3, 4 and 8) lay on the site of the former lake, in the lacustrine sands (fig. 2). It is a level spot, open, well sheltered with light steppe vegetation. The contemporary surface has a degraded black earth, penetrated by roots, about 30 cm. thick. Below this (0·3–0·8 m.) is a loam of bright chestnut colour of low humidity. Barrow 3 had a layer (10–12 cm.) of gravelly loamy material at this level, derived from the neighbouring cliff face on the right side of the valley. Lower (0·8–7·0 m.) is a fine-grained whitish quartz sand, well sorted by water, and then a thin layer of fine-grained loam and finally fine-grained clean quartz sand alternating in places with a fine silt.

At a depth of about 7 m. there was a deep deposit of loam with a large admixture of gravel.

Barrow 1 was constructed on the edge of the lateral moraine which was composed of boulder-pebble-clay deposits, and the second barrow was on top of the

3

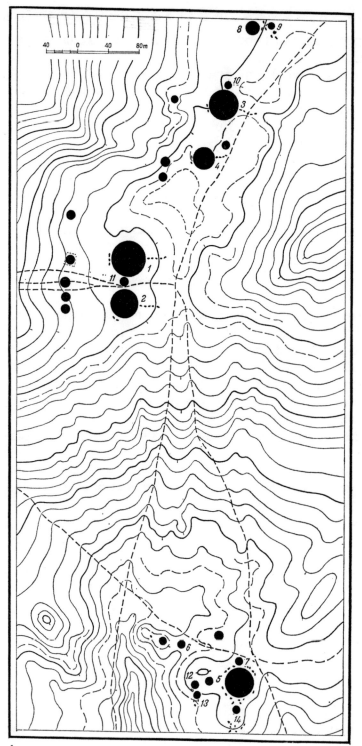

2. Plan of Pazyryk group of barrows.

moraine. These deposits were observed to their full depth of 6·5 m. at the centre of barrow 2 and at the edge of the mound.

Barrow 5 lay on a terrace-like area 460 m. south-south-east of barrow 2 and 30 m. below it, close to the mouth of the valley. It had been built on laminated lacustrine sands stratigraphically earlier than the sands of the upper valley where the other barrows are. Their depth under the mound is not great, up to 1·7 m., and below this is a solid clay deposit.

The vegetation of the valley and slopes gives an impression of xeromorphism, both in its appearance and the inventory of species. There is a complete absence of annuals and almost complete lack of biennials. Of 104 species collected in the valley only two plants were biennials. The preponderant mass of plants have a strong deep root system as, for example, sage (*Phlomis tuberosa*), which was very widespread.

The plants were undersized, with small leaves and flowers. The grass height was low, on the average 40–45 cm., and only on the north side of the valley was it higher and more continuous with the formation of proper turf. In the middle part of the valley, where the first four barrows are situated, and on the southern part, the turf cover was weak and discontinuous, leaving bare patches.

The vegetational features enumerated indicate a dry soil, strong drainage and sharply continental climate in the valley bottom.

The preponderant types of plants were *Gramineae, Compositae, Labiatae, Ranunculaceae, Rosaceae, Caryophyllaceae* and *Iridaceae*.

All or almost all the species belong to the steppe groups of mountainous, rocky and semi-desert plants; in Pazyryk valley these were basic, and most often encountered.[1]

The vegetation of the valley is characterized by marked seasonal changes: in early spring, when the iris, Altai anemone and campion are flowering, the ground is covered by a blue-grey carpet; in summer, the varied steppe-meadow grasses flower luxuriantly; and finally in the early autumn wormwood and feather grass are conspicuous.

[1] The list of species is as follows: Gramineae: *Festuca sulcata* Hack. (steppe fescue); *Agropyrum cristatum* P.B. v. *imbricatum* M.B. (combed couch grass); *Avena desertorum* Less. (steppe oat); *A. fatua* L. (wild oat); *Trisetum flavescens* L. P.B. (yellow oat grass); *Poa angustifolia* L. (narrow-leafed spear grass); *Stipa rubans* P. Smirn. (feather grass). Compositae: *Antennaria dioica* L. (cat's paw); *Leontopodium sibiricum* Cass. (Siberian edelweiss); *Artemisia sacrorum* Ledb. (holy wormwood); *A. rupestris* L. (cliff wormwood); *Senecio pratensis* D.C. (meadow ragwort); *Galatella angustissima* Lindl. Labiatae: *Thymus serpyllum* L. (thyme); *Phlomis tuberosa* L. (sage); *Schysonopeta multifida* Briq. Ranunculaceae: *Pulsatilla patens* Mill. (campion); *Aconitum barbatum* Patr. (bearded aconite). Rosaceae: *Filipendula hexapetula* Gilib. (dropwort); *Potentilla subacaulis* L.; *P. sericea* L. Caryophyllaceae: *Diantus seguieri* Will. (Seguiere's pink); *Melandrium aprica* Turcz. Iridaceae: *Iris ruthenica* Ker-Gawl. (Russian iris).

[Where it has not been possible to identify an English name reliably it has been omitted. TRANSLATOR.]

The vegetational composition, the marked change of seasons, sharply expressed xeromorphism and low height of the grass, combined with sharp continental climate and dry, well-drained soil, are all characteristic features of mountain steppe. The vegetation of such steppes possesses a high salt content favourable to the growth and increase of pasturing animals. So in spite of the feeble grass at the present time such steppe is highly valued. It was no less prized at the time the barrows were thrown up, since, as we shall see below, no essential change in vegetation has taken place from that time to this.

The flora on the barrows themselves, and especially that on their edge, is little different from that of the valley as a whole. The surface drainage around the mounds was in all cases excellent, since everywhere, except in barrow 4, there was a slight (considerable in the cases of barrows 2 and 5) slope away from the mounds. The best drainage of ground water was under barrows 3 and 4.

On the rocks of the cairns lichen grew slightly (*Squamaria robina Will.*, *Placodium*). On the north shaded side lichen grew more extensively; sometimes it covered the stones with a continuous layer, making them look red.

Of plants that grew only on the edges of the barrow-cairns Siberian barberry (*Berberis sibirica* Pall.) may be noted. The particularly splendid iris flowers (*Iris ruthenica*) that grew in spring around the cairns, no doubt due to the relatively greater dampness of the soil adjoining them, should be mentioned.

Park-like larch woods predominate not only in the hollows of the valley but also on the adjoining prominences. Larch with some fir covers the watershed between Pazyryk valley and the River Balyktyul. Larch woods were the dominant vegetation at the time the barrows were constructed; among many hundreds of trees employed in the barrow structures we will find an almost exclusive use of larch with a small number (not in all the barrows moreover) of fir logs. Shrubs, flowering plants and mosses from the barrows are all represented among contemporary species. Pollen analysis of the buried soil under the barrow mounds, besides varied grasses and pine with cedar (larch pollen does not survive) showed nothing remarkable.[1]

The presence in all the large barrows of huge strips of birch bark covering the burial chambers, as well as numerous objects made of birch wood, should be noticed. At the present day birch does not grow in the Great Ulagan valley, for

[1] Results of pollen analysis:

	0·0–0·05 m.	0·25–0·30 m.	0·35–0·4 m.		0·0–0·05 m.	0·25–0·30 m.	0·35–0·4 m.
Tree pollen				Artemisia	–	–	2
				Chenopodiaceae (?)	1	–	–
Pinus sibirica	6	–	6	Undefined	–	2	1
Picea	–	–	1	Spores			
Non-tree pollen				Green mosses	–	2	4
Gramines	–	–	4	Ferns	2	–	–

6

its uppermost limit appears to be 1,500 m., higher than which it does not occur in the eastern Altai. On the other hand birch does grow in the lower reaches of the River Bashkaus and in the valley of the Chulyshman, and could have been brought thence. Therefore we have no grounds for inferring changes in the vegetation, and consequently not in the climate either, since the barrows were constructed.

The climate of the eastern Altai, in particular of the Ulagan hills and steppe, is characterized by low average annual temperatures, long duration of winter and low temperatures during winter months. A thin layer of late snow is blown on to the open places by wind. Light winter cloud cover causes a great loss of heat by radiation, strong chilling and deep freezing of the ground. The predominant calmness in the cold time of the year produces an inversion of temperature distribution and consequently refreezing in the valleys. The summer is short, relatively dry and cool, and has high midday temperatures alternating with cold nights.

Thus all the climatic conditions required for the formation of frozen ground are present in the eastern Altai. Yet, due to an insufficiently low mean annual temperature and the extraordinarily variable surface conditions, this region does not lie in the zone of permanently frozen ground. We do not see it on the south-facing slopes that are strongly heated in summer, but it is a normal occurrence on northern slopes of valleys and hills. Frozen soil (*merzlota*) is visible at various points in the Great Ulagan and Balyktyul valleys adjacent to the place that concerns us. Nevertheless in Pazyryk valley itself, apart from in the barrows we dug, frozen soil does not occur, nor did it do so at the time the barrows were made. Hence it is very natural to ask when and by what means did the permanent refrigeration arise that led to such remarkable preservation of the tombs themselves and everything buried in them? In order to answer this question it is necessary to be acquainted briefly with the method of construction of the barrows.

In all the large Pazyryk barrows at the bottom of the burial shaft (with an area of about 50 sq. m., in barrow 4 about 30 sq. m.), at a depth of about 4 m. there was a log chamber with a floor area of about 17 sq. m. (in barrows 1, 2 and 5, 13 sq. m. and 8 sq. m. in barrows 3 and 4), with a height of 1·8–2 m. (except in barrow 4, the height of the chamber of which was only 1·2 m.). The upper half of the tomb shaft was filled with layers of logs and substantial rocks. The tomb shaft was covered by a cupola-shaped earth mound varying from 0·9 to 2 m. high at the centre, over which lay a cairn of stones 1·3–1·7 m. high and 36–46 m. in diameter. In barrow 4 the cairn was only 1·1 m. high and 24 m. in diameter.

Observations on the distribution of frozen soil made while digging showed that this existed at the topmost level of the buried surface if dug in the first half

7

of the summer, and 0·4–0·5 m. lower if dug in the second half of the summer. The depth of frozen soil was variable: in barrow 4 it hardly reached the bottom of the tomb shaft, in barrow 1 it was slightly below and in the others a good deal, at least 1·5 m., below the tomb bottom.

Generally the frozen soil took the shape of a lens beneath the barrow, the upper edge being related to the superincumbent cairn and not extending beyond its perimeter. In the centre of the barrows in the robbers' craters the lens thinned out somewhat and reached its greatest thickness under the inner ring of stones thrown up by the robbers. Hence the top surface of the frozen ground tapered off towards the edge, while the lower surface was slightly convex.

Measurement of the ice content of the soil showed that it diminished outwards from the barrow centre; the degree of congelation depended on the distance from the centre of refrigeration and the source of the waterlogging of the ground.

The climate of the Ulagan uplands, the basic factor producing barrow congelation, is sufficiently favourable for refrigeration given certain secondary factors, but in normal conditions permafrost does not exist in Pazyryk valley. The barrow congelation under the mound is to be attributed mainly to the cairn of stones, the factor that promoted the development and, above all, maintained the refrigeration. The cairn acted as a heat insulator protecting the earth from heat in the summer and thus delaying and weakening the thaw. Under winter conditions the cairn was the focus of maximum heat radiation on account of the uneven but more rapid cooling of the stone, by comparison with the ground surface, due to the free convection within the cairn. Although at the beginning of the winter some store of warmth in the cairn slightly held up the cooling process, in the spring heating was greatly delayed. The mixing up of warm air with cold happened much more quickly than cold with warm.

The cairn, a poor heat conductor, influenced the temperature alternations in the daily and annual sequences, softening extremes and preventing large absolute changes. Allowing gentle penetration of rain in the warm time of the year it sharply decreased evaporation; acting indeed in the opposite way by condensing moisture, the cairn increased the general dampness of the ground, at the same time strongly hindering heat conduction. Finally the cairn acted as a light shield, reducing the penetration of light.

As a result of the combined action of the factors described a special microclimate was created in and under the cairn, quite distinct from the microclimate of the natural surface, which favoured the development and maintenance of congelation.

Besides the cairns the general construction of the barrows encouraged refrigeration. Rising above the ground surface they became colder in winter,

8

and the earth mound over the tomb shaft froze, the freezing reaching even lower. The voids between the logs and stones of the roof in the upper half of the tomb became cold cells, cooled from the base of the mound above. In the lower half of the shaft the burial chamber covered over by birch bark strips was free of ice. In the voids of the roof and in the chamber there was produced continuous contact convection of air. Air, cooled in the voids of the ceiling, escaped into the chamber, and the warmer air of the chamber drifted up to the zone of contact with the cold surface. This process was continuous, intensifying at a time of low temperature contact (winter) and weakening at a time of maximum (summer) warming of the ground surrounding the barrow. The cairn and the log and boulder filling above the roof covered by bark stabilized the seasonal cooling.

Thus in the course of some years the combined action of climate and peculiarities of barrow construction produced a temperature equilibrium under the cairns and a lens of frozen ground.

The convection process, described above, could cause condensation of moisture by contact with the ceiling or within the log and stone fill, which, together with seepage through the voids, was responsible for the ice formation on the floors of several of the burial chambers. After the plundering of the tombs the robbers' crater in the mound and trap in the roof caused several changes in the thermal conditions within the barrows. It created, albeit briefly, conditions for refreezing of the tombs, reduced the contact area of refrigeration in the centre of the barrow and filled the burial chambers with ice.

As already remarked above, lenses of frozen soil were found under all the large barrows. Since all the barrows had been plundered the question obviously arises: after they had been robbed did they then freeze up or did freezing take place earlier, directly after the interments? Was the freezing not the direct result of the plundering, more precisely the result of the crater which the robbers left that allowed direct penetration of cold winter air into the chamber?

That the robbing was done long ago is well testified by the formation of a soil cover over the gaps made by the robbers' pits, while the marks of blows left on the aperture cut in the log cover indicate the use of bronze celts. Nevertheless all the evidence points to the barrows having been robbed after refrigeration had taken place, which would require some years. Had the congelation been completed in a single winter (which is wholly improbable seeing that the maximum seasonal freezing of ground in the given climate cannot exceed 2 m. depth) then the horse bodies, even if they had been buried at the beginning of the summer, should have been fully preserved. In reality things were quite different. The horse bodies even in barrows 1 and 2, where preservation was relatively good, had undergone considerable decomposition before they had finally frozen up. Only the bones survived of the animal food placed in the burial chambers; the

9

meat had entirely decomposed. Consequently there must have been an appreciable lapse of time before the temperature in the chambers fell permanently below 0° C. On the other hand at the time of the plundering of the tombs, even in barrows 3 and 4 the buried corpses—embalmed it is true—were relatively well preserved. We found them in excellent preservation in barrows 2 and 5. In barrow 1 the robbers had removed the body (or bodies) which consequently must also have been in good condition. In barrow 3 the skeleton, thrown out of the coffin on the floor, was articulated, and the same can be said of the skeletons in the coffins of barrow 4; at the time of plundering the buried bodies in the last two barrows could not yet have turned into skeletons.

It is obvious furthermore that the plundering took place quite openly, proceeding at leisure, executed by small groups of perhaps two or three individuals. Clear traces of robbing, like great open pits and piles of upcast, cannot be concealed, so this could not have taken place if relatives of the deceased were close by. The plundering could only have been undertaken by newcomers when the tribe responsible for making the Pazyryk barrows had for one reason or another left this area.

Study of the ice filling the chamber in barrow 2 has given extraordinarily interesting results, and resolved the question. The ice in this tomb had been produced in two phases: in a phase at the original barrow congelation and in a phase after the plundering. The first phase is represented by a layer of ice exceeding 40 cm. in thickness in the central part of the chamber and in its north-west corner, reducing towards the east, where it was about 25 cm. thick. This ice had formed in the chamber before the plundering. It was quite clear, translucent, slightly porous, identical with that between the logs above the chamber. It lay in the shape of a plano-convex mound, as a result of the swelling of the floor, with its apex to the north-west of the centre of the chamber. The robbers' debris lay on a quite distinct surface of translucent ice. On it lay the log coffin lid, taken off and turned upside-down by the thieves, and the corpses thrown out of the coffin with various other things. The legs of four little tables were set hard in the ice and had remained held fast even after the robbers had ripped off the tops of three of them. The side of the coffin showed chop-marks almost to the bottom; it had been by no means easy for the thieves to accomplish their work since the ice had penetrated the coffin, making it difficult to free the contents.

Ice of the second phase, caused by water pouring through the hole cut in the roof by the robbers, filled the whole chamber. This ice was of a yellow colour and filled with air bubbles of elongated form mainly running vertically in discontinuous chains. The division between this ice and that of the first phase was sharply distinguished by greater transparency and fewer bubbles in the latter. The new ice had not formed at one time, since in section it was layered; no less than three clear layers of smudgy yellow ice can be traced, showing lines of flow of the water from the robbers' trap opening and circulation against the chamber walls. Freezing took place simultaneously with the flow, so that ice was formed from the outside inwards. This would only have taken place if the water coming through the trap entered a chamber where a kernel of refrigeration already existed.

It had been a rather different story in barrow 1. There the ice on the bottom of the tomb, formed before the plundering, was thin, about 5 cm. thick. It was clear, and the felt frozen into it on the wooden floor, not to mention the debris on top of it, are evidence of its formation before the robbers' intrusion. Collapse from the crater, that happened evidently soon after the plundering, had choked up the trap-hole in the tomb's roof and so prevented the entry of atmospheric precipitation into the chamber. Consequently there was no complete icing up in this chamber as in barrow 2. The laminated ice of the second phase that filled the tree-trunk coffin and inside of the chamber owed its origin to condensation.

In barrows 3, 4 and 5 the ice of the first phase was clear, translucent and of the same structure as in barrow 2; it filled the interstices between the rocks and logs in the shaft. An actual layer of this ice, about 4 cm. thick, was observed only in barrow 3. All the chambers of these barrows were filled by ice of the second phase, formed from water coming through the plunderers' forced entry. No distinct lamination was observed in this ice.

In the first three barrows the log coffins stood not directly on the floor but at some height on the ice of the first phase. This lifting had been caused during the formation of the first-phase ice by the expansion of the crystals.

The large barrows of the Pazyryk group, as we shall see below, were not of one date. The time between the construction of the first and the last could have been a hundred years,[1] but the plundering was all done at once. The identical method of gaining access to all the burial chambers, even down to small details, points to this.

In a circle of 10–15 m. diameter in the centre of each barrow the cairn was removed and the stones thrown out around its circumference. In the earthen mound below, the shaft reduced from 4–5 m. to 2·2–3 m. diameter at the level of the buried soil. In the upper level of the logs a rectangular trap of 1·4 m. by 1·9 m. to 1·9 m. by 2·6 m. was chopped through. In the roof immediately over the chamber, where normally five logs were cut through, the aperture was from 0·5 m. by 1·05 m. to 0·7 m. by 1·16 m., and in the lowest tier, where only two logs were cut out, the trap was only 37 cm. by 48 cm. to 43 cm. by 90 cm. Only in barrow 1 was the trap not rectangular but oval in shape, measuring 40 cm. by 60 cm.

[1] According to the tree-ring dating the time that elapsed was forty-eight years; see Introduction, p. xxxvi. [TRANSLATOR.]

Chopping in the solid ice among the logs of the roof was not an easy matter, so probably during the robbing of barrow 5 the thieves lit fires, which caused all the logs in the centre of the barrow down to the roof of the burial chamber to be charred or burnt.

Having penetrated the burial chambers the robbers found them free of ice except barrow 2 which, as explained above, was partially filled with it. So they could easily take out the contents except from that one.

The chambers of all the barrows (except no. 2) had been almost entirely emptied. Clothing, decorated wall-hangings of felt, household gear—even earthenware bottles—were removed. In barrow 3, as we shall see below, even the arrowheads were taken off the shafts, which were all that was left. Where anything survived it was accidental, carelessly dropped or, as in barrow 2, was stuck in the ice of the first phase; if there had been no ice evidently nothing would have remained even there.

The horse burials had never been disturbed by the plunderers. They were evidently not interested in them, as they must have been well aware of their contents. Apart from Pazyryk, in the valley of the Great Ulagan and its tributaries there are many cemeteries with ordinary burials of just the same kind of the same period as the Pazyryk barrows. The ordinary burials, which differ from the large barrows basically only in dimensions and absence of congelation, have almost all been robbed. It can be assumed that in digging these the robbers had found the horse burials there and consequently knew what to expect elsewhere.

The only case where an attempt appeared to have been made to penetrate the horse burials was in barrow 1, where the robbers had chopped a window, measuring 1·05 m. by 1·2 m., in the north wall of the inner log face of the chamber and taken stones out of the intervening space. Then they chopped through one log in the outer wall of the chamber, making an opening of 12 cm. by 21 cm., after which they stopped further work. It is abundantly clear why they stopped. First, the job of clearing the horse burial out was beyond the resources of a small gang, and for a big gang there was not room to work. It is one thing to clear out the chamber unimpeded, but quite another to extricate from a solidly frozen mass horse bodies and objects deposited with them behind the double thickness of tomb walls beneath hundreds of tons of overburden. In the barrows of the basin of the River Ursul, where the burial chamber walls were of one thickness, the robbers reached a horse burial, although they limited themselves to partial plundering of the remains. In the second place it would be known to the thieves that they could count on finding nothing more valuable there than saddlery and a certain number of thin gold plates.

12

2. BARROWS OF THE
PAZYRYK GROUP

IN THE comparatively limited area of Pazyryk valley there are about forty structures: big and small barrows with superincumbent cairns, flat stone pavements of circular and oval shape, enclosures, stone circles and alignments of vertical stones (fig. 2). Among them five large barrows can be distinguished: two in the north (nos. 3 and 4), two in the middle (nos. 1 and 2) and one in the south (no. 5). Besides the five large barrows there are nine small ones (nos. 6–14) of just the same type.

The large barrows were dug as follows: the first in 1929, the second in 1947–8, the third and fourth in in 1948 and the fifth in 1949 (*Pls. 1–30*).[1] In the last year three small barrows were excavated (nos. 6, 7 and 8). Five low cairns marked on the plan but not numbered were examined at various times, but in each case below the stony soil the ground appeared to be undisturbed. In 1924 I dug one of the stone enclosures, but again there were no traces of a burial in it, as was the case in similar enclosures that have been dug at other places in the Altai. Only in one enclosure on the left bank of the Great Ulagan, 2·5 km. below its junction with the Balyktyul in a pit at 0·4 m. below the ground surface, the bones of a man and a sheep, together with an iron horse bit, arrow-heads and buckles, were found in 1924.

Circles of six to eight rocks partially embedded in the ground have been dug in the Altai from time to time by A. V. Adrianov and myself, but they have yielded no finds with which one can assess their significance or age.

All the large Pazyryk barrows have a low earth mound covered by stones. The ratio of barrow height to diameter is more or less constant at 1 : 10. In the barrow centre there was inevitably a depression, the result, on the one hand, of subsidence in the ground and the material filling the tomb shaft and, on the other, of the robbers' digging.

The relatively small height of the barrows is attributable to the fact that in the mound only the soil that was dug out from the tomb shaft was used, over which

[1] For separate descriptions see Gryaznov, A, 1950; Rudenko, A, 1948, 1950, 1951.

the stones of the cairn were spread fairly evenly. The latter was made only slightly deeper from the perimeter inwards towards the centre.

All the barrows of the period treated were of the same type. The common structural features were as follows: (i) a rectangular tomb shaft oriented east–west; (ii) a human burial in a log chamber on the south side of the shaft; (iii) horse burials in the northern half of the shaft, outside the chamber; (iv) a low earthen mound covered by a cairn of rocks.

In the small barrows with cairns of 13–15 m. diameter the log chamber was only three logs high which, as we shall see below, hardly gave room for the interment with its insignificant household goods, while outside it two or three horses were buried. In the medium barrows, approaching the large in size (barrow 4), with a cairn diameter of about 24 m., there were proper burial chambers containing the corpse in a log coffin, and interment of a substantial number of horses.

In the great barrows with a cairn diameter of 36–46 m. the burial chamber was of double thickness with a system of posts and beams supporting the vast load of logs and rocks above, which filled the upper half of the burial shaft.

These great barrows are distinguished from each other by a number of peculiarities, so that no two are completely alike. We shall study the large barrows in more detail beginning with their external form.

It should be noted that from each of the first four large barrows a line of upright stones extended eastward. In the case of barrow 5 there was no such row, but on the other hand it had a ring of flat uprights around it with some areas of stone paving (fig. 3) not observed in the other four barrows. The stones in the ring were set at intervals varying from 3·5 m. to 5·7 m., and stood 2·5–3 m. back from the edge of the cairn. The areas of stone paving led directly from the barrow edge radially outwards. Such external features occur in large cairns in the valley of the River Ursul, e.g. at Tuekta.

The areas of the tomb shafts were practically identical, 51–55 sq. m., in all the large barrows except barrow 4, in which the shaft had an area of only about 30 sq. m. The depth of the shaft below the buried ground surface was about 4 m., except in barrow 3 where it reached 5·2 m. In barrow 1 the shaft was square and in the others rectangular, the east–west dimension being greater than the north–south one. The area at the shaft bottom was normally somewhat smaller than at the orifice because its sides were not vertical. The extra depth of the shaft in barrow 3 is probably due to the sandy ground beneath it being softer than that below the other mounds. In the relatively small barrow 4 the shaft dug in just the same soft ground was only 4·1 m. deep and hardly exceeded the 4 m. depth of the larger barrows.

Tools used for digging the tomb shafts, to judge by the discoveries in them,

3. Plan of Pazyryk, barrow 5.

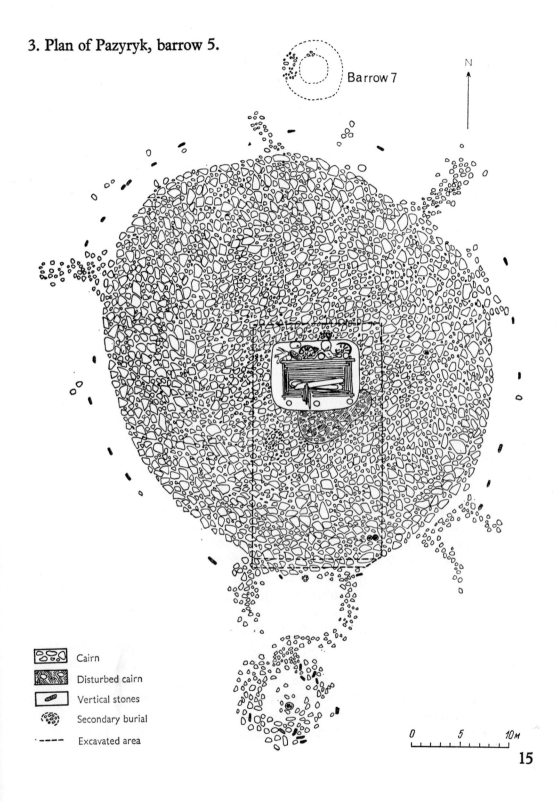

Barrow 7

N

	Cairn
	Disturbed cairn
	Vertical stones
	Secondary burial
- - - -	Excavated area

0   5   10 m

15

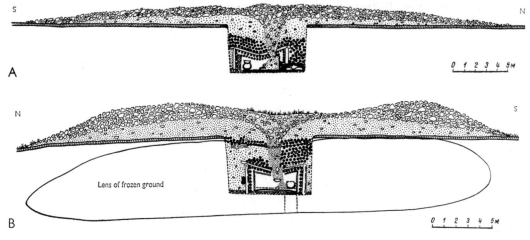

4. Sections of barrows 1 (A) and 2 (B).

were wedges, mallets, antler picks and wooden shovels. In barrow 1 only a fragment of the working end of a shovel survived. In barrow 2 shovels were found during the dismantling of the filling over the burial chamber among the logs on the north side. One was short (115 cm.), a second long (127 cm.) (*Pl. 36*B). The working part of both shovels was narrow (about 12 cm.) and long (35–38 cm.) and the handle straight with a circular section (5 cm. in diameter). The blades of both had been broken during work, otherwise they would not have been thrown in with the logs, since they would have been needed for throwing up the mound.

In several places in the shaft of barrow 2, mainly in the log filling, there was a great quantity (about 100) of wooden wedges and several wooden mallets. Such wedges and mallets have been observed in other barrows, and without a doubt they were used in digging the burial shaft. The wedges (*Pl. 36*C), varying in size from 30 to 73 cm., were flat, oval in section, with a bevelled end, their butt ends bearing signs of strong battering with a mallet. They must have been re-sharpened with an axe as they blunted with use, but when the butts splintered from blows they were thrown away.

The mallets had been made from the trunks of larch trees, in some cases from a root at the base of the trunk. They were generally massive, heavy, 46–70 cm. long, the working part with a diameter of 12 cm. and the handle 25 cm. long. These tools must have had long use; on some a mass of dents was visible, made by blows on the wedges. They had been thrown away after battering from long use had split them. Several such mallets were found; *Pl. 37*A (*left*) shows one made from the top of a larch root and examples made from the bole.

16

Digging holes with the aid of mallets and wedges was practised where the ground was hard. So the latter were particularly numerous in barrow 2, the shaft of which had been dug into boulder clay. They occurred in less quantity in barrow 5, where the lower half of the shaft had been dug through stiff clay. In barrows 1, 3 and 4, with shafts excavated in lacustrine sands, there were only single wedges, and in barrow 1, besides what has already been mentioned, there were fragments of a mallet.

In filling the shaft the worn-out wedges and mallets, like the broken shovels, were thrown back into it, but antler picks had been treated with more reverence and put in the tomb with the other grave goods. A pick found in barrow 8 consisted of the tine and part of the shaft of an antler (*Pl. 37B*). It was polished from long use and had been fixed originally in a wooden handle.

While digging the shaft and dressing back the sides cracks must have sometimes appeared, and in order to check these and prevent collapse the faces had had to be shored. In barrow 2, in the upper quarter of the shaft, wedges had been driven into the sides to support struts holding the walls back. In barrow 3 vertical posts had been set up against the sides, except the south side, pressed back against the wall near the top by thin logs held at their ends by stakes (*Pl. 36A*). Such reinforcement was especially necessary in this barrow due to the sandiness of the ground and the great depth of the shaft.

The considerable depth of the shafts rendered access without a ladder difficult; ladders were found in barrows 4 and 5. In barrow 4 steps were found in the eastern part of the shaft between the burial chamber, at its north-eastern corner, and the horse burial. They were upright and consisted of a log (*Pl. 38A*), 3·17 m. long, 9–10 cm. in diameter at the top and 14–15 cm. at the bottom, in which nine steps had been notched out at intervals of 32 cm. The ladder in barrow 5 was with the wagon parts in the horse burial in its eastern half above the horse bodies. It consisted of a log 4·13 m. long, 11 cm. in diameter at the top and 16 cm. at the bottom, with eight notches roughly 6 cm. deep.

The burial chambers in all the large barrows, except barrow 4, were double, that is, had walls and ceilings of double thickness. In barrow 4, as already mentioned, it was single. Although of broadly similar construction, each of the double-walled chambers had its own peculiarities.

The chambers of barrows 1 and 2 (figs. 4, 5) can be regarded as structurally identical. The main common distinction of these two was that the floor of the chamber was above the shaft bottom, which was covered with a layer 10 cm. thick of broken stone on which the log chamber stood. In barrow 2 this stone base was covered by a further thin layer (5 cm. thick) of black soil, not found in barrow 1. In both cases the floor was made of thick planks, the inner walls of the chamber of dressed logs, interlocked by setting in deep notches at the corners,

17

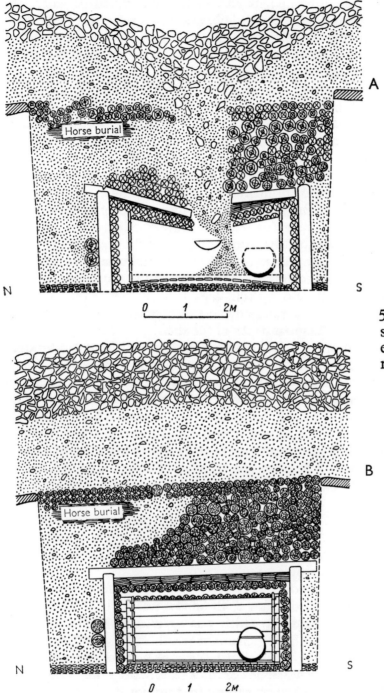

Horse burial

N

S

0   1   2M

Horse burial

N

S

0   1   2M

5. Section of burial shaft in barrow 2, as excavated (A) and reconstructed (B).

and the outside wall similar but of undressed logs. In barrow 1 upper and lower ceilings were of squared timbers, and in barrow 2 the lower logs had been dressed underneath to give a flat ceiling in the tomb.

In barrow 1 the space between the walls was filled with broken stone, in barrow 2 the space was left empty. The chambers were covered over with layers of birch bark, then by a layer of larch bark and finally by foliage of 'smoky tea' (*Potentilla dasiphora fruticosa* L. Rybd.).

The log box tomb of barrow 1 was not exactly a rectangle and its opposite walls were not of uniform length. The average internal dimensions were 3·35 m. by 4·87 m. with a height of 1·4 m., while the dimensions of the outer box were 4·45 m. by 6·15 m. with a general height of 2 m. The floor, on which the lower log of the inner box lay, consisted of nineteen planks about 6 cm. thick with an average width of 15 cm. The long walls (north and south) of the inner box consisted of nine, and the transverse sides of ten, dressed members. The ceiling of thirty logs rested on the transverse walls of the box.

The outer box rested directly on the bottom of the tomb shaft, and its sides were made up of eleven dressed members. The thirty logs of the ceiling lay with their thicker (root) ends on the thicker eastern wall.

The internal dimensions of the chamber in barrow 2 were 3·65 m. by 4·92 m. with a height of 1·53 m., while its outer box measured 4·15 m. by 5·7 m. with a height of 2·1 m. The floor on which the inner box stood consisted of seventeen planks, 5–6 cm. thick and of very variable width, 12–24 cm. The dressed members numbered eight longitudinal and seven transverse in the inner box with a roof of twenty logs; in the outer there were ten members in the walls and twenty-eight logs in the roof.

The burial chamber of barrow 5 was constructed on just the same plan as those of the first two but it was longer (fig. 6). The inner box, which was 1·4 m. high, measured 2·3 m. by 5·2 m.; the outer box 3·4 m. by 6·4 m. and 1·9 m. high. The floor consisted of thirteen planks of exactly the same thickness as in the first two barrows. The inner box had walls of eight members and a ceiling of thirteen logs, the outer box of ten and eighteen logs respectively. A distinctive feature of this chamber was that the inner box was constructed of trunk logs (not branch logs as in the other two barrows) dressed flat on the inside face. As in barrow 2 the space between the boxes in barrow 5 had not been filled up, leaving out of account a few objects put in there. On the other hand the space between the outer box and shaft wall had been filled up with pounded stone on the west and east sides entirely, and partially on the south side, which did not occur in the first two barrows.

The burial chamber in barrow 3 (fig. 7) has this much in common with that of barrow 1: the space between the inner and outer boxes was filled with pounded stone. Its floor was made of planks, but the walls of both boxes were

19

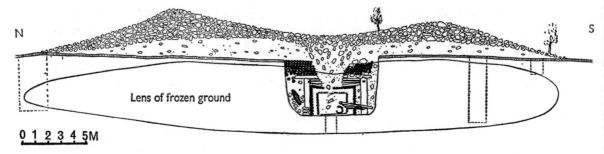

N S

Lens of frozen ground

0 1 2 3 4 5M

6. Sections of barrow 5 and its burial shaft.

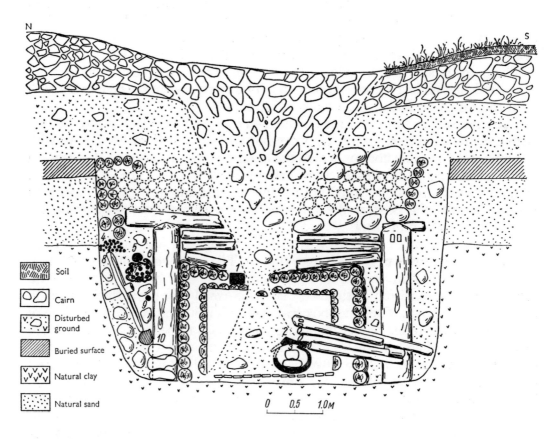

N S

Soil

Cairn

Disturbed ground

Buried surface

Natural clay

Natural sand

0   0.5   1.0M

1, 'Pillow' or stool;   4, rods from trolley;   8, wheel of carriage;
2, tree-trunk coffin;   5, wooden steps (ladder);   9, draught-pole of carriage;
3, embalmed bodies of man   6, felt wall-hanging;   10, bodies of horses.
and woman;   7, rods from carriage;

20

made of plain logs, fitted with notch upwards at the corner, and with no trace of any dressing whatever either on walls or roof.

The inner box of the chamber measured 2·08 m. by 3·45 m. and 1·08 m. high, the outer box 3·45 m. by 4·42 m. and 1·68 m. high. The floor consisted of fourteen planks about 5 cm. thick. The inner box stood seven logs high with a ceiling of fifteen logs; the outer box had ten members with eighteen logs in the roof. A peculiarity of the chamber of barrow 3 was a free space of about 0·5 m. between the roofs of the inner and outer boxes, which was not the case in the other tombs.

The burial chamber of barrow 4 (fig. 7) in its arrangements repeated the construction of the inner chambers in barrows 1 and 2. Its single thickness of wall was built of dressed members, its roof of logs and its floor of thick planks. Its internal dimensions were 2·14 m. by 3·75 m. with a height of 1·2 m. Its floor had eleven planks, wall seven members and roof sixteen logs. As in barrow 5 the space between the chamber and shaft sides, except on the north side, was filled with pounded stone.

The roofs of all the tombs without exception were covered with birch bark, but it did not survive to the same extent in each case. In barrow 4 its existence was merely established, in barrow 1 it is known that several layers existed, in barrow 2 there were six layers and in barrows 3 and 5 there were four layers. The method of roof covering was not the same in all cases. Thus in barrow 3 the covering was not plain strips of birch bark, but sheets made from strips sewn together with twisted bast thread. Such a sheet was from 2·23 m. to 2·27 m. long made up of birch-bark strips 0·42–0·7 m. wide. The sheets were laid in the following way; the first with outer face of bark downwards, second with inner, third outer and fourth inner face down. Where the edge of one sheet touched the edge of another there was a lining of moss. This moss consisted of the same species as now grow in the neighbourhood of the valley, among them *Phytidium rugosum* (Hedw.) Lindb.; *Pleurozium schreberi* (Willd.) Mitt.; *Ptilium crista-castrenris* (Hedw.) De Not. The chamber in barrow 5 was covered by two double bark sheets (*Pl. 33*), which extended over an appreciably larger area than the chamber itself (5·2 m. by 8·2 m.). Each sheet consisted of a large number of birch-bark strips sewn together, their outer faces adjoining each other. Where the strips touched they were sewn together by twisted bast thread (*Pl. 33*). As the area of the sheets was greater than the chamber's roof area their edges hung free down to the sixth log of the outer box of the tomb. These free edges of birch sheets were squeezed tight between the outside of the outer box and the upright posts against it, so it follows that the latter must have been set up after the chamber had been covered with birch bark.

In barrows 1–3 a layer of larch bark, outer face upwards, lay on the birch bark. Above the birch and larch bark, except in barrow 5, a fairly thick layer of

21

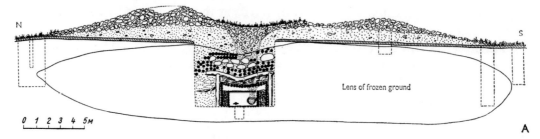

7. Sections of barrows 3 (A) and 4 (B).

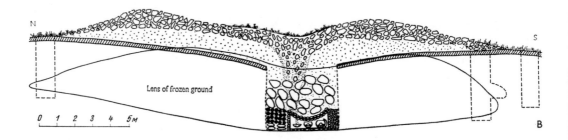

foliage of the shrub 'smoky tea' had been laid. It is difficult to judge the original thickness of this layer, but in its compressed form it was in the order of 10 cm. in the first three barrows, but less in the fourth.

By the north and south walls of the chambers, except in barrow 4, as already mentioned, stood three upright posts with elongated hollows, running north–south, notched into their tops, in which were lodged horizontal logs of the same diameter as the posts. The function of these was to act as beams taking the load off the tomb.

In barrows 1 and 2 the height of the posts was 2·1 m. and 2·65 m., with a diameter of 35 cm., and the beams had exactly similar thickness. In barrows 3 and 5 the posts were 2·6 m. and 2·65 m. high and considerably thicker, about 50 cm. in diameter, with the thicker (root) ends upwards. The horizontal pieces were over 40 cm. thick. The posts were set directly on the shaft bottom without any special seating. Barrow 1 was an exception in which the posts on the north side had packing stones around the base. In barrow 2 in the filling of the northern half 1·25 m. from the bottom two logs were laid one on top of the other behind the posts and parallel to the chamber side.

The size of the gap between the outer surface of the chamber roof and the lower face of the horizontal beams varied. In barrows 1 and 2 it was approximately 20–35 cm., in barrow 3 about 40 cm. and in barrow 5, 70 cm. The beams had sagged under the load of the top filling in barrows 1 and 2 and slightly

22

penetrated the roof below. In barrow 3, because there was still an open space of 40 cm. below them, the beams were very bowed. In barrow 5 there was a different arrangement, and three layers of short logs had been laid beneath and parallel to the beams. So the latter, although 70 cm. above the tomb roof and bearing the superincumbent filling of logs and stones, had scarcely bowed at all.

The horse interment, as an inflexible rule, was in the northern third of the burial shaft. In barrows 1, 4 and 5 the horses had been put in the bottom of the burial shaft. Some peculiarities of the horse burials in barrow 5 will be discussed below. In barrow 3 the northern third of the shaft had been filled to the level of the roof of the outer box. The larch bark and 'smoky tea' of the chamber roof partially overlapped this part of the burial shaft, on which some of the horses had been laid. Later, due to subsidence, the horse bodies had come down to the level of the roof of the inner box of the chamber.

In barrows 1, 3 and 5, when the horizontal members were put up on the posts, as mentioned above, the horses had already been deposited in the burial shaft. This is proved by the projection of the beams beyond the posts over the horses' bodies—of 0·5–1 m. in barrow 1, in barrow 3 up to 1·3 m. and in barrow 5 up to 0·5 m.

In barrow 2, exceptionally, the horse bodies were deposited very high up after the shaft at this point had been filled up to four-fifths of its depth. They lay about 0·7 m. below the buried ground surface, resting on juniper and larch branches.

After the interment of the human and horse bodies the upper part of the tomb shaft was filled up with layers of logs and a mass of large rocks with a slight amount of soil.

In barrows 1 and 2 this part of the tomb was filled exclusively by logs. The depth of logs in barrow 1 above the horse burial was up to 2·5 m., and above the burial chamber up to 1·5 m. There were about three hundred logs, which were for the most part uprooted trunks with the roots towards the west. In barrow 2 there were approximately nine layers of logs above the burial chamber, the tenth and eleventh layers covering both chamber and horse interment, making the total number of logs about two hundred and forty. As the length of the logs (6·5–6·9 m.) in barrow 2 laid transversely was less than the width of the shaft at the top, besides the upper two layers eight logs were laid along the east and west walls of the shaft at right angles to the rest.

Due to subsidence in the shafts at the time of the excavations the upper layer of logs was 0·4–0·5 m. below the buried ground surface, the void thus created having filled with soil.

Barrows 3, 4 and 5 were distinguished from the first two by the fact that the upper part of the shaft was filled not only with larch logs but with a great number of boulders and angular rocks.

In barrow 3 two regular layers of logs were laid on the transverse beams with additional third and fourth layers against the northern and southern faces of the shaft. Above the logs there was a great quantity of stones in two layers, over a hundred. Above the stones was another layer of logs (sixteen) but with gaps, not continuous. The logs were mainly uprooted tree trunks about 6 m. long, the layers laid alternately, root towards east, then towards west and so on.

In barrow 4 there were only one layer of logs covering the tomb and four layers over the horse burials; above was a filling of stones and soil.

In barrow 5 above three layers of logs laid north–south over the tomb was a bed of boulders, about sixty stones, and in the northern part of the shaft over the horse burials were two boulders weighing 2·8 and 3·2 tons. Above the stone bed there were again five tiers of logs, on an average thirty in each, lying transversely, and over this the earthen mound containing a number of boulders, several of them large, up to three tons in weight. In the whole construction we can reckon about two hundred and fifty logs and nearly a hundred large boulders.

To complete the filling a low earthen knoll was heaped up over the shaft, the material of which had derived from digging it. This conclusion is based not only on the mechanical consistency of the mound but also on its volume. Over the mound a cairn was piled, which consisted in all the barrows mainly of angular rocks, predominantly of red tufaceous sandstone (with traces of clay-haematite-celite), gathered from natural outcrops on the valley slopes. Quite a lot of boulders of granite-porphyrites (granites, microlinear-biotite-hornblendes; assorted porphyrites, that is, cerosite-zeolite epidotic ore with carbonate) and quartzites (quartz, micro-quartzite and cerosite) collected from the slopes and in the valley itself.

The cairns were made up of both large boulders and pebbles; in the interstices between the large rocks there were small amounts of river pebbles and fairly coarse gravel.

The tomb shaft as a rule lay at the centre of the barrow, but in heaping it up attention had not always been paid to making sure that the centre of the mound coincided with the shaft below. Consequently in barrows 3 and 4 the tomb shaft was to the north-west of the true centre of the barrow.

Three small barrows excavated in Pazyryk valley, like all the rest, had been plundered, as was obvious before the excavation. Barrow 6 lies 60 m. west-north-west of barrow 5. The cairn's diameter was 14–15 m., height 0·7 m., diameter of the plunder hole 6 m. and depth of its hollow 0·5 m. The earth thrown out had been put back, for a secondary interment had been made in the robbers' hole. The burial shaft measuring 3·4 m. by 3·4 m. was orientated towards the east, and was filled up with the lacustrine sand into which it had been dug. At the bottom of the shaft, 2·2 m. below the buried surface and on its southern side, traces of a log box (2·2 m. by 3·2 m.) of three members (0·5 m. high) were observed with its long walls orientated east–west. To judge by the

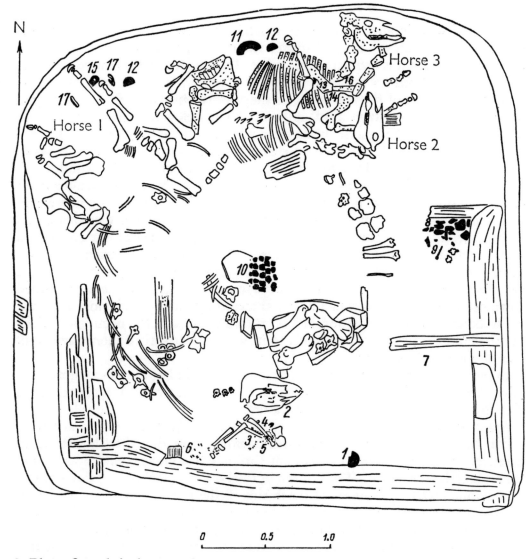

N

8. Plan of tomb in barrow 6.

1, Chinese mirror; 2, 3 and 6, beads; 4, cowrie shell; 5, red lacquer; 7, gold beads; 8 and 10, earthenware bottles; 9, knife; 11 and 12, antler saddle plaques; 13–16, antler saddle pendants; 17, gold leaf.

bones an adult (probably a woman) and an adolescent girl had been buried there. The girl lay on the south side on her back, head towards the east. Behind the north wall of the tomb three horses had been deposited. One of them lay on the shaft bottom against the north wall on its left side, head towards the east; the other two were above it, lying on their right sides, one facing east and one north-east (fig. 8).

25

Barrow 7 was situated 5 m. to the north of barrow 5 and separated from it only by a slight hollow 4 m. in diameter and by the low bank surrounding it. A trench 4 m. square was opened in the centre of the barrow within the edges of the depression left from its robbing. Traces of a cairn were observed only in the north-western part of the barrow. The shape of the burial shaft, 2 m. by 2 m., filled mainly with lacustrine sand, appeared 0·5 m. below the surface. The depth of the shaft was 1·9 m. and its walls were orientated at 45° to the lines of longitude. On the south side was a box two logs high, its bottom decked with wood, and roofed with planks. In it were the bones and skull of a child or youth.

Barrow 8 lay 106 m. north-north-east from barrow 3. Its cairn had a diameter of 14 m. and was 0·65 m. high above the ground. In the centre was a depression 8 m. across and 0·45 m. deep. In the cairn there was a secondary human burial with a horse. At a depth of 1·25 m. below the buried surface the shape of a burial shaft of irregular quadrilateral form, 3·2 m. by 3·5 m., orientated east–west, was observed. At 2·65 m. below this surface in a decayed box of three logs a woman was buried on her back, head towards the east, with arms extended down her sides. The barrow had been plundered by extensive digging, and most of the bones of a horse skeleton had been thrown out. In the north part of the shaft behind the box grave, and next to it, were the disturbed thorax and right arm of a woman's skeleton.

In order to provide a fuller picture of the normal kind of burial in the barrow-cairns accounts are given below of four such barrows: two at Aragol and two at the village of Katanda on the River Katun'.

Aragol is situated on the right bank of the Great Ulagan above its flood terrace 5 km. from Pazyryk. One of the three barrow-cairns dug there was 8 m. in diameter and 0·6 m. high. At a depth of 3 m. in a box grave 0·9 m. by 2 m. and 0·4 m. high lay a skeleton. The bottom of the box was planked and the roof was of the same material. Behind the north side of the box lay two horse skeletons one on top of the other, heads towards the east (fig. 9). The shaft was filled with stone and soil. All the evidence indicated that this tomb had never been robbed. The second barrow was larger, 12 m. in diameter, the cairn 0·5 m. high, with a depression 0·5 m. deep in the middle. In the burial shaft, at a depth of 3·1 m. below the surface, remains of a box tomb were observed measuring 1·6 m. by 2·5 m. with long sides running east–west. There were remains of a plank floor on the bottom, and the box (probably two logs high), which was about 35 cm. high, contained the bones of two individuals lying in confusion. In the northern part of the burial shaft two horse skeletons were found, both with heads towards the east.

The barrow cemetery at Katanda lies on the left bank of the Katun', a kilometre along the river from the junction with the River Katanda. The first of four barrows excavated there was 9 m. in diameter with a cairn about 0·4 m. high and a central depression 20 cm. deep. The burial shaft, which measured 1·5 m. by

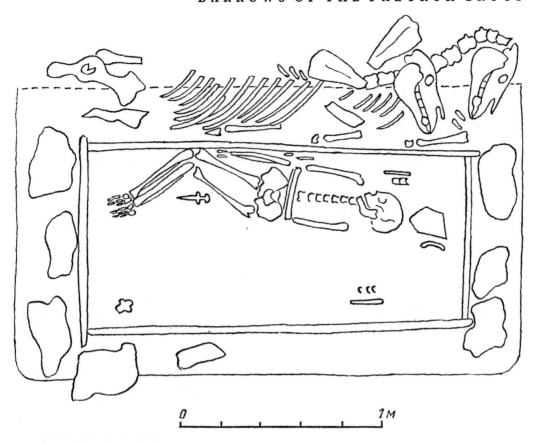

9. Plan of tomb at Aragol, barrow 1.

2·5 m., was orientated east–west and was 3·25 m. deep. Judging by the surviving skeletal remains there had been a man, a woman and a child buried there. Above them, in the northern part of the shaft, lay two horses, one with head towards the east and the other with head towards the west. The shaft was filled with stones and soil. The second barrow was larger, 13·5 m. in diameter, 0·65 m. high and central depression 0·35 m. deep. The shaft was 2·35 m. by 3·4 m. at the top, 2 m. by 3·11 m. at the bottom, 3·4 m. deep and orientated east–west. On the bottom of the shaft was a stone pavement on which lay the skeleton of a woman with head towards the east. North of this and parallel to it, head also towards the east, lay a horse skeleton. Up to a depth of 1 m. the shaft was filled with soil and, above that, stones.

Thus we see that in ordinary barrows with superincumbent cairns, in poor men's graves, the methods of interment were basically the same as in the large barrows. At the bottom of a shaft was a log box in which a person was buried, and beyond the box in the northern third of the shaft was a horse burial. The shaft was filled with soil and stones, and above was a small mound covered by a cairn.

A series of favourable circumstances offers an opportunity to define the time of year when the burials in Pazyryk took place. The presence of congelation suggests late autumn or even early winter as the burial time. One can hardly suppose that burial took place during winter or early spring when the ground is frozen to a considerable depth. To have excavated the burial shaft in frozen ground, particularly in clay, with wedges and mallets, would be extremely difficult, even if not quite impossible. Many facts point to the early summer and autumn as the time when the burials were made in these barrows.

In all the barrows, except barrow 4, hair survived on the horse bodies which could not possibly be regarded as the winter coat. Of the nine horses buried in barrow 5 only one, the one which had the rich saddlery and head decoration with crest, was well groomed. This animal had probably been stalled during the winter and fed on concentrated feeds. All the other horses were to some degree emaciated, as they are during spring and early summer when they have been left outside to feed in the previous winter. In barrow 3, in the moss packing between the strips of the birch-bark sheet covering the burial chamber, flowers were found of white-yellow scabious (*Scabiosa achroleuca* L.). The phase of development of this plant showed that it had been collected in the first half of summer, at the end of June or beginning of July. Moreover in the same moss packing shoots of *Hylocomium splendens* indicate early growth and are to be referred to the spring/summer.[1] The partially rooted trunks of larch and the bark covering the chamber of this barrow also point to the spring/summer period for the cutting and peeling off of the bark, because in late summer and autumn the bark of larch cannot be peeled off in broad strips. The canine teeth of the young horses in barrows 1 and 2 indicate an age of three and a half years, which is further evidence that they were killed in the autumn, not winter.

In the ordinary burials, as we know, the corpse was laid directly on the bottom of a small log tomb, on its back, head towards the east and arms and legs extended. In all the large barrows the dead were put in a special coffin made of a larch tree trunk. Such was the case in the five Pazyryk barrows, at Shibe and Berel. The bodies at Pazyryk and Shibe had been embalmed, although mummified corpses survived only in barrows 2 and 5 at Pazyryk and partially at Shibe.

The coffins had been hollowed out of larch tree trunks up to 1 m. in diameter at the root end. The coffin in barrow 2 was 4·2 m. long, 87–95 cm. wide and 72 cm. high; that from barrow 1 was somewhat smaller, 3·7 m. long with

[1] The mosses were identified in the Botanical Institute of the Academy of Sciences.

average width and height 80 cm. and 65 cm. respectively (*Pl. 37*c). Barrow 3's coffin was almost the same size but somewhat shorter, 3·25 m. The coffins in barrow 4 were even smaller: 3 m. and 2·5 m. long with average widths of 70 cm. and 60 cm. and heights of 40 cm. and 37 cm. respectively. The coffin in barrow 5 was quite exceptionally long, 5 m., with average width and height of 70 cm. and 50 cm.

The external surfaces of the coffins had been dressed smooth with an axe, the inside hollowed out with an adze of slightly concave blade. In all cases the bottom was flat. At both ends of the coffin there was always a pair of strong lugs, through the apertures in which thick cords were undoubtedly passed for lowering the coffin into the tomb. They would also have been necessary in carrying the coffin about.

The walls of the coffin are 3–4 cm. and the bottom 9–13 cm. thick. The ends are 25–30 cm. thick. The coffins of barrows 1 and 2 differ from the others in that the ends are not parallel, not vertical as with the others.

The coffin lids were also made of larch trunks. They are carefully dressed, and their dimensions correspond to the coffins except that they are 10–14 cm. narrower; their height varies from 22 cm. to 30 cm., and thickness 3–4 cm., so they are much lighter than the coffins. In section the lids are all domed except that from barrow 5, which is gable-shaped.

The dimensions of the lids somewhat exceeded those of the orifice of the coffin, which they entirely covered over. The lids were secured by square pegs that passed through four holes, two in each end, both in lids and coffins.

To hollow out such coffins and make such lids from a brittle wood like larch, especially old wood sometimes rotted in the centre, was no easy matter. So if there were splits in the central part of the wood, the heart of the tree, as, for example, in the coffin in barrow 2, these were wedged up and smeared over with resin. If there were cracks or splinters along the edge of a lid or coffin, as happened with the lid in barrows 1 and 2 and in the coffin of barrow 5, the damaged places were bound with thongs secured through special holes drilled along the edge of the cracks.

In barrows 1 and 2, in distinction from the other three, the whole outer surface of coffin and lid was pasted over with narrow (4 cm. wide) strips of birch bark, cut from young birch trees. The strips were arranged diagonally, intersecting one another to form a pattern of rhombs.

A peculiarity also of the coffins of the first two barrows was the decoration of the sides by leather cut-out silhouettes in the shape of cocks in barrow 1 and deer in barrow 2.

The representations of cocks fixed along the side of the coffin in barrow 1 took the form of pairs of birds heraldically confronted. The pairs ran above the lugs at either end and along the long sides (to judge by what survived on the south side) in tens, spaced at a constant interval. The decoration had been applied

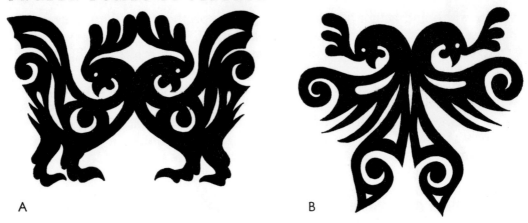

A   B

10. Cut-out leather cocks from barrow 1 $(c. \frac{1}{3})$.

before the lid was made, since the latter covered half of it. The birds were cut from thin leather, the outside (the flesh side) surface covered with tinfoil. The greater part of the double figures had been cut from a single piece of leather, but there are cases of the two confronted birds being separate pieces fixed in juxtaposition to each other by woollen thread.

The double, heraldic confrontation, chest to chest, of profile birds has two variants. First, there are full figures with legs with typical cock's head, wattle and deliberately exaggerated comb (fig. 10A). The claws and raised tail are typical of a cock. The second variant, also a confronted pair of cocks, is now to some extent stylized so that the head is the only clue as to what is represented, and the composition has altered; instead of confronted figures the idea has been changed to make one figure only with outspread wings and turned-down tail, with a double head (fig. 10B). Notwithstanding their conventionalization, the wings and tail in the first variant show all the typical peculiarities, but in the second variant wings and tail are interpreted as entirely conventional ornamental motifs. The conflated single cocks are in essence the same as the double, but with a slight falling-off in details.

On the upper edge of the side of the coffin of barrow 2 were fixed leather cut-out silhouettes of running deer (fig. 11). As the coffin edge had been chopped the deer survived only at the ends. The deer, which were secured by miniature iron nails, went round the coffin in an anti-clockwise direction. As in barrow 1 the figures were fixed with the smooth surface of the thin leather inwards, the flesh side outwards. Hence it can be inferred that, as with the cocks, tinfoil was stuck on the face, although an insufficient amount was collected to allow analysis.

11. Cut-out leather deer from barrow 2 ($c. \frac{1}{6}$).

To distinguish whether it was reindeer or red deer that were intended is not possible, since the craftsman was not concerned with showing species variations; he was depicting a general deer. They have most in common with reindeer. The short elk-type body has been well caught and the broad palmating antlers are characteristic of reindeer. The remarkable lightness of movement of these masterly figures is achieved by triangular openings cut in the upper thighs.

In the burial chamber of barrow 2 the floor was covered by thick black felt, and the walls, except on the north, had been draped with the same black felt. The upper edges of the long (as long as the wall) felt were tucked back 6 cm. and tacked to the wall between the fourth and fifth members of the box, either with wooden pegs or copper nails with or without heads (*Pl. 34*). The nails and pegs had been hammered into the cracks between the timbers. The wall felt was fixed not only at its upper edge but at the corner and at its lower edge. The north wall, as mentioned, was not covered with felt, and at its bottom only the felt which covered the floor was fixed.

The walls in barrows 1 and 5 were also draped with felt, but it is a pity that in barrow 1 only one piece of felt, albeit a fairly large bit, remained, while in barrow 5 the tomb plunderers had destroyed nearly all of it, and only a few small scraps survived.

The wall felt in barrow 1 was also secured at its upper edge by wooden pegs and copper nails, with or without heads, between the first and second log down. It consisted of a strip of thick dark grey felt about 63 cm. wide with a border, 39 cm. wide, sewn to it consisting of three bands. The middle band was of white felt and the edge bore triangular festoons of white, red, yellow and blue thin

31

12. Lion's head on wall-hanging in barrow 1 ($c. \frac{1}{2}$)

felt. The festoons on upper and lower bands consisted of triangles, inter-digitating with one another, sewn on with twisted sinew thread. Along the middle white band were red and blue thin felt cut-outs of profile lions' heads (*Pl. 148*A) with blunt nose, half-open and fanged jaws and well-modelled eyes. The mane is shown with separate locks (fig. 12). Along the upper edge of the border a thick dark grey cord was sewn on, made up of four twisted threads (*Pl. 148*A).

All the walls of the chamber in barrow 5 were hung from the top with a white hanging of fine felt bearing representations of lion-like figures with a human trunk, and of birds. These hangings were secured at the top by long thin wooden pegs between the first and second members down of the box, driven into the crevice between the logs at intervals of 20–30 cm.

It has been mentioned above that the plunderers pulled these hangings down from the walls and tore them to shreds, and it is only thanks to the fact that part of such a carpet remained intact in the horse burials that its pattern can be partially recovered.

On the upper and lower edge of this wall-hanging was a sewn-on border with a pattern formed from polychrome felt cut-outs (*Pl. 149*B). We shall meet this decorative pattern again in the pendant saddle plates and in other decorations. Its basic elements consist of heart shapes with a flower in the middle, and between them, on a red applied background, sickle shapes and triangles with a circular cut-out on one side.

Above the border, one behind the other, are sewn-on figures of winged lions with human bodies, which will be more fully described in the chapter on art.

Above the half-lion are half-human figures and in the spaces between them representations of birds which unfortunately cannot be fully restored. The bird's head with circular eye has a hooked parrot-like beak. The best preserved is the back half of a bird on tall thin legs with hooked claws (*Pl. 149*A).

32

The flat wooden pegs which supported the felts and felt hangings on the walls were of various sizes and shapes. Their usual length was from 8 cm. to 15 cm. (*Pl. 38*B, C). Some were flat and broad, with a large head, others flat but narrow with hardly perceptible head, and lastly some oval in section without a head. Some after being split off a block had been merely sharpened at one end, others carefully whittled down with a knife.

The cast copper nails mentioned above had a square shank roughly sharpened at one end, or almost circular with an oval, almost circular, head. The casting was rough, often leaving voids in the metal. The heads of such nails, from barrow 2, had been cast separately from the shanks. The latter were fitted to a corresponding rectangular mortice on the head and then welded, as can be seen on the nails shown in *Pl. 38*D. These nails are 9·5–11·6 cm. long.

Since all the large cairns so far excavated have been looted there never has been any possibility of establishing all details of the burial in the log coffin.

What do we definitely know? First, in every case where the body was still in the coffin it lay on its back in an extended position with head towards the east. Secondly, where there was a double interment (man and woman), in two cases they were in one coffin (barrows 2 and 5) and in one in separate coffins (barrow 4). At Shibe the old man and youth lay together in one coffin. Thirdly, the corpses were not dressed as in ordinary life. In barrow 2 the man's shirts (one in shreds) were found in the south-west corner of the chamber and the body had evidently been buried without its shirt. Head-dress (barrow 5) and footwear (barrow 2) were obligatory, but breeches were probably not worn. The palm of the right hand usually rested on the pubic area, the left, bent at the elbow, on the chest. The man buried in barrow 5 not only had his right hand resting on his pubic area but the hand was held there by a thread attached to the finger passing under the skin above it. This would hardly have been possible if the corpse had been wearing breeches. The bodies had been buried in dress worn over the shoulder with the arms not in sleeves. Besides shoulder attire the bosom of the woman in barrow 2 was covered by a single-piece apron which, with her cloak, made a simple costume. In some cases the corpses had worn metal torques, ankle and wrist bracelets and earrings. In one of the barrows dug by S. V. Kiselev at the village of Karakol a woman was found actually wearing a torque. In barrow 2 at Pazyryk it is probable that the tomb robbers hacked off the heads of the man and woman in order to remove torques. The woman in this barrow had had both legs hacked off at the knee joint and also the right hand. How both the man and the woman had been laid in the same coffin we cannot tell, but, judging by the length of coffins in cases of other pairs and their small width, the bodies were laid not side by side but one behind the other. Before laying the corpse in it the coffin bottom (as, for example, in barrow 2) was

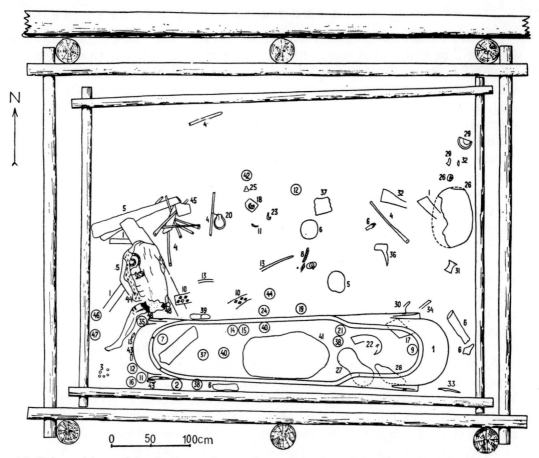

13. Disposition of the finds on the surface of the ice of the first phase in barrow 2.

1, tree trunk coffin and chips from it
2, leather deer
3, legs of first hexapod stand
4, legs of second hexapod stand
5, parts of man's corpse
6, parts of woman's corpse
7, woman's severed foot in shoe
8, parts of the woman's hair
9, 'diadem' bearing cocks
10, black fur with decorations, from head-dress
11, pieces of torque
12, gold pendants from ear-rings
13, pieces of decorated belt
14, silver belt-plate
15, silver horse pendant
16, the same with strap

17, leather pouch with silver mirror
18, bronze mirror in fur case
19, pouch of steppe cat fur
20, leather flask containing hemp seeds
21, 22, deer's head in griffin's beak
23, 24, wooden griffins' heads
25, carved deer's head
26, top of small table
27, wooden 'pillow'
28, cover for 27
29, shards of bottle
30, horn handle of wooden vessel
31, horn drum
32, pieces of harp
33, iron knife

34, wooden handles
35, antler arrow-heads
36, horn mallet
37, piece of pile carpet
38, woman's hose
39, man's felt stocking
40, tatters of man's dress
41, pieces of woman's costume and stamped copper decorations
42, stamped copper decorations
43, sleeve of female costume
44, sable fur
45, pieces of black colt's fur
46, pieces of dyed fur
47, beads on brown fur
48, red and brown cloth.

34

covered by a thick felt, folded double, and over this was spread a soft woollen rug with long nap, upon which the corpses were laid. In barrow 2 the body was covered by the free edges of the rug, and then a special strip of strong cloth was laid over it along the full length of the coffin.

What was the full original complement of articles placed with the corpse and what was their disposition in the chamber? This also is very difficult to answer because of the activities of the tomb robbers. The plunderers, once inside the chamber, were free to ransack it completely, which they did in almost all the barrows. From barrow 1 even the corpse or corpses were pulled out. The only exception was barrow 2, where the ice prevented the looters from robbing as freely as in the other cases. Some of the grave goods were found in this barrow in the upper layer of the robbers' debris, some on the surface of the first-phase ice (fig. 13), and, finally, some on the chamber floor (fig. 14). Combined with whatever else survived in the other barrows this allows us in some measure to reconstruct a picture of the original grave goods and their disposition in the chamber.

Besides clothes and adornments placed in the coffin with each body a wooden 'stool', or 'pillow' as we formerly called it (because it was near the head end of the coffin in barrow 2), was found in each tomb.[1] In barrows 1, 3 and 4 such an object was found at various points on the chamber floor, while in barrow 5 the thieves had put it on a log of the inner ceiling of the chamber in their trap opening. In all the barrows there were little low tables with detachable tops. In barrow 1 only one table leg survived; in barrow 2 there were four such tables; in barrows 3 and 4 two each; and in barrow 5 three tables. They only occurred *in situ* in barrow 2, where they were placed in the east part of the chamber next to the coffin. To judge by the remains that survived the table tops served as dishes on which food, goat- and horse-meat, was put. Beside the tables close to the north side of the tomb in barrow 2 stood two tall earthenware bottles. Judging by the surviving shards there was one such bottle in each of the other tombs. In barrow 2 between the tables and bottles two wooden vessels rested on circular stands on the floor. The vessels, wooden and earthenware, were undoubtedly filled with fluid, probably a milk drink, koumiss and possibly milky vodka. In addition the deceased were furnished with cheese, of which remains were found in barrow 5, while in the horse burial in barrow 2 there was a whole pouch filled with cheese. In each barrow there was probably one, and in those with double burials two, bronze censers with six-legged covers. In barrow 2 one censer stood in the south-west corner of the chamber and above it the frame of a tent-like cover with six legs, and another censer, with just the same framed leather cover, and a leather flask containing hemp, stood in the middle of the western half of the tomb. In the other barrows neither cover nor censer was found, but the rods of the cover frames did survive. The single stone lamp which was

[1] [Translator's note. See note on p. 69.   M.W.T.]

35

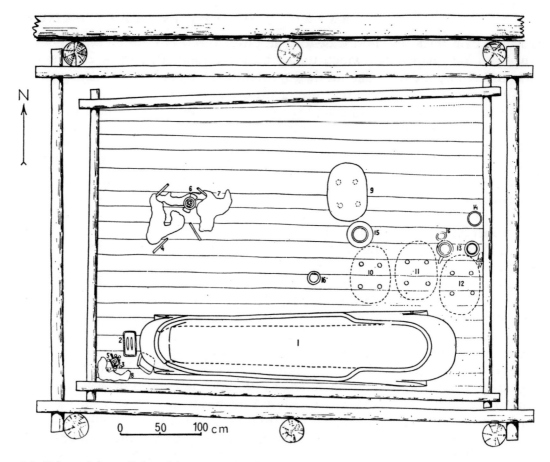

14. Disposition of the objects on the floor of the chamber of barrow 2.

1, tree-trunk coffin
2, stone lamp
3, legs of first hexapod stand
4, legs of second hexapod stand
5, copper censer on feet
6, copper censer on pedestal

7, leather covering cloth
8, man's shirt
9, little table with tiger-shaped legs
10, legs of another table
11 and 12, carved and turned table legs

13, wooden vessels
14, neck of earthenware bottle
15, earthenware bottle
16, felt ring-rests for vessels

found stood on the tomb floor in barrow 2 in the south-western corner beside the censers. In three barrows one-sided composite drums made up of two halves of an ox-horn were found. In barrows 2 and 5 they had survived well except the membrane, but in barrow 3 only traces of a disintegrated drum of this kind were found. Like the stringed musical instrument of harp type, split into two, from barrow 2, the drums in all probability were in the coffins, and later thrown out on to the floor by the tomb robbers.

36

The above list of objects found in the different barrows needs to be completed. In the coffin of barrow 2 were found a torque in the form of a bent copper tube decorated with winged lions carved out of wood and gold plated, and wooden figures of deer and griffins also covered with gold-leaf; a horn comb; a leather pouch containing a silver mirror with antler handle; a little rectangular leather pouch and flask, both bearing applied leather decoration; a leather purse of hemispherical shape; an iron mace; a wooden finial in the shape of a griffin holding a deer-head in its beak, a silver plaque with the picture of a lion falling upon a goat, and amulets in the shape of horses. Another such plaque was found in the chamber outside the coffin among the debris fallen through the robbers' trap. In the coffin were a fragment of gold earring and part of a fur cap, parts of clothing and shreds of felt and textiles.

Outside the coffin at different points in the chamber, and probably thrown out by the looters, were found an iron knife and two wooden knife-cases in the south-east corner of the chamber, an antler mallet on the ice to the north of the tables, together with the fragments of the harp already mentioned. In various parts of the chamber, mostly by the robbers' trap, were found two antler arrow-heads, a bronze mirror in a leopard-skin case, several beads, a strap with figures of cocks sewn on it, a whole series of bags and pouches (one containing seeds of cultivated coriander), various wooden cut-outs of animals, gold-plated, copper-stamped leather animals, shreds of thin felt edgings with polychrome applied decoration, bits of clothing and sheep fleece, and amulets.

In barrow 3, besides what has been mentioned, there were also pieces of sable clothing, a male head-dress, a piece of patterned silk, a silk purse and arrow-shafts. They were scattered about the tomb, for the coffin was empty.

In the chamber of barrow 4 a massive antler chisel came to light in the robbers' access passage, and in addition a leather cut-out of a big-eared horned bird and, in one of the coffins, several stone beads were found.

In barrow 5, besides articles already mentioned, there were found (fig. 15) a wooden head-dress worn by the buried woman, pieces of goat- and sheep-skins at various points on the floor, rods of six-legged censer covers, a small felt pillow stuffed with deer hair, a goat horn with a little wooden spoon inside it, part of a felt stocking, a rectangular dressed board with straps on its short ends and, in a crack in the floorboards, a biconical turquoise bead.

Thus only barrow 2 gives a more or less full picture of the set of articles with which the deceased were furnished to enter the world beyond the grave. The outfit comprised all that was necessary to satisfy the needs of everyday, mundane life.

In describing the methods of interment in the large barrows we must recall a detail in barrow 5. After freeing the burial chamber of ice it turned out that the coffin on the south side of the chamber had its lid held down by the chopped off ends of seven logs embedded in the chamber wall. Originally this prompted the

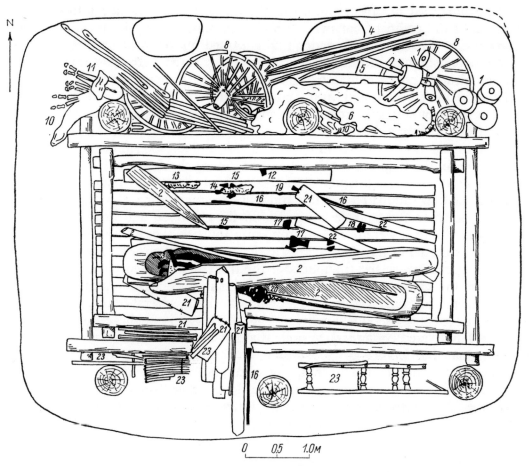

15. Plan of burial shaft in barrow 5 and disposition of objects within it.

1, wheels of trolley;
2, tree-trunk coffin and lid;
3, interred corpses;
4, rods from trolley;
5, steps;
6, large felt carpet;
7–9, parts of carriage;
10, horse bodies;

11, pile carpet;
12, shard of bottle;
13, goat's skin;
14, fleece;
15, table legs;
16, rods of hexapod;
17, horn drum;
18, felt cushion;

19, horn vessel with wooden spoon;
20, female head-dress;
21, boards with strap lashings;
22, logs of chamber's ceiling;
23, pieces of the carriage.

thought that the robbers after ransacking the coffin felt a terror of the dead they had disturbed and, in order to seal the coffin, wedged it in this fashion (*Pl. 30*). Subsequent research showed such a view was not tenable and that the lid had been wedged thus after the interment had been completed.

38

In the second log from the bottom of the box, exactly in the middle, an aperture had been cut. However, appreciating that this would come up against the central upright outside that supported the log filling over the chamber, work on making an aperture was moved west, so that the new opening was between the middle and western supporting posts. For this purpose the second third and fourth members up of the inner box and the third, fourth and fifth members up of the outer box were cut through. A window about 70 cm. broad and 60 cm. high was thus produced. This opening had been cut after the chamber had been constructed but still not erected in the tomb shaft. The cutting had been done on the inner box from inside and on the outer box from outside, as was clearly visible from the axe marks and method of cutting in the logs that narrowed inwards towards the intervening wall space. Neither in the chamber, nor outside it by the window, was there a single wood chip; consequently the work must have been done outside the burial shaft. After the sealing of the coffin lid had been carried out at some distance from the south wall of the chamber seven chopped-off logs, 1·54–1·75 m. long, were put into the aperture with their thinner ends outwards, the inner ends pressing on the closed coffin lid and the outer projecting outside the chamber. Then these logs were wedged into the wall with pieces of trolley axle, board and wedges. Since the level of the upper edge of the second member of the outer box was somewhat lower than the upper edge of the first member of the inner box, the 'wedge' sloped slightly outwards from a higher inner end.

It is not easy to judge the original full complement of articles placed with skeletons in the small barrows. After plundering, apart from objects of clay, metal and antler, nothing survived.

In barrow 6 with the skeletons were found (fig. 8) a Chinese mirror, various beads, four shells of *Cypraea moneta*, remains of red lacquer, gold pins, shards of two clay vessels and an iron knife. Barrow 7 yielded part of a maral's antler, potsherds, copper tubelets, remains of clothing and cylindrical stone beads. In barrow 8 all that survived was maral antler tools, square stamped copper plates and a gold-plated copper runner bead. Barrow 1 at Aragol (fig. 9) yielded a gold earring, a bronze dagger, two bronze knives, a bronze halberd and hook; and barrow 2 a bronze knife and hook, two gold plates (showing heads of saiga antelope) and two earthenware vessels. In the two barrows at Katanda, besides items of saddlery, there were only an antler 'lion's head' pin, an iron knife and a shell of the mollusc *Cypraea moneta*.

Although poorer in content, by far the best and most fully preserved of the grave goods were what had been deposited in the northern part of the burial shafts, for in not a single case among the large Pazyryk barrows had the horse burials been disturbed by the plunderers.

All the horses had been killed by a blow with a pole-axe in the forehead, usually into the crown. A rigid arrangement of the horses' bodies in the tomb had not been intended, since their allotted space did not always measure up to their number. Where there was room they would be put in some order, but when, as, for example, in barrow 5, there was only a narrow space left in the shaft, they were put on top of one another, not only horizontally but also

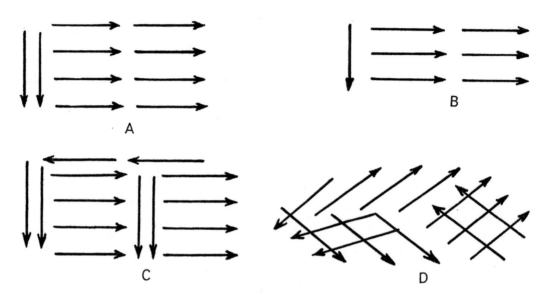

16. Disposition of horse bodies in barrows 1–4.

vertically. So the horse bodies were mixed up not only with logs and boulders, but in the subsidence under the weight of the superincumbent load they had been displaced and compressed. Consequently the original arrangement had been altered.

The disposition of the horses and their normal attitude, fore and back legs pressed up and head thrown back on the neck, were dictated probably by the need to save space. In barrow 1 eight horses were deposited lengthwise, heads towards the east, in two rows of four. In the remaining free space on the west side of the shaft another two horses were laid side by side, heads towards the south (fig. 16A). In barrow 2 seven horses were arranged in the same way, two rows of three lying east–west with heads towards the east, and one in a transverse direction on the west side of the area intended for horse burials (fig. 16B). Since the horse bodies were lowered into the shaft simply on a rope, to lay them in straight rows would have been difficult, and evidently it was not attempted. So the heads were not always raised; sometimes they were thrust forward and the horses in a row often overlapped each other.

The arrangement was more complicated in barrow 3 (fig. 16c), where, as in barrow 1, eight horses were put in two rows of four, heads towards the east. In the space between these rows and on the west two pairs of horses were laid, head towards the south. There were still two horses to fit in; they were laid one behind the other against the north side of the shaft facing the opposite direction to the others, heads towards the west.

Entirely different from that just described was the disposition of the horses in the burial shaft of barrow 4 (fig. 16D). In this barrow, after the erection of the burial chamber, only a relatively small space was left in the north part of the shaft, and so narrow that to lay a horse crosswise was impossible. It was not practicable to put them in two rows of four and consequently this arrangement had to be abandoned. Nine horses were laid diagonally, six with heads towards the north-east on the north side of the shaft and three with heads towards the south-east by the burial chamber. Such a diagonal position in an extended line gave each body its own place, and did not take up too much width, since the broader parts of the body, such as the pelvis, did not coincide with the same part on the adjoining horse. There were still five horse bodies left for which there was no room in the shaft, and it was necessary to form another layer, the bodies again diagonally laid but heads towards the west instead of the east, that is, the opposite direction and at right angles to the lower layer. A very compact deposit was achieved in this way, which after the filling-in of the shaft produced an impression of a confused mix-up of adjoining skulls and pelvises, vertebrae and extremities, especially as the flesh had not survived in this barrow.

In barrow 5 in the north part of the shaft behind the burial chamber there was only a very narrow space at the bottom, which could accommodate nine horses arranged in rows longitudinally. So in the eastern half of the shaft three horses were put one on top of another. The lowest horse lay on its belly, head towards the west with muzzle twisted back towards the east. The upper horse lay in just the same position with head thrust out. In the next row, also lying longitudinally, head towards the east, behind the middle post, was a single fourth horse. In a third row lay a fifth and a sixth horse, one on its belly, head towards the west, and the other parallel to it, on the north side of the shaft on its right side with head towards the east. Between the head of this one and the large fourth horse, a seventh horse lay transversely on its back. The two last horses were put in the north-west corner of the shaft. One lay on its back with feet thrust up, head towards the west; the other was seated on it, back towards the east, with

41

legs and head extended so that its head turned the corner of the burial shaft, slightly rising above it (fig. 17).

We can see the same sort of thing in the small barrows; the horse bodies sometimes lay one on top of another, head towards the east, sometimes towards the west, and when there were three horses one was sometimes laid transversely.

Thus a certain order can be observed in the disposition of the horse bodies in cases where the place intended for them in the shaft allowed sufficient space, but where this was lacking the order was inevitably upset. One matter leaves no room for doubt: with the orientation of the horses, as with the human bodies, there was a consistent preference for directing the head towards the east. From the east towards the west was the body arrangement. All horses wearing head-dress with decorative crests were buried in the first row, in all cases with heads towards the east, with the exception of barrow 5, where just such a horse had its head towards the west. Horses with decorative head crests occurred in pairs in barrows 1–3 and singly in 4 and 5.

With the exception of barrow 5, in which four draught-horses were buried, all the others were animals for riding.

Together with the horse were placed its bridle, saddle and head decorations. The saddles and bridles buried in the large barrows had been taken off the horses prior to burial, as also had the head decorations, but in the small barrows they were buried still wearing them. This was the case in barrow 6 and in the Aragol barrows. Although in the former case the robbers had taken the bronze bits, the copper oxide on the head of one of the animals showed that it had been bridled when buried. In the Aragol barrows the bits were still in the mouths of the horses. All the horses with head-dress also wore leather-covered felt or plain leather covers over the manes, which were not taken off before burial. Two horses in barrow 1 besides head-dress and mane-covers had also special tail-covers. Bridle, saddle and head-dress were evidently placed with the horse to which they had belonged (*Pls. 39* and *40*). The bridles of the four draught-horses in barrow 5 were all put together.

In the horse burials of barrows 1, 2 and 4 whips were found in addition to the saddlery.

In all the barrows, except no. 5, there were wicker shields, three each in barrows 1 and 3, and two each in barrows 2 and 4. When they were found with saddles they were fastened to the right side. In barrow 1 in the horse burial there were a fur pouch shaped like a flask and a fur cushion; in barrow 2 there was a leather pouch covered with fur containing cheese. In all barrows, except No. 4, parts of trolleys running on solid wooden wheels were found, and in barrow 5 a four-wheeled carriage with draught pole. Finally, in the horse burial in barrow 5, there were two carpets, one pile and the other felt.

In those cases where there was not enough room in the northern horse-burial

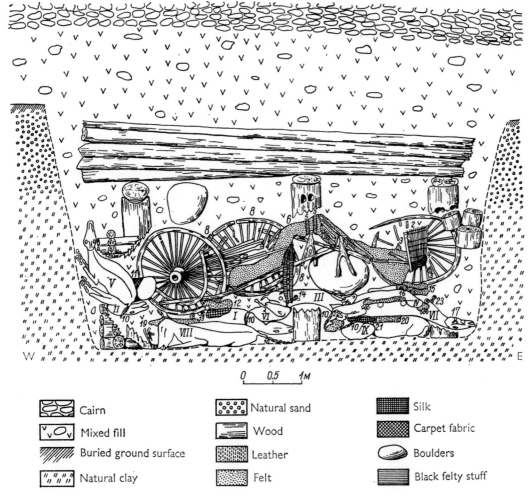

Cairn	Natural sand	Silk
Mixed fill	Wood	Carpet fabric
Buried ground surface	Leather	Boulders
Natural clay	Felt	Black felty stuff

17. Vertical disposition of horses and objects in the north part of the burial shaft in barrow 5.

1, trolley wheels

2, body of carriage

3, swans from carriage

4, black felt canopy of carriage

5, pieces of black felt

6, felt carpet

7, sticks with spatulate ends

8, carriage wheels

9, draught-pole of carriage

10, horse tails

11, pile carpet

12 and 13, saddle and bridle from horse I

14, bridles of draught horses II, III, V and VI

15, saddle from horse IV

16 and 17, saddle and bridle from horse VII

18 and 19, saddle and bridle from horse VIII

20 and 21, saddle and bridle from horse IX

22, head-dress from horse IX

23, bridle from horse IV

I–IX, horse bodies

43

part of the shaft behind the tomb for articles that had to be deposited, usually parts of the trolleys, they were put above the chamber or in the southern part of the shaft between its side and the chamber wall. Thus in barrow 5, behind the south wall of the chamber between the upright posts, the platform of the carriage had been placed with other objects, namely one of the rods of a six-legged censer cover, a piece of maral antler and smaller parts of the carriage.

3. PHYSICAL TYPE OF
THE POPULATION

THE LITTLE information available about the population of the Altai Mountains during Scythian times has been summarized by G. F. Debets.[1] The majority of skulls of the period belong to a European type and, although insufficiently clearly documented, are predominantly brachycephalic. Of all the skulls he studied Debets especially distinguished the male skull from barrow 6 at Tuekta (excavations of S. V. Kiselev), which he regarded as resembling those of modern Kazakhs. He considered this as unquestionable proof of tribes of southeastern origin having reached as far as the Altai by this time.

Since the excavations of the Pazyryk barrows we have more representative male skulls available for study; one from Shibe, three from Tuekta, four from Kurai, one from Katanda and two from Pazyryk (barrows 3 and 4).

The discovery of embalmed corpses in barrows 2 and 5 at Pazyryk is especially valuable, giving a vivid picture of the physical aspect of the ancient Altaians.

Looking over the small series of skulls enumerated (*Pl. 43*), their extreme variation is noticeable. There are brachycephalic (Pazyryk 4 and Kurai III, 9), sub-brachycephalic (almost half), one mesocephalic (Kurai III, 4) and three sharply dolichocephalic (Shibe, Kurai III, 3, Katanda) skulls.

With regard to height only, the skulls from Shibe and Tuekta 6 are low (chame- and tapeinocranial), while the skull from Katanda is high (hypso- and orthocranial). All the rest are average. A medium length of face (mesoprozopia) is in general characteristic for the whole series; some, however, show a relatively long face (Pazyryk 3, Shibe, Katanda). A general trait of the Altaian skulls is their orthognatism, often strongly marked.

The form of the nose varies sharply. Although a medium width (mesorhines) predominates, there are cases of markedly narrow noses (leptorhines) at Pazyryk 3 and Shibe and wide noses (platyrrhines) as at Pazyryk 4. The orbits are relatively high on the skull from Shibe, the others of medium height (mesokonchs).

Although in general the skulls in the series are of europeoid type, there are

[1] Debets, A.

45

some among them with markedly mongoloid features. Among the latter are the skulls from Pazyryk 4, Shibe, Tuekta 6, and to some degree Katanda. For these skulls a relatively flat and broad face, weakly developed *fossae caninae* and flat nose are characteristic.

The female skulls are excluded from Table 1 (pages 48–9) first, because of their rarity and, secondly, because of their atypical character as a guide to racial characteristics. In our classification there is one female skull each from Tuekta 10, Katanda and Kurai v,[1] and two from Pazyryk 4 and 5. Of the latter the skull from Pazyryk 4 is that of a juvenile, fifteen–sixteen years old, and severely deformed, while that from barrow 5 still retains its ligaments and skin and so cannot be studied (its mandible has in addition been damaged).

In general all the female skulls exhibit europeoid orthognatism, with medium-wide face and average nose width, but the skull from Tuekta 10 is almost broad-nosed, and from Katanda, on the contrary, narrow-nosed, and also has excessively high orbits. The cranial index of the series varies greatly. The skulls from Tuekta 10 and Pazyryk 4 are markedly brachycranial (index 86), from Katanda and Kurai v sub-brachycranial (index about 81·5), and from Pazyryk 5 dolicho-cranial (index about 73).

Besides the skulls we have three mummified heads from Pazyryk: two male from barrows 2 and 5 and one female from barrow 2 (*Pl. 44*). From the point of view of anthropometric study these heads present the difficulty that they cannot be treated as skulls. As a result of the deformation of the soft parts of the head, measurements of the skull and face cannot be compared with those made on living subjects. All the same they are extremely valuable in giving an incomparably better picture of the physiognomy and type of face than a skull. Moreover the surviving hair provides further material for racial diagnosis.

The age of the man in barrow 2 was about sixty, as indicated by the obliteration of the pulpary chamber and the severe wear on the front teeth, the coronary parts of which had worn to exactly two-thirds of their original size.[2] He was a markedly mongoloid type, and had a large occiput with cephalic index of 83–4, and extremely broad (skull diameter 156 mm., face height 146 mm. and anatomical height 96 mm.) and flat face with strongly projecting malar bones. The interval between the eyes (38 mm.) and the width of the nose (48 mm. high,

---

[1] Debets, A, Pls. 44 and 45.

[2] The heads of the man and woman from barrow 2 were studied by G. M. Ivashchenko in the Stomatological Department of the Military Medical Academy. X-ray photographs have shown that the man's first molar on the right in the lower jaw was defective, that is, it did not grow and emerge during life, so the milk-tooth remained in the socket. Possibly therefore there had been a follicular cyst during life surrounding the crown of the first molar, causing pressure that produced a lesion of the surrounding bone. As a result of the pressure of the ungrown tooth on its neighbours and the pressure of the milk-tooth on the pulp of the third molar the man must have experienced terrible toothache during his lifetime.

34 mm. wide) were considerable and the root of the nose was depressed. The epicanthus was poorly displayed, but he probably had one.

The woman from barrow 2 was getting on in years, over forty. Her physical type was quite different from the man's in the same barrow. Her cephalic index was significantly lower, about 80. The face was narrow and long (malar diameter 134 mm., with a face height of 141 mm. and anatomical height of 99 mm.), with a sharp profile. The malar bones projected slightly having regard to the slight malar diameter. The nose projected fairly sharply. If in the woman's type we can detect slight mongoloid traits (relatively high face, narrow nose), they are very trifling.[1]

A man of over fifty-five years of age was buried in barrow 5, of a type sharply distinguished from that buried in barrow 2. The mesocephalic head (about 78) was marked by a high forehead and long, orthognathous, sharply profiled face with projecting chin. The maral bones, although broad (maral diameter about 146 mm.), did not project. The nose was very long and narrow (approximately 32 mm. by 54 mm.), strongly projecting and hooked. One often encounters this type today among Kazakhs and Kirgiz, which evidently constitutes one of the central Asian types between the rivers Amu-Darya and Syr-Darya.

As I have already remarked, the hair is a very important diagnostic feature of race. The man from barrow 2 retained hardly any hair, as he had been shaved, but it was possible to study the roots and stubble. These gave the impression of fairly stiff black hair, but not so circular in section and not so stiff as that of northern mongoloids. The hairs of his false beard were dark chestnut in colour, which would be very interesting if we could be certain that it was his own hair.

The hair of the woman in barrow 2 was black, but soft and wavy, not stiff like that of mongoloids. The hair of the man from barrow 3 was bright chestnut, what I would call dark blond, and fairly soft. The man in barrow 5 had black, wavy or even curly hair, while the woman in the same barrow had thin and soft, dark chestnut hair.

Study of sections of the strands of hair from the Pazyryk barrows revealed that in thickness and form it differed from the characteristic hair of mongoloids.

From barrows 2, 3 and 4 we have complete skeletons beautifully preserved. However, for want of sufficient comparative material, I limit myself to describing the long bones and establishing the height of the individuals that interest us. The details are set out with corresponding measurements from other Altai burials in Table 2 (pages 50–1), the skulls of which are dealt with in Table 1.

---

[1] Ivashchenko observed clear traces of lesion of the bone and sides of the alveolar cavities exposing the side and root of the tooth in the woman's jaw. This was particularly the case in the front teeth of the lower jaw, which had moved out of vertical (striking each other). This evidence permits the inference that during life this woman suffered from alveolar pyorrhoea.

TABLE 1

BASIC MEASUREMENTS *numbered after Martin*		TUEKTA 6	TUEKTA 8–2	TUEKTA 11	KURAI III, 3
1.	Longitudinal diameter	186	189	180	197
8.	Transverse diameter	150	154	146	141
17.	Vertical diameter	131	135	135	139
5.	Nose-base diameter	100	—	105	106
9.	Least forehead width	90	108	94	102
40.	Length of base of face	97	—	97	96
45.	Malar diameter	144	140?	144	138?
48.	Height of face	78?	73?	71	72
55.	Height of nose	55	51	51	54
54.	Breadth of nose	28	25	28	26
51a.	Orbital width	40	39	39	39
52.	Orbital height	35	34	33	35
32.	Forehead angle	76	85	77	84
72.	Angle of face	91	84	89	90
75(1)	Angle of nose bones	23	28	28?	—
	Norma verticalis (Frassetto)	Sr.	Ept.	Sr.	Pt.
	Superciliary bone (1–6) Martin	4	3	4	3
	Fossa canina (0–4)	2	3	1	2
	Lower edge of aperture	F.p.	F.p.	F.p.	Ant.
	Spina nasalis anterior (1–5)	1	3	—	—
8 : 1	Cranial index	80·7	81·4	81·1	71·6
17 : 1	Height-length index	70·4	71·4	75·0	70·6
17 : 8	Height-width index	87·3	87·2	92·4	98·6
9 : 8	Forehead-width index	60·0	70·1	64·4	72·3
40 : 5	Occipital index	97·0	—	92·4	90·6
46 : 45	Upper face index	54·2	52·1	49·3	54·1
5 : 55	Nose index	50·9	49·0	54·9	48·2
52 : 51a	Orbital index	87·5	87·2	84·6	89·7

KURAI III, 4	KURAI III, 9	KURAI V	KATANDA	PAZYRYK 3	PAZYRYK 4	SHIBE
183	180	181	183	186	179	204
145	151	146	138	150	158	149
135	—	125	141	139	134	136
99	—	101	108	110	104	105
96	94	101	101	89	105	103
100	—	—	100	107	98	104
139	—	134	135	145	147	151
70	—	—	75	79	74	90
50	—	—	—	55	54	63
24	—	—	—	26	30	25
39	—	—	—	41	41	41
34	—	—	—	34	35	33
85	—	—	79	77	79	84
81	—	—	87	85	83	92
30	—	—	25	22	23	22
Ov.	Sn.	Ov.	Ov.	Ov.	Sr.	Ov.
3	4	2	3	3	3	4
4	—	—	2	3	1	1
Ant.	—	—	Ant.	Inf.	Inf.	Ant.
4	—	—	3	5	4	4
79·2	83·9	80·7	73·8	80·7	88·2	73·1
73·8	—	69·1	77·0	74·7	74·9	66·7
93·1	—	85·6	104·4	92·7	84·8	91·3
66·2	62·3	69·2	74·8	72·6	66·5	69·1
101·0	—	—	92·6	89·0	94·2	99·0
50·4	—	—	55·6	54·5	51·0	59·6
48·0	—	—	—	47·3	54·6	39·6
87·2	—	—	—	83·0	85·0	92·6

TABLE 2

			TUEKTA	
		6	8/2	11
	Height (after Pearson) in cm.	166	161	159
RATIOS	$(H_1 + R_1) : (F_2 + T_1)$, between limbs	69·7	70·3	—
	$T_1 : F_2$, tibia to femur	81·4	82·2	—
	$R_1 : H_1$, radius to humerus	79·4	74·0	75·1
	$H_1 : F_2$, humerus to femur	70·5	73·7	—
	$R_1 : T_1$, radius to tibia	68·8	66·2	69·6
FEMUR	1 Extreme length	461	425	—
	2 Length in natural position	456	422	—
	8 : 2 Rigidity index	21·0	21·3	—
	(6 + 7) : 2 Size index	13·4	14·0	—
	6 Front-back diameter	33	30	—
	6 : 7 Pilaster index	118	107	—
	10 : 9 Platymeric index	69·5	79	—
	10 Upper front-back diameter	25	26	—
TIBIA	1 Length	371	347	330
	10c : 1 Rigidity index	21·0	22·5	22·1
	9a : 8a Platycnemic index	70·5	70·5	71·5
	12 Angle of retroversion	15	10	15
	13 Angle of inclination of articulating area	11	8	11
	8a Front-back diameter	34	34	35
HUMERUS	1 Length	321	311	306
	7 : 1 Rigidity index	21·2	21·5	22·2
	6 : 5 Sectional index	73	83	69
RADIUS	1 Length	255	230	230
	5 : 4 Sectional index	70·5	68·5	81
	4 Front-back diameter	17	19	16
ULNA	1 Length	278	253	251
	13 : 14 Platolenic index	70·5	88	81·
	14 Front-back diameter	27	25	27

| | KURAI | | | PAZYRYK | |
III, 4	III, 9	V	2	3	4
167	168	164	176	181	174
70·0	67·6	70·9	63·7	66·1	69·0
79·1	80·9	81·0	79·4	83·0	79·1
72·0	73·2	75·5	73·4	73·9	74·9
72·8	70·6	73·1	70·0	69·5	69·6
66·4	63·9	68·1	64·2	62·0	65·8
467	472	442	510	524	511
462	470	442	508	523	510
19·3	20·2	19·9	17·9	18·7	17·6
12·3	13·4	12·2	14·0	15·5	14·5
29	33	25	30	33	28
104	110	83	120	114	100
96·5	88	71·5	96·5	81·4	75·7
28	30	25	38	28	26
365	380	358	401	434	404
20·3	20·3	19·6	18·0	18·0	18·6
68·5	77·0	60·0	71·7	82·6	75·3
8	13	10	9	13	8
4	7	4	4	6	5
35	35	35	35	34·5	34·5
336	332	323	355	364	355
19·6	21·1	18·6	20·0	20·8	19·2
87	73	74	71	75·5	68
242	243	244	260	269	266
72	72	81	76·4	67·6	70·3
18	18	16	17	18·5	18·5
265	262	265	283	297	286
76	85	79	90	93	93
29	26	24	27	27	27

The tallness of all the men buried in the large barrows, whom we regard as tribal or clan chiefs, is remarkable. The chief in barrow 2 was 176 cm. tall, in barrow 3, 181 cm., barrow 4, 174 cm. and barrow 5, 175–6 cm. The height of the last was determined by measuring the body, making necessary corrections. The man in the Shibe barrow was just as tall (178 cm.). His height was calculated from his tibia. The men buried in the ordinary graves were shorter, 164 cm. on the average.

Besides other somatological differences the powerful build and slight platymeria were noticeable in all specimens except that from Tuekta 6, where it was moderate. Also noticeable is the platycnemia in relation to the small angle of incline of the articulating area of the tibia, particularly in the Pazyryk specimens. This would be compatible with a pastoral life where men spent more time on horseback than hunting in the mountains.

The women were of average or below average height. The two women at Tuekta were 149 cm. and 164 cm. tall, the ones at Katanda 151 cm. and Pazyryk 5, 158 cm.

The data available are insufficient, it seems, to assess the physical type of the Altai population at the time under discussion. Nevertheless it is possible to draw some general conclusions. First and foremost it is the unusual variety of types, in spite of the very limited range of specimens available, that deserves mention.

The europeoid type is particularly well represented, in the ordinary graves especially, and in Tuekta 8, Kurai III, 4, Pazyryk 3. No less a distinctive element is mongoloid; both dolichocephalic (Shibe and Pazyryk 5) and brachycephalic (Pazyryk 2 and 4). In the skulls from Tuekta 6 and Katanda I am inclined to see rather local forms than representatives of pure mongoloids. Dolichocephaly with some mongoloid traits is probably of south Siberian origin or comes from central Asia between the two rivers; while brachycephaly, according to Debets,[1] can be compared with the Siberian branch of the Asian trunk (Tungus type). Debets relates the appearance in the Altai of a mongoloid type to Hunnish expansion.

This idea was extended by Kiselev,[2] who regards the man buried at Shibe as a member of the Hunnish aristocracy entering the Altai at the time of the hegemony of the Hunnish union. He similarly contrasts the mongoloid type of the old man at Shibe with a local europeoid type of the native population.

I cannot detect the presence of a branch of the Asian mongoloid trunk in the Altai. The tallness, broadness of face in combination with brachycephaly, the absence of stiff hair—all these signs are incompatible with our picture of the north-eastern mongoloids. On the other hand it is well known to us that mongoloids were widespread towards the west (Ananin folk in the west Kama

[1] Debets, A, pp. 141–3.   [2] Kiselev, A, 1949, p. 182.

area) long prior to Hunnish expansion, and the mongoloid character of the Argippaei was known to Herodotus. Consequently entry of the mongoloid type into the Altai need not be connected with the expansion of the Huns.

All the male burials in large barrows, particularly those at Pazyryk, are distinguished from the ordinary ones by the tallness and powerful build of the individuals interred. This is not surprising if it is taken into account that the latter were members of ruling families of barbarian society, that is tribal chieftains for whom physical strength and agility had especial importance. In these aristocratic families we would expect, indeed, a greater variety in physical type than among the rest of the population. In these circumstances obligatory exogamy may be assumed, normal in clan society, and the custom for a lord to take a bride from the top social level of another, often very remote, tribe.

In conclusion we must once more emphasize the variation of physical type in the population of the Altai Mountains in the period under discussion; there is an appreciable mongoloid admixture, but in a diluted form; indeed just as can be seen today among modern Kazakhs and Kirgiz.

THERE HAS BEEN no significant change of climate or environment in the Altai Mountains, as already mentioned, over the last two thousand years. The mountains would be covered by steppe vegetation in this geographical position were it not for their great height above sea level. The vertical distribution of steppe, forest and high mountain vegetation depends as much on surface relief as exposure of the slopes. The southern slopes, which are everywhere drier and without forest, bear a steppe xerophytic flora, while the northern slopes bear continuous woodland. The combination of open steppe valleys with their wormwood/grass vegetation and high plateaux in the subalpine area with very rich mountain meadows favoured the development of pastoralism to an extraordinary degree. So with the adoption of stock-rearing by the population of the Altai in general, and of the Ulagan plateau in particular, it became the main source of livelihood. The variation of vegetation within small areas at the same time facilitated the breeding of a range of different animals. Especially favourable to the relatively primitive pastoralism of that time was the absence of snow on the open steppe slopes of the mountains, so that in winter stock could find its own food. For this reason in pastures surrounded by mountains the animals did not need special attention, and the horse herds could be left to look after themselves, needing only a general oversight.

Judging from the excavation, horses and large-horned cattle (including yaks) and two small-horned animals, goats and sheep, were bred at this time. In a number of barrows objects of ox horn have been found, in particular the one-sided drums and, in barrow 3, the sacrum and vertebrae of a cow. Yak wool was found in barrows 2 and 5. Rams' sacra and articles made of their wool were found in all barrows; in barrows 2 and 5 there were sheep's fleeces and in barrow 5 a goat's hide.

On the excavation evidence first place among domestic animals was held by the horse.

The significance of this animal in the life of pastoral people can be appreciated

55

by observing the life of the eastern Kazakhs and Kirgiz. The horse was the basic unit of exchange, the value of large- and small-horned animals being assessed in direct proportion to this unit. The bride's dowry (*kalym*) was counted out in horses, the fines for murder and wounding were assessed in horses. The horse was the only animal the value of which was reckoned as equivalent to that of a man.[1] It was just the same in antiquity; among the Wu-huan a man sentenced to death could compound his sentence by a payment of horses.[2]

Horses were bred not only for meat and milk, for their skins were used for dress, as we shall see, and vessels and straps were made from the same material. This animal had special significance as a means of locomotion: for traction and, above all, for riding. The ridden horse was one of the important prerequisites of the development of pastoral herding. As we know, the people of the steppes, and consequently the Altai tribes also, have for a long time been predominantly an equestrian society. In the Altai the life of everybody, men and women, was so closely bound up with riding horses that these animals had to accompany the dead into the next world.

Apart from fleshless skeletons in several Pazyryk barrows, actual horses' bodies were found, furnishing in the completest way details of the animals' appearance and quality. V. O. Vitt has made a specialist study of the Pazyryk horses,[3] and here we shall confine ourselves merely to a very brief account of the conclusions that he reached in his researches.

The wide variety of horses in some burials is most remarkable. Together with small plain herd animals, there were thoroughbreds, powerful cantering animals and typical riding horses.

The absence of horses of certain colours among those buried is conspicuous, notably dapple grey, mottled bay, skewbald, roan, grey and the like. The majority were chestnut and brown, sometimes with gold hues, less commonly a kind of bay, rarely jet black, but without the white patches so usual on brown horses at the present time. Vitt explains this avoidance of such horses in antiquity in this way: until man had mastered the blacksmith's art, the quality and strength of the horn on the horse's hoof had an exceptional importance, and horses with white patches on their extremities have a brightly coloured hoof horn that easily breaks.

It is noticeable that in the chieftains' tombs the number of thoroughbred horses is so large that in the Altai at this time not only the use but also the breeding of such animals must have been a recognized practice. More than likely is the suggestion of Vitt that such horses were not bred in the Ulagan valley, nor in the Pazyryk district where climatic and economic conditions were not favourable, but in areas with a more genial climate as, for example, in the

---

[1] Radloff, B.
[2] Bichurin, A, pt i, p. 144.
[3] Vitt, A.

valleys of the rivers Ursul and Karakol. The Pazyryk horses could have been obtained by purchase or exchange by the Ulagan people from kinsmen or members of the same tribe in the central Altai.

At all events we must recognize that the people of this area at that time possessed beautiful horses 150 cm. and more tall. Their quality may not have exceeded that of all the other horses of the ancient world, but the best from the excavation were not excelled.

Although this type of horse disappeared in the middle of the first millennium A.D., nevertheless in the middle of the last century Altaian horses were highly esteemed by the nomads of eastern Kazakhstan for their robustness and high quality.

In herd horse-breeding the stallion only began to copulate with the mares in the fifth year, so it was usually castrated in the fourth year. Such was the practice among Kazakhs, Kirgiz and Altaians, but in the period under discussion they did otherwise. All the riding-horses buried in the tomb were geldings, but they included three-and-a-half, three- and even two-and-a-half and two-year-olds. Furthermore the young horses were amongst the best and strongest breeds of horses in the tomb. The presence of such young immature horses, castrated at two years old, is attributed by Vitt to the desire to remove artificially the more powerful horses from the local breed.

Second place in the economy, judging by their representation, was held by sheep; they offered meat, skin, wool and, probably, milk. The shape and the extreme dimensions of the fourth sacral vertebrae (put as food in the tombs) suggest the animals belonged most likely to the variety of 'slight fat-tails'. In size they were no bigger than gipsies' sheep, but the strength and construction of the sacrum speak of relative suppleness and agility; these were evidently sheep that were capable of considerable travel.[1]

Although the osteological material is still insufficient to determine the breeds of sheep then kept in the Altai, the woollen articles and surviving fleeces lead us to suppose that sheep with rough wool and fine fleeces were reared simultaneously. Study of the wool of two skins with long white fleeces showed that in one case it was a summer coat of a young individual consisting exclusively of down with a fibre thickness varying from 10 to 14 μ. It was the same fine down in the second, a spring coat.

Study by V. N. Kononov of the wool used for cloth and in the thin kinds of felt has revealed that it consisted only of down. The small diameter of the fibre, the shape, the pieces of skin attached and the superposition are all analogous to the down of the best breeds, giving fine wool with fibre thicknesses of 11–26 μ.

In addition to the fine-fleeced sheep the ancient people of the Altai, as just

[1] Prof. S. N. Bogolyubsky has studied the bones, mainly sacra, and the conclusion about the breed of sheep is his.

mentioned, also reared a coarse-woolled sheep, the wool of which they pressed into thick felt. White was evidently the predominant colour, but dark grey sheep which yielded a black wool were also reared.

The importance of sheep-breeding is indicated by the fact that mutton was the favourite food. In the food placed with the corpse sometimes there were remains of horsemeat (sacrum), very rarely beef, but without fail in all graves, even the poorest, remains of mutton (sacrum with vertebrae).

Incomparably less important appeared to be goat-breeding. Only in barrow 5 was a goatskin found, of grey hue, such as is still very widespread in the Altai. The down, as with sheep, was very fine.

To what degree large-horned beasts were bred we do not know, so little information having survived about them and their appearance. All we can say is that the cows identified by Bogolyubsky from the skin in barrow 3 were of medium size, and the yaks, to judge by the wool found, were black.

Having regard to the basically settled life of the population it can be supposed that large-horned beasts, cows, were owned by each family and in very limited quantity horses and sheep. Rich families would rear horses and sheep on a large scale.

Prior to the introduction into the Altai of contemporary breeding practices the aboriginal population did not separate their herds, but allowed all animals to pasture together. Such was probably the case in antiquity, for the Altai is so rich in pasture of so varied a kind that even large herds of mixed stock can feed in the same area. In addition, thanks to strong winds during winter, the snow is blown off the rocky areas and open mountain terraces and animals can reach their food through this thin cover.

While the main mass of stock had to find its food underfoot the whole year round, some animals would be stalled during the winter. This would have been particularly the case with young stock (calves and lambs), and also fine-woolled sheep and selected thoroughbred horses.

On the horny walls of the hoofs of many horses from the excavation uneven creases can be seen, the so-called 'rings', testifying to famines survived, found commonly, as is well known, in winter conditions of open-air feeding 'under-foot'. It indicates that the majority of horses during the winter received little or no supplementary feed. At the same time the hoofs, or more exactly the horny walls of the hoofs, of the best, or as Vitt calls them the true saddle-horses, do not show this feature. Evidently during winter special conditions were created for them, different from those experienced by the others. The ancient Altaians valued these chosen horses and, possibly, kept them into old age, sometimes over twenty years old, which was only possible if they were looked after carefully.

One point detains us particularly: did they have domesticated birds at this time? That there were fowls, undoubted evidence is offered by the realistic representations of cocks of different kinds found in barrows 1 and 2. The birds are so faithfully depicted that it could only have been done by someone familiar with and breeding them. A second question: were the birds reared for eggs and meat (which is unlikely) or because of special qualities of the cock? In Mesopotamia hens had appeared long before; we see them on Babylonian graves of the seventh to sixth centuries B.C.[1] It is well known that Zend speakers honoured the cock, believing its crowing drove off evil spirits of the night. The cock was considered a sacred bird in Persia, where it figured at funerals. Fire, the dog and the cock were regarded by the Persians as the three protectors. In the sixth century B.C. chickens penetrated from Persia through Asia Minor into Greece, and it is not improbable that at about the same time they reached the Altai.

The barrow finds offer no essential evidence about hunting as a permanent occupation of the people, nor about methods of hunting. Engels remarked that among pastoral peoples hunting takes a secondary place, and, previously necessary, now becomes a luxury.[2] So it was in the Altai Mountains, as distinct from the steppe peoples, where it still had not lost a certain economic significance. It constituted an entertainment for the aristocratic upper level of society, but for the mass of the population hunting was probably a subsidiary occupation.

Saddle and other cushions, and the figures of swans from barrow 5, were all stuffed with deer hair. Such a use of deer hair in all the barrows could only be possible given the condition that deer were regularly made use of. We found maral horns or objects made of them in every barrow. The beautiful, fairly realistic representations of elk, deer, mountain goats and rams, boars and saiga antelope indicate that the local inhabitants were thoroughly familiar with these animals. The fur of steppe cat was found in the barrows as well as that of squirrel, sable and otter, while at Katanda there was also ermine, and at Shibe remains of a dress of squirrel or sable fur.

In the Pazyryk barrows we have various articles of leopard skin, called *bars* in the Asiatic parts of the U.S.S.R., which were found in the Altai until quite recently. Animals that are common in the Altai fauna like wolf, roebuck and hare, beautiful representations of which we found in the barrows, were also probably game that was hunted.

If hunting deer, elk, goats and other ungulates had as its motive the need for meat and skins, then this was a consumer need, but hunting fur animals, particularly sable, might have had a commercial significance. It is not accidental that in all the burials of tribal chiefs or elders in which fur survived we find clothing made of sable. It is possible that such furs as sable and squirrel were used for dress not only in the Altai but in the steppes to the west and south, and the Altai in such circumstances could have been a centre for this trade.

[1] Layard, B, 1867a, pp. 304, 305.   [2] Marx and Engels, A, vol. xvi, pt i, p. 38.

The hunting of birds (to judge by representations of swans, geese and black grouse) met an exclusively consumer's demand and, because of natural conditions in the Altai, could not have been particularly fruitful. Eagles may also have been obtained, as suggested by feathered arrows found in the barrows, and beautifully realistic representations of this bird, converted, it is true, into a mythical griffin.

The means and methods of hunting might have been quite varied, relying upon centuries of experience. The *battue* of riders must have been widespread, for it is always and everywhere associated with riding. Such hunting in the past, not to mention the eighteenth century, was widespread in the Kazakh steppes and throughout central Asia. The chief weapon in such hunts was the bow and arrow, in the use of which all Scythian tribes [1] were skilled, including the Altaians, and of the Buryat and mounted Tungus Pallas wrote that they were 'so skilled that even at full gallop the arrow did not miss its mark'. [2]

It must be assumed that the people were not concerned with fishing, since natural conditions were not favourable. There still remains the problem of agriculture.

In the district of Ulagan, where the Pazyryk barrows lie, the climate is too severe to allow cultivation of the soil. It was no milder at that time, or the barrow congelation would not have taken place. Today wheat will only ripen in insignificant areas of the valleys of the Chulyshman and Bashkaus. It is difficult to concede that the earlier population of the Ulagan plateau could have done any cultivation at all.

It is possible, however, that then, as now, agriculture was practised in the central Altai Mountain area, particularly in the valley of the Ursul, where the climate is milder and warmer than in the Ulagan tableland. It is essential to point out, however, that up to now no barrow of this period has yielded either corn seeds or querns. Consequently cereals were either not cultivated at all or in very limited amounts.

Stock-breeding was therefore the basic occupation, and the food of the inhabitants of the area consisted mainly of milk products and meat. This is confirmed by the finds in the barrows of cheese, bones of different domestic animals and vessels that had undoubtedly been filled originally with milk products. The cheese, surviving in great quantity in a special leather bag in barrow 2, and also found in barrow 5, is indisputable proof of its important place in the people's food. Analysis has revealed the presence of casein and fat,

---

[1] Herodotus records that the Scyths taught young Medes how to shoot the bow, and that the Amazons went hunting with their menfolk and shot from bows. Herodotus, A, bk i, 73; bk iv, 114, 116.

[2] Pallas, A, pt iii, first half, p. 280.

but it was not possible to determine from which milk the cheese had been made. This was the more difficult in that in the preparation of the cheese cows', yaks', sheep's and goats' milk could have been mixed together, all these animals being kept. I would point out that among the contemporary pastoral peoples— Altaians, Kazakhs and Kirgiz—in making cheese the milk of the animals mentioned is mixed, by rich as well as by poor families.

It is highly probable that the ancient Altaians milked mares and made koumiss from their milk. Herodotus tells us about the preparation by the Scyths of koumiss from mares' milk: 'They blind all their slaves to use them on the milk . . . the drawn out [mares'] milk is poured by the Scyths into deep wooden vessels and then they arrange the blind slaves about these and cause them to shake the milk.' [1]

The large and small narrow-necked earthenware bottles found in the tombs were more than likely filled with koumiss. Had they held curds and whey, or some other such drink made of cows' milk, then there would have been, in frozen conditions, particles of curds on the bottom of the vessels.

Meat of all the domestic animals was eaten—horse, sheep and large-horned cattle. In the barrows the sacral bones of all these animals were found; as is well known, pastoral peoples of today regard these parts of the meat as a great delicacy.

About the preparation of food by the ancient herdsmen we know nothing, but Herodotus gives us some information about Scythian methods:

'Since the Scythian land is entirely devoid of trees, the Scyths have contrived the following method of cooking meat: they skin a sacrificed animal, clean the meat from the bone, and throw it into a cauldron of local manufacture, if such is available (these resemble Lesbian vessels, but are slightly larger); then they set alight the bones and cook the meat over them. If a cauldron is lacking they stuff the meat into the animal's own stomach, add water and heat it up over the burning bones.' [2]

In the barrows we excavated, which had been looted, no copper cauldrons were found, but there was a small cauldron of Scythian type in barrow 2. The large cauldrons found accidentally in the Altai, taken with the description by Herodotus of the Scythian method of cooking, lead us to suppose this method was also practised in the Altai. But a reservation must be made about the use of animal bones as fuel as described by Herodotus. Bones, as is well known, will not burn by themselves, and he must be describing something else, the incineration of the bones of a sacrificed animal which must not be thrown away. So when a victim was brought to sacrifice the flesh was taken off the bones, which were then incinerated. In cooking meat of non-sacrificed animals one does not

[1] Herodotus, A, bk iv, 2.   [2] Ibid., 61.

remove it from the bone, but cooks the two together; otherwise we should not have found animal bones in all the barrows.

There remains something to be said about narcotics. It was mentioned above that two sets of apparatus for inhaling hemp smoke were found in barrow 2. We shall discuss this in more detail when dealing with Herodotus' description of purification after burial. Here it will be merely remarked that smoking hemp, like smoking hashish, took place without a doubt not just as a ceremony of purification after burial but in ordinary life; hashish was used as a narcotic. Not without reason Hesychius of Alexandria in his Lexikon, referring to Herodotus, calls hemp 'the Scythian smoking which has such strength that it brings out in a sweat anyone who experiences it. They burn hemp seeds'.[1]

Both men and women probably smoked, since we found two sets of apparatus for smoking with the burial of a man and a woman. They possibly also used the seeds of hart's clover (*donnik*), found in barrow 2, for smoking.

With regard to houses it can be assumed that at this time three types of dwelling existed in the Altai: birch-bark tents, felt tents (*kibitki*) and log cabins. In describing one of the eastern tribes, the Argippaei, Herodotus wrote: 'Each of them live under a tree which in winter they cover over with thick white felt, and in summer leave open.'[2] The ancient Altaians naturally did not live under trees, but undoubtedly they must have had conical huts or tents similar to the contemporary Altaian *shatyr*, covered by larch bark, birch-bark mats or felt. This is the more probable in that such tents, together with more sophisticated dwellings, arc in usc today among the pastoral peoples of Asia from the Caspian Sca to Mongolia. Let us recall the conical, albeit miniature, hexapod felt covers found in all the large barrows, used in smoking hemp. Their rods were like the frame of the light Kazakh shepherds' *kos*, with the upper end lashed with a thong, which could be assembled and covered with felt in a minute. We have seen such *kos* still in use among Adaev Kazakhs as recently as 1926.

Having regard to the felt and the huge sheets of birch bark and larch bark on top of the burial chambers we may reasonably assume the use of such materials also in huts. In this connection the birch-bark sheets in barrows 3 and 5 deserve attention. Not only were they of great size, particularly in barrow 5 where strips were sewn together (internal surface of the bark facing out), but also in order to retain the pliability of the bark it had been boiled beforehand. In spite of having passed thousands of years in the tomb it had not lost its elasticity. At the present day we can see how birch bark is prepared like this for use on a dwelling.

There were probably other kinds of temporary dwellings, perhaps portable.

[1] Hesychius of Alexandria, A.　　　　　　　　[2] Herodotus, A, bk iv, 23.

Herodotus [1] and Hippocrates definitely refer to movable dwellings on wheels among the Scythian nomads. According to Hippocrates, 'the Scyths call themselves nomads, as they have no houses but live in wagons. These are very small with four wheels. Others with six wheels are covered with felt; such wagons are employed like houses, in twos or threes and provide shelter from rain and wind. . . . The women and children live in these wagons, but the men always remain on horseback.' [2]

From this it is evident that the Scyths, besides huts covered by two or three layers of felt, lived in wagons constructed like the huts. It is still difficult to say what was the nature of their construction, but one may suppose they resembled the structures erected on the ground and tents on wheels used by steppe nomads (Nogai and Turcomans) at the end of the last century. The remains of the frame of what was evidently such a felt cover (*kibitka*) were found in barrow 5, and reveal a highly accomplished type of dwelling, not excelled constructionally by the best in use among the Kazakhs at the present day.

The light four-wheeled carriage found in barrow 5, which was drawn by four horses, could hardly have been a movable dwelling, although it was evidently covered over. Of the parts of the frame of a portable dwelling found with it that were just mentioned insufficient remained to decide whether it was intended for erection on the ground or on a wagon.

However, such dwellings could not have been in general use in the Altai for three reasons. First, constructional material for horizontal or vertical timber building together with bark was available in unlimited quantities; second, as we shall see, migrations over long distances were not necessary. Finally, to cover dwellings with felt would require a large quantity of wool, which could be furnished only by the numbers of sheep possessed by rich families—that is, just the sort of families to whom the big Pazyryk barrows belonged.

On the other hand we know that at this time there were skilled carpenters at work. The log tombs are evidence that the Altaians knew how to make log cabins with notches at the interlocking log ends, either with plain logs with knots removed carefully fitted together, or with dressed logs. In some cases after construction the inner surface of the logs could have been dressed to make a finished cabin, the inside corners being not right angles but rounded. The cabins as a rule were constructed away from the site intended for them, and, as is done today, in the preceding year. Before transfer to their permanent site the logs were marked to assist reassembly. Such had been the case in the box tombs in barrows 2 and 5, where all members were marked, both of walls and roof. The floor was made of thick planks, the roof of logs, partly dressed on the inside. What the roof cover would have been it is difficult to say. At all events the tomb ceilings were covered with larch bark, a layer of smoky tea and sheets

---

[1] Herodotus, A, bk iv, 46, 114, 121.   [2] Hippocrates, A, pp. 25 ff.

of birch bark; the inference is that the latter material was also used on the roofs of houses.

The dimensions of dwellings would depend on the length of larch logs used in the walls. In some cases the rooms could have been fairly large and high. In the horse burial in barrow 5 a large felt hanging (4·5 m. by 6·5 m.) was found which we have the following grounds for believing to have been a wall-hanging. First, we know that in three of the largest Pazyryk barrows (1, 2 and 5) the tomb walls were draped with felt; so it follows there was a practice of draping the house walls. Second, on the hanging we see two rows, one above the other, of the same scene repeated: a goddess on a throne with a spray of blossom or sacred tree in her hand and a rider in front of her. Such carpets are not put on a floor. In the chamber of barrow 2 the floor was carpeted simply with thick felt of rough workmanship and quite undecorated. Furthermore on the large carpet from barrow 5 there were a series of felt, hanging, fan-shaped decorations that would not have been suitable to lay on a floor. Finally, if it did not hang on the wall of a house, but covered a tent or marquee, then the rows of figures would not have been one above another, but running in opposite directions along its lower longitudinal edge (*Pl. 147*).

In rich houses carpets would not only hang on the walls, but would also cover the floors. In barrow 5, besides the felt wall-hanging, there was a pile carpet showing signs of intensive wear, which had probably lain on a floor. The felt wall-hanging will be described in detail in the chapter on the local art and the pile carpet in the last chapter.

Having regard to the double walls and double ceilings of the box tombs can it be assumed that the log houses of the living had double walls and ceilings? I think not, since houses of such a kind are not known to me, nor are there reports of them either in contemporary ethnographical literature or in historical sources. Indeed they were not necessary; careful fitting of the logs and a felt lining were sufficient to retain the warmth. The double walls and ceilings in the chieftains' tombs were designed to increase the strength of the structure, so that it could withstand pressure from the sides and above.

There is nothing definite that can be said about outbuildings or about animal stalls. Nevertheless, bearing in mind the uprights with horizontal beams erected over the tombs, one is prompted to think that cattle stalls could have been constructed similarly.

Houses were lit by stone oil-lamps; one such lamp was found in barrow 2 in the south-west corner of the burial chamber (*Pl. 41*). It was made out of a solid rectangular block of sandstone with four solid feet and a raised rim, and two elongated hollows for the fat (*Pl. 52*A). Several stone lamps on four feet of a slightly different kind have been found in excavations in the valley of the

River Ursul.[1] A whole series of similar lamps, accidental finds in the region, are preserved in the regional museum at Gorno-Altaysk. Among them are rectangular examples on four feet similar to those from Pazyryk, and plain stones without feet with a hollow for the fat, rectangular, oval or rhombic in shape. Such stone lamps were evidently in widespread use at that period in the Altai.

Apparatus for making fire has still not been found, but there can hardly be any doubt that this was done by rotating one piece of wood against another. Such a device was found in one of the Noin-Ula barrows of a later date. Had a strike-a-light been used, even if the steel had not survived one would expect to find the flint.

The most widespread article of furniture at this time was a low, four-legged, collapsible table with an oval dish-like top. Such tables were found in all the Pazyryk barrows, and even in barrow 1, which had been almost entirely ran-sacked, there was still the leg of such a table remaining. In barrows 3 and 4 there were two tables, in barrow 5 three and in barrow 2 four. Although in general they are similar, all these little tables vary in construction and dimensions. In all of them, as mentioned, the four legs are column-shaped and have a tenon in the end that fits into a mortise in the underside of the top. These tenons are either circular or square in section or in the shape of a truncated, four-sided pyramid. The table tops were all, without exception, oval in shape with a rounded more or less raised rim, consequently giving the top the form of a dish. The tenons of the legs fitted either into apertures cut through the wood to the same shape as the tenon, or into mortises cut in the thickness of the top on the underside. If it was a loose fit either the tenon was wrapped in thin leather or the mortise was chipped wider and a little wedge driven in. The table heights varied markedly from very low (18–23 cm.) in barrow 5 to relatively high (40–47 cm.) in barrows 2 and 3.

The one table leg that survived in barrow 1 had an overall height of 37 cm., without tenon 34.5 cm., and a diameter of 6 cm. It was carved with eight encircling hollows of round profile with seven intervening sharp arrises. Part of the hollows had evidently been stuck over with fine birch bark and part with tinfoil (*Pl. 51*A).

The four little tables from barrow 2 were each about 45 cm. high with oval tops, measuring on average 52 cm. by 65 cm. They were cut from a solid piece of wood with a slightly concave top and rim raised about 4 cm. The convex under-neath face of the top had four projecting knobs with mortises in the centre for the tenons on the tops of the legs. These mortises were round or rectangular according to the shape of the tenon. All the tops were coloured red with cinnabar. One top had not been detached (*Pl. 50*A), the other three had all been removed, only two (both damaged) in fact still being in the tomb.

[1] Kiselev, A, 1935, p. 101, fig. 12.

While these three tables were still in position (their legs held fast in the ice) the robbers had used them as blocks for hacking off the heads of the corpses, and the woman's legs and right hand. One of the tops bears deep cuts showing traces of blows with an axe. Moreover two tables were hewn through to the leg, in one case split vertically, although the remaining three legs were intact and in position.

The legs of all four little tables survived. Two sets of legs are round, carved or turned, and two have the shape of tigers. The carved legs (overall height 33 cm., height without tenon 29 cm., diameter 5·5 cm.) have eight annulated swellings with sharp arrises (*Pl. 51*F). The legs turned on a lathe (overall height 35 cm., effective height 33 cm., diameter 5 cm.), are circular in section and have five hollows with three arrises in each, which separate four intervening globular segments and two at top and bottom (*Pl. 51*L). The latter were covered by tinfoil. On the round legs the tenons fitting into the mortises on the tops were also round in section.

The legs on the remaining two tables, carved in the shape of tigers, are thinner and more refined on one than on the other. The animals stand on their hind legs with the front legs extended forward and muzzle supporting the top. In the examples illustrated in *Pls. 50*B, *51*G, H the forehead is well modelled and the eyes clearly carved; the mouth is open, nostril distended, and upper lip puckered into three deep creases; the ear in relief is shown with a marked lobe. The long tail is coiled at the end. The front paws both on the side surfaces and underneath are carefully modelled, but the back ones only on the side and then more schematically.

In the table legs in *Pl. 51*I–K the front paws are shown in full; the fore part of the muzzle has been so carved that only the root of the nose and part of the creases of the upper lip are shown. While on the legs described above the fore-paws touch the lower jaw, in this case the paws pass either side of that and touch the upper lip. In spite of the great elegance of the bodies of these animals the heads are relatively coarser, thicker and larger in size; the ears are in relief with sharply marked lobe. The forepaws are shown more schematically, the rear paws are carved at the front and sides. The knee joint is indicated by cuts. The tail with twist at the end is significantly shorter than on the table legs represented in *Pl. 51*, G, H. The whole surface of the first legs shows the traces of the cuts of the knife used to carve it; the surface of the other has been rubbed smooth.

Since these legs were made by free carving, not from a pattern, apart from a broad conformity in each set, they differ considerably in detail, keeping only a general unity of style. On the other hand, in spite of essential differences between the legs of one table and those of another, they seem to constitute variants of one and the same permanent theme. The tenons of the legs were rectangular;

they must have been fixed to the top in such a way that the backs of the tigers were turned outwards and parallel to the short axis of the table top.

The tables from barrow 3 (fig. 18) were the same as those from the first two barrows. They are both low (about 40 cm.) and set on four carved legs with an oval top (52 cm. by 62 cm.). On the convex under-surface of the top there were four knobs with mortises for the leg tenons (*Pl. 51*B, C). The carved legs of both tables are of one and the same type, but one set is short and thin and the other higher and larger (overall height 27 and 30 cm., diameter 4·8 and 5·3 cm.). The legs of both tables were decorated by pairs of rings with arrises dividing the annulated leg into four barrel-shaped segments, not counting the top and bottom. The tables were entirely coloured with cinnabar to a bright red.

The tables of barrow 4 were smaller in size and simpler in design by comparison with the tables of the first three barrows. One had carved legs (*Pl. 51*E) and the other plain ones, circular in section (*Pl. 51*D). The top of the first table was not found but, judging by the tenons on the legs, its lower surface must have had mortises. The leg takes the shape of truncated cones at top and bottom, separated from a biconical middle by two pairs of rings with sharp arrises. The second table was of the same type but without mortise on the underside of the top, which is distinguished from all the others in having quadrangular holes driven through it to receive the leg tenons. In addition its legs were quite plain, not annulated, scarcely thicker above than below. The overall table height was 32 cm., the top measuring 47 cm. by 51 cm. (fig. 19).

In barrow 5, as already mentioned, the surviving legs indicated three little tables, only half of one top having survived. Evidently, as in barrow 2, the tomb robbers used the table tops as trays on which articles were carried out of the

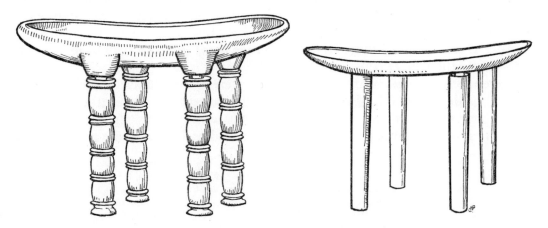

18. Little table from barrow 3 (*c.* $\frac{1}{9}$).   19. Little table from barrow 4 (*c.* $\frac{1}{9}$).

tomb. In barrow 2 one of the tops was actually found in the forced entry above the tomb.

The basic feature of the tables in barrow 5, more marked than in all the other barrows, was their lowness. The circular legs of two tables were of appreciably greater diameter above than below (5 cm. and 3 cm.) and had an overall height of 21 cm. with tenon (*Pl. 52*D), giving a table of a mere 23–24 cm. high. The legs of the third table had a diameter of 4·6 cm. at the top and 5·4 cm. at the bottom, with a height at the junction with the top of 16 cm. (*Pl. 52*D). Therefore the height to the edge of the rim did not exceed 20 cm.

Judging by the form of the tenons (square truncated pyramids) there must have been mortises, not through perforations, for fixing the legs to the tops.

Comparison of the tables from all barrows reveals the skill and care put into the making of these from the first three barrows in contrast with the last two, in particular with those in barrow 5.

It may be remarked that all the table tops were detachable and the raised rim gave them a dish shape. Detachable tops were very handy for transport, but it was evidently not for this reason that they were given the shape they had. In all essentials they can be regarded as dishes on legs on which food was served, for with their delicately concave shape they could not have performed any other function. Their lowness indicates that their owners ate seated on the floor on mats similar to those found spread out on the floor in the chamber of barrow 2.

Since these tables, in particular those from the early barrows, have a thoroughly finished and mature form it is reasonable to suppose that this could have been achieved only during a long passage of time. We do not know of such tables from an earlier period than this. Tables and thrones with similar carved circular legs, resting on lions' paws and with annulated ornament, are well known in Assyria and Achaemenid Persia,[1] but these are not the dish-tables of the Altai Mountains. Later, tables with detachable tops are known from the Noin-Ula barrows in Mongolia, but whether these acted as dishes we do not know since the tops are missing from the legs.[2]

An entirely individual device for sitting were the primitive stools, the so-called wooden 'pillows', also found in all the Pazyryk barrows without exception. Originally when two such flattish objects with circular edges were found in the first two barrows, and moreover at the head end of the coffin in barrow 2,

[1] See the little tables on the bas-reliefs from Khorsabad in Perrot and Chipiez, B, vol. ii, figs. 24 and 28. They are especially numerous on the bas-reliefs of Persepolis where Artaxerxes is shown on his throne or giving audience, and in the procession of tributaries. See Herzfeld, B, figs. 364 and 365, Pls. 67, 68, 77. See also details of the royal Achaemenian tombs in the necropolis of the Takht-i-Jamshid and the bas-relief of the Apadana with a hundred columns in Dieulafoy, B, 1885, vol. iii, Pls. 4 and 19.

[2] C. Trever, *Excavations in N. Mongolia* (1932), Pl. 27.

20. Part of a stool-cover or pillowcase showing applied leather work, from barrow 2.

we were led to suppose they were a kind of pillow for putting under the head. Furthermore the example from barrow 2 had a special 'pillow-case' of leather and fur. However, when just such objects were found in the remaining three barrows, it became clear that they could not be pillows for putting under the head.[1] Their considerable height and sharp edges would only have allowed sitting on, and probably only for men, since in all the barrows with a double burial, man and woman, there was only one stool.

The wooden stools found in barrow 1 (*Pl. 53*A) and 2 (*Pl. 53*B) are of the same shape with a slightly waisted middle; the former (21 cm. by 40 cm., 8·5 cm. high) only slightly larger than the latter (17·5 cm. by 36 cm., 8 cm. high). The surface of these stools is axe-dressed, the traces of the blows being quite distinct, and has not been smoothed off as in all the other wooden objects. Probably this is due to the fact that the former had covers. From the remains of such a cover in barrow 2 (*Pl. 58*) it can be concluded that one surface was the fur of steppe cat, and the other smooth, finely dressed leather. Its sides were decorated at the corners with large applied rosettes (fig. 20) and the leather surface was decorated with an intricate pattern of applied coloured leather.

The stools found in barrows 3, 4 and 5 are of a different type from those found in barrows 1 and 2. First, their upper and lower surfaces are flat or slightly convex; secondly, as mentioned above, they have sharp, not smoothed, edges; finally, they are all relatively higher. Their dimensions were, from barrow 3, 20 cm. by 36 cm. and 14 cm. high (*Pl. 53*C); from barrow 4, 14 cm. by 29 cm. and 16 cm. high with convex upper surface (*Pl. 52*B); finally, from barrow 5, 24 cm. by 50 cm. and 19 cm. high (*Pl. 52*C).

Apart from the low dish-tables and stools just described, there was no other furniture and possibly they had no other. In barrow 5, however, there was a

[1] [Translator's note. Rudenko has been prompted by his discoveries at Tuekta to some extent to revert to his original 'pillow' theory. Rudenko, A, 1960, p. 114.]

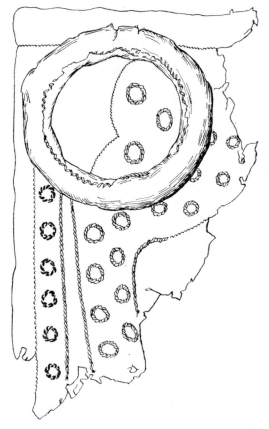

21. Corner of a felt coverlet with a ring-stand from barrow 2 (*c.* $\frac{1}{3}$).

small flat felt cushion, stuffed with deer hair, but its purpose is uncertain. It was stitched along its edge and down the middle lengthways (*Pl. 56*). In addition in the middle of each side a short strap was attached to it.

Vessels were made of wood and clay. Wooden vessels, which survived only in barrow 2, were of two types, both cut out of the solid. One took the shape of a small mug (height 14·5 cm., greatest width 13–14 cm.) with upper edge slightly turned out, and had a spherical bottom and short, high handle (*Pl. 54*c). Another was almost spherical (13·5 cm. high, maximum diameter 15·5 cm.), with strongly everted rim. The handle was long and curved with a horn (*Bos taurus*) mount terminating in a horse's hoof (*Pl. 54*A). The handle had been covered with gold-leaf. Between mount and the vessel's body there was a wide perforation through the handle, evidently for a strap to be passed through for suspension. The first vessel was made of wood from the trunk, the second from a growth on the wood. Externally the workmanship was good, while the inside had been worked with a special burin with curved blade.

In barrow 2 there had been another wooden vessel of which only the horn handle survived. In a socket at the base of this handle was a biconical wooden peg for fixing it to the body (*Pl. 54*B). A vessel shaped like a cup or ladle with short handle had been placed in barrow 3, but it had survived extremely badly and become very distorted.

The shape of the round-bottomed wooden vessels has numerous analogies in the pottery, gold and silver vessels found in pre-Scythian and late Sarmatian burials of the north Caucasus,[1] in Black Sea Scythian burials [2] and in pictures of vessels in Persian and Assyrian bas-reliefs.[3] This points to the durability of the type in Hither Asia and the culturally related areas.

Prior to the excavation of the Pazyryk barrows it was not clear how these vessels were kept upright. It has turned out that they stood on special felt rings or straw rings sewn up in felt. The vessels in barrow 2 stood on just such rings, about 2·5–3 cm. high, twisted from strips of fairly thick black felt sewn up in red or black fine felt, plainly sewn with twisted or plaited sinew threads. Their diameter varied and depended on the diameter of the vessels that they supported (14–18·5 cm.). Six such rings were found in barrow 1, from which it can be concluded that not less than six vessels, including clay ones, had been placed in the tomb. As a rule the rings were free to be put anywhere (*Pl. 54*C), but sometimes they were sewn on to a felt coverlet. Fig. 21 is a schematic representation of the corner of such a coverlet from barrow 2, which is made of thick black felt decorated with a pattern of twisted woollen threads and has a black felt ring sewn on to it.

Earthenware vessels were represented in all barrows by a uniform type of tall, narrow-necked bottle. In the big barrows they were large, in the ordinary ones small. To judge by the remains only barrow 2 had two large bottles; in the others they occurred singly.

The bottles in barrow 2 were both the same shape and size. One had been smashed by the robbers, and the other was still whole, standing in the ice when the tomb was opened, but so badly cracked that in thawing it could only be taken out in pieces (its base was badly shattered). This bottle was flat bottomed (12 cm. across the base) with a fat belly (28·5 cm.), narrow neck (11·5 cm.), expanding at the top (17 cm.); it was 50 cm. high (*Pl. 55*B, C). It was hand made of grey paste with large grits of fine gravel. The latter were unevenly spread, in places only grains being visible, in others a mass of gravel with grain sizes up to 6 mm., and in some cases chips up to 11 mm. long. This pot, like all the Pazyryk bottles, had not been made on a wheel but by hand, using either the coil method (8 cm. thick in the middle) or joining four separate parts (base, neck

---

[1] See the well-known Maikop silver cups, and gold from the Novocherkassk hoard illustrated in Smirnov, A, Pl. 1, 1–12; Pl. 2, 9–11.

[2] Rostovtsev, A, Pl. 1.
[3] Perrot and Chipiez, B, vol. ii, fig. 24; Herzfeld, B, Pl. 78.

22. Cut-out leather cocks decorating a bottle in barrow 2 (*c.* $\frac{2}{5}$).

and two intervening rings). The inner and outer faces of the vessel had been covered with a yellow-reddish slip and carefully burnished, the outside being particularly finely done. Its walls were 14 mm. thick in the lower part near the base, 8 mm. in the broad part, 7 mm. at the neck and 9 mm. at the rim. The firing, done on an open fire, was uneven.

The second vessel from this barrow was of the same shape and dimensions. Its base survived particularly well, and in comparison with the whole pot was extraordinarily small. Its diameter was 8 cm., and the diameter of the flat surface on which the bottle stood 6 cm. It was this bottle that stood in the felt ring sewn to the coverlet mentioned above. Both bottles were evidently used exclusively to hold fluids, perhaps koumiss; they could not have been used on the fire.

The neck of the first, whole, bottle had been stuck over with a broad band of very thin leather (possibly there was a crack at the rim), and on the belly six silhouettes of cocks, cut from thin leather (but thicker than that bound round the neck), had been pasted.

One pair of cocks stood facing each other, but a second pair, on the opposite side of the vessel, had their heads turned in different directions. The figures were stuck on with the smooth, inner side of the skin downwards, and the outside face of the skin was covered with tinfoil. The tail of one of the cocks was sewn on with a double stitch in woollen thread. The cocks had not been made

72

uniformly with a stencil. They are shown in motion with left claw slightly raised (fig. 22). In spite of a certain conventionality of reproduction the characteristic features of the birds are masterfully caught: head with wattle and comb, and raised tail.

The earthenware vessels in the ordinary barrows, in particular in barrow 6 at Pazyryk and barrow 2 at Aragol, are the same kind of bottle, but of smaller size (*Pl. 55*A), with a somewhat more accentuated belly and narrower neck. The pot from barrow 6 at Pazyryk is 30·4 cm. high with a belly diameter of 16·4 cm. and a very narrow (6 cm.) neck below a strongly flaring mouth (rim diameter 10·7 cm.). The bottles from barrow 2 at Aragol were 20 and 23·7 cm. high with relatively fat bellies of 17·3 cm. and 18·3 cm., 5·8 cm. and 7 cm. at the neck and 6·7 cm. and 8 cm. at the rim. It is remarkable that they all had a constant base diameter of 6 cm., and so could have fitted the same ring rests.

A well-levigated grey paste with comparatively small sand and gravel grits was used in these hand-made pots, made in the same fashion as the big ones. Firing had been uneven in an open fire.

All kinds of fur and leather bags, pouches and purses were found in some quantity, particularly in barrow 2. Such a variety of leather and fur containers, resembling very closely the well-known containers of Asian pastoral peoples, betrays the basic occupation of the people as stock-rearing, and also confirms the considerable antiquity of the pattern of leather vessels still in use among pastoral peoples today.

In the horse burial of barrow 2 was a bag made of thick leather, a sort of broad, flat flask (30 cm. by 40 cm.) with relatively narrow neck, in which cheese had been kept. The external surface was covered by a mosaic pattern of cut-out shapes of white and bright blue fur with a pattern between in a cherry-red colour. The motif of the pattern is vegetable—the lotus flower (*Pl. 150*B). In the barrow 1 horse burial a large (37 cm. high) leather container with narrow neck, resembling the flask, was found. It is sewn together from pieces of leopard skin (*Pl. 59*B) on one side, and on the other (*Pl. 59*A) is a mosaic pattern consisting of shapes of white and blue fur, sewn on to a thin leather background. The motif of the design is rhombs, in the middle of which are ovals containing an X-shaped excision, flanked by triangles with their bases following the outline of the ovals (*Pl. 150*A).

The burial chamber of barrow 2 yielded two leather flasks with narrow necks like bottles; one was found in a leather bag at the end of the coffin, and the other in the fallen debris below the robbers' trap. The first (21·5 cm. high), with small round bottom (diameter 3 cm.) and narrow neck, had been sewn from four strips of fairly thin leather, flesh side outwards, giving the appearance of chamois leather. The seams were reinforced by a double strip of thin leather of greyish-red colour, and the decoration was done with the same finely dressed leather. A band of little circles between two parallel lines divides the flask into upper and lower halves, with four trapeze-shaped areas in each half. In each area is the same sewn-on lotus pattern, the origin of which becomes intelligible by comparison with other representations of the same flower. In the background beneath the flower are triangles with a round notch, and beside the flower a stylized antler (*Pl. 152*B). The applied pattern is sewn on to the background by thin sinew threads, which had been used to stitch the whole flask. Although the seams are tightly, impermeably sewn the flask could scarcely have been used for fluids; more probably it was intended to hold grass seeds or roots like those found in other similar containers.

The second flask was also flat and circular in shape, with a narrow neck, sewn together basically from two pieces of leather with, as before, the underface outwards, with a strip of leather (with fur side outwards) sewn round the flask holding them together. As in the first case a narrow doubled band of leather sewn on with sinew threads reinforced the seams. On each flat surface of the flask there were sewn-on cut-outs of thin leather depicting a griffin holding a black grouse in its claws and biting at it with its beak (*Pl. 61*C).

This appliqué work and the circular rim were cut from a single piece of leather with fur side outwards. The silhouettes of the birds stand out sharply on the lighter underside of the leather forming the background, and beneath the excisions in the cut-out figures of birds, leather of the same quality and colour as that applied has been set. Consequently some details of the birds have been somewhat obscured.

Let us pause to examine this composition. The grouse is depicted with lowered wings and distended tail, head twisted back and feet in the air. The griffin, tail distended and wings outstretched, has plunged its claws into the neck and chest of the grouse and bites with its beak at one of its claws. The tall, long comb of the griffin is very characteristic. On the leather band around the edge of the flask are sewn-on leather rhombs with rhombic excisions inside. To the top edge of the neck is attached a tiny thong. Grains of hemp were kept in this flask, which was secured to one leg of a hexapod frame.

In the eastern part of the tree-trunk coffin in barrow 2, at the head end, lay a large pouch (20 cm. by 30 cm.) or saddle-bag made of thin, finely dressed leather (fig. 23). In it were found a silver mirror, a flask (the first described above), a small flat pouch and other objects. The middle part of this bag was secured by a thong to a stick in such a way that the bag was separated into two halves on either side, thus forming two capacious pockets. The projecting ends of the stick were modelled into feline heads. The upper side of this double pouch was straight, the lower rounded. It was carried by a strap that divided into three, two parts secured at the ends of the stick near the animal heads and

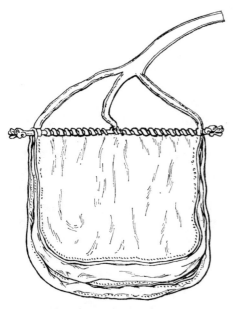 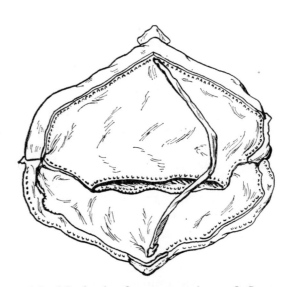

23. Leather bag from barrow 2 (*c.* ⅕).

24. Method of construction of flap-pocket on pouch in barrow 2.

the third in a special lug in the middle of the stick. The latter divided into two strips at the middle of the stick, and their ends were sewn to a wooden ring. The bag is made out of a single piece of leather with side gussets sewn with sinew threads.

Feline heads in the round like this have an especial interest: the teeth are bared, the upper lip creased, nose broad, ears big and muzzle deliberately rounded (*Pl. 136*c). We shall be encountering heads like this more than once in the future.

A rectangular (13·5 cm. by 23 cm.) little pouch, with curved upper edge and so slightly expanded middle, was found in the bag described above, which in construction and ornament has much in common with the flask illustrated in *Pl. 152*B. It consists of a piece of chamois leather decorated round its edge with applied stiff leather and a decorated leather pocket sewn on to its middle (*Pl. 151*B). The pocket is stitched on three sides, the fourth remaining open. The right expanded side of the pocket is convex, which increases its capacity. The original colour of the background leather was cream (chamois) and the applied leather dark cherry. The motif of the pattern is vegetable, a kind of lotus; a pair of similar flowers differ in size because of the shape of the pocket. The right-hand larger flower is shown with petals upwards, the left with them down. Both flowers are set within a spiral of rosettes. It is to be noted that the lotus-like

75

flowers, as in the decoration of the flask in *Pl. 152*B, rest on supports of branching circles. The shapes rhythmically repeated on the border are griffins' heads, which we shall also encounter more than once later on. This little pouch was evidently a toilet ancillary to hold jewels or other personal adornments.

Of interest by its refinement is a little pouch with flap, found again in the debris in barrow 2, together with torn cloth and pieces of other objects. One half of it was badly damaged, but its complete shape could be reconstructed without difficulty, as well as its varied decoration (*Pl. 153*A). The bag was made of stiff leather with an inside pocket of fine leather, and an outside flap covering the pocket. On the top border above the flap was sewn a band of thick leather with excised ornament on it. The pocket is bigger than the pouch, so that its free upper part was held, but it was tight below. In order to get into the pocket you had to raise the flap and then pull back the upper part of the relatively narrow opening at its top (fig. 24). The flap was covered on the outside with leopard's fur and was trimmed with a band of fine felt, dyed red. On to this band had been sewn little copper geese, or ducklings, covered with gold-leaf, which were found at various points not far from the pouch. The places where they had been sewn were easily distinguishable by the traces of the sinew threads that had stitched them on. Beneath this, under a specially shaped lug cut out of skin, a perforation had been made for a strap with its end divided into three and plaited. This strap secured the flap at the bottom of the pouch.

 25. Stamped copper birds from barrow 2 ($\frac{1}{1}$).

The miniature figures of geese or ducks with raised wings and turned-back head consisted of plates of thin copper stamped in relief and stuck together with resin. Covered on the outside on both sides by gold-leaf, they could be sewn to an object whichever way up preferred (fig. 25).

In this pouch, as in the leather purse described below, seeds of cultivated coriander had been kept.

The seeds of cultivated coriander (*Coriandrum sativum*) found in barrow 5 at Pazyryk have an especial interest. The genus *Coriandrum* was widespread in antiquity in the eastern Mediterranean lands, Egypt and Asia Minor, whence it penetrated into India. It is one of the oldest cultivated plants surviving to the present day. In antiquity coriander was chiefly valued for its medicinal and aromatic properties. Its seeds occur in Egyptian tombs from the XII dynasty.[1]

---

[1] Apart from XII-dynasty tombs it occurs also in those of the XXII dynasty and in Graeco-Roman times. Schweinfurth, B.

Its medicinal properties are referred to by Homer, Hippocrates, Herodotus and others.

At the present time, within the extensive area of distribution of coriander, one of its most concentrated areas is Asia Minor where there are more poly-morphs and 'artificial' varieties than in any other. Coriander seeds are par-ticularly rich in oil of ether content (0·8–11·1 per cent) the value of which is assessed by its content of linalool alcohol (90–92 per cent).

Foreign to the flora of the Altai, coriander (more precisely its seeds) could only have reached there as an import from the south, from central and Hither Asia.

An unusual form of purse was hemispherical, taking the shape of a wasps' nest with hood (*Pl. 61*A). It was stitched from a single piece of thick leather. The bottom (5·5 cm. in diameter) was flat, but the neck constricted (about 1·5 cm. across) and the half-round hood closed right over it. In the middle of the bottom was a short projecting strap which held the hood when it was open. In the leather side were holes and the remains of a little strap by which the purse had been attached to something. The bottom and hood were covered by engraved decoration (fig. 26), the bottom with rows of zigzag lines as if imitating fur, and the hood with trefoils. In the middle above was a kind of cross made up of four trefoils. Around the edge they were cut in definite lines. In the slashes between the leaves of the trefoils gold plates were stuck.

Besides the skilfully made pouches and purses described above, in barrow 2 there were a very plain fur pouch and many plain purses. A hemispherical pouch (20 cm. by 27 cm.) was sewn up out of two pieces of sable fur, one side of whole skins of a darker colour, the other of small rectangular pieces of a lighter colour (*Pl. 57*).

The leather purse illustrated in *Pl. 61*B secured with a strap above was used to hold a black dye; such dye, as we shall see below, was used to colour the arti-ficial beard of the man buried in barrow 2.

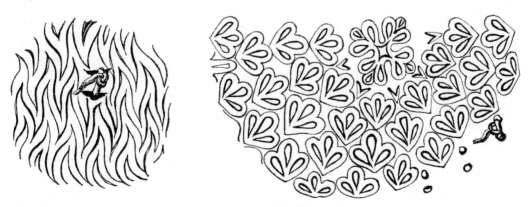

26. Ornament on leather purse in barrow 2 ($\frac{4}{5}$).

In ransacked tombs, where thieves had taken even the tiniest metal articles, one could not reckon on finding large copper cauldrons used for boiling food. Only in the ice of barrow 2 two copper vessels, the censers, accidentally survived. One took the form of a 'Scythian cauldron' (*Pl. 42*), the other being rectangular (*Pl. 35*B). The first, of spheroidal shape (*Pl. 62*B), was small (14·8 cm. high) and stood on a pedestal. The handles welded on to the middle were very large in relation to its body. On the rim were six low ornamental knobs.

The second censer (*Pl. 62*A) of rectangular shape (11·5 cm. by 12·3 cm. at the top and 9 cm. by 10 cm. below) was shallow (3·5 cm.) and stood on four annulated legs. A handle of the same shape as the legs was welded to a short side, and on the others were lugs, evidently for suspension.

In barrows 2 and 5 hollow inner horns from the end of domesticated goats' horns were found. In barrow 2 the horn was wrapped in a piece of leather (*Pl. 60, above*) and in barrow 5 it contained a little spoon (*Pl. 60, left*), hardly different from those used with a snuff-box among the contemporary population of central Asia. In barrow 3 at the right shin of the buried warrior, and evidently kept in the upper boot, was a wooden object (fig. 27), the purpose of which is uncertain.

27. Spatulate object of wood from barrow 3 ($\frac{1}{2}$).

A leather cover concludes the collection of household goods; it was spread over the hexapod frame to cover the censer shaped like a 'Scythian cauldron' in barrow 2. It measured 150 cm. by 175 cm. and had suffered badly at the time of plundering, particularly its central part. Nevertheless it proved possible to reconstruct it almost entirely. In fig. 28 the cover as a whole is shown above, and below, on a larger scale, its decoration, the attack of a winged, horned lion-griffin on an elk.

The central rectangle of this cover consists of several pieces of thin leather stitched together, and it is trimmed with leather. On each of the four edges a leather strip is sewn on bearing the scene mentioned, which originally also adorned a leather strip across the middle, now only partially surviving. The outside edge of the cover was decorated with just the same narrow leather band as decorated the other side. The repeated panels were separated from one another by narrow leather strips on which were sewn leather circles. A mosaic technique has been employed; the pattern of leather cut-outs, originally probably of varying colour, was at one and the same time sewn together and on to a leather backing.

The scene depicted on the cover is both decorative and vivid. The wretched elk with bent muzzle and long ears has a beard and huge, typically elk-like

28. Leather cover from barrow 2.

antlers. It has fallen on its front legs, the back ones twisted up. On the shoulder and crupper are conventional comma, full-stop and half-horseshoe marks, which we shall meet again more than once later on, and in addition stylized triangular excisions. The griffin is resting with its back paws on the back legs of the elk, its front paws gripping its back and teeth biting into its withers. Individual features of the griffin are its 'ox' horn with tip twisted back, raised wing with end directed slightly forward and long tail with typical brush on the end. The body of this monster is also marked, like that of the elk, by conventional slashing, including triangles and ox-horns. Although the repetition is almost stencil-like, certain differences can be detected in each picture which might be interpreted as two scenes in a series on a very large scale.

We have reached the conclusion, then, that the basic occupation of the people in the Altai at this period was stock-rearing, with hunting in a subsidiary role (rudimentary agriculture was probably practised if only to produce winter fodder for stock); the probable types of house have been described and we are acquainted with the domestic utensils; it remains to pose the question of the people's way of life.

In the Altai Mountains settlements of this period have not yet been discovered, but in the steppes to the west they are well known. There are a number of points to confirm that the people of the area led a basically settled or semi-settled existence.

These views are based on the ethnographic evidence from contemporary tribes. Let us begin with the Kazakhs. In the spring the Kazakhs moved on to the southern slopes of the foothills, where the pasture at this season of the year grows richest. As soon as the sun began to scorch the grass they climbed to the higher open slopes until they reached mountain pastures, where they spent the hot part of the summer. In winter the Kazakhs returned to their winter quarters.

Pastoralists in the foothills transhumed into the mountains, but people of the steppe had their winter quarters in the south and in the summer time moved north with their cattle, sometimes over hundreds of kilometres, where we can say they had their normal pastures. The stock were separated; horses and sheep went by different routes and joined up only at the terminal points.

Quite a different picture presented itself in the Altai Mountains, where the grass is so luxuriant everywhere that even the largest herds moved only over small distances. The less prosperous group remained in the same place all the year round. In the Altai, therefore, stock were not separated, and all animals pastured together; the Altaian pastoralist lived in a permanent settlement. One matter must be commented on: the open steppe is the only place where stock-breeding is possible without hay stored for winter, and in the Altai such areas are very limited, separated from each other by more or less impenetrable mountain barriers. Mere narrow mountain tracks, along which it was impossible to herd animals, cut off the tribes and clans from one another and led to an isolated, shut-off way of life.

As evidence of a more or less settled way of life in the Altai Mountains, besides a series of probable analogies, some indisputable facts can be adduced. It is difficult to accept that in a mountain-forest landscape, with slight steppe areas in the narrow river valleys, as we find in the Altai, where an unlimited quantity of building material was everywhere ready to hand, the forest would not have been utilized for the construction of dwellings. Evidence that the mountain people had permanent log houses is furnished by the technically very accomplished structures of dressed logs or thick planks that served as burial chambers in the barrows. Some stock, such as thoroughbred horses and fine-fleeced sheep, horned cattle (apart from yaks), particularly calves, would have had to be kept in covered enclosures during the winter. Thoroughbred horses, furthermore, are maintained on concentrated feeds. Finally, there are the heavy earthenware bottles, found in the large barrows, and the thin-walled, remarkably fragile, bottles from the ordinary barrows—pottery is not compatible with nomadism.

5. CLOTHING AND PERSONAL
ADORNMENT

THANKS to the congelation in the Altai barrows already described, not only remains of clothes but various personal adornments survived, even the tattooing on the corpse of a man buried in barrow 2. In that barrow a well-preserved, almost intact, man's shirt was found as well as pieces of another (*Pl. 63*). The cloth was of a linen weave of hemp or kendyr fibres, one half of the shirt being made of a thinner and brighter material than the other darker and thicker half. The brighter cloth was one uniform piece, but the darker of two kinds: a coarser cloth in the body, and a relatively fine cloth in the sleeves and gusset. The width of the body was 44·5 cm. The shirt was long (104 cm.) and broad (130 cm. along the lower edge) and very wide (93 cm. at the shoulder); the long sleeves (58 cm.) narrowed at the bottom. The head aperture was broad (32 cm.). The shirt was made up of four pieces, two at the front and two at the back, sewn together at the shoulders, sides and middle. The sleeves had been sewn on without gusseting. Below the hem on the sides four gussets were sewn in, one consisting of two pieces (fig. 29).

The main seam in the shirt was stitched with a fine red woollen braid and cord. A flat woollen cord (only about 2 mm. wide) was stitched longitudinally from the top downwards, from the neck to the hem front and back, in the shoulder seam and at the juncture of arms and body. A circular cord (1·5 mm. diameter) was used on the sides from hem to lower edges of arms, the thread being continuous and unbroken over the whole length. The head aperture and cuffs were hemmed with a broad red woollen braid (10 mm. wide). The cords used for sewing together the parts of the shirt were all of very tough twisted sinew. The bottom of the shirt was hemmed, but the cuffs were turned back 5 mm. and under, and stitched through.

The material and the make-up of the second shirt were the same, but the braid used for stitching the head opening was narrower (7 mm.) and the braid down the shirt and on the shoulders slightly wider (3 mm.). The twisted red woollen cord was precisely the same.

83

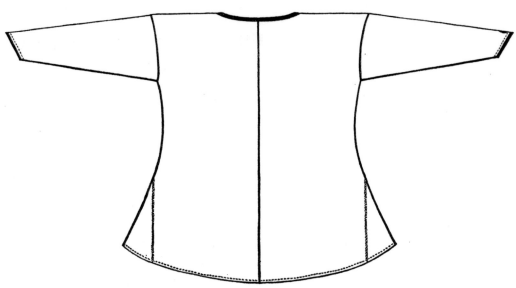

29. Make-up of shirt from barrow 2.

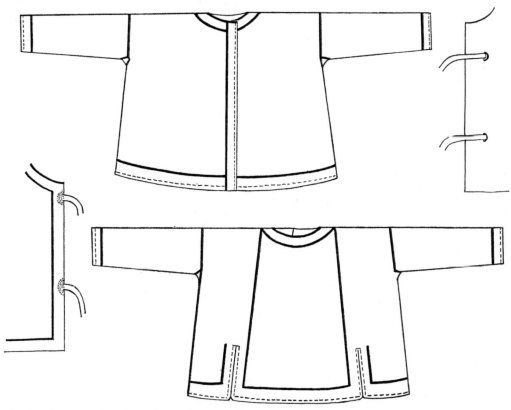

30. Make-up of caftan from barrow 3.

84

The man's shirt from barrow 2 at Pazyryk resembles the barbarian's (Scythian) shirt as it is depicted on the well-known terra-cotta from Kerch.[1]

Breeches have not been found in any of the barrows,[2] but the upper garment of male attire is represented by five examples: two from barrow 2 at Pazyryk, one from 3 and two from the barrow dug by V. V. Radlov at Katanda.

Only the back survived from one of the garments in barrow 2, and it can be assumed it is part of a caftan, typical of the attire of pastoral folk. It was short (90 cm. long) and made of sable fur. The external side has been treated as chamois leather, but to give it longitudinal rigidity parallel lines of fine sinew threads have been stitched on it with meticulous care. It may be remarked that sometimes the reinforcing and decorative stitching ran beside each other at intervals of about 4 mm., and in a length of 1 cm. there may be twenty stitches. The thread only passes through the superficial underside of the skin, except where the sewing corresponds with the longitudinal edges of the pieces of fur, when the stitches pass right through. The square-toothed edges of the pieces of fur have seams that are barely discernible.

The most remarkable feature of this garment is the applied leather cut-out decoration with gold disks stuck on it (*Pl. 151A*). In its surviving part this appliqué consists of a pair of deer's heads back to back with long, extended, branching antlers, with the tines terminating in stylized, big-eared birds' (griffin-like) heads. Although decorative and schematic, these are still typical of Altaian art in the period under study; we have already seen them adorning household objects and we shall see them again in the tattooing. The gold disks, furthermore, looking like eyes (where they survive) give the head an especial expressiveness. From the crown of the antlers narrow leather bands with gold disks fall out to left and to right, to some extent framing the composition in which the deer are the leading motif.

The hem, to judge by the surviving tatters, was bordered with a leather band on which were sewn stylized antlers cut out of leather and covered with gold. The border of the garment was edged with fur dyed blue (*Pl. 150D*). It is probable that a piece of fur, dyed an azure colour, belonged to it originally (*Pl. 150E*). This fur, probably ermine, is made up of small pieces sewn together with very fine sinew thread. Small leather disks (9 mm. diameter), pasted over with gold-leaf, are sewn on to it 1 cm. apart in diagonal rows at intervals of 3 cm.

In barrow 2 parts of another sable garment survived, with fur inside and outside. It is interesting that, in spite of the fact that the underside of the skin was not visible, the fur was stitched right through by sinew threads in parallel rows lengthwise, as in the previous example. Undoubtedly the main purpose of such

[1] Tolstoy and Kondakov, A, vol. ii, p. 63, fig. 46.

[2] [Translator's note. Breeches have subsequently been found by Rudenko in Tuekta, barrow 1. Rudenko, A, 1960, pp. 118–19.]

stitching was to give the fur rigidity. Only one sleeve survived (*Pl. 155*A), which is sewn like all the clothing with wool inside and outside. The cuff of this sleeve is made of skin of a dark bay colt, to which have been sewn two rectangular leather plates pasted over with gold-leaf. Although the end of the sleeve was broad enough to have allowed the hand to pass through freely, it had been sewn up at its lower edge, so the garment must have been thrown over the shoulders like a cloak.

A broad but short caftan found in the horse burial in barrow 3 is of great interest. It was made of a double thickness of very thin white felt and in make-up resembles the shirt in barrow 2. Its width at the shoulders is 1·18 m., and at the hem 1·4 m., but the length from collar to hem is only 1 m. The long (0·7 m.) and broad (0·29–0·23 m.) sleeves with small gusset at the end are tapering (fig. 30). The neck is broad and open. Behind and below are two slits; there was provision for tightening from right to left by means of two pairs of cords of numerous twisted wool fibres secured underneath (*Pl. 66*B, *below*). The top of the caftan was made of large pieces of felt, the lining of small pieces, and the sleeves of single pieces stitched at the lower edge. On the upper border, around the collar, on the cuffs and the back there was a decorative border seam shown as a continuous line in the figure, the punctuated line indicating the real seams. The decoration was carried out by passing thin white wool thread through the upper felt and tightening it, in the same way as the caftan itself was made, which produced narrow creasing. On the right outer border of the caftan a fleece band 6 cm. wide ran down between the layers of felt. This longitudinal stitching on its edges had the effect of producing a rigid relief border. The cords were secured in the following way: one end of the bunch of fibres was passed through a slit between the two felt layers and then secured by stitching right through (fig. 30).

There had evidently been a similar caftan in the burial chamber, where the cord illustrated in *Pl. 66*B, *top* was found.

In addition to the caftan a loose-fitting hood was found made of thin white felt, and two rectangular pieces of doubled felt (9·5 cm. by 14 cm.), with diagonal and circular stitching 1 cm. back from the edge. Possibly these had been pockets sewn on to the caftan, but in what place it would be difficult to say.

The costume from Katanda that took the form of a frock-coat has been described more than once, and a special study has been devoted to the caftan.[1] So we need only pause briefly to describe them.

The caftan is a long garment with very narrow and long decorated sleeves made of sable, the top with a scaly mosaic pattern made of ermine, recalling encrustation. Over the fur were fixed hundreds of wooden plates and buttons, covered with gold, which gave this light, portable costume the air 'of smith's

[1] Vidonova, A, p. 155.

work, heavy and glistening'.[1] This ancient Altaian costume can be compared to the dress of some of the nomads of Mongolia, eastern Europe and central Asia.

In one of the barrows at Noin-Ula (Mongolia) a pointed felt cap resembling that from Pazyryk was found.[2] The soles of the Noin-Ula shoes, like the woman's shoe from barrow 2 at Pazyryk, bore a decorative pattern.[3]

With regard to the dress of the tribes of eastern Europe and central Asia, Herodotus in a well-known passage said: 'The Sacae, a Scythian tribe, have sharp pointed caps on their heads, sticking up, made of felt; they wear breeches.'[4] This record is in full accord with such representations of Sacae from the period as we have. On the well-known rock-carving at Bisutun nine prisoners stand before Darius with halters round their necks and above the last is inscribed: 'This is Skunka, the Saka.'[5] He wears a girdled caftan and on his head is a tall, bent-back, sharply pointed cap. The same head-dress can be seen on a second relief decorating a terrace at the Persian royal palace at Persepolis.[6] These Sacae wear a short sword and on the left a bow-case, soft shoes and narrow breeches. The same costume, but with wide and long trousers, is shown worn by the Sacae on a Persian cylinder seal.[7]

The upper part of Scythian dress (as depicted by Greek craftsmen) was a short fur caftan, the fur turned inward and the skirt pressed into pleats by a strap girdle. The outside face of the caftan was quilted longitudinally and sewn over with decoration. In some cases a short cloak is shown slung over the shoulders and fastened with a brooch on the chest or right shoulder; the breeches are either narrow and of fur, or wide and probably of felt. The narrow fur or leather breeches were sewn over with decorations, possibly with plaques. The Scythian breeches were tucked into soft leather bootees and, like those worn by the Sacae, strapped at the ankle. The short upper of such bootees, like the upper part of the costume, sometimes bore sewn patterns. This footwear, as has been said, was tied either only at the ankle, or at ankle and the foot arch by the same strap. It had no sole or heel.

To judge by representations, Scyths (men) wore their hair long, sometimes tied with a thong; like the Asian Sacae they did not shave off either moustache or beard.

In the great felt wall-hanging of local manufacture from barrow 5 at Pazyryk, as already remarked, there is a picture of a rider in a costume which has a number of things in common with the Scyths as depicted by the Greeks, but significant differences also (*Pl. 154*). The short caftan of blue colour has a constricted waist, standing collar and sleeves narrow at the cuffs, and along hem and edges and also on the shoulders there is a decorated border. Attached to the

[1] Vidonova, A, p. 155.
[2] Rudenko, A, 1962a, Pl. 16, 4 and 5.
[3] Ibid., Pl. 13.
[4] Herodotus, A, bk. vii, 64.
[5] Turaev, A, p. 1.
[6] Herzfeld, B, Pl. 79.
[7] Tolstoy and Kondakov, A, vol. ii, p. 13, fig. 6.

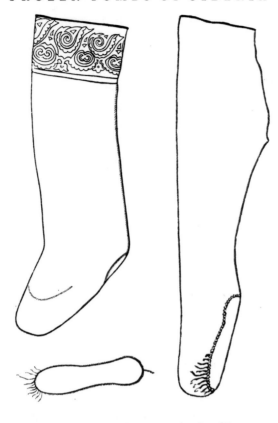

31. Man's felt stockings, one plain and one decorated at the top, from barrow 2.

neck is a short billowing cloak of brown colour. The narrow, tapering breeches are of the same colour, the footwear being depicted as one piece with them, separated only by stitching. The bow-case, following usual Scythian practice, is worn on the left.

The actual dress found in the frozen Altai tombs, although broadly similar to the costume of the Sacae, Scyths and to some extent the Huns, a dress suitable for mounted herdsmen and warriors, differs essentially from theirs, as we shall see.

The costume from Katanda with narrow sleeves, just mentioned, is very interesting. I have already had occasion to compare its make-up and shape with the ancient candys, the dress worn by the Persian aristocracy in Achaemenid times.[1]

This costume differed from all the other known Persian costumes in that the long narrow sleeves were not used, but hung freely down the sides. We can see it in bas-reliefs and sculptures at Persepolis and Lycia and on gold plates in the Oxus treasure. A candys was of bright colour, and Xenophon, who speaks of Πορφύρεος κάνδυς, reports that the Persian cavalry only put their arms into the

[1] Rudenko, A, 1944, no. 6.

sleeves on days of inspection. Dalton thought that the candys could have been an article of Median dress taken over by the Persians and other Iranians. Justin remarked that the Parthians wore the candys.[1]

In this instance, therefore, we are in all probability dealing not with typical native, but rather with central Asian, Parthian, costume, which could easily have been taken over by the Sacian aristocracy, which in the sixth century B.C. and later had close, even blood, links with the Parthian nobility. Subsequently this type of dress, the so-called oriental or central Asian gown, came into widespread use, not only among the settled population of central Asia but also amongst the steppe nomads.

The second costume from the Katanda barrow, also of sable, covered by silk material, was like a frock-coat with an apron over the chest. The only analogy for this kind of dress is the *mirelen* of the taiga Evenki.

Men's footwear did not survive in any of the Pazyryk barrows, but in 1950 in digging a large barrow in the central part of the Karakol valley I found a man's fur boot with tall uppers and soft leather soles. Barrow 2 at Pazyryk yielded men's felt stockings of two kinds. The first type were long (59 cm. from top to ankle), made up from soft, but fairly thick, white felt with seam down the back, sewn-on sole with semicircular cut at instep, sewn up with tough thread. Since the sole is narrow and short (we shall see this in the women's footwear) the material of the stocking is gathered up into creases at the front end (fig. 31). The stitching was done with fairly thick twisted hemp fibres. The top of the stocking was edged with a band (10 cm. wide) of dark red, very thin felt, on which in turn is sewn relief ornament of pieces of polychrome (brown, green and white) felt. The ornament is mixed plant (one of the lotus variants) and animal, consisting of stylized cocks'-combs (*Pl. 153*B). The upper edge of the stocking is trimmed with a narrow leather ribbon.

Men's stockings of the second type, also made of white felt, were even longer (overall length 75·5 cm., width at top 18 cm. and at bottom 10 cm.) and of another cut, but also with sewn-on sole. A piece of felt, corresponding to the shape, was doubled over and back, overlapping somewhat at the edge back to the heel, then sewn together with fine sinew thread (fig. 31).

The lower end of another stocking like this, but of fairly soft black felt, sewn with twisted woollen thread, was found in barrow 5.

Men's head-dresses were found in barrows 2 and 3. The first, from barrow 2, was made up of stiff, but not particularly thick (3 mm.), brown felt. To judge by the surviving half this head-dress was tall, with broad circular flaps extending over the nape of the neck and ears. This is the kind of hat we see depicted on the heads of Scyths by Greeks and on Sacae on the Persian bas-reliefs, and which we encounter in the Noin-Ula barrows. Such head-dress has survived among

[1] For the candys see Dalton, B, pp. 51, 52.

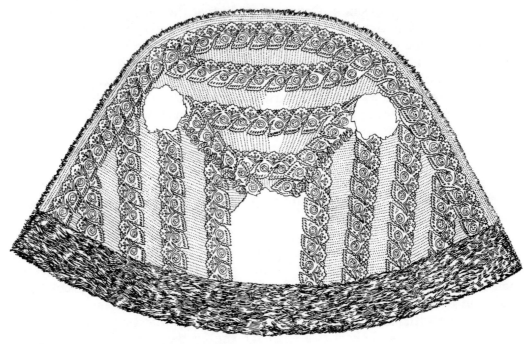

32. Woman's costume from barrow 2.

the Asian pastoral peoples to the present day. For external decoration the lower edge of the hat bore leather disks covered with gold-leaf, set at 1 cm. intervals and held on by sinew thread.

The head-dress found in the centre of the floor of the chamber of barrow 3 is a kind of helmet, or cross between a hat and a balaclava helmet, covering the nape and ears, with two side flaps (*Pl. 155*B). It is made of two pieces sewn together (stitched down the middle) of white felt, yellowed by time, and two pieces of thin leather cut to the same pattern. Apart from the seam between the two halves, neither in the felt base nor in the thin leather covering is there any kind of seam. Evidently the sodden, sewn-up shape had been placed over a spherical wooden block and pulled and pressed on it, so that it took the required form and, when dried out, could be removed. Between the leather covering and the felt border there was a free area about 1 cm. wide. Along the border, front and back, beyond the free area there was an edging 1·5 cm. wide of the same felt as on the base. This edging, joined up at the corners of the hat, was covered with a second layer that extended downwards in fan shapes. Above the border along the edge of the leather covering were fine thong braids. On top of the helmet a square 'towerlet' was sewn on, made of four uniform leather cut-outs and covered with gold figures, and in its centre there had been some kind of

90

33. Sleeve of woman's costume from barrow 2.

pinnacle covered with gold. Of this only a fragment of the base survived, firmly attached by twisted sinew threads, with which the whole head-dress had been sewn.

On the outer surface of the leather casing, to left and right, faint traces of drawings of monsters of some kind can be detected, coloured partly bright red, and partly by leather scales, covered by dark red lacquer.

It is extraordinarily interesting that this head-dress is of identical type to that represented on the Scythian warriors on the gold plate of the sword scabbard from Chertomlyk, in the scene showing a fight between Scyths and Greeks.[1]

A female upper garment from barrow 2 consists of a comparatively short (96 cm. long) caftan (fig. 32) with narrow decorated sleeves (fig. 33) as in the man's costume at Katanda. It is made of squirrel skin, fur inwards. The external face is entirely sewn over by long stitches of sinew thread or covered by applied leather cut-out patterns. The border is edged with a fairly narrow band of black colt's fur with a border of otter's, and another unidentified animal's fur dyed blue. Along the hem there was a fairly wide band of black colt's fur (fig. 32).

The basic motif of the applied decoration, made of dark red, beautifully

[1] Tolstoy and Kondakov, A, vol. ii, p. 146, fig. 123.

91

34. Detail of ornament on apron from barrow 2 (*c.* $\frac{2}{3}$).

dressed leather, was something not unlike cocks' combs, within which were sewn gold-covered copper rams' heads in rings. The rest of the ornament was of plant inspiration, lotus flower (*Pl. 152*A), resembling that which we met on the man's stocking (*Pl. 153*B).

No kind of brooch was needed with this costume; it would probably be thrown over the shoulders like a Russian *dushegreika*.

To complete the costume just described there was an apron of which only the upper half, with a narrow band of otter fur trimming, survives. The apron is a long garment, expanding from a rounded top down towards the feet (*Pl. 156*). To judge by its surviving part the bottom was not straight, but had a triangular opening in the middle. It is a composite make-up of pieces of squirrel and sable fur. The outside edge is trimmed with a band of otter fur, screened by a band of streaky fur dyed blue. The external face of the apron, except for two intermediate strips, is entirely covered with applied leather cut-out patterns.

This decoration consists of an elaborate combination of lotus motifs with ox horns, in the centre of which are leather cut-outs, covered with gold-leaf, of rams' heads. The composition, which is highly intricate, is shown in *Pl. 156* and can be divided into the following basic components.

92

The central figure (fig. 34) consists of a sideways lotus flower and a symmetrically arranged composition of lotus flowers on their sides with rams' heads in nimbi. Below (fig. 35A), in the middle of the apron, is a pair of rams' heads, and under them two sideways lotus flowers below birds' heads. Still lower, one above another, an intricate interplay of the same motif is repeated (fig. 35B): heraldically opposed rams' heads with lotus flowers by their sides; below this stylized composite lotus flowers treated in the same way as we shall see them on the woman's footwear; below this a sideways bird's head and lotus flowers. By the side, right and left, a series of subjects are contrasted one with another: lotus flowers cupped in a pair of leaves, and below, intersecting in the nimbus around the ram's head, dismembered and complex lotus flowers (fig. 36).

On the lower edge of the apron was the applied leather ornament illustrated in fig. 37.

As in all other similar applied work the pattern had not been cut out with a stencil, and each element differed from the others in this or that detail.

Very interesting also are the remains of some kind of child's clothing from a small barrow, no. 7. Unfortunately it has survived badly, but all the same makes a striking impression (*Pl. 157*C). So far as one can judge it appears to be some kind of apron. A piece of fur has sewn decoration on it; a bow-shaped figure of two bands of thin leather has rows of gold-covered copper hemispherical plates sewn on to it. The relatively broad space between the narrow bands of leather is filled by a series of stamped, gold-covered, copper heads of saiga antelope shown in profile. The decoration within the bow consisted of a vertical band of two narrow strips of thin leather as on the edge, with hemispherical plates, covered with gold, sewn on them. Between these narrow strips is a vertical row of gold-covered copper plates of horseshoe shape sewn with convex end upwards. The area left free is filled by a pattern of spirally twisted 'horns', leaf-shapes and gold-covered hemispherical plates.

Of the ornament on the piece of skin beyond the bow-shaped part just described, only isolated elements survive, inadequate to reconstruct the pattern. We can judge its intricacy by the single example shown in *Pl. 157*D, where, besides strips covered by disks, we have polychrome leather triangles and festoons, and leather ribbons covered by red lacquer and framed in twisted gold wire.

A pair of woman's display boots, to which we now turn our attention, undoubtedly belonged to the same costume, robe and apron, from barrow 2 described above. They are soft bootees with short flaring tops. The vamp consists of one piece of leather dyed red with seam at the back, to which the sole is stitched by thick sinew threads, so that the front part at the toe is crimped into pleats. As a result of this goffering at the front the dimension of the boot was increased. The top of the boot, like the vamp, is made of fine, beautifully

A

B

36. Detail of ornament on apron from barrow 2 ($c.\frac{2}{3}$).

35. Detail of ornament on apron from barrow 2 ($c.\frac{1}{2}$).

37. Detail of ornament on apron from barrow 2 ($c.\frac{2}{3}$).

dressed leather not sewn up behind, but only to the top of the vamp, and consequently it covered only the front part of the shin.

These bootees are entirely covered with ornament. Along the seam between vamp and top there is a band of red woollen braid, decorated by leather figures, covered with gold-leaf, that look like ducklings. The ornament of the upper is shown in side view in fig. 38, and from the front in extended view in fig. 39. The sewn decoration has been carried out in sinew thread wrapped in a strip of tinfoil. To the basic sewn-on pattern decorative excisions in the leather have been added in places. The lotus provided the motif of the ornament. The pattern in fig. 39 (extended) is made with the same appliqué technique as we saw on the apron. On the chamois leather background of the top is sewn a pattern in finely dressed red leather. The motif is a thrice-repeated variant of the same lotus-like flower in intricate and elegant patterns. The upper edge of the boot front bears a fanciful border.

The soles of these bootees are highly original (*Pl. 64*A). Narrow and short on their outside surface, they are embroidered with a red woollen material and edged by double bands of sinew thread about 1 mm. thick. Between these an almost continuous row of small black beads was sewn on, threaded on thin twisted sinew thread, which at every fifth bead looped through the sole. In the front part of the sole and at the heel large rhombs are stitched on in the same sinew thread, subdivided internally into twenty-five and sixteen small rhombs respectively, each of which has a piece of crystalline pyrites sewn into its centre. In the middle of the sole, under the arch of the foot, is a little rhomb with one pyrites crystal in the middle. At the intersections the rhombs are secured by triple stitching.

Of exactly the same cut as the bootees just described were the stockings or socks of thin fine felt found inside them. They were made from a single piece of felt with a narrow sewn-in sole and short seam only at the back of the heel. As in the man's stocking the front part, pulled into the sole, was crimped with pleats. The sewing has been done with very fine sinew thread in small stitches, the upper edge being decorated with festoons. Two thin socks were worn simultaneously: first a longer one (fig. 40) with a semicircular slit at the instep tightened with thread, and over it a shorter one with a W-shaped cut (fig. 41). Thus below the top festooned border was a second like it. Furthermore, above the two socks an additional festooned ribbon was placed.

The second pair of boots from the same barrow was of quite another style. They also were bootees, but with complete broad and short tops (25 cm. high) of leopard fur with leather vamps. These bootees also undoubtedly belonged to a woman, since one still contained her severed foot. From the various pieces it was possible to reconstruct one bootee fully (*Pl. 155*D). It was soft, with top reaching the knee and with a heel of thick (2 mm.) rigid leather. The under

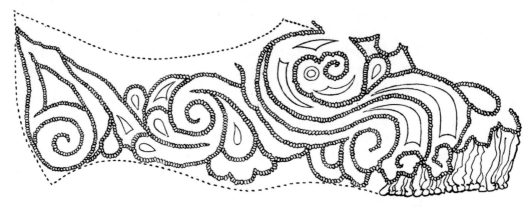

38. Ornament on uppers of woman's bootee from barrow 2 ($\frac{3}{5}$).

surface of the sole was entirely covered with incised decoration (*Pl. 152*C); the basic motif was the lotus both on the broader front part and on the narrower heel. The vamp, which was made of a single piece of relatively dark leather, had a seam only behind and was secured to the sole by thick sinew threads, while, like the boots already described above, it was crimped at the front into pleats. The outer surface of the vamp was smooth, but between it and the top there was a band of red woollen braid sewn in (1·7 cm. wide). On the upper edge of the top was a pattern in sinew thread, bound round spirally with narrow strips of tinfoil and gold. It was partially covered by a band of red woollen braid sewn on above it (*Pl. 64*B).

The decoration of the soles deserves our special attention. It only had much point if people sat with legs arranged so that the heels were turned out, as is usual among steppe peoples of Asia, and was usual in antiquity in Hither Asia. This was possible if the floor of the house was spread with carpets or soft felt, which, as we have seen, was the custom among the Altai nobility in the period being considered.

Of female head-dress we have two examples from barrows 2 and 5.

In 1947 several pieces of fur of a black colt were found in barrow 2, entirely covered by cut-outs of thick leather decorated with rhombs. Below each rhomb two triangles of thin red leather were sewn into the fur, and fixed above them gold-leaf that covered the rhomb (*Pl. 155*C). In 1948 several similar pieces with ornamental rhombs were found in the same tomb, sewn together in the shape of a hood. N. V. Isachenko reconstructed the head-dress, which I consider to be female (*Pl. 65*C). It emerged also that the cut-out-cocks ornament which I had previously regarded as a 'diadem' appeared to be part of the same article (*Pl. 65*A). The head-dress is a kind of hood of double-thickness fine leather, covered by black

39. Ornament on woman's bootee from barrow 2 ($\frac{1}{3}$).

colt's fur, to which are stitched four bands of the same material sewn together, ornamented with rhombs, the whole reaching down to the shoulders and upper back. Above this, forming a kind of rim, was the decoration of cocks just mentioned; found at the eastern head end of the coffin it deserves a special description.

There were ten little cocks at 2-cm. intervals secured to a felt plait wrapped in fine leather (diameter 6 mm.). They are cut out of thick leather and have heads turned back and tails and wings raised. On the obverse face, within the silhouette, details of head and wings have been incised. The lower part of the leather, the base of the figure, has been split longitudinally into two halves. These halves, festooned on their lower part, are held to the plait by stitches of sinew thread. The wings are split in the same way into two halves (*Pl. 65*B). As a result, the pieces of flat but thick leather have produced figures with a sculptured look. All the cocks have their heads turned towards the same side. On the lower edge of the plait dangling pendants of sable fur are attached with a mosaic ornament on their outer face, consisting of pieces of white and blue-dyed ermine fur, pieces of grey leather and a fur border of blue colour (*Pl. 150*C).

No less original a head-dress was taken from the head of the woman in barrow 5. It is made entirely of wood, fairly low (height 6·8 cm.), of oval shape and of precisely the same size as the woman's head, but flat on top. It is made

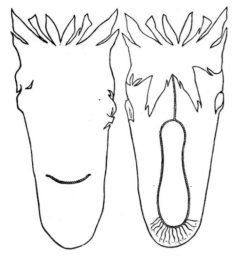
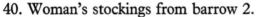
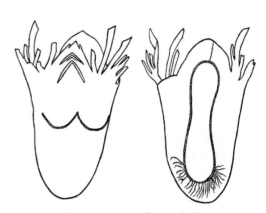

40. Woman's stockings from barrow 2.   41. Woman's stockings from barrow 2.

out of a single piece of cedarwood, except on the side where two little boards projected over the ears. Six circular apertures, 13–18 mm. in diameter, have been pierced in this wooden hat: two over the nape of the neck, two above the coronary suture and two over the sagittate suture. Through the latter projected two tresses of hair, plaited (*Pl. 66A*).

The carved wooden boards (above the ears) were seated in grooves and secured in place by sinew thread. On top the hat was covered by a piece of leather, cut to precisely the same shape as its bottom. This was fixed to the hat by twisted sinew thread together with two hollow cylinders set over the sinciput carved from wood and neatly glued.

The hat and the hair style, which we will describe below, are part of the same head-dress.

In barrow 2 parts of at least three different belts survived, but we lack the evidence to allow us to decide whether they belonged to men or women. They are all strap belts, and for rigidity or for ornamental purposes (more probably the latter) are embroidered with fine, twisted sinew thread, stitches 1·5–2 mm. apart, which gives the strap the appearance of cloth.

Part of a belt (55 cm. long, 4·5 cm. broad), the end of which is shown in *Pl. 67F*, is sewn along its edge with treble stitching of sinew thread wrapped in a narrow strip of tinfoil in such a way that the interval between stitches is 4 mm. The external surface of the belt is covered by sewn-on decoration of thong braid, the edge trimmed with sinew thread wrapped in a similar way in tinfoil.

98

In the recesses in the pattern, the shape of which recalls commas, and on the belt end, above and below, leather cut-outs of comma shape, stuck over with gold plates, are secured with double stitches. The motif of the pattern is a garland of intercoiling plants.

There was a second belt made with the same technique. The strap is quilted with twisted sinew thread, its edge hemmed with treble stitching of the same thread, wrapped in a strip of tinfoil. The applied pattern had been produced in the same way; the ornament consisted of rhombs, within which were repeated combinations of triangles and 'commas' and 'horseshoes' in half-rhombs along the edge. Within the triangular, comma and horseshoe-shaped recesses leather cut-outs of corresponding shape, covered with gold-leaf, were stitched on (*Pl. 67*A).

A peculiarity of this belt is its silver ornamental plates and pendant straps. One of these, a narrow strap (13 mm. wide), was threaded through an opening in a plate at its lower end and right through the belt, while a wider one (24 mm. wide, 22 cm. long) passes through a specially cut opening in the belt beside the plate. These pendant straps are embroidered with sinew thread and hemmed along the edge in the same way as the main belt. At the rounded lower (outside) end of the broad pendant strap is a small circular opening, and on the end of the second narrow (inner) half a strap tip that passed through the opening just mentioned. From these straps it was undoubtedly intended to hang a quiver, dagger, knife in sheath or short sword of the acinaces type.

The silver plates (43 mm. by 46 mm.) deserve special attention. They are both cast, and bear a relief representation of the same scene, a lion or lioness seizing a mountain goat. The picture on the second plaque is a reverse, mirror image of the first; hence they belong to the same belt, although they were found apart (*Pl. 67*A, B).

Along the border of the plaque run ornamental circles with twists, and at each corner is a round hole for attachment to the belt, with a special slit below to pass the suspender strap through. The goat is seated on its back legs and has its front leg raised. The lion (or lioness) rests on its rear paws with its front ones, as the composition requires, flung upwards. With its huge jaws it has seized the muzzle of the goat—a detail met also in the decoration on a saddle of barrow 1 and bridles from barrows 1 and 4. A characteristic trait of the male goat, apart from its typical body structure, is the emphasized shape of the horns with their annulations. The curve of the lion's neck is emphasized by 'herring-bone' lines, running from the front of the head down the neck to the back. The disproportionately large head of the predator is especially effective. The gaping jaws with sharp creasing of the skin, particularly on the upper lip, the eyes in sharp relief with conventional brows, the small ears; all these are leonine. The musculature of the body of both goat and lion is emphasized by circles, commas and

42. Decoration of cocks on a strap in barrow 2 (c. $\frac{2}{3}$).

half-horseshoes, and it is interesting to note that these are outlined by rope orna-ment that is clearly visible under the magnifying glass, as if it were imitating the threads outlining felt appliqué work. Originally cast, the plates have been finished by stamping.

Beside the system of conventional signs to indicate details of body and shape by stops, commas and half-horseshoes, it is worthy of note that the 'herring-bone' lines going from the lion's head to its tail can be compared with the con-ventions for indicating fur on the lion's body in Assyrian bas-reliefs. The attitude of the lion with head turned back and front paws thrown up has an analogy in one of the winged lion-griffins depicted on a gold plaque from the Oxus treasure.[1]

Part of a third strap (43 cm. long, 2·7 cm. broad), also probably a belt, bears no particular decoration (*Pl. 67*G). On its rounded end is a loop for tightening, and a few centimetres from this near the lower edge is a slit with a pendant strap threaded through it. A double pendant of thick leather with applied leather at the ends, covered outside by red lacquer, was also decoration for some kind of belt.

Also in barrow 2 were two little silver horses—most likely pendants decorat-ing a belt. One of these silver pendants was found on the bottom of the coffin (*Pl. 67*D). It consists of two plates riveted together, one with the relief repre-sentation of a horse, the other smooth. The horse, with magnificently realistic head thrust forward, ears pressed back and legs stretched out, looks as if it is leaping. The mane is trimmed. Like the silver belt plates this pendant had been cast with details completed by stamping. There is a half-horseshoe on the crupper and behind this a loop for suspension.

The second little horse was from the burial chamber (*Pl. 67*E). In contrast to the first it is entirely cast, and, although in size and shape the two are almost identical, some details of manufacture are different. The head with pressed back

[1] Dalton, B, Pl. XI, no. 28.

ears is well modelled, the mane trimmed, the legs, extended forward as with the first, touch the muzzle, while the rear legs are retracted. There is no half-horseshoe on the crupper as we saw on the first. This pendant is attached to the end of a long, thin, narrow strap, stitched through and hemmed with sinew thread, wrapped in a narrow strip of tinfoil. On the outside of the strap leather disks are stitched on, covered with gold-leaf.

Between the coffin and the cone of debris in the centre of the chamber of barrow 2 was a thick strap (6 cm. by 53 cm.), its outer face trimmed with thin leather, on to which were sewn with sinew thread leather cut-out figures of cocks (fig. 42). What the purpose of this strap was—belt or shoulder strap—we do not know, but the cocks are interesting. They are cut out in low relief from thick leather: the head, legs and tail in outline and body and comb with ornamental excisions. Stylistically these openwork cocks resemble those that were pasted on the earthenware bottle from the same barrow. The attitude, shape of body and head, the large comb with slashing are the same, but the tail is distended and the body bears triangular, stop and half-horseshoe shaped excisions. All the cocks were covered by gold-leaf. Where the gold-leaf survived it had been sewn on by threads that went through the leather cut-outs; evidently the latter had been covered with gold-leaf before they were sewn on.

There are some very interesting bronze belt decorations, more precisely

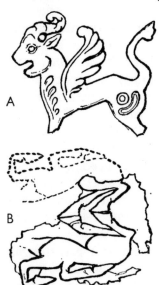

43. Stamped copper ornaments from barrow 2 ($\frac{7}{8}$): a lion-griffin (A) and deer (B)

44. Copper pendant from barrow 2 (c. $\frac{3}{4}$).

101

45, 46. Stamped copper plates from barrow 2 ($\frac{1}{2}$).

buckles through which straps passed, from burials in the Aragol valley and near Biysk. That from Aragol barrow 2 (*Pl. 67*H) has only a slit, but that from near Biysk (*Pl. 67*C), evidently used as a proper buckle, has on its outside face cut-out decoration of a goat with twisted crupper. A precisely similar bronze buckle was found by S. V. Kiselev in a barrow at the village of Tuekta.[1]

In describing one of the pouches from barrow 2 we have already met copper figures of geese covered with gold used as decoration (fig. 25). Examples of this technique, stamped copper covered with gold foil, used for decorations, were found in some quantity in this barrow. The precise function of the objects is not always clear, but in most cases they probably were dress adornments. There were two types: two-sided made of two plates, and one-sided made of one. The two plates in the two-sided ones were stuck together with resin and depicted flying birds and a winged and horned lion-griffin (fig. 43A). The wings of the latter are raised up and their tips point forward, while on its head, with open jaws, are horns with knobs on the tips; this is how the lion and griffin were represented in Achaemenid Persia. The tail with typical brush on the end is raised on high. On the back sticking out in relief are the characteristic stop and half-horseshoe, and on the shoulder commas.

Amongst the carved wooden pendants decorating bridle and breast-strap from barrow 5 we shall see an appreciable number of heraldically confronted, chest to chest or recumbent, figures of deer and elk. Similar figures, but stamped on copper, were found in the burial chamber of barrow 2. The first, of copper, is a badly preserved plate with figures of a pair of deer or elks (fig. 43B), and the second, part of some kind of composite theme, shows two rams (fig. 44). At the

[1] Kiselev, A, 1947, vol. ii, p. 166, fig. 52.

102

upper edge of the latter, attached to one side by a strap, there survives a fragment of a thick leather cut-out decoration, resembling part of a wing.

A very interesting open-work composition of stamped copper covered with gold-leaf shows confronted figures of goats (fig. 45), or more precisely of the front half of these animals. Another shows eagle-griffins (fig. 46).

The goats' heads with open mouths, large stylized ears and sharply twisted horns, although conventionalized, are reasonably expressive; the bodies, except the raised legs, have been executed extremely schematically. The manes, not actually possessed by this animal, outline the figures from the ears down to the lower edge of the plate, and have a decorative character.

The subject is more fully and individually treated with the clasping griffins. The front feet are birds' claws, but the rear are tiger-like paws, as is the whole of the rear part of the animals, with turned-under feline tail. Both figures are bent over facing beak to beak, and claw to claw. The head, ears, shape of body and musculature are all indicated by conventional signs, including stops, commas and half-horseshoes on front and rear part of the body. The comb-mane is treated in the same style. One cannot fail to notice the encircling nature of the feline tails, just like those we shall see in the monsters tattooed on the chief from barrow 2. At first glance at the two plates it is clear that these are motifs with a long history of development before they achieved such an individual and stylistic degree of maturity.

The closest analogy to this plate can be seen in the clasping lions in the lower part of the gold scabbards from Lity barrow [1] or in the bronze ornaments from the Tamansk peninsula.[2] It is not often found in the art of the Black Sea Scyths, but it is well known on the ancient cylinders and seals of Hither Asia.[3]

Stamped copper plates covered with gold used to decorate clothing are known from a number of ordinary burials. By way of example we may cite the heads of saiga antelope on the costume from barrow 7 at Pazyryk (*Pl. 157*C) and barrow 2 at Aragol (fig. 47A), and square plates from barrow 8 at Pazyryk (fig. 47B) decorated in relief.

47. Stamped copper decorations: saiga head from barrow at Aragol (A); squares from barrow 8 at Pazyryk (B) ($\frac{1}{1}$).

A   B

[1] Pridik, A.
[2] Rostovtzeff, B, 1929, Pl. 6, fig. 5.

[3] An example is a Hittite cylinder of the 2nd millennium B.C., where lions and sphinxes are shown struggling with claws upraised. See Ward, B, Pls. V, 24; VII, 49.

When considering dress and adornment we cannot omit the question of hair styles.

The man's and woman's heads in barrows 2 and 5, where they are relatively well preserved, are more or less shaven. The woman's head from barrow 2 was entirely shaven. The man's head from the same barrow was shaven at the front, but whether there had been hair on the occiput we do not know, since he had been scalped. On the shaven heads from barrow 5 the woman had some hair on a small part on the crown and the man on the back.

Shaving the head of a corpse was possibly required prior to trepanation to remove the brain. The latter is the more probable in the case of the woman in barrow 2, whose plaits were found with the head (*Pl. 69*A). The hair above the plait was twisted into a bun with a felt stuffing (*kom kom*), and soaked in some sticky matter. From the knot it was divided into two plaits, which were twisted spirally with felt braid and diagonal strapping. In addition the two plaits were entwined with a fringe of special locks of hair (*Pl. 69*B, C). At the ends of the plaits double spun ribbons were worn. This woman's tresses had been chopped through at several points when the ornaments were removed from them.

The hair of the woman in barrow 5 remaining on the back of the head was also divided into two plaits, a thin one at the front and a thicker one behind. These were further subdivided into three tresses, each plaited into two tresses, which were passed through the circular openings in the wooden hat. Then these were wound around an artificial plait of horse's hair, which consisted of at least twelve braids, twisted into two tresses of black horsehair, bound round and stitched through with twisted woollen thread. The woman's two tresses were wound around the rigid plait several times and then tied at the end with two narrow ribbons of thick white felt (*Pl. 66*A). In order that the hair and artificial plait did not undo when tying the knot in front an iron pin was put through it at the back. In addition, at the end of the artificial plait, a pendant tress of the woman's hair (37 cm. long) was secured by twisted woollen thread, the actual length of hair being 25 cm. This plait was made up of two original tresses of hair and three soft coils of twisted woollen yarn, intertwined into three separate plaits and tied in a knot at top and bottom.

Besides a mirror and other toilet accessories an iron rod, forked at the end, was found in barrow 2. I had already assumed before digging barrow 5 that it was a hairpin. Now that an identical, but broken, iron rod has been found in the woman's hair in that barrow it confirms that the first forked rod from barrow 2 was indeed a hairpin (*Pl. 68*F).

It is still not at all clear whether the shaving of the head, albeit partially, was normal or a part of the burial custom. It has to be borne in mind that the hair and the hat from the woman in barrow 5 form one unit, so there is some reason for supposing that partial shaving of the head was normal with women.

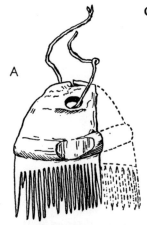

48. Horn combs: from barrow 2 (A) and a barrow near Biysk (B) ($\frac{3}{4}$).

Speaking of the Wu-huan a Chinese chronicler made the interesting observation: 'They regard it as more convenient to shave the head. Before marriage the women let their hair grow long and divide it into two tresses; they put on a head-dress. . . .'[1]

Shaving the head was a custom among men, as the especially interesting observation of Herodotus about the Argippaei, close neighbours of the Altaian tribes, recorded: 'They say that all of them, men and women, are bald-headed from birth.'[2]

Returning to the woman's hair style, mention should be made first of the intricacy of its construction and secondly of the introduction into the plait of braid, felt and horsehair and the use of a supplementary artificial plait. It seems that the hair styles of the women from barrows 2 and 5 differ to such an extent that one can with some confidence speak of them as belonging to different tribal groups.

The men's beards and moustaches were evidently either shaven off or plucked out, but on the other hand at least some of them wore artificial beards. In barrow 2 an artificial beard of human hair was found under the man's head, in the form of a sort of fringe sewn on a leather strip with straps for attachment (*Pl. 69*D, E). It had been dyed with an intense black matter, bits of which had been left in the beard, so that after rinsing the hair took on a dark chestnut colour.

Regarding this artificial beard we cannot pass on without reference to the human faces on the pendants of one of the bridles from barrow 1 (*Pl. 92*A–D). Although not portraits perhaps, yet one's attention is inevitably caught by the absence of moustaches and the presence of thick beards.

Hair was combed, for two combs have been found. The first from barrow 2 is made of horn and is roughly bow-shaped (fig. 48A). One side is smooth, the other has a rib above the teeth. At the upper end, broken at one edge, is an oval aperture through which a little strap is threaded. The second comb which I illustrate

[1] Bichurin, A, pt i, p. 143.   [2] Herodotus, A, bk iv, 123.

49. Gold earring from barrow 2 ($\frac{1}{1}$).

(fig. 48B) was found in my excavations near Biysk, done at the same time as the Pazyryk excavation. This miniature horn comb is a very delicate piece of work with fine teeth. Besides the ornamental circles on the side of the handles the lightly incised spiral at the centre is interesting.

Men and women wore earrings. On the men from both barrows 2 and 5 the lobe of one ear only was pierced for an earring; therefore men wore only one earring, in the left ear. Both rings had been robbed from the Pazyryk barrows, but one survived in an ordinary Aragol burial (*Pl. 68*A). It was penannular, about 16 mm. in diameter, made of a gold rod of rectangular section, to which a little ring, 7·5 mm. in diameter, was soldered on below. S. V. Kiselev found just such gold earrings under a barrow-cairn at the village of Karakol in the valley of the River Ursul.[1]

The women in the Pazyryk barrows were pierced in both ears for earrings, but these survived only in barrow 2 and then not fully (Pl. 68B; fig. 49). The earrings consist of a cylinder (6 mm. high, 8 mm. in diameter) made of a gold plate. On the upper and lower edges of the cylinder thirty-six tiny globular grains are welded on, and in the middle five circles of grains, thirteen in each. In the slightly convex bottom of the cylinder a little ring is welded on from which the main pendant is suspended. In addition, on the edge of the cylinder, three smaller rings are welded on at equal distances, from which hang three miniature circular pendants (diameter 3·5 mm.) with a solid bottom filled with light blue paste. Underneath, little pyramids of four globular grains are welded to each one. The large pendant is square in section and consists of four equal plates, which expand downwards and bear cells filled with blue paste, as if they were meant to look like flies.

Below each plate is yet another little ring from which a pendant hangs. The latter is semi-lunate in shape and supports an elongated plate, divided by partitions into four cells, each again filled with blue paste. These rings were

[1] Kiselev, A, 1935, p. 102, fig. 17.

106

50. Reconstruction of torque from barrow 2.

undoubtedly worn suspended from a penannular ring, and we found a crimped rosette cap with circular opening in the middle and cells round the edge filled with blue and red paste.

In the preliminary report on the excavations at barrow 2 in 1947, when only the lower parts of these earrings were available, I expressed an opinion, based on several points, that the earrings were imports from Hither Asia. Now that we possess almost complete examples of them, with their minute, artificially contrived decoration of granular beads, this view becomes even more probable. They are executed in a technique resembling that used in the gold adornments of a noble lady of the Achaemenid period, whose burial was discovered at Susa by de Morgan.[1] Her earrings were decorated with exactly the same cloisonné enamelwork, while just the same kind of grains decorated the gold mounts of her necklace pendants.

The earrings from barrow 2 had been damaged during the lifetime of the owner; one of the lower pendants was broken and two of the upper parts were missing. A little ring had been welded on to the intact part, by which it had hung. The lug of a second pendant had been broken; after preliminary lashing of the pendant it had been secured to the earring by fine resinated sinew thread.

It follows that even if there were not jewellers capable of creating such earrings in the Altai, at any rate there were probably craftsmen there capable of mending them.

No bracelets were found in the Pazyryk excavations, but undoubtedly, at least in barrow 2, they were worn, both at ankle and wrist. In the Altai Mountains they are known only as plain bent copper rods from Kumurtuk on the lower Chulyshman, 10 km. from its mouth into Lake Teletskoye.[2]

An extraordinarily interesting find was the parts of the neck torque in the tree-trunk coffin and burial chamber of barrow 2 at Pazyryk (fig. 50). When in 1947

[1] de Morgan, B, Pl. v, figs. 3 and 4; p. 50, Pl. vi, fig. 78; p. 49, fig. 77.   [2] Kiselev, A, 1947, Pl. 30.

at the head end of the coffin the head of a horned lion-griffin was found, together with wooden cut-outs of deer and big-eared griffins covered with gold, I formed the opinion that they had all belonged to a diadem. Further finds in 1948 showed that we were dealing with a neck torque which, although badly damaged by the looters, can be fully restored. It consists of a hollow copper tube bent into a ring, at the free ends of which are fixed wooden and horn carvings covered with gold, representing, one behind another, three winged and horned lion-griffins with detachable sculptured heads. The lions' bodies are somewhat sketchily treated, with claws and wings in the already familiar conventionalized manner of representation. The attitude is characteristic of the recumbent beast with head raised and tail with brush-end turned back. The raised tail balancing the figure and the wings pointing forward are done in the same way as the standing figures of lion-griffins from barrow 2 with which we are already acquainted. The digits on the front paws are portrayed more realistically than the schematic ones at the back. Two sculptured heads were found, both somewhat damaged, but fully restorable (*Pl. 68*D, E). The heads have jaws slightly open, a small nose and the upper lip creased double. The face is flat with a high, straight forehead, the lower jaw is well modelled, and the round eyes have been sharply cut. The long pointed ears, with traditional kink at the base, at their upper ends touch the low annulated horns, the ends of which rise up and finish in knobs.

The closest analogy to this representation of griffins is the gold recumbent lion-griffin from the Oxus treasure.[1] Like the Altaic specimen, it had a head carved in the round. The slightly open jaws and small nose, the creasing on the upper lip, the pointed ears with twist at the base, the muzzle and the eyes are all the same, although the annulated horns with knobs on the end are longer. The body of the Oxus specimen is in flat relief, but the posture is different. The raised tail with brush on the end and the wings are essentially the same. Although similar in basic traits, the Oxus griffin is markedly more complicated in additional ornamental motifs and the working out of minute details. If it were under discussion as to which were the prototype, then one would have to accept the Pazyryk griffin as the model, not the Oxus one.

An analogous torque was found by S. V. Kiselev in the same barrow near Karakol in the Ursul valley where the gold earrings discussed above were found.[2] This torque consisted of bronze tubes, ribbed externally and held firm internally by a strap. The ends of the torque were decorated by wooden carvings of lions' heads which, like the torque, were covered with gold-leaf. In the lions attached to the ends the representation of the mane by special curls has a particular interest, since we shall meet it more than once in other representations of this animal.

Shells of *Cypraea moneta* (cowrie) (*Pl. 68*C) and transparent and opaque

[1] Dalton, B, p. 86, fig. 50.　　　　　　　　　　[2] Kiselev, A, 1935, p. 102, fig. 16.

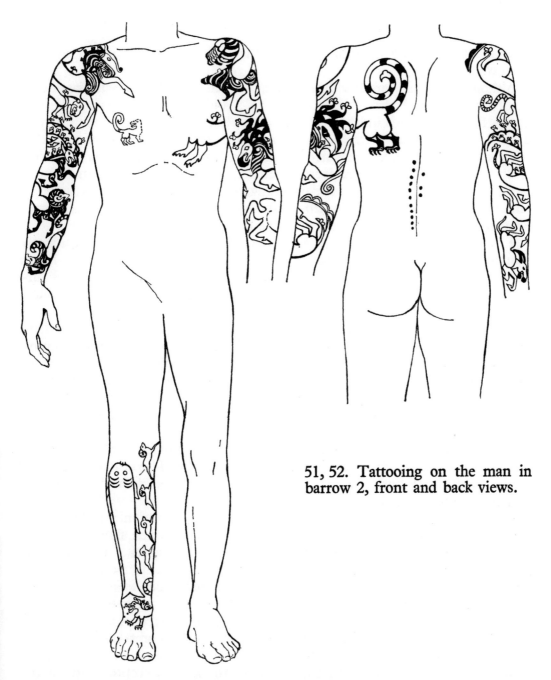

51, 52. Tattooing on the man in barrow 2, front and back views.

beads (*Pl. 158*) were evidently used to a slight extent for adornment. Besides cylindrical beads of white marble, which are usual both in rich and ordinary burials, beads were found in barrows 2, 5 and 6, but transparent beads only in barrow 2. The shells of *Cypraea moneta* can be more accurately regarded not as adornments so much as amulets, since they normally occur singly in each barrow.

Although the beads are few they are very varied. Round dark blue glass beads (diameter 5–7 mm.) were found in barrows 2 and 6; glass, elongated, double-bored, light blue beads in barrow 6; light blue but of a glasslike paste in barrow 2; large (14 mm. long) barrel-shaped glass beads of light blue colour with blue streaks and red fillets in this barrow; and round yellow paste beads in barrow 6. In the same barrow there were seven flat, biconical pieces (diameter 7–8 mm.) of orange sard. A bead of dark orange sard from barrow 2 was large (13 mm. in diameter), of flattened form, with ten grains (five along each side) in two pentagonal zones, above and below, with a biconical boring.

The only find made in barrow 5 between the boards of the floor (evidently dropped by the robbers) was a turquoise bead of elongated shape (16 mm. long), six-sided, thickened in the middle and tapering at the end. Cylindrical turquoise beads were found in 1950 in Bash-Adar barrow 2 in the Karakol valley (*Pl. 158*).

Transparent beads, as remarked above, were found only in barrow 2, where there were very small translucent beads threaded with others of cherry colour on thin twisted wool with black beads at the end held by a knot. Glass beads, as we have seen, were sewn over the soles of fashionable ladies' bootees. Azure and violet beads also decorated the case of one of the mirrors of barrow 2. Both the opaque and transparent beads probably came in as imports from central Asia.

Besides the adornments worn on the ears, hands and possibly legs, tattooing of the body was also practised in the period under review. The tattooing revealed on the chief's body buried in barrow 2 at Pazyryk was one of the most remarkable discoveries made by the 1948 expedition.

The tattooing had not survived intact, as the body was in a poor state of preservation, particularly the left side of the chest where the skin and muscle fibre had perished. However, here above the heart the forepart of a monster was depicted, more exactly the head (the basic feature in all the tattooing) of a lion-griffin or some other imaginary creature. The body of the beast passed under the man's left arm, and over the left shoulder-blade lay its back part with long raised tail, twisting into a spiral and terminating with a bird's, or a snake's, head (figs. 51, 52). Although the head and front portion of the animal did not survive, and the forepaws were severely deformed, some idea of the lost parts can be gained from the right arm or right leg below the knee. Excepting part of the right shoulder, the tattooing on the right arm survived, which it covered entirely from shoulder to hand. It is shown extended in fig. 53. At the bottom is a donkey or onager with back twisted round; at the same level is a winged monster with a feline tail; above is a mountain ram with twisted crupper; then in the

53. Tattooing on the right arm
of the man in barrow 2.

54. Tattooing on the left arm of
the man in barrow 2.

same attitude comes a deer with eagle's beak, long antlers, the tines terminating
in birds' heads, which also run along its neck and tip of its tail. Above the deer is a
fanged carnivore, not winged, but resembling that found on the left side, and,
at the top on the shoulder, a deer with crupper twisted round, antlers with
birds' heads and long tail on the tip of which is a bird's head.

111

The tattooing on the left arm is worse preserved (fig. 54), and, in so far as we can interpret it, consisted of three independent figures, two deer and one mountain goat, with front legs in a springing position, crupper twisted round and back legs raised in the air. The most interesting and best preserved of these is the central figure of a deer.

On the right leg the tattooing was clearly discernible (fig. 51). The left leg had been severely hacked by the robbers, and the undamaged parts of the tattooing were insufficient to make sense of the figures. The basic figure on the outside of the right shin, running from knee-cap to ankle, was a fish. Below the fish on the foot running from the top surface round under the inner ankle and behind over the heel was the figure of a fanged and horned monster with feline tail, which has three birds' heads on its neck. Several little balls are noticeable flying, as it were, out of its mouth. I think these disks have no direct connection with the creature; similar disks, one long and one short row, are tattooed on the man's back, following the general line of the vertebrae down to the waist (fig. 52). These and the others were probably put there with a therapeutic aim, to counteract pains in this area from one or another cause. Such a use of tattooing is well known to ethnologists; I have personally seen it among Siberian peoples, particularly among Khanty and Eskimos.[1] On the inner shin parallel to the fish is a row of four hurrying mountain rams or goats with horns pressed down. These animals, with legs touching one another, form a single dynamic composition. Above this there is yet another, not properly intelligible, figure of a squatting horned and winged animal with a long tail terminating in a bird's head.

The tattooing just described could be done either by stitching or by pricking in order to introduce a black colouring substance, probably soot, under the skin. The method of pricking is more likely than sewing, although the Altaians of this time had very fine needles and thread with which to have executed this. In the preparation of clothes of exceptionally fine squirrel and sable skin, as we have seen, minute stitches were passed through the material from the inside. Sinew thread was used only in the most superficial skin layer and never taken through to the external furry side. The considerable depth of the colouring substance in the body inclines one to the view that the tattooing was done not by sewing but by pricks. Undoubtedly also it had been carried out on the ageing chief long before his death, possibly in his youth. We are dealing with a stout man with strongly developed subcutaneous fat tissue. The ordinary fat layer, directly under the skin, was not coloured, although the muscles under them in the area directly below the tattooing were intensely blackened. At the time he was being tattooed the chief, if not exactly thin, was not as stout as he became before his death.

[1] Pallas, A, p. 54; Sorokin, A; Rudenko, A, 1929, pp. 16–17; 1949d, p. 149.

112

During life the soot or black matter of the tattooing always looked lightish blue on white, and dark blue on swarthy skin. At its discovery the tattooing was almost black on the grey skin of the body.

What was the purpose of this tattooing?

At that period tattooing had a varying significance among different people. According to Herodotus, among the Thracians 'cuts in the skin signified noble birth; not having them, absence of it'.[1] Xenophon relates that among the sons of the rich Mossynoeci 'their bodies were drawn over and the front part tattooed in colours'.[2] According to Pomponius Mela the Agathyrsi 'bore drawings over the face and body, more or less according to their degree of noble blood'.[3] At a later date this custom was noticed among the Din-Lin and their successors, the Kirgiz, among whom being tattooed is a privilege for the very brave. In Classical times slaves had the name of their owner tattooed on them. Furthermore Herodotus recounts a case of conspirators, in the reign of Darius I, communicating by means of tattooing.

To Aristagoras, tyrant of Miletus, 'came a slave with writing on his head sent from Susa by Histiaeus, telling him to revolt against the king. Wishing to give Aristagoras this order, as the roads were guarded Histaeus could do it only in one safe way: he shaved the head of his most trusty slave, pricked the letters on the skin and then let the hair grow. As soon as the hair was grown he sent the slave to Miletus with a single instruction that, when he reached there, he ask Aristagoras to shave him and look at his head, and what was pricked there told him to revolt'. [4]

The tattooing of the chief in barrow 2 at Pazyryk most probably signified noble birth or was a mark of manhood or perhaps both. Furthermore the lion's or griffin's head depicted on the chest over the heart is not coincidental, since it is the basic figure of all the tattooing. In addition the majority of the other figures are monsters including in themselves signs of the tiger, deer, eagle and snake (its head on the tip of the tail). These figures all had some kind of magical significance not yet understood; they were perhaps protective (apotropaic) signs. However, apart from these the presence of a row of running mountain rams would seem to indicate that at the level reached by Altaian society tattooing could be used purely decoratively.

It may be mentioned that there is some evidence for the existence of tattooing in the Near East and eastern Europe. According to Hippocrates 'the whole mass of the Scyths, as many as are nomads, cauterize their shoulders, arms, and hands, chests, thighs and loins, for no other purpose', explains the famous doctor, 'than to avoid weakness and flabbiness and to become energetic'.[5]

[1] Herodotus, A, bk v, 6.
[2] Xenophon, A, *Anabasis*, bk v, 4, 32.
[3] Pomponius, A, bk ii, 4, 32.

[4] Herodotus, A, bk v, 35.
[5] Hippocrates, A, 26.

Herodotus wrote of the royal Scyths that 'they make cuts in their hands as a sign of mourning for the dead, slit a part of their ears and thrust an arrow through the left hand'.[1] Scars on the body after this kind of operation cannot be regarded as tattooing. Very late writers record the practice of tattooing among neighbours of the Scyths, the Agathyrsi. Thus Pomponius Mela wrote that they 'draw over the face and body . . . drawing which even washing cannot remove',[2] and Ammianus Marcellinus added that this tribe coloured the whole body blue.[3] According to Pliny 'the Dacian and Sarmatian men paint their bodies'.[4]

Several examples of mirrors have been found in the Pazyryk barrows.

One of the two mirrors in barrow 2, of plain bronze, survived in its leopard-skin case. This mirror (*Pl. 70E*), which has numerous analogues, is oval in shape, with one side completely smooth and the other slightly convex, and has a short (1·7 cm.) flat, tanged handle, forming part of the mirror. It is very thin, about 1 mm. thick. The handle was wrapped in a fairly long rectangular piece of leather, tightly sewn along one side and thus firmly held to the handle. The case in which it was found (*Pl. 70D*) was sewn up with sinew threads from leopard skin, as mentioned, fur outwards. A gold disk was attached to the middle of one side and around it were concentric rings of blue and black beads.

The second mirror from barrow 2, made of silver, was highly original (*Pl. 70A*). If the first, which was found in the burial chamber, can be regarded as a man's, then the second is undoubtedly a woman's, since it was in a leather bag with other toilet articles. It is large (15 cm. in diameter) and round, not in one piece but made of two halves riveted together with a void between. The obverse is completely smooth, the reverse worked in relief with a ridge 12 mm. high round the edge and another similar but smaller surrounding a projecting cone in the middle. The reverse side is decorated around the edge with little incised circles with points in the middle. Between the inner and outer ridges are twelve concentric incised rings, the interspaces filled by alternating series of vertical and diagonal lines.

The two halves are secured at the edge by seven rivets. A short, flat tang forming part of the obverse plate is fitted with an ox-horn handle. A socket had been bored for this tang into the ox-horn which is clearly visible in the X-ray photograph (*Pl. 70B*). In longitudinal section the handle is eight-sided with smoothed arrises, flattening and broadening towards the bottom.

I know of no analogy for this mirror. Composite mirrors riveted from two plates are known in China, where they are regarded as the most ancient of all Chinese mirrors so far known; but in these the obverse is not smooth but decorated with openwork. It is known also that Chinese dancers performing at

[1] Herodotus, bk iv, 71.
[2] Pomponius, A, bk ii, 10.
[3] Ammianus Marcellinus, A, 14.
[4] Pliny the Elder, A, bk 22.

court held a mirror in their hands. The concubine of the tribal chief buried in barrow 2 was, as we shall see below, a musician who played on a multi-stringed *pizzicato* instrument resembling a harp. All this, however, does not bring us any nearer to finding an origin for our remarkable silver mirror.

A very important find in barrow 6 was a Chinese mirror of white metal (*Pl. 70c*). This is one of the well-known kinds of Chinese mirrors, the so-called Tsin type with the following special characteristics: thinness and brittleness, a very shiny reflecting surface and a small tubular lug in the middle. There is no inscription and the pattern is delicate and often very intricate. Within the limits of these common traits the mirrors vary in details, often in ornament. Although ours is broken (slightly more than half of the mirror has survived) we can make a full reconstruction since the vital central part with lug remains (fig. 55).

Our circular mirror is 11·5 cm. in diameter, thickness about 1 mm. and in places 0·5 mm. The edge is almost flat, but has a slightly raised rim. The lug is seated in a slightly raised square in the middle of the mirror. The whole field is covered by a uniform relief pattern, consisting of the so-called 'wings and feathers' pattern, amongst which in beautiful relief are four figures of capital T's tilted towards the edge. Between these letters are pairs of heart-shaped leaves. As will be shown in the final chapter this mirror belongs to a group of early Tsin mirrors from the period of warring princedoms (provinces). Exactly the same mirrors have been found in China in the Huai valley and at Loyang.[1]

[1] Umehara, B, Pls. 8, 9; Swallow, B, fig. 14.

55. Mirror from barrow 6 ($\frac{2}{3}$).

Although we have put mirrors in this chapter, with other personal possessions, one must bear in mind that they could have had another, magical, significance, especially in view of the Chinese origin of some of them. In China, as is well known, mirrors were not only looked into but were also considered as having magical powers that warded off evil spirits. Doctors used them in the diagnosis of illness, fortune-tellers for foretelling the future, warriors took them into battle against their chests, the bride came to her spouse holding one to her heart, and so on.

6. MEANS OF
LOCOMOTION

THE OBLIGATORY burial of horses in all the barrows with the human burial, without exception regardless of sex or social position, either draught- or riding-animals, indicates the quite exceptional significance these creatures had at this period as a means of locomotion.

Horse-breeding has a long history. Although the earliest records of domesticated horses come from China and India, the centre of ancient thoroughbred horse-rearing was, it seems, Assyria. Since special treatises on horse-breeding had already been written among the Hittites in the fourteenth century B.C., it can be concluded that the practice arose in that area at a much earlier date. The oldest representations of horses in Hither Asia from the second millennium B.C. show them harnessed to chariots, but they only became of significance in rural life appreciably later. In the first half of the last millennium B.C. horses were harnessed to royal hunting carts, and then to special war chariots on wheels.

Real cavalry evidently appeared on the Eurasian steppes at the beginning of the last millennium B.C. In Hither Asia in the middle of this millennium it replaced war chariots, and from then on played a large part in military matters.

In the last millennium B.C. the horse was ridden not only in war but in normal life, and was used also for draught purposes. All the pastoral tribes were pre-eminently riders. This is quite natural, since it was only horse-riding that made possible the creation of that pastoral, nomadic way of life in the steppes and foothills of eastern Europe and Asia, about which we spoke above.

Draught animals among the nomadic tribes, in particular among the Scyths, were predominantly oxen.[1] Nevertheless, as we shall see below, both in the Altai and in central Asia, horses were not only ridden but also harnessed for traction. The large number of horses buried in a single barrow is noticeable; in an ordinary barrow one to three horses and in a rich barrow (of a tribal or clan chief or elder) seven to fourteen horses, and in one case even sixteen.

Marks have been recognized on the ears that identified the different ownership of the horses (fig. 56). On this evidence I came to the conclusion twenty

[1] Hippocrates, A, 25.

117

56. Ownership marks on ears of horses from barrows 1 and 5.

years ago in the preliminary report on the excavation of barrow 1 that the horses had not belonged to the buried person. I cited as an analogy the account of Herodotus, in which the Scyths bore a king's body in a cart from one subject people to another, and the corpses of humbler Scyths among their friends, who arranged a lavish feast for the mourners where all regaled the corpse. I suggested part of the regaling could have been a gift of horses.[1] Such a suggestion was wrong and ill-founded.

In the text of Herodotus [2] it is clearly meant that the lavish feast was prepared for the mourners, and the corpse shared part of the regalement, that is, the food; those believing in life after apparent death thought the departed would need to eat.

Food was placed in the tomb with the corpse to sustain him during his journey to the next world, and in addition all the personal possessions that he would require there. There are no grounds for supposing that any kind of extraneous gift was buried with the corpse.

In the tombs of noble persons at Pazyryk all the horses were geldings; not a single stallion or mare was found. According to Strabo the Scyths rode exclusively on geldings.[3] This can be readily understood if we bear in mind that we are dealing with horses ridden by pastoral folk. Among the Kazakhs only the poor used stallions or mares for riding; the well-to-do rode geldings exclusively. The same can be said of the Altaians, the better-off of whom never rode mares and stallions.[4] The number of riding-horses that a reasonably well-off owner of horse-herds (let alone the chiefs) among pastoral people might expect to own at any one time would be several. For example, rich Kazakhs usually had not more than three riding-horses at the house, but they would be changed several times

[1] Rudenko, A, 1931, no. 2, p. 30.

[2] Herodotus, A, bk iv, 71.

[3] Strabo, A, bk vii, 4, 8.

[4] Radloff, B, pp. 282 and 446.

118

in the year, and frequently in the winter.[1] The same thing happened among the modern Altaians. The pastoralist who set a high value on his riding-horses was extremely reluctant to let a stranger ride one, and normally after the death of the owner his personal horses were never ridden again. If we study the age of the horses buried in the Pazyryk barrows we notice that in each interment there were one or two young animals three and a half, or even two and two and a half years old, several of middle age, and some old, fifteen to twenty years or more. Hence it is clear that in each burial, besides the regular horses, we have in addition horses which were being trained for riding, and veterans; none of them would have been ridden again once their owner had passed into the next world. The relatively large number of horses in the burials need not be a matter for surprise if we remember that a man and a woman of noble birth were being buried together. Let us recall that in barrow 5, although a man and woman were interred together, there was a total of only five riding- and four draught-horses.

Let us now turn to the ear-marks. Without a doubt different marks on the ears mean that the horses had been in different herds and in their time had belonged to different owners, but the buried horses would be choice riding-animals, which could have been bought, swapped or received as a gift in the chief's lifetime.

All the horses whose bodies were well preserved (barrows 1, 2 and 5, partly 3) had their manes and the upper part of their tails clipped. The custom of clipping the manes on riding-horses was very widespread at this period. It was practised in Hither Asia [2] and among the Black Sea Scyths. In the famous frieze on the silver vase from Chertomlyk, showing scenes of catching horses, those with untrimmed manes are from the herd (*tabun*), for trimming of the mane was obligatory for riding-horses. The ridden horse illustrated on the felt carpet from barrow 5 (*Pl. 154*) has its mane trimmed. Judging by surviving representations it seems that the ridden horse in Hither Asia, in particular in Assyria, and in Achaemenid Persia, had its mane trimmed, but this was not done on draught-horses.

The motive for trimming the manes on ridden horses was that the wind blowing in the mane impeded the rider when shooting his bow.

The tails of the horses of Scyths were docked, but in those from Pazyryk the hairs had been cut at 25 cm. from their root. The tails were normally plaited from three tresses, less often twisted in a spiral (*Pl. 71A*), and only one was plaited from five tresses (*Pl. 71B*). Several horse-tails from barrow 1 were tied in a knot (*Pl. 72*). In the middle of the plaited tail there was usually a leather fillet faced with gold.

[1] Radloff, B, pp. 445, 446.

[2] For numerous representations of horses on Assyrian and Achaemenian bas-reliefs see Perrot and Chipiez, B, vols. ii and v.

It is worth noting that on the carpet already mentioned the tail of the horse is clearly represented as docked and then plaited, just as the tails were found on the majority of horse bodies at Pazyryk.

Bridle, saddle and hobbles are the normal equipment for controlling a riding-horse. No hobbles were found in the excavation, but there can be no doubt they were available at that time; we need only recall the famous scene on the Chertomlyk vase of the Scyth hobbling his saddled horse.

In the contemporary specialist literature the halter and bridle as used today constitute one single unit called the headstall (*ogolobe*). The headstalls at Pazyryk consist only of bridles, which, as we shall see below, differ essentially from modern bridles. So the names applied to the constituent parts of contemporary bridles cannot be exactly applied to the Pazyryk examples. A modern bridle consists of an encircling strap beginning at the right ring of the bit, going up and passing round the back of the head behind the ears and then coming down to join the cheek-strap. The latter, which is a short strap, begins at the left ring of the bit and finishes a little above the noseband. Above is a strap over the forehead, below are the noseband and chinstrap. The bridle is kept on the head by the throat-lash.

In the Pazyryk bridles (figs. 57A, B; fig. 58), as in all the Altaian bridles of the period being considered, there were no straps at the chin or across the forehead. There were two longitudinal side-straps, starting from the cheek-pieces and joining up at the horse's sinciput behind the ears on the left side. The noseband was either attached to these side-straps, or intertwined with them, down to the top holes in the cheek-pieces. In the latter case the side-straps were secured in the lower apertures in the cheek-pieces. The throat-lash consisted of two straps (fig. 58). From now on for clarity I will confine the name side-strap to the part above the junction with the noseband, if the latter is secured to the cheek-pieces. I will call the lower ends of the side-straps and the ends of the noseband from their junction downwards 'cheek-straps'. For the remaining straps and other parts of the bridle I will employ the generally accepted names.

The contemporary type of headstall, halter and bridle, has been in use a very long time. The oldest representations of a headstall known to us date to the first half of the last millennium B.C., and are Assyrian, later Persian. Halters are undoubtedly earlier, possibly reaching back to pre-metallic times and the original domestication of the horse. In Assyria we meet bitless bridles with nose-band and chinstrap, side-straps and throat-lash.[1] Assyrian bridles, like the later

---

[1] A representation of such a halter is engraved on a shell (*Tridacta squamosa*) found in south Mesopotamia, on which the cheek-straps are already divided into two. See Perrot and Chipiez, B, vol. ii, p. 670. There are pictures of halters of an even simpler kind with noseband but without cheek bifurcations, e.g. in the horse on the bas-reliefs showing led prisoners in the palace of Sennacherib. In the bas-reliefs at Nimrud showing a fortress the horses wore halters with forehead-strap (ibid., pp. 201 and 511).

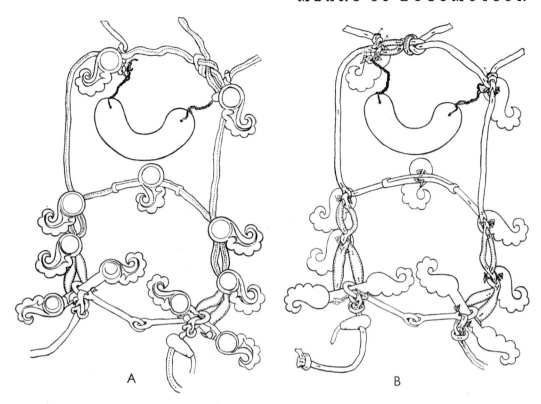

57. Bridle from barrow 3: upper side (A) and underside (B).

Persian ones, consist of side-straps which split at the junction with the cheek-pieces into two or three bands, noseband with or without chinstrap, sometimes forehead-strap and throat-lash.[1] This type of bridle, with or without forehead-strap, is known among the Black Sea Scyths from representations of horses, e.g. on the silver vase or on the gold plate from the sword sheath from Chertomlyk barrow,[2] and on the rhyton from Merdzhany.[3] These offer merely a vague view of the bridle; the High Altai excavation allows us to study real examples.

The bridles, as just remarked, normally consist of three straps: two side-straps changing into cheek-straps below and a single noseband strap. In the design of the bridle with three straps, as mentioned already, there are two variants. In the first the noseband strap plays no part in the formation of the cheek-straps (fig. 58). In this case its ends were threaded into slits in the side-straps and there secured. The cheek-strap then divided into two at the cheek-

[1] Perrot and Chipiez, B, vols. ii and iii.
[2] Tolstoy and Kondakov, A, vol. ii, figs. 114 and 123.
[3] *Reports of the Imperial Archaeological Commission* (1913), XLIX, Pl. 11.

121

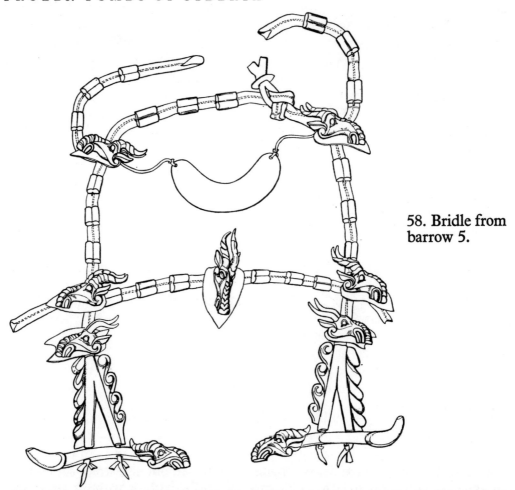

58. Bridle from barrow 5.

piece. In the second variant the ends of the noseband are plaited at two points with the cheek-straps (extensions of side-straps) by looping through two slits (fig. 57); in the intervening space they were sometimes sewn together by sinew thread (fig. 59). Below this the two straps separate and pass through two specially cut slots in the cheek-piece, and are secured underneath it by knots or by strap-fastenings. The right-hand and longer side-strap is tied to the left side-strap with a special knot, which made it possible to adjust the size of the head-stall to conform with the size of the horse's head. The knot was either simple (figs. 60A, 65), or on one of the upper ends of the side-straps there was a special loop through which the end of the second side-strap was threaded and then made fast (fig. 60B). This loop worked by threading the upper end of the first strap into a slit, previously made in it some distance from its end; the loose end was secured below at the junction of side-strap and throat-lash.

122

The right strap of the throat-lash was larger than the left. They were secured to the side-straps at about 20–26 cm. above the junction with the noseband, and are simply threaded into slits in the side-straps and tied merely with loops, or more often held more firmly by intertwining and threading through loops in both straps (fig. 61A). On the free end of the right throat-lash strap there was usually a special loop to take the narrow end of the left throat-lash strap.

In spite of the absence of a forehead-strap nearly all the bridles have a frontal plate, suspended with twisted leather braid or thongs, tied to the ends of the throat-lash at its junctions with the side-straps (fig. 62). The plate itself was hung from holes at its edges, or circular plates (*Pl. 73*) sometimes from a sunk lug at the back (*Pl. 73B*).

The bits were secured to the bridle by means of cheek-pieces. In bridles which had a lead-rein (*chumbur*), this was secured to the left ring of the bit by a double loop, and the rein was secured to the right-hand ring in precisely the same way (fig. 61B). At the left end of the reins from barrows 3 and 4 an antler, less often a wooden, slider block was fixed. Through a circular hole in this slider the strap of the lead-rein was passed and tied in a plain knot at 20–25 cm. from the bit (fig. 57B). Thus the rein-block could slide along the lead-rein between the bit and the knot. Although the right end of the rein was fixed to the right ring of the bit, and the lead-rein similarly to the left, the attachment of the left end of the rein to the slider was extremely feeble. Inside the slider block the end of the rein was fixed and secured to it only by a light thong, threaded through its side. Hence it is clear that the horse could only be controlled by the right rein and the lead-rein. Uniting the left end of the rein by means of a slider block with the lead-rein had only one purpose, to prevent this end of the rein dangling loose, either when stationary or when on the move.

In barrows 1 and 2 there were no slider blocks on the rein, a loop at the left end of which slid along the lead-rein strap between a knot tied in the latter and the bit. In barrow 5 no lead-reins were found and both ends of the rein were attached directly to the rings of the bit.

The position of the lead-rein on the left side and the knots of the side-straps and throat-lash on the same side indicate that in that remote period, as today, the bridle was put on the horse from the left side, just as the horse was mounted from the left side.

A lead-rein, fixed to the bit on the left side, was used also by the Huns to the east and the Black Sea Scyths to the west, as can be seen on the well-known plate from Kul-Oba.[1]

The cheek-pieces can be subdivided according to the material of which they were made: antler, copper or bronze, bronze shanks with decorative wooden terminals and, finally, those made entirely of wood. The antler cheek-pieces,

[1] Tolstoy and Kondakov, A, vol. ii, p. 89, fig. 69.

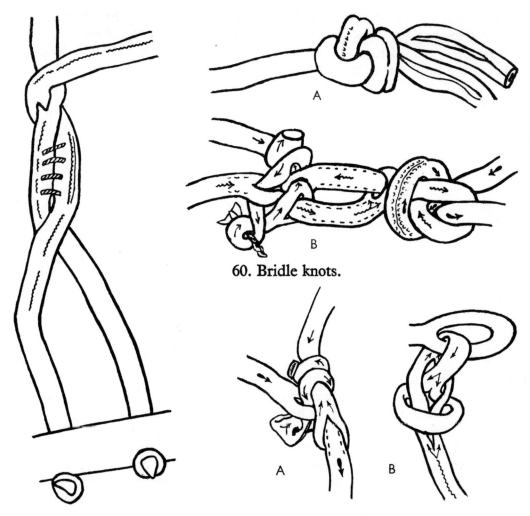

60. Bridle knots.

59. Method of securing side-strap and noseband.

61. Joining straps of throat-lash (A) and of lead-rein with bit (B).

found in barrows 2, 3 and 4, have oval openings to receive the ends of the cheek-straps. In the bronze cheek-pieces, found only at Aragol barrow 1, the holes are round, and in the wooden and composite ones they are of elongated rectangular form. Threaded through these holes the ends of the cheek-straps were held by a special knot, tied by threading the end back into a slit cut in it, or by a thong passed through a cut in the end of the cheek-strap. The latter is particularly characteristic of the bridles from barrow 5.

The antler and bronze cheek-pieces were passed through the bit-rings, and the composite bronze ones with wooden terminals could easily be put in the bit-rings, the terminal simply being taken off and fitted on again. Where the cheek-piece was wholly of wood it could be slipped through the bit-ring, provided one or both terminals were not big, which was the case with the majority. Where, however, the decorative terminals exceeded the aperture of the bit-ring one of them could be chopped off and then after putting the piece through the ring stuck on again. Since the ends of the piece were pasted over with gold-leaf this damage was not visible.

The bridle-straps were made of thick, finely dressed leather. In barrows 1 and 2 they were plain, 1–1·6 cm. wide, but in barrows 3 and 5 they were folded double. In the latter instance the strap was 2–2·5 cm. wide with edges turned in towards the middle and then stitched with twisted sinew, the seam then being polished smooth. Thus one side of the strap had a level face, the other was interrupted longitudinally by a seam. Plain, not double, straps occur in the bridles of barrows 3 and 5 in a single case; the throat-lashes are plain, but usually trimmed with fine leather in such a way that the edge above the longitudinal seam is very slight.

The lead-rein straps in barrow 1 were plain and in barrow 3 bent double and stitched along the middle.

Even in the same burial the methods of dividing the cheek-straps at the cheek-piece and of securing them to the latter may show an unexpected variety of detail. In all bridles of barrow 1 there is a division of the side-straps into cheek-straps, and the junction with the cheek-piece is covered on the outside by wooden forks; in barrows 3 and 5 there are two ways, in five variants, of uniting cheek-piece to headstall. In the first type the side-straps divide, in the second the attachment of cheek-piece to headstall is effected by the use of the noseband. In the first type there are two variants: when the bifurcation of the cheek-straps is decorated by a fork (fig. 58) and secondly, when the cheek-strap ends take on a sort of spade shape and are threaded through the prongs of specially carved wooden forks (fig. 63).

In the second type there are three variants. In the first, wide (not sewn) straps of headstall and nosebands are secured to the cheek-piece ends undecorated (fig. 57). The second differs from the first by the presence of attached wooden forks (fig. 58). In the third variant side and noseband strap from the lower part of their intertwinement are threaded by decorative concertinas of goffered leather. In the latter case each strap can have its own individual 'concertina' (*Pl. 97*B), or they start by both sharing the same, and after the bifurcation have their own 'concertinas' (fig. 64). The number of pleats in the concertina varies: in short straps five (*Pl. 97*B), long ones twenty-six, of which half are doubled (fig. 64). The concertinas can be made from a single or several pieces of

125

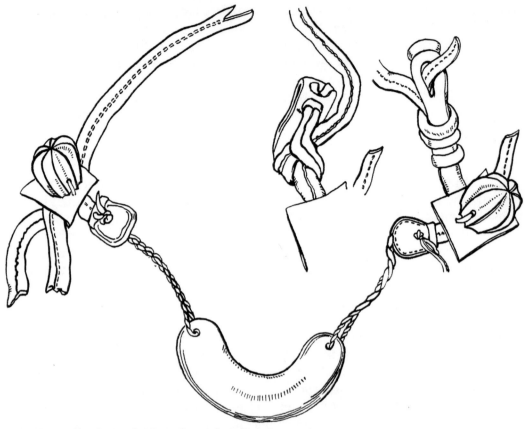

62. A bridle frontal plate from barrow 5.

leather (fig. 64). Where there are such bridle 'concertinas' (fig. 65), after intertwining but before dividing they were usually sewn together.

The peculiarities in the construction of the Altaian bridle have an especial
interest. Bifurcation of the headstall straps is only found where check-pieces
were used. In Assyria the straps broaden downwards and divide into two, even
three, lobes to join the bit by way of a cheek-piece.[1] Such branching of the
straps at the cheek-piece was characteristic of Scythian, as well as contemporary
Persian, bridles;[2] cheek-pieces, as is well known, came into use because of the
demand for rapid and precise manœuvring by cavalry.

The earliest bits with cheek-pieces known to us, which come from Luristan,
were solid and not two-piece. The cheek-pieces consisted of large cast-bronze
plates taking the shape of various animals. In the later Luristanian bits the

[1] Weber, B, figs. 22, 37, 38; Layard, B, 1867b,
pp. 27, 233, 234, 240, 311; Perrot and Chipiez, B,
vol. ii, pp. 47, 283, 491.

[2] Herzfeld, B, Pls. 77–9.

126

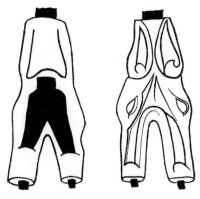

63. Wooden bridle fork from barrow 3 ($\frac{1}{3}$).

64. 'Concertinas' on bridle straps (c. $\frac{1}{3}$)

cheek-plates diminished in size, but the general type with figures of different animals, particularly griffins, continued.[1] In Assyria the cheek-pieces were not cheek-plates and had an elongated shape, although they still sometimes took the shape of an animal.[2] Elongated cheek-pieces shaped like animals occasionally turn up among remains of the Black Sea Scyths.[3] We know them in the Altai. The most widespread (at least of those known to us from this period) are simply antler tines. Sometimes the tines have been shaped into animals, particularly birds. Such simple antler cheek-pieces are very characteristic of the High Altai and were found in three large Pazyryk barrows.

In the Ulagan district bronze cheek-pieces have been found only in Aragol, barrow 1, together with bronze bits of the same type as found in the Pazyryk barrows (*Pl. 74*A). They are long (17·2 cm.), circular in cross-section, slightly bent and thickened at the ends. In the expanded middle part are round holes for

---

[1] Dussaud, B, vol. i, pp. 257–61; vol. iv, Pls. 28–38.

[2] Perrot and Chipiez, B, vol. ii, p. 753, fig. 411.

[3] e.g. cheek-pieces from one of the Seven Brothers' barrows: *Report of the Imperial Archaeological Commission* (1879), p. 134 and (1880), p. 14.

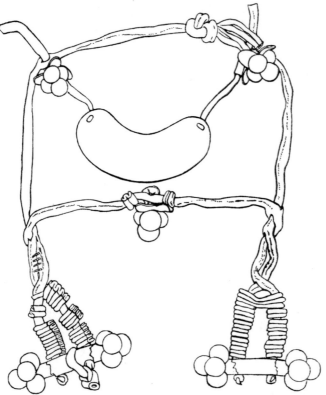

65. Bridle from barrow 3.

the ends of the cheek strap, which were secured, however, in the same way as in the bridles from Pazyryk barrow 5, by threading a short thong into a slit in the forked part of the cheek-strap. Similar cheek-pieces, but this time of iron, were found by S. V. Kiselev in the barrow-cairn near the village of Tuekta.[1]

The great majority of cheek-pieces were evidently made of wood and they are not found in the ordinary burials simply because they have perished. I do not know of any cheek-straps from this period fixed directly to the bit-ring, and, if no such bridles existed, then a cheek-piece was a necessity. I may add that in Aragol, barrow 1, some bronze bits were found with the cheek-pieces described above, but others, also of bronze, with remains of wooden cheek-pieces.

The vast majority of cheek-pieces from the frozen barrows at Pazyryk were of wood. Amongst these we can distinguish straight and S-shaped. From the subject of their decoration they can be divided into several groups: animals, front parts of animals or their heads, palmettes, rosettes and other simple figures. The ornament on the cheek-piece usually corresponds to the decoration of its bridle, and we shall examine the two together.

[1] Kiselev, A, 1947, p. 165, fig. 4.

The bits at Pazyryk were all of the same type: two-piece, cast copper or bronze (with a slight admixture of tin), or wrought iron (*Pls. 74* C, D, and *103*E). Bronze bits were comparatively few: in barrow 1 of ten bits only one was of bronze, in barrow 2 of seven only two, in barrow 3 of fourteen, five, in barrows 4 and 5 all bits were of iron. It should be emphasized that in ordinary barrows bronze bits predominated. Thus, to judge by the copper oxide found in the mouth of the horse from barrow 6 at Pazyryk, the bits were of bronze, and in both barrows at Aragol there were bronze bits.

The Pazyryk saddles belong to a thoroughly evolved and evidently widespread Scythian type. All the saddles have pairs of straps secured to the edge of the cushion, front and back, an upper girth-strap, breast- and crupper-straps (fig. 66). Nevertheless the saddles of the first two differ somewhat from those of the last three barrows, and so we shall consider them separately.

The saddles of barrows 1 and 2 consisted of two joined cushions, four wooden bows (two each at front and back of the cushions), a sweat-cloth of felt and a felt covering.

Each saddle cushion is sewn together from two large pieces of leather, forming its top and bottom surfaces, and two small pieces covering the back and front of the cushions, the saddle 'arches'. All the seams, apart from the inner longitudinal one, show light stitching with sinew thread. The upper and lower parts of the cushion are stitched along the edge from the inside, but leaving about a score of centimetres on the inside unstitched. After the cushion had been stuffed with deer hair, or less often with grasses of the sedge type, it was sewn up with a thong. In order to keep the hair or grass stuffing flat the cushion was quilted longitudinally along three seams with a heavy stitch, using a wool-hemp-hair cord or a leather thong.

In the same way the arches were quilted along two or three seams from the outer to the inner edge. In barrow 2 in one case it was from the upper edge to the outer. The length of the cushions was 50–58 cm. The finished cushions were sewn together along the edge of the pieces of leather forming the bottom covers, a margin of 5–8 cm. wide having been left free on the stuffed, sewn-up cushions. They were so joined that between the stuffed parts was an area of leather (over the horse's backbone) about 10 cm. wide in front and about 6·5 cm. wide at the back.

In one saddle from barrow 2 there were short conical runners arranged in threes on the front and back arches, holding the knots at the ends of the threads of the cushion quilting.

In addition to the central seam the saddle cushions were held together by two relatively narrow straps, laid directly over the front and back arches and fixed to the cushions by thongs.

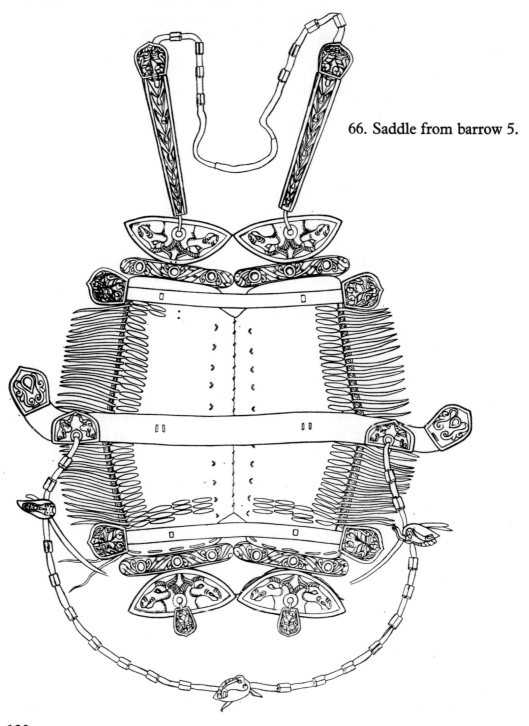

66. Saddle from barrow 5.

The front and back walls of the cushions (the arches) were trimmed with a red (less often yellow) woollen serge-type cloth, and in barrow 1 either thin coloured felt or leather was also used. Over the sewing either thin leather open-work, cut decoration, or in barrow 2 plaiting (network) was applied (fig. 67).

The girth-band consisted of two straps: a broad upper strap laid on the cushion of the saddle and held at some distance from its outer edges by special thongs passing through the thickness of the cushions, and a lower strap under the belly. The latter was fixed to the upper strap on the right, but on the left it was adjustable when the horse was saddled. A horn girth buckle with prong but no return clip was found in only two cases, in barrow 2. The buckles were pear-shaped with double slits for the girth-strap (Pl. 94F).

In some saddles from barrow 2 there were horn pendants (Pl. 94C–E) sewn to thongs hung at the rear saddle arch where the crupper-strap was attached. On others, as also in the saddles from barrow 1, low conical horn runners were fixed (Pl. 94G) through which the flat straps of the crupper were threaded.

Saddle-covers had the same shape as the cushions and were cut from soft, thin, black or (more usually) white felt, dyed blue or red. They were piped along the edge, usually with leather, and fixed to the saddle edge at four points by thongs. In addition to these four thongs the felt covers were held in position by the wooden arch bows (narrow and triangular in section) fixed at their ends and sometimes in the middle (Pl. 75), to which the covers were attached at eight points by thin thongs.

The sweat-cloths were of the same shape as the saddle, cut from white, soft but (as distinct from covers) fairly thick felt. The sweat-cloths were sewn on under the saddle of which they formed part.

The breast- and crupper-straps only survived well in the saddles from barrows 1 and 5. The breast-strap consisted of a long strap secured at either end to the upper girth-strap slightly below the edges of the cushions. At some 15–20 cm. from the girth-strap, attached to the breast-strap, were two straps that rose vertically over the horse's withers and were stitched together with a thong.

The crupper-strap was broader than the breast-strap (the former about 22 mm., the latter about 12 mm.). The ends, as mentioned, were threaded through conical horn runners at the rear arch of the saddle, and then fixed to the top surface of the cushions. Except at the end near the saddle the remaining part was trimmed with fine leather.

The saddle-covers, breast- and crupper-straps bore various adornments which we shall discuss below.

In barrow 3 no complete saddle survived, although there were quite appreciable remains, mainly hair stuffing, horn or wooden decorations and small bits of straps. They suffice to give a fairly clear picture of the type of

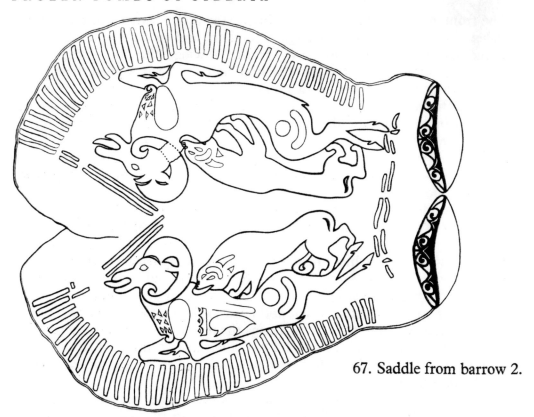

67. Saddle from barrow 2.

saddle. In barrows 4 and 6 no traces of saddles, except horn facings, were preserved, but in barrow 5 they had survived as well as in barrow 1.

Comparison of the saddles, their fittings and decoration, in the last four barrows makes it evident that they all belong to one and the same type, which differed somewhat from the saddles of the first two barrows.

The dimensions, shape and technique of manufacture of the saddle cushions in barrows 3–6 are much the same as in the first two. The hair stuffing is quilted longitudinally along three or four seams by large stitches of twisted wool or hair thread. The front and rear arches are quilted with the same cord but transversely. They are, however, larger, on average 10 cm. high and up to 20 cm. or more broad at their base.

The arches are edged in most cases with woollen cloth of red, rose and brown colour. The cloth was of two types: plain serge weave, and the same but decorated with diagonal ribbing. In some cases the pommels were trimmed with fine leather and covered with red lacquer.

A distinctive feature of saddles of the second type, besides the high arches, was the wooden spacers between the cushions at front and back under the

132

arches. They consist of solid boards with projecting tongues at either end (*Pl. 76A–B*), placed between the cushions into which the tongues were embedded. As in barrows 1 and 2, above the cushions directly over the inner edges of front and back arches, thick straps about 3 cm. wide were fixed to the edge of the cushions by narrow thongs. The spacers just mentioned were lashed to the middle of these straps; they may indeed be regarded as a first step towards the future frame, or tree, of the saddle.

To the ends of the straps holding the wooden spacers horn or wooden pendant plaques were fixed. The broad upper girth-strap (up to 6–7 cm. wide), secured by thongs to the cushions at two points (as in the first two barrows), hung 20–25 cm. below the edge of the cushions. Directly below the cushion edges on the

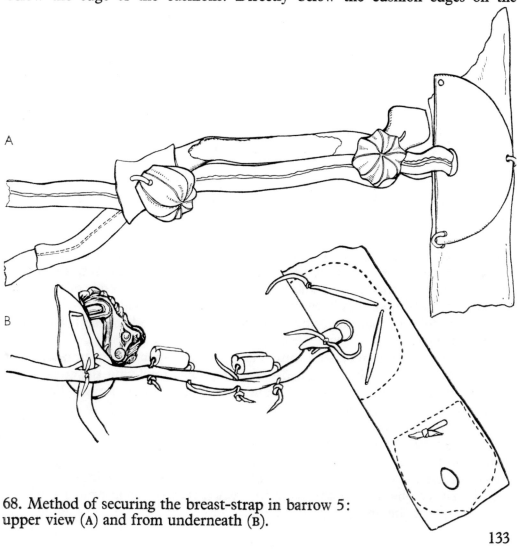

A

B

68. Method of securing the breast-strap in barrow 5:
upper view (A) and from underneath (B).

133

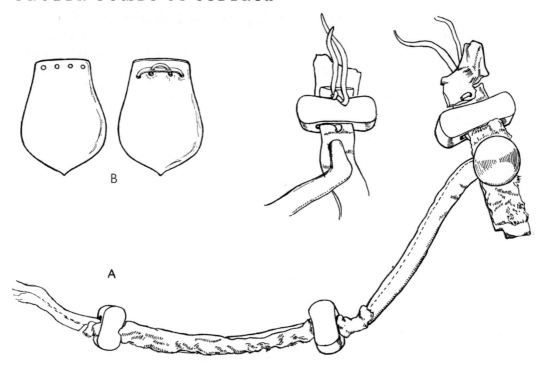

69. Method used in barrow 5 of attaching the breast-strap to the girth-strap with slides (A) and pendant shields (B).

outside were fixed semicircular horn plates perforated on the straight side (in one case leather was substituted for horn). The ends of the breast-strap were threaded through the opening and made fast (fig. 68). At the ends of the girth-strap on the outside similar horn (in one case leather) plates of shield-shape were fixed, with holes in their lower half through which the ends of the lower girth-strap were passed.

I have entered into details on this, since four strap-pendant horn plates, two semicircular and two shield-shaped—with openings for fixing the ends of the breast- and lower girth-straps—are found as sets in ordinary burials. This gives a clue as to the type of saddle used. In these sets there are usually in addition two narrow pendant plates from the front arch.

A second peculiarity of the saddles being considered are arc-shaped horn facings on the top edge of the arches and large horn or wooden facings on the outside of the arches. We shall become acquainted with these facings below, and here I shall confine myself to saying that when they occur in ordinary burials they also give a clue to the type of saddle.

134

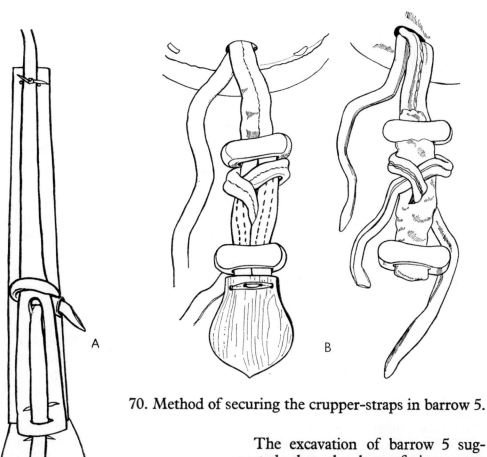

70. Method of securing the crupper-straps in barrow 5.

The excavation of barrow 5 suggested that the horn facings were replaced by exactly similar thick leather cut-outs, but the opposite could have happened; the leather facings on large saddle arches might have been replaced by stronger horn ones. At Pazyryk both were used simultaneously.

Saddle-covers (leaving their decoration aside for the moment), sweat-cloths, girth-buckles and breast-straps were all of the same type as found in the first two barrows. Only the crupper-strap is distinctive.

In the first two barrows the crupper-strap was fixed at its two ends directly to the saddle cushions, but in the later barrows a more sophisticated method was used. At the back ends of the saddle cushions a relatively short strap (30–35 cm.) was fixed, gradually expanding at its end (up to 3·5 cm.) and with a long slit in it (fig. 70A). The ends of the crupper-straps were secured to this, on the right usually with a permanent knot, and on the left making use of a loop so that

135

in case of need it could be shortened or lengthened (fig. 70B). Horn or wooden slides were sometimes applied here.

The crupper-strap, like the bridle and breast-strap, was stiff, doubled over and sewn along the outer surface, but in some cases it was single and trimmed with thin leather.

The saddle-straps to which the crupper-strap was attached were sometimes decorated at their ends, or all along the whole surface, by sewn-on plaques (fig. 66).

Besides the ancillaries and decorations mentioned, in one saddle from barrow 5 (fig. 88) a wooden rod was found fixed to the left side, with its ends carved with feline heads (*Pl. 136F*). Its purpose eludes me, but its shape deserves attention. Similar rods (e.g. in the leather pouch from barrow 2, fig. 23) were usually decorated with animals' heads facing in opposite directions, but in this case the rear head is carved so that instead of looking back like the front one it looks forward.

In fig. 88 a general representation is given of all the details mentioned above of the saddle from barrow 5. In the drawing there is yet another feature distinguishing saddles of this time from those of barrows 1 and 2: the method of fixing the breast-strap, discussed above.

In some cases, at the point where the breast-strap joined the girth on its outer side, a semicircular, or more often a round, ornamental plaque was fixed (fig. 69A). On the lower girth-strap ends sometimes long slits were made for passing the end of the upper girth-strap through when the horse was saddled (fig. 71).

Saddles similar to the second type have been found outside Pazyryk in the barrow at Shibe,[1] where not only horn facings for large arches but also wooden spacers were found, and in addition in a barrow at Karakol.[2] Thus this type of saddle enjoyed widespread use in the High Altai at this period.

Although the bridles found at Pazyryk may have been developed in all details in Hither Asia long previously, this is certainly not true of the saddles. Assyrian saddles, familiar from bas-reliefs, consist merely of a cloth with a very broad breast-band, all of one piece.[3] So girth- or crupper-straps were not required, although the latter were sometimes used.[4]

71. End of lower girth-strap.

[1] Preserved in the Hermitage, Leningrad, no. 4888.

[2] Kiselev, A, 1949, Pl. XXXII, fig. 12.

[3] Weber, B, fig. 38; Layard, B, 1867a, p. 166.

[4] Layard, 1867b, p. 240.

Later, Median and then Parthian and Persian saddles were of this type. In his story about the customs of the Persians at the time of Cyrus the Younger Xenophon says: '...now they had more covers on their horses than on their beds, because they were concerned not so much about riding as having a soft seat'.[1] This type of mat saddle, more precisely a shabrack, seen in the pile carpet from barrow 5 (*Pl. 174*) is depicted on the well-known silver disk from the Oxus treasure.[2]

Since we do not know any other, older saddles, the type from Pazyryk can be regarded as the oldest and most widespread type used in the period under discussion, not only among Asian tribes but also among the Black Sea Scyths. We have not a few representations of Scythian saddles: on the Chertomlyk vase, on a plate from Kul-Oba, on the silver cup from Solokha and on the rhyton from Merdzhany.[3] To attempt detailed documentation from these pictures would be futile, but a common method of construction shared with the Altai examples cannot be open to doubt. The majority do not show a crupper-strap, except in the Merdzhany barrow, Great Kuban oblast.[4] This need not signify, since there is alternative information on saddles of the Altai type used by Scyths in the archaic period. The horn plates and cheek-pieces from the barrows at Zhabotin,[5] in the middle Dnieper valley, dating from the end of the sixth and the beginning of the fifth centuries B.C., are widely known. Although the purpose of the cheek-pieces has never been doubted, the connection with saddlery of the narrow carved horn plates, decorated on the external face, has not been elucidated. However, there can be no doubt that we are dealing with the horn facings from saddle arches, on the ends of which and in the middle, just as in the Altai, there are perforations for attachment.

After the excavation of barrow 1 at Pazyryk the opinion was put forward in the literature, particularly abroad,[6] that the saddlery in the Altai barrows had been specially made for the funeral. Such a view is quite baseless.

In a burial, with the corpse are placed the things belonging to it most closely related to the rite of the dead, so to substitute specially made things for real ones would be absurd. Innumerable ethnographic parallels show that wherever a corpse was furnished with articles necessary for the next world they were his personal possessions. There are cases of the manufacture of miniature articles to replace real ones or even paper cut-outs of animals and people, but these are related to a cult, and have no special connection with the

[1] Xenophon, A, *Cyropaedia*, bk vii, 8, 19.
[2] Dalton, B, Pl. ix, no. 24.
[3] Tolstoy and Kondakov, A, vol. ii, figs. 69, 114, 123; Rostovtzeff, B, 1922, Pl. 20; *Reports of the Imperial Archaeological Commission* (1913), issue 49, Pl. 11.
[4] *Reports of the Imperial Archaeological Commission* (1913), issue 49, Pl. 11.
[5] Rostovtzeff, 1929, Pl. 7, figs. 1, 2 and 5.
[6] Salmony, B, p. 19.

burial rite. These either belonged to the soul of the departed, as it were, temporarily until the second final burial of the spirits in the clan (as can be seen among the peoples of north-west Siberia), or served as symbolic offerings (as is the case in China).

Let us now turn to examine the Pazyryk grave goods, which some archaeologists have regarded as specially made for the burials.

I have already denied this to some extent when I assumed the wooden cheek-pieces to have been in everyday use. I would add that metal was dear, so where a substitute was available it was used. In two cases in barrow 1 two different cheek-pieces were used in the same bridle, which would hardly be likely had they been made for the burial. Obviously in both cases one was broken and lost, and replaced by one resembling it from another bridle. One cheek-piece from the same barrow was broken and then had been carefully lashed around the break with a thong. This would not have been done if the cheek-pieces were made especially for the burial ceremony.

Detailed study of the bridle-straps reveals their extraordinarily careful manufacture, especially in barrows 3 and 5. The craftsman had worked as if he were the owner, trying to make everything neat, strong and securely stitched. That the bits had been in daily use, and not especially made, is often proved by the obvious scratching, even attrition, on them. In some cases the bridle-straps had been lined with fine coloured felt to make them softer. Not uncommonly, bridles constructed in two different ways were found in the same barrow (3 and 5), which could hardly have been the case if they had been made on a specific occasion for the burial.

There are equally good grounds for regarding the saddles as those in ordinary use. Like the bridles all the saddles have been meticulously made. Some bear clear traces of repairs, like patches on the saddle cushions. Wooden spacers serve a purpose in a riding-saddle, but are quite unnecessary in dummies, particularly as they are invisible; furthermore some of them are polished as if from long use. The method of fixing the crupper-strap to the saddle, allowing it to be lengthened or shortened at will, is only meaningful in a saddle in use. Finally, it would only have been necessary to use simple wooden facings, and not make them laboriously of horn, on the saddle arches of a dead man's horse.

An impression that the Pazyryk saddlery was not intended for everyday use might be prompted by the large number of wooden decorations, covered by gold-leaf and tinfoil. Nevertheless it has to be borne in mind that tinfoil, and particularly gold-leaf, had extraordinarily wide application in the Altai (and not in the Altai alone) at this time for covering various decorations of copper, bronze and wood, particularly dress adornments. Naturally, therefore, wooden decorations on saddlery were covered with gold-leaf. The information vouchsafed us by Herodotus that the Massagetae had 'head-dresses, girdles and bands decorated with gold', and 'made bridles, bits and cheek-pieces out of gold'[1] must be read, in my opinion, in the sense that it is seen in the Altai, that is, decorated with gold-leaf; it could hardly be that the Massagetae had access to so much gold that these articles were made entirely of it.

The results of the excavation in 1950 of barrow 2 at Bash-Adar in the Karakol valley were particularly revealing in this connection. There, in addition to wooden saddlery decorations covered with gold, cast copper decorations covered with gold-leaf were found. It is particularly interesting that in two sets, cheek-pieces, bridle and saddle (breast) pendants, one cast in copper and another carved out of wood, were identical copies. Those gold cheek-pieces of the Massagetae, referred to by Herodotus, were probably copper covered with gold, similar to our Altai examples.

Another supposition is possible: bridles and saddles in everyday use were deliberately decked out with decorations as part of the funeral ceremony. The latter is the more feasible if we remember some of the scenes depicted on several saddle covers of barrows 1 and 2, one of the covers from barrow 5 and also several of the saddle pendants. I would merely observe that anyone who has visited the tent of a rich steppe pastoral nomad or the hut of one of his mountain cousins can see on the left of the doorway saddles bedecked with rich ornament, which are the pride and joy of their owner. Why should not the ancient Altaians have been able to decorate their everyday saddles in the same way?

Let us now make a brief barrow-by-barrow description of the sets of decoration on the saddlery from the Pazyryk graves.

Looking at the sets of saddlery decoration from barrow 1 the striking point is the absence of any correspondence between the decorative motifs used in the bridles and saddles. In the wooden decorations on bridle and breast-strap, however, a match can be seen, e.g. if the subject on the bridle, say, is a palmette or deer then this is repeated on the breast-strap. The decorative motifs of the saddle cover and its pendants, on the other hand, have nothing in common with those on bridle and breast-strap. Since this feature is also exhibited in the saddlery in the other barrows we shall mainly consider the bridle and breast-strap decorations in this chapter, and only to some extent the saddle decoration, which will be dealt with in the chapter on art.

On the bridle and breast-strap decoration there was usually one overriding motif, but this is not always so, and quite often the decoration was inspired by two or three themes.

The first set from barrow 1 consists of graceful S-shaped cheek-pieces terminating in palmettes (*Pl. 77*), with bridle and breast-straps decorated also

[1] Herodotus, A, bk i, 215.

with palmettes (*Pl. 79*). This variant of the palmette, petals in a fan-shape cupped in spirally twisted leaves, is known from Hither Asia and Scythia.[1] The frontal plate is circular with a hemispherical projection in the middle. The wooden forks covering the bifurcation of the cheek-straps bear no ornament.

In the second set straight cheek-pieces terminate in multi-petalled palmettes that open directly from the cup (*Pl. 80*). Double palmettes together with figures of elks decorate the bridle and breast-straps. The open-work plates with the figures of elk split and spread out, as it were, their heads twisted back, are very interesting. They have tiny tails and legs with retracted, exaggerated hoofs. The heads carved in the round are detachable and have leather ears and horns. Some of the figures are flat. Both in the middle of the noseband and breast-strap the two halves of the animal are fixed at a slight angle to each other. Although much conventionalized in the body, the elks are done fairly realistically in the heads. The motif employed on the cheek-strap forks is a variant of 'running waves'. The frontal plate is lunate, decorated with cable pattern in the middle.

The third set (*Pl. 81*) has S-shaped cheek-pieces also decorated with lotus-like palmettes, but now in a new third variant. The bridle-strap junctions and the breast-strap are decorated with triple-layered, leather cut-outs very expressively depicting goats' heads (*Pl. 81*D). A peculiarity of this set is the presence of a forehead band, its only occurrence at Pazyryk. A remarkable central decoration was used on the breast-strap—a carved leather bird (*Pl. 81*C). It is a griffin with extended wings and distended tail made out of thick leather, as also was its protruding chest sewn on with sinew threads. The wings and tail feathers are represented by incisions on the leather. The griffin's head (*Pl. 81*B), with tall comb and eagle's beak, is sculptural, three pieces of thick leather having been employed for it. The chest, two strips over the division of wing feathers, and the head were covered by gold-leaf. The griffin was suspended by four thongs from the breast-strap. Its decorative quality and simplicity of line render it beautiful. The tail, shaped as a palmette, is interesting because it has an exact replica in the tail in a similar bird composition next to the feeding cervid on the well-known silver breastplate from the Seven Brothers' barrows.

There are pendant palmettes identical to those from the first set among bridle and breast pendants of the fourth set (*Pl. 82*A), but accompanied this time by mountain rams. Cheek-pieces in this set consisted of remarkable figures of mountain rams with sharply twisted horns and a beard-like under-mane which nature itself might have intended as an ornament (*Pl. 82*B). The animals are shown as if jumping with front legs retracted and rear legs extended backward.

The craftsman gave special attention to shaping the head, in which he achieved both realism and decoration. The shape of the body is generalized,

---

[1] Perrot and Chipiez, B, vol. ii, p. 138; Herzfeld, B, Pls. 63 and 84; Dieulafoy, B, 1892, Pls. 4 and 10; *Report of the Imperial Archaeological Commission* (1877), Pl. 1, fig. 5; Pridik, A, Pl. 5, fig. 1.

with emphasis on certain distinctive muscular contours, particularly the shoulder girdle. The pendants on the bridle and breast-straps in the shape of rams' heads facing (*Pl. 83*B, D) are highly decorative. The forehead is broad, the horns are of inserted leather, the ears small and hidden by the horns. The under-mane spreads out both ways with twists on the ends giving it a lyre shape. Such heads occur in two varieties: a more detailed working-out of the incised mane, with marked nostrils, or rough, differently incised work. The frontal plate is leaf-shaped and convex in the middle. The wooden forks for the cheek-straps are decorated with a series of opposed curls.

A single theme, the mountain ram, was used on the open-work decorations on bridle and breast-straps in the fifth set (*Pl. 84*A). The straight cheek-pieces have profile rams' head terminals back to back (*Pl. 84*C), which in fact hardly differ from those in the fourth set. They are carefully carved, but have a round eye with tear duct, the annulation of the horns is shown differently and the mane is shorter. The treatment of the pendant plates reflects ingenuity and skill; the rams are shown in a conventional form. They have a large, slightly lowered head with inserted leather horns that are so broad, extending over the lower mane, that they conceal the body, as it were. Just below the muzzle four retracted little feet with hoofs are visible. These pendants are all flat except one in the middle of the noseband, which is convex, and the horns, which are not leather inserts but relief carving done in a single piece. Amongst the breast pendant plates of this set there is a kind of scene of a ram in the jaws of a horned carnivore (a wolf), which is of exceptional interest. In the centre is the ram's head with round eye and tear duct, sharply twisted and annulated horns and distinctly marked mouth and nostrils. This head is gripped in the jaws of the carnivore, the mandible of which touches the mandible of the ram, while its upper canine is plunged into the ram's muzzle. The head of the carnivore has a well-cut eye and nose terminating in a curl, and to retain the symmetry the under-mane of the ram also finishes in a twist. From under the carnivore's mane project the two forefeet of the ram. Besides the ingenuity of design by which a representation of 'a ram, seized by a carnivore' could be confined within an almost square plate, we should note the uniformity of the composition, which is achieved by the same treatment of horns, under-mane and the rams' legs placed as a counter-weight to the front part of the muzzle of the carnivore (*Pl. 83*C). Extremely characteristic is the curl on the tip of the carnivore's nose, which we shall meet again in the future. The fork is decorated by a 'running waves' motif (*Pl. 84*B).

In the sixth set very varied motifs have been employed on the cheek-pieces, as well on the pendants of the bridle and breast-straps. The bridle (*Pl. 85*) is the only one in barrow 1 with a bronze bit and one of the two in which the cheek-pieces do not match. Both cheek-pieces are straight, but on one the terminals

141

are identical but in the other they are not. In the first (*Pl. 86D*) the back-to-back griffins' heads have eagles' beaks, clearly delineated mouth, a ruff of knobs and a tall denticulated comb along the beck. The second cheek-piece is quite unusual (*Pl. 86C*). On the straight shank the lower head is exactly the same as on the first cheek-piece, but with an additional ruff around its neck; the other head, instead of looking up, looks forward and is quite differently made. The eyes are not round, but elongated, the beak is more strongly hooked with extra ornament along the top of the mouth, and the top crest and comb gradually fade away to nothing. Both heads had inserted leather ears, for which special sockets had been bored.

The relief figures of griffins *en face* with sculptural detachable heads on the bridle-strap junctions reveal remarkable skill and decorative qualities (*Pl. 86A, B*). The wings are spread, the tail is bifurcated and a central claw is shown conventionally. The head with half-open, typical eagle's beak, has the same decoration along the top of its mouth as one of the cheek-piece terminals. The round eye has a distinct cere; the leather ears and toothed comb are inserted. The pendant in the middle of the noseband is not flat, but has the body surfaces at slightly varying angles to each other. In the details two variants can be distinguished. The motif employed on the straps between junctions on the bridle is the ram in the jaws of the carnivore that we have met (*Pl. 83D*), while the breast-strap pendants are palmettes of the same type as in the first set. The frontal plate is round and convex, and 'running waves' with toppling crests decorate the cheek-forks.

The S-shaped cheek-pieces of the seventh set (*Pl. 87B*) bear beautiful stylized heads of long-eared griffins with crest and comb. The mouth is ajar, the great beak is hooked and there is a marked cere. The bridle and breast-strap decoration consists of little finely carved boards (*Pl. 87A, C*), and at the strap junctions, in the middle of the noseband and breast-strap, plain lotus-type palmettes (*Pl. 83A*). There is a round frontal plate, while the wooden cheek-forks bear no decoration.

The theme of the decoration in the bridle and breast-straps of the eighth set (*Pls. 88, 89*) is a variety of deer. The deer on the cheek-pieces (*Pl. 88B*), like the ram in the fourth set, is shown springing with retracted forelegs bent at the knee and rear legs stretched out. The head is extended forward with the branching antlers pushed back on the spine and the pressed-back ears emphasize the exertion of leaping; the exaggeration of the rear hoofs achieves a balance. At the strap intersections, in the middle of the noseband and on the breast-strap, opened-out versions of these deer are fixed with inserted sculptural heads (*Pl. 89B*) and openwork in between. The deer with insertable heads have much in common with the elk examined in the second set; it is a matter for discussion whether elk or deer are represented. The basic difference is only in

142

details, in particular the position of the forelegs and the substitution of two short tails by three-petalled palmettes.

The intervening ornaments are more original (*Pl. 89*c). Here we have deer depicted chest to chest, but without legs and with a palmette between them. The huge antlers running down over the back and the head are like those on the deer on the cheek-pieces, but in this instance the antlers exceed the size of the body. The antlers and palmette at the end constitute a frame for the pendant. What was intended, reindeer or red deer, it is pointless to discuss, since the craftsman has not concerned himself with peculiarities of species; it is a question of a generalized form.

A deer with retracted legs, thrust-forward head and antlers crowned with tines extended along the body, so that the antlers become a motif of their own, is characteristic even of the archaic period of Scythian art. We can see a beautiful example of it from the barrow at Kostromskaya,[1] on the projection from the sword scabbard in Melgunov's treasure,[2] in a whole series of stamped figures on the axe facing, as well as on the well-known gold cup, from Kelermes,[3] on plates decorating horse head-dress in a barrow from former Kiev province,[4] in the gold deer from Kul-Oba barrow [5] and in many other similar pieces. However, we do not know of a similar treatment of deer antlers in the Altai.

The frontal plate in this set is circular, as we have seen before, while the wooden cheek-fork is ribbed.

The decoration in the ninth set is of an individual kind. The two themes are a leopard's head with boar's tusk in its mouth and a four-petalled rosette. The S-shaped cheek-pieces have as a terminal a feline, leopard-like head with a boar's tusk in its jaws (*Pl. 90*A). It has sharply incised savage eyes with distinct eyebrows, short cat-like ears and puckered upper lip. The pendants attached to the strap intersections, at the middle of the noseband and breast-strap, are the same, sculptural heads of leopards with inserted leather ears and strongly hooked boars' tusks in their mouths (*Pl. 90*B, C). The heads have been more carefully made than in the cheek-pieces, with deeper incisions. There are four-petalled rosettes cut from thick leather. The frontal plate is round.

The decorations on the tenth set (*Pl. 91*) are singular. The cheek-pieces are straight, with round rosette terminals, varying in design and evidently originating from different bridles. In the right-hand cheek-piece the rosettes are completely uniform, and consist of a central hemispherical swelling, encircled by a ring of fourteen–sixteen small knobs. In the left cheek-piece the upper rosette is identical with those on the right, with fourteen knobs around the edge; in the lower terminal the central swelling is smaller and ringed by petals. The especial

[1] *Report of the Imperial Archaeological Commission* (1897), p. 17, fig. 46.

[2] Pridik, A, Pls. 3 and 4, fig. 1.

[3] Rostovtzeff, B, 1922, Pl. 7.

[4] Bobrinsky, A, vol. iii, p. 134, fig. 71.

[5] Antiquities, A, Pl. xxvi, fig. 1.

72. Open-work leather cut-out plates from saddle arches: A–E, I, J from barrow 1; F, G from barrow 2; H, barrow 3 ($\frac{1}{3}$).

interest of this set is the representation of human heads, or, more accurately, masks. They fall into two types. The first, of which there is only a single example fixed to the middle of the noseband (*Pl. 92*D), is convex, and not flat

144

like all the rest. It is a relatively narrow, long face with eyes set slantwise and narrow nose. There is no moustache, but the beard, which finishes high up, is pressed to the ears by special curls. The remaining flat masks (*Pl. 92*A–C) are broad-faced and high cheek-boned, with ears sticking out and, although bearded, are also clean-shaven on the upper lip. There are several variations, all more or less broad-faced. The intervening open-work pendants for bridle and breast-straps consist of a series of opposed curls. The frontal plate is half-moon shaped and has a cord edging.

The leather cut-outs facing the outside of the narrow saddle-arches in barrow 1 are shown in fig. 72A–E, I and J. The motifs are fairly varied. They are either running waves, or various combinations of spirals, or vegetable, that is, a more or less composite palmette and a four-petalled rosette. The leather cut-out adornments sewn on the crupper-straps are also varied (fig. 73).

A normal decoration of the saddles in barrow 1 was bunches of three fairly long thongs or woollen cords, less often ribbons of felt, attached to the rear of the saddle on both sides (*Pl. 79*B), from which hung hair tassels. The cup of the tassel takes various shapes, and the brush was usually horse-hair dyed red (*Pl. 90*I, J). These pendants, which were attached either to the strap joining the

73. Leather cut-outs decorating crupper-straps from barrow 1 ($\frac{1}{3}$).

saddle cushions at the back, or directly to the back of the cushion, were fixed to a thong at each side by means of a transverse pin at the end.

From barrow 2 there were decorations from only six bridles (the bit of a seventh

145

being found without any), which in general had survived in very poor condition in this tomb.

The most interesting is a set of horn bridle decorations. The cheek-pieces, found in the rings of an iron bit (*Pl. 74*D), were fairly long, scarcely worked tips of deer antler tines with their natural curvature.

A remarkable frontal plate from this bridle consists of a bold composition of two heraldically opposed geese (or, more exactly, one goose split into two), with head thrown back and a pair of feet, which are in the jaws of a long-eared, horned carnivore. This design fills the frontal plate (*Pl. 159*A). In studying it one realizes that the two halves, each showing a goose in the jaws of the beast, are not represented facing but in profile. This was done intentionally by the crafts-man. A second point deserves attention: the peculiarities of the style of work on the geese and predators' heads. While the geese are depicted fairly realistically (particularly the drooping heads), the carnivore's head is rendered in a con-ventional manner: muzzle with puckered upper lip, large savage eyes with exaggerated eyebrows, large ears with characteristic twist and horns with knobs. Here we see worked out in individual native style the familiar lion-griffins of the Middle East. Even if the shape of the monster had been borrowed from the south, in the Altai it received a quite different treatment, although some of the widely applied methods used in the former area have survived. Executed in low relief, the recesses of the design on the plaque have been painted with yellow and red mineral colouring.

The horn bridle plates of this set are oval, almost round, big and small, and bear one and the same incised lotus pattern (*Pl. 159*B, c). Within a central oval is a slit and two circular holes for fixing the plate to the straps. Above and below between the stems are the lotus flowers with five petals on the big, and four on the little, plaques. To right and left are three-petalled flowers cupped in leaves with curled tips. As in the frontal plate the recesses in the excised pattern are coloured red and yellow.

The theme of the second set of wooden bridle decorations is a cat. The S-shaped cheek-pieces have terminals in the form of the forepart of a cat (*Pl. 93*C). The head with open mouth is carved in the round; the front paw supports the chin; ears and whiskers are indicated by one denticulated twist; the upper lip has the characteristic pucker. The bridle pendants of this set are represented by sculptured feline figures on horseshoe-shaped bases, painted bright

74. Leather bridle decoration from barrow 2 (*c.* ½).

75. Leather bridle decorations from barrow 2: from cheekstraps (A); from cheekpieces (B); from strap intersections (C) ($\frac{3}{4}$).

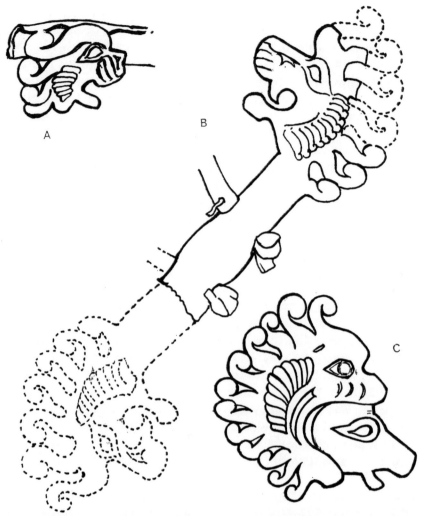

red with cinnabar (*Pl. 93*A, B). The figures were lashed by thin thongs to the bases and the latter sewn to the bridle with thongs. The cats, depending on the strap they decorated, squatted on the right or left side with back legs curled up and front ones extended, the neck extended upward as if in an alert position. As in the cheek-piece terminals erect ears and whiskers are formed by a single ribbed arc. The upper lips on the expressive muzzles are strongly puckered.

The frontal plate is a simple disk with central protrusion exactly as in barrow 1, but differs from it in that it is coloured red and the convex part is covered with gold-leaf.

In the next three bridles, apart from the bits, only the wooden cheek-pieces survive. One pair is S-shaped with goose-head terminals (*Pl. 94*B). In spite of

147

the schematism of the representation of the heads in dimensions and beak shape, the emphasis on the cere has definitely revealed the species. A pair of straight cheek-pieces with heads of mountain rams as terminals (*Pl. 94*A) has much in common with the cheek-pieces of the fifth set in barrow 1, only in this case the horns are differently shaped and the under-mane does not stick out so strongly. Quite different is the treatment of the ram's-head terminals of the other S-shaped cheek-pieces (*Pl. 93*E). What is noteworthy in this case is the absence of an under-mane, the individual shape of the annulated, sharply bent horns and the excellently carved hooked ram's muzzle. Here we are probably dealing with a domestic ram, a rare subject compared with wild rams. With the cheek-pieces were a circular frontal plate, rams' heads and wooden forks. The convex central part of the frontal plate was edged with cord ornament (*Pl. 90*H). The muzzles of the rams' heads (*Pl. 93*D) are the same as those on the cheek-pieces (*Pl. 93*E), but because the insertable leather ears and horns have been lost it is difficult to be certain that we are dealing with rams' heads. Wooden bridle decorations carved to a comma-shaped pattern (*Pl. 90*F) also belong to this set. The wooden fork concealing the bifurcation of the cheek-straps is the same as in barrow 1.

Unusual finds in barrow 2 were cheek-pieces and bridle decorations cut out of leather. These bridles were very badly preserved, but detailed study of the remains revealed that they had had leather cut-out facings over the branching of the cheek-straps (fig. 74). On the cheek-strap were leather cut-out lions' heads (fig. 75A). Similar lions' heads, but larger, with deer's heads in their jaws, had been fixed to the strap intersections on the same bridle (fig. 75C). Most surprising was the discovery of badly disintegrated, but identifiable, cheek-pieces cut from leather with lions' head terminals (fig. 75B). All the heads had the mouth open (fangs being shown in the case of the cheek-pieces), with puckering on upper lip, and whiskers and mane indicated by curved hooked lines.

In addition to leather bridle decorations the breast-strap in the same set bore leather cut-out decorations, consisting of rows of palmettes with human masks at intervals, the top part of the head being lotus-shaped (fig. 76). We shall return again to this subject in the chapter on art. All these leather cut-out decorations were covered by gold-leaf.

Two saddles from barrow 2 had leather cut-out facings on the saddle arches, as in barrow 1 (fig. 72F, G). On several arches were horn pendants (*Pl. 94*C–E). We shall become more closely acquainted with similar pendants in discussing the decoration on the saddles from barrows 3 and 5. As in barrow 1 tassels (*Pl. 90* D, E) with or without cups were hung by thongs or woollen cords behind the saddle, and there were also wooden buckles and horn runners (*Pl. 94*G) attached by straps.

The decorations of the saddle cushions showing individual animals or

76. Leather decoration of breast-strap from barrow 2 ($\frac{2}{3}$).

struggles between them, together with similar examples from barrow 1, will be described in the chapter on art.

In barrow 3, as already recorded, leather scarcely survived, and so there were only three or four bridles and several pieces of straps, but not a single complete saddle. Nevertheless using the finds made together of the different decorations, and their subjects, it is possible to study the individual sets of decoration, while the remains of saddles give some idea of their construction.

A set of horn parts and bridle decorations with iron bits from barrow 3 consisted of cheek-piece, spheroidal runners, one in the shape of a horse-hoof, and a slider. The cheek-pieces are only slightly worked maral [1] antler tines (*Pl. 95*A). On the outside they were ornamented by triangular cuts above, below which they were covered by red lacquer. The spheroidal runners (diameter 2·5 cm.), also made from antler tines, have a circular perforation for the bridle-strap. All the runners have been made to look like eyes with pupil, iris and white (*Pl. 95*B). The central part (pupil) and the side triangles (whites) have been incised and covered with red lacquer. Of seven such spheroids one is large (diameter 3 cm.), four medium (2·5 cm.) and two small (2 cm.). Their shape is markedly spheroidal and the side opposite the 'pupil' touching the horse's head is flat. The runner from the throat-lash, shaped like a hoof, also has an ornamental incised triangle covered by red lacquer (*Pl. 96*F).

The horn slider (*Pl. 95*C) from the rein is oval in section, with a socket for the rein at one end and an oval opening at the other for the lead-rein.

The bridle decorations just described constitute, with the saddle adornments, a single set of horse decoration. The large horn facings of the saddle arches at back and front can be described first. They are trimmed by rose-coloured wool cloth of serge type. In this set the four facings (corresponding to the arch sides) take the

[1] [Translator's note. Maral is the name for the variety of red deer found in this area. M.W.T.]

shape of gently curved half-horseshoes (*Pl. 96A*). On the outside are carved pairs of heraldically opposed profile elk heads. In spite of the marked degree of their stylization, due to the confined area in which they were done, they catch with unmistakable clarity the typical traits of the subject being portrayed: the heavy curved muzzle, the half-open mouth with fleshy lips, the heavy lower jaw, the large eyes under the base of the antlers and the large fan-shaped ears. There are ornamental cuts on the nose and mandible, which in general repeat the outlines of these parts of the head. The antlers are shown sketchily by the brow tine and palmation with an ornamental knob in between. Skilfully fitted into closely confined limits, this pair of elk heads has a finished artistry of design. The excised areas of the pattern were covered with red lacquer, and consequently the bright yellow heads of the elks stand out sharply against this red background. For fixing the facings to the arches holes had been bored through from the outside at either end and in the middle.

Below the facings were additional ornaments: special pendants on the front arch (*Pl. 96E*) and round, flat runner beads at the rear (*Pl. 96C, D*). The small narrow pendants have a round hole in the top, and in the lower broader part a heart-shaped one. On the outer surface pairs of symmetrically disposed antler tines are incised. The symmetry and flowing lines harmonizing with the shape of the object give the pendants an especial beauty. The disk beads are exquisitely shaped, each one slightly distinguished from the others by its decoration. On one of them, with an oval opening in the middle between the margin and hole, three commas, with pointed ends like teeth, facing in the same direction, have been incised. Between inner and outer borders on the smaller beads there is a zone bearing incised horseshoes, dividing it into six lobe-shapes, of which three, as in the first bead, are covered by red lacquer. The straps for securing the crupper-strap were threaded through these runner beads.

At the ends of the straps joining the saddle cushions at back and front more substantial pendants had been hung (*Pl. 95F, G*), on which the decoration was the same as that of the pendants on the front saddle arch, incised antler tines, but in this case they have a twist at the bottom.

At the ends of the upper girth-strap were shield-shaped horn pendants similar to those already described, but without the heart-shaped slit (*Pl. 95H, I*). Its absence allowed the craftsman to give a more elaborate curl to the bottom, which gave this ornament its own style. All the incisions in the pendants just described were covered with red lacquer.

The semicircular plates in this set that were attached to the upper girth-strap at the saddle cushion are of great interest. They have oval openings for tying the ends of the breast-strap and bear representations of a facing feline head (*Pl. 96B*). The feline muzzle has been fitted into the obligatory semicircle with rare skill. Evidence of conventionalization is as marked in these as in the elk heads, but the significant features of the animal have been entirely caught. In the middle is the broad, heart-shaped nose, the great, half-open mouth with top lip formed by peculiar curls, the great, elongated eyes with tear ducts and the large, pointed ears with their characteristic twist. The composition can be compared with the well-known carnivore's muzzle depicted in the centre of a large hemispherical ornament from the Katanda barrow (*Pl. 140*C) or that on the horn plaque in the Frolov collection at the Hermitage (*Pl. 138*D).

The massive horn girth buckle (*Pl. 96*G) has its point on the front with an X-shaped slot for the girth-strap.

Four horn slides from saddle-straps for fastening the ends of the crupper-strap belong to this set (two large and two smaller) (*Pl. 95*D, E). The slits in the slides have been drilled with brace and bit of about 5 mm. diameter; six over-lapping holes were drilled in each case and then the intervening ridges whittled off (unevenly) with a knife. They were decorated outside by triangles, the incisions being filled with red lacquer.

One of the simplest sets of carved wooden bridle ornament from barrow 3 is shown in fig. 65. This bridle with bronze bit consists of two side-straps, nose-band and two throat-lashes. The strap-ends at the cheek-piece are decorated with strap 'concertinas', coloured red. Two of the latter with three pleats each are set on each side of the central decoration of the noseband. The straight cheek-pieces are carved at the ends into pyramids of four balls (three at the base and one on top). The straight shanks of the cheek-pieces, as with most of the wooden ones, are pasted with fine leather on three sides, the side touching the mouth of the horse being excepted. The pendant ornaments are just the same, a pyramid of carved wooden balls, fixed to three-petalled leather rosettes which are covered on the outside by red lacquer. On the back of the pendants, as on most of the similar decorations, special lugholes had been made for attachment to the bridle. The frontal plate is half-horseshoe shaped, flat underneath and slightly convex on top, and has two pairs of holes above for suspension by thongs. The slider is of antler with a hole for the rein-strap.

The next bridle set with an iron bit consisted of cheek-pieces, frontal plate of half-horseshoe shape, ornaments in the shape of six-rayed stars ('burdocks') in relief, hoof-shaped and pentagonal drop-shaped runners and a slider for the reins. The cheek-pieces have skilfully carved terminals of 'paw' shape (*Pl. 97*B). The 'burrs' were fixed to the strap intersections, mounted on leather disks covered by red lacquer. The frontal plate is of usual form, but bears incised ornament (*Pl. 98*B) coloured red, and the remaining parts, like the 'paws' and 'burrs', are covered by gold-leaf. Incised triangles, coloured red, decorate the hoof-shaped runner and the slider (*Pl. 98*F, G). The socket in the slider for the rein-strap was deep and conical, and the strap itself was secured by passing a thong through it, which was knotted at the edge of the aperture. A characteristic

151

detail of this bridle set is that the side-strap and noseband between their inter-sections are not only stitched together but covered outside by pieces of clipped white sheepskin.

The ornament on the wooden bridle decorations is equally simple, the motif being a little rosette. The bit is of iron. The cheek-pieces are straight with rosettes on the ends (*Pl. 97*c). Six hemispherical knobs are arranged in a ring within the rim and around a larger protuberance in the middle. The branches of the cheek-straps are decorated by plain 'concertinas'. Similar rosettes, but with seven knobs, decorate the strap intersections, the rosette being of two sizes, 4·7 cm. or 5·3 cm. in diameter (*Pl. 98*D). The circular frontal plate has a central protuberance.

Another bridle has a very interesting subject for its decoration—a swan. The bit is of bronze. The cheek-pieces are bronze rods, square in section, with figures of swans with turned-back heads fitted to the ends (*Pl. 97*A). The head and neck, and especially the beak, are exaggerated in size in relation to the body. The figures are shown in the round, but give only the general shape of the body. The beak with clearly indicated cere is coloured red, the eyes are indicated by excision and the aural openings by semicircles. Pendants of the same swan decorated the bridle-strap intersections (fig. 64). On the swans' shoulders, in the cheek-pieces only on the outside, but in the pendants on both, were bored conical holes into which had been fixed leather wings that unhappily no longer survived. Mention has already been made of the 'concertinas' near the cheek-pieces. On the right strap of the throat-lash a runner survived, shaped like a horse's hoof similar to that already described. The half-horseshoe shaped frontal plate and the slider were of the usual kind.

A bridle with a bronze bit in which the decoration had an unusual subject was illustrated earlier, from back and front, in order to describe the construction of a bridle (fig. 57). By analogy with a series of similar decorations known to us in the Altai and among the western Scyths this motif (*Pl. 98*H, I) can be regarded as a bird's head at the limits of stylization. Essentially all that remains of the head is the eye on a round protuberance and a hooked beak below. The cheek-piece terminals take this form, as do all the pendants.

In this bridle, as has been mentioned, there are a series of sewn details. In particular the side-straps and noseband below their junction and down to the cheek-pieces are stitched through along the edge with sinew thread, and in the middle of the noseband there is a supplementary decorative strap stitched on.

Another bridle from barrow 3 with bronze bit takes a special place, the decorative subject this time being mountain rams (*Pl. 99*A). The bridle-straps have not been folded double and stitched, as was the case with all the others from this barrow. Except the strap intersections and the middle of the nose-band, which are hidden by figures of rams, the rest of the straps are entirely covered by globules threaded on them. Together with globules, the other straps are threaded also with pendants of half-moon shape (*Pl. 98*A) and figures of rams like those in the upper part of the set. The breast-strap was therefore also decorated with rams and globules.

The cheek-pieces of this bridle (*Pl. 99*D) consist of bronze rods, just like those decorated with swans described above, to the ends of which are fitted wooden figures of the foreparts of mountain rams carved in high relief. In these somewhat roughly executed figures special attention has been given to the eyes and under-mane. The muzzle has been executed with some care. The neck is slightly humped, and on the retracted legs the hoofs have been carefully carved. The broad spatulate ears and large annulated horns are of leather and detachable, the method of attachment varying. The eyes were inserted into bored conical holes, but the horns, which had their own sockets, were secured by a thong threaded through an aperture at their base.

The pendants on the strap intersections and in the middle of the noseband consist of similar figures, but now the whole animal is represented (*Pl. 98*E), with forelegs raised up, the crupper twisted round so that the rear hoof touches the head (*Pl. 99*C). Due to the inserted ear and horn this leg is not visible, but without them the whole animal can be clearly seen. This stylistic device of representing animals in this especially striking way, by twisting their hind quarters round, is usual in the Pazyryk barrows. In this case, however, it was employed in order to fit the figure into a shape as close to a circle as possible, the shape desired for the plaque. The craftsman has acquitted himself brilliantly. Given a rather exaggerated head and extended neck with mane he has indicated the rest of the animal beautifully by a few bold strokes. Neck, back and hind quarters are represented by flowing lines; two or three lines indicate the chest, the shoulder girdle and the curved spine in the twisted back. The forelegs are quite naturally lifted, and rear ones in just that position we can observe rams and goats adopt when they scratch their heads. It hardly needs saying that there is some degree of conventionalization caused by artistic requirements, the rear hoof being bent back to balance the front hoof. Since each figure was carved separately they differ from one another in details.

The decoration on the bifurcation of the cheek-straps is individual, corresponding to the forks of the first two barrows. It consists of the sectionally split (as it were) and opened head of some kind of animal, a carnivore to judge by the shape of its ear and the way the eyes are represented (fig. 63).

There is a large frontal plate of half-horseshoe shape.

The globules threaded all along the bridle and breast-straps were alternately coloured red or covered with gold-leaf, and similarly the half-moon pendants were alternately reddened or covered with gold-leaf.

The globules are slightly spheroidal and have the perforation always following

153

the grain of the wood. Probably a hole was drilled in a stick of the right dimensions which was then cut up and carved into this globular shape.

The wooden slider block and the hoof-shaped runner (*Pl. 99*B) are of usual form.

There is a complete and very varied set of bridle and saddle decorations, of which the basic motif is an elk head. Its bit was an iron one. The large straight cheek-pieces have elk-head terminals, the insertable horns of which unfortunately no longer survive (*Pl. 100*A). The heads are well modelled, with wide nose, slightly opened mouth, fleshy lips and relatively large eyes and ears. The tip of the nose and the tongue are coloured red, and the ears and eyelids partially so. The elk heads in the bridle pendants are the same as in the cheek-pieces (*Pl. 100*B, C), but there is a curious variation in their methods of attachment. Out of nine pendants seven have different forms of attachment: sunken lugs of various kinds, perforations, and combinations of the two. In *Pl. 78* two examples are shown, double perforation and a lug. The frontal plate (*Pl. 100*D) took a curious form in this case, triangular, perhaps heart-shaped, with a notch in the upper edge.

The fork concealing the branching cheek-straps generally resembles the one in the bridle previously described (fig. 63). The split head of the carnivore, through which the straps passed, is similar, but some details, particularly the ears, are different (*Pl. 100*A). Like the elk heads in the pendants the mouth, eyelids, curl of the ears and the area between the ears have been reddened.

The ornaments in this set are abundant and varied. The saddle arch facings bear pairs of heraldically opposed elk heads as we have seen in similar horn facings, but in this instance all the decorations are of wood (*Pl. 101*A). The large size of the facings is noticeable (although slightly bowed they are 16·6 cm. wide), which corresponds to the large size of the arches. Comparing these facings with those described above it is clear that they repeat the same motif. A peculiarity of the wooden examples is that the heads bear no antlers, apart from a suggestion in the form of a small ridge over the head. These facings, like all the rest in this set, are coloured in the recesses, while the projections at the edge and on the head are covered with gold-leaf. One detail noticed was that the eye in the right elk head was not finished (*Pl. 101*A). The craftsman evidently forgot in this case to incise the outline of the eye as was done on the other heads.

Under the facings, as with the saddles with horn ornaments, drop-shaped, flat pendants were attached bearing a stylized antler design (*Pl. 102*C). Similar designs were used on the broad scutiform pendants fixed to either end of the front and back straps joining the two cushions, and at the end of the upper girth-strap (*Pl. 102*A, B). The last two are somewhat larger. It is not clear where the four semicircular plaques belong that show a slightly different variant of the stylized antlers (*Pl. 101*B, C). Since the plaques just listed occurred in two sets we have to assume that two saddles bore similar decoration.

154

The upper rim of the front saddle arch bore an interesting decoration, resembling what we shall see in one of the saddles from barrow 5. This consists of lion cubs, or strictly speaking their heads, the fore part of the body including the shoulders and the tip of their turned-back tail approaching the head (*Pl. 102*E–G). The little muzzles are thick and wide, and the half-open mouth shows a fleshy tongue. The nose is narrow and the eyes well cut with sharp creasing above the brows, while the mandible is hemispherical and the ears have the characteristic curl. These profile figures fixed one behind another, alternately painted red or covered with gold-leaf, were stitched on to a strap sewn round the edge of the saddle arches.

The decoration of the crupper-strap is interesting, consisting of plaques covering the straps near the back arch of the saddle, and of bilobate runners on crupper- and breast-straps. The plaques, of elongated trapeze shape, have figures of hares excised on them, their heads directed towards the broader end (*Pl. 102*I, J). The figures are characteristically hare-like, with short, softly outlined muzzles, large long ears, and short tails. The paws are typical for the hare, two-digited in one case, three-digited in the other. The animal is shown startled, and with the crupper twisted round. A characteristic feature, but not often found in such figures, is a spiral ribbon along the twisted spine. Although depicted in the same attitude the hare in one case is longer than in the other, but in neither case does the figure fill the area available on the plaque. The free space is occupied in one case by three, in the other by four, teeth, which may be a convention for grass or bushes. The recesses were reddened and the border covered with gold-leaf.

Bilobate runner beads (*Pl. 101*D) decorated the breast- and crupper-straps, and, like the lion cubs, they are alternately reddened and covered with gold-leaf. Their average length is 2·4 cm. and width 1·5 cm., and they are flat underneath, convex on top but with a longitudinal groove that makes them bilobate in section. A thin thong passed through their perforations; the whole chain was secured to a thin strap by a thong in such a way that nothing of it was visible outside, but underneath it was intertwined with the strap above, winding between the beads. This thin strap with the beads was then fixed on the breast- and crupper-straps.

There is another bridle with decoration based on the head of the saiga antelope (*Pl. 103*E). The straight cheek-pieces have expanded ends of rhomboidal shape, almost flat on the inside but keeled on the other. Red leather is stuck over the inside and gold-leaf on the outside of the expanded ends. The sculptural saiga heads are carved in the same way as the elk heads were, but with deep creases on the blunt, large-nostrilled snout, round eyes with tear ducts and large ears (*Pl. 103*B, C). The insertable horns are of leather. In the half-opened mouth the tongue is reddened, but the rest of the head is covered with gold-leaf.

155

At the strap junctions and in the middle of the noseband the heads are stitched on with the help of thongs passed through perforations in the mandibles under the eyes.

A runner in the shape of a young saiga's head is especially interesting (the tiny horns are shown by bumps). On account of the head being extended the ears are relatively longer and narrower than in the large heads, the eyes not circular, and due to its length the snout has five instead of four creases. The half-open mouth is reddened. A thong passed through the perforation was tied at the front end with a knot and extended inwards into the mouth (*Pl. 103*D).

The frontal plate is of the usual half-horseshoe shape (*Pl. 103*A); the cheek-straps are decorated by a leather 'concertina' coloured red (*Pl. 103*E).

Because of the skill employed in its manufacture, the subject and its peculiarities of style, a set of bridle and saddle decoration that makes use of a horned lion's head must be set apart from the others. The bit is made of iron. The shank of the S-shaped cheek-pieces is rectangular in section, and has a splendid horned head of a lion or cat in profile at the upper end and a griffin's head on the lower end (*Pl. 104*A). The open jaws reveal great fangs, the upper lip is strongly puckered, the muzzle is blunt and feline, the large eye is in relief, the long ear is treated in typically carnivore fashion with a curl at the base and the horns are short, annulated and bent back at the ends. The head may be conventionalized, but it is worked out in detail; with the griffin the conventionalization of treatment is carried much further. Essentially only a schema of the head is shown: eyes, beak and comb or ear represented by a curl, and just a hint of the lower jaw. Nevertheless it is extremely expressive. This is the way the griffin heads were shown on the tips of the antler tines and on the necks of the monsters in the tattooing, on the tine tips on the back of the costume from barrow 2, and in the cheek-pieces from barrow 5, with which we shall become acquainted below. We know of many other griffins' heads treated similarly to those of the Altai in the art of the Black Sea Scyths.

The pendants from this set consist of the same lions' heads as on the cheek-pieces, in profile and *en face*, slightly differently treated (*Pl. 104*B, C, G). The profile heads are almost identical to those on the cheek-pieces except that the lower edge of the ear is not smooth but notched. The heads look right or left according to the side of the bridle on which they were fixed, those looking straight ahead being attached to the noseband. The latter have fairly broad noses, like the profile ones, with distinct nostrils; the upper lip is puckered; the large eyes have tear ducts; the ears and horns are raised, the latter with a curl or rather a knob on the end. All the details of manufacture are the same as with the profile ones. The profile heads, as usual, were attached at the strap junctions by means of a sunken lug on the back, but the facing heads were attached by a thong passed through them at the root of the nose.

156

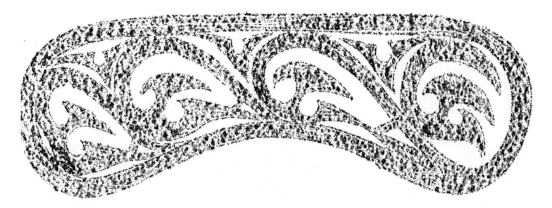

77. Gold-leaf decoration from front saddle arch in barrow 3 ($\frac{2}{3}$).

78. Gold-leaf decoration from saddle-strap in barrow 3 ($\frac{2}{3}$).

79. Gold leaf decoration from upper girth-strap in barrow 3 ($\frac{2}{3}$).

157

80. Gold-leaf decoration on upper girth-strap from barrow 3 ($\frac{1}{2}$).

81. Gold-leaf decoration from front saddle arch in barrow 3 ($\frac{1}{2}$).

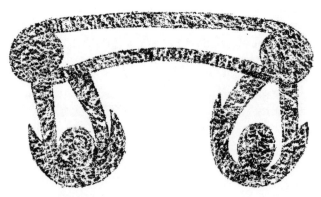

82. Gold-leaf decoration on saddle arch in barrow 3 ($\frac{1}{2}$).

83. Gold-leaf decoration on saddle arch in barrow 3 ($\frac{1}{2}$).

The wooden fork for the cheek-straps is of the same type as the forks from barrow 1, except that it was fixed to them not by a lug at the back but by a pair of perforations at its ends (*Pl. 104*H). The motif of the ornament is 'running waves' and a sloping comb above. The rein slider is of the normal type (*Pl. 104*E).

The pendants decorating the saddle-straps, facing horned lions' heads, resemble the bridle ones, except that they are carved with a horseshoe-shaped base and are not in such high relief (*Pl. 104*D, F). One pair is larger than the other. The bases are decorated in red colour while the heads, as throughout the set, are covered with gold.

The saddle, the front arches of which were decorated by half-horseshoe shaped leather cut-outs ornamented with stylized antlers (fig. 72H), had wooden pendants bearing the same decoration. Those attached to the front arch were identical to those on the saddle the arches of which were adorned with elks' heads (*Pl. 102*C). Similarly the pendants on the saddle-strap were the same as on the other saddle (*Pl. 102*A, B), the same stylized antlers, but forming a more intricate pattern.

The decoration of the saddle was highly unusual: the arches had fine leather covering the brown felt, decorated by an open-work pattern of half-horseshoes cut from gold-leaf with red lacquer in the recesses, as shown in fig. 77. Just the same pattern of long gold strips occurred elsewhere, relatively narrow on the front and back straps that joined the cushions (fig. 78), and wide on the upper girth-strap (fig. 79). The pendants on these straps made use of the same antler motif, but in a simpler version (*Pl. 105*C) than on those discussed above. On the narrow pendants at the front arches the same motif was used again (*Pl. 105*F).

In *Pl. 102*D one of these pendants is shown at the end of a strap which is fixed to a wooden saddle spacer bar. This strap is of double thickness leather below and a strip of felt above, both layers being stitched together by sinew thread along the edge. The pendant is attached by means of a narrow thong.

The saddle, the arches of which were covered with fine leather pasted with red lacquer with a gold-leaf pattern stuck on, obviously had been very richly decorated, but it was only possible to determine the decoration on the front arch. The latter was decorated, not only in front but also on the top edge, with applied gold-leaf cut-outs using the pattern shown in *Pl. 163*A. There was a remarkable, broad (7 cm.), open-work, gold-leaf, applied strip on the upper girth-strap (fig. 80). The intricate pattern on this strip consists of stylized antlers with grooved ox-horns, triangles with a round notch at the base, commas with grooves in the shape of commas but of smaller size. The scutiform pendants on the straps of this saddle (*Pl. 105*B) bear decoration similar to that on the arch facings, which can be regarded as a variant on the ox horn. One was found with a saddle-strap to which it was attached, the strap being doubled and sewn down the

159

middle. Over the strap on the outside was sewn a strip of thin red felt, and on this, at 4·5 cm. from the lower end, was a leather disk covered with gold, and below was a fine felt runner, also covered with gold. To the same set belongs a semicircular plaque with a grooved decoration of ox horns (*Pl. 105G*). All the plaques of this set are reddened in the grooves and their projecting surfaces covered with gold-leaf.

In passing we can briefly describe the methods of attaching the pendants to the saddle-strap found in barrow 3. When the pendant had a pair of apertures a thong was threaded through these and tied on the back of the strap. When there were three or more holes attachment was carried out as follows: a narrow doubled thong was passed through the hole in the pendant and the strap; a loop was made at the back and a short leather sprig passed through it and then the strap tightened up.

The last set of wooden saddle pendants from barrow 3, consisting of two narrow ones fixed to the front arch and six broad ones attached to the saddle-straps, has a decoration that almost defies description (*Pl. 105A, E*). In the narrow pendants the ornament could perhaps be described as incised triangles and squares, but in the broad ones it is difficult to separate out the distinct elements.

A series of motifs in the decoration of front saddle arches in barrow 3 were recorded during the excavation. Besides those mentioned above we have the following patterns. On an oval piece of leather covered by red lacquer there were three gold disks with circular openings in the middle, the central disk being larger than the other two (*Pl. 163F*). Another motif was a gold S-shaped figure in an oval gold frame against a background of red lacquer (*Pl. 163D*). A third motif was a cut-out of gold-leaf of half-horseshoe shape with circles at the ends and a void in between (fig. 81). A fourth was the same arc, but with balls suspended from it (fig. 82).

The decoration on the next three arches is just as plain, but distinguished merely by the range of materials employed. On *Pl. 163B* there is a semicircle above a broad strip of dark brown felt trimmed with a band of blue felt; on the brown strip are blue circles. The upper segment is bright yellow felt trimmed around the arc with a strip of blue felt, and along the chord are pasted a series of rectangles cut from tinfoil and gold-leaf. Another arch was covered by brown felt (*Pl. 163C*) with a blue felt half-horseshoe in front and a gold circle in its middle. The back part was also covered by a half-horseshoe of white (yellowed in the tomb) felt, piped with twisted woollen cord, which had three rows of rectangles pasted on it, two of gold and one of tinfoil. Another arch was covered by yellow felt (*Pl. 163E*) and has a half-horseshoe in front, piped with woollen cord and with a gold comma in the middle. The upper edge is covered by a band of blue felt in the middle of which is pasted a comma of gold-leaf with curls of the same material along the edge. The inside of the arch is also piped and decorated with a series of gold and tin rectangles.

Some saddle plates were decorated with gold-leaf cut-outs of half-horseshoe shape, similar to those cut from leather, but with a toothed ornament in the horseshoe (fig. 83). There are also oval gold facings with an internal toothed edge.

Besides the varied, elaborate saddle decorations just described there were some quite plain facings from two saddles. These are mainly facings on arches of trapezoidal and bow shape (*Pl. 106*). There are four of these and others in the sets, corresponding to the number of cushion faces, which the horn bows covered along the edge on top. These facings resemble those we have already met and are half-horseshoe shaped, but their lower edge instead of being rounded is right-angled. The semicircular notches under such facings were deeper and had a conical runner to attach them. With such facings the horn bows take the same shape as the upper edge of the facing.

The trapezoidal facings have a slightly convex edge and rounded corners on top with bent, almost right-angled, corners at the bottom. In the centre is a hole. In this set the bows which cover the upper edge of the arch reproduce the shape of the upper edge of the facing (*Pl. 106*A, B). It should be noted that the same number of holes were drilled in the top and sides of the bows as in the facings; clearly facing and bow were secured to the arch plate at the same time and with the same thong. Saddle arches with such facings were extra firm and rigid.

Plain horn pendants cannot be assigned to a definite saddle, and I shall confine myself merely to enumerating their types and indicating their significance.

Pairs of narrow pendants (*Pl. 107*E, F) come from the front arches of two saddles. Four large, long and narrow pendants (*Pl. 107*A) adorned strap ends, and the shield-shaped pendants of medium size, examples of which are illustrated in *Pl. 107*B–D, served the same purpose. Large, wide pendants (*Pl. 107*L–N) were from upper girth-straps.

Semicircular facings (*Pl. 107*J, K), with pairs of oval apertures along the straight side, had been stitched on to the girth-strap at the edge of the saddle cushions and the ends of the breast-strap made fast to them. There are such pendants from three saddles: from the two described above with horn facings on the arch plates and from a third not identified. From crupper-straps of one of these saddles there are horn slides (*Pl. 107*I). One of the two horn plates with holes in the end (*Pl. 107*G) was probably a spacer, while *Pl. 107*H illustrates a low conical horn runner.

From barrow 4 not a single bridle or saddle has survived, but we can draw some inferences about them from the surviving horn and wooden accessories and decorations. All the same, what did survive is of great interest, and the wooden cut-outs decorating the bridles make a significant addition to those from the first three barrows.

To judge by the bridle, and especially the saddle, facings and decorations, the bridles and saddles from barrow 4 were identical to those of barrow 3.

There were two sets of bridle decorations: one quite plain and another of the same manufacture as in barrow 3 but simpler. In the first set the cheek-pieces were simply unworked antler tines (*Pl. 108*C). Quite as plain are the barrel- and hoof-shaped antler bridle-strap runners (*Pl. 108*F–H). The horn reins slider is of normal shape (*Pl. 108*I).

The antler cheek-pieces of the second set are flattish oval, not round, in section, and bear excised decorative triangles on both sides at both ends (*Pl. 108*A, B). The bridle-straps were adorned with ball-shaped runners of two kinds: those with ocular decoration, and those that were entirely plain and smooth (*Pl. 108*D, E). The reins slider is oval in section (*Pl. 108*L).

A peculiarity of the reins sliders, like that already mentioned in the others in barrow 4 (*Pl. 108*J), is that the method of attachment to the rein differs from that used in barrow 3. Instead of a socket for the end of the rein, a perforation had been made which was used to tie it. In addition, as we shall see, in barrow 4 flat sliders were found, which was not the case in barrow 3.

Two saddles had been furnished with horn facings and pendants. One saddle with high arches had facings and bows of a type already familiar to us from barrow 3 (*Pl. 109*A–C). Under the facings of the front arches narrow pendants were fixed (*Pl. 109*G), and under the rear facings low conical runners (*Pl. 109*F). The saddle-straps were decorated with scutiform and semicircular horn facings (*Pl. 109*I, M). The arches of the second saddle had no facings, but two narrow pendants were attached to the front arch (*Pl. 109*H). On the ends of the front and rear saddle cross-straps small scutiform pendants of two kinds (*Pl. 109*J, K) were suspended, while on the upper girth-strap very individual kinds of plates were attached, through which the end of the breast-strap protruded (*Pl. 109*L). The lower girth buckle was of the same kind as found in barrow 2, except that its end was not curved but straight (*Pl. 108*M). Tiny, short slides (*Pl. 109*D, E) have survived. The attachment straps were provided with the same wooden toggles as in the other barrows (*Pl. 102*H).

I turn now to describe the wooden decorations of the bridle. Wooden cheek-pieces of S-shape from one of the bridles have a high-relief representation of a wolf's head at the top end and an excised triangle at the lower expanded end (*Pl. 110*A). The head has a narrow nose, puckered top lip, pointed ear and large eye. Remarkable high-relief figures of wolf with turned back head and twisted hind quarters decorated the strap junctions of this bridle (*Pl. 110*B). The craftsman has not attempted a realistic representation, but has exaggerated the head

162

to about two-thirds the size of the whole figure. The mouth is shown open, fangs bared, upper lip puckered, as with a growling animal. The nose is long and thin, the eye in relief, the ear has a curl at the end, while the lower jaw is shown with two creases. The feeble little body terminates in a long curling tail, and the unnaturally retracted legs have been treated in a conventionalized manner. A characteristic peculiarity of this figure, already observed in the hares from barrow 3, is the curved line along the backbone that harmonizes with the writhing figure of the beast. Apart from the hares I know of a spiral line only on a gold plate in the Siberian collection of Peter the Great, where a horned and winged griffin has bitten into the withers of a horse.[1] In spite of its excessive stylization the figure of this convulsively writhing animal with disjointed backbone has been caught in a remarkable way and all the typical features preserved. The task that had to be solved, to fit the shape of the animal into a bridle plate, has been accomplished with distinction. In the set there were eight such plates, four with the wolf's head turned in one direction, and four in the opposite direction, depending on which side of the bridle they were to be fixed.

The second set of bridle decorations also employed the wolf as their theme. The S-shaped cheek-pieces have a wolf's head at the upper terminal (*Pl. 110*D, E) and an incised triangle on the lower expanded end (*Pl. 110*C). The wolf's head is the same as that described above except that the upper lip is not puckered [2] and the muzzle is more pointed. The plaques adorning the straps of this bridle show the head of a roebuck held in the jaws of a wolf (*Pl. 110*F). The long-snouted wolf muzzle, a few details apart, has been basically reproduced in the same way as in the wolf in the last set. The roebuck's head is schematized but fairly expressive. The craftsman has, as usual, paid particular attention to the eyes: those of the roe deer are typical and those of the wolf particularly wolfish. The pretty little muzzle of the former is good. The long extended ear of the roe deer and its lower jaw are so drawn that the twist of the ear coincides with the angle of the mandible. The inside of the ear, the creases on the lower jaw of the wolf and the head of the roe deer are coloured red and the rest of the surface covered with gold, while all the other bridle adornments from this barrow have been entirely covered by gold-leaf. The set being described had eight wolves' heads, four looking in either direction. The frontal plate is narrow and serpentine, sharply convex, almost semicircular in section (*Pl. 110*G).

A unique bridle set has a cat or kitten as the motif of its decoration. The profile heads of cats on the upper cheek-piece terminals (which are badly decayed) have a narrow nose, large eye, half-open mouth and large circular ear with a curl inside (*Pl. 111*C). The lower terminals bear the usual form in this

---

[1] Rudenko, A, 1962b, Pl. VIII, 7 and 8.

[2] [Translator's note. There appears to be some confusion here, for the description and plate do not tally. This description applies to the cheek-pieces from the first set, unless the letters in the plate should be transposed. M.W.T.]

84. Carved wooden kitten from bridle decoration in barrow 4 ($\frac{1}{1}$).

barrow, an incised triangle (*Pl. 111*A). The bridle-plates consist of high-relief representations of a cat with a large sculptural head (*Pl. 111*E, G), the direction in which it faced depending on how it was attached to the bridle. In spite of the repeated examples (eight in all) no two figures are identical. The animals are all shown in the same recumbent position, with front paws extended forward and tail depressed. In some the muzzle is up, with others down; sometimes the head is raised, with others turned to one side and slightly inclined. By comparison with the dimensions of the body the heads are exaggerated. The eyes are large and, as always, sharply cut. The broad muzzles have a characteristically feline nose with slight hook and the ears protrude as in the cheek-pieces. There are whiskers on the cheeks. The front paws, as in the hares in barrow 3, are three-digited, while the back ones are the same as in the wolf. On the shoulder girdle the characteristic comma has been incised, and on the back the half-horseshoe, the ribs being indicated by deeply incised brackets. On one of the cats there are two commas on the shoulder girdle and on the back a stop and three half-horseshoes (fig. 84). The figures were covered with gold-leaf, except the points, commas and half-horseshoes, which were covered with red lacquer.

Similar bridle ornaments in the form of a recumbent animal, but made of metal, are known among the Black Sea Scyths.[1]

The frontal plate of this set was round with a hemispherical protuberance in the middle.

[1] S. N. Zamyatnin, A, fig. 14, 4. Figures of hares from the excavations of Bobrinsky in Krivorukov, near Zhurovka (formerly Chigirin-sky in Kiev district): *Report of the Imperial Archaeological Commission* (1905), issue 14, p. 27, fig. 64.

An extremely interesting set contained high-relief, facing heads of a feline carved in horn medallions. The cheek-pieces, like all the others from this barrow, were S-shaped with profile, large-eared, horned lions' or cats' heads at the upper terminal and an engraved triangle on the rounded, expanded lower end (*Pl. 111*B). Here we see the familiar feline head with large eye, hooked nose, slightly open mouth and puckered upper lip. The horn with a knob on the end is pressed down and covered by the long, narrow ear. In the circular bridle-plaques the heads are shown just as in the cheek-pieces but face on (*Pl. 111*D, F). The heads are enclosed by three concentric circles, stepped down and outwards, which gives them a quality of relief or of being hemispherical. Their eyes are large and slanted, the nose wide with nostrils indicated and the upper lip puckered. The horns with knobs on the end are partly hidden, as in the cheek-pieces, by long ears with characteristic twist at the bottom. Some of the plaques are smaller than the rest.

It is of some interest to compare the horned feline heads of this set with similar heads from barrow 3 (*Pl. 104*). The subject is the same, although in barrow 4 the ears pass over the horns, whereas in barrow 3 they were beside the horns. There are stylistic differences: the heads of barrow 4 are closer to nature than those of barrow 3.

A bird's-head motif employed in another set is original. The S-shaped cheek-pieces have a large-eared bird's head at the upper end, the lower being spatulate and bifurcate (*Pl. 112*E). The combination in this profile head of a circular bird's eye and eagle's beak with an evidently mammal's ear typically curled at the base is noticeable. The pendants consist of the same bird *en face*, the head being carved in the round; the body, wing and tail are so conventionalized that, were it not for the head, we would have regarded the rest as some merely ornamental motif not connected with birds. The head, indeed, is not wholly birdlike (*Pl. 112*G, H). The hooked beak is clearly a bird's with its well-indicated cere, as also are the round eyes, but as on the cheek-pieces there are ears. From the head there are expanding projections; one short with a knob on the end, another long (wing and tail) with a curl, touching the short projection above on the opposite side. The latter is on the right or left side according to how it was fixed to the bridle. Each figure was covered by gold-leaf and fixed to a leaf-shaped leather pad reddened with lacquer. The frontal plate of this bridle was of narrow, serpentine shape, like the one described above.

The decorations on the bridle of the horse put in the north-east corner of the burial shaft were markedly different from the rest. Their peculiarity lay not so much in the originality of motif of the monster used, nor in its manufacture from wood and leather, but in the existence of a special carved wooden crest representing the great head of the same monster that adorned the bridle-straps (*Pl. 113*B, C).

At first sight the cheek-pieces of this bridle recall the already familiar ones

85. Leather cut-out bridle decoration from barrow 4 ($\frac{1}{3}$).

with wolf-head upper terminal. Closer examination, however, reveals essential differences. This is especially so with the more humpy nose, slightly flattened at the end. The puckering on the upper lip is longitudinal, not transverse, and the most important thing to notice is the presence of large boar's tusks curving upwards (*Pl. 112*A). It is not a wolf's head, therefore, that is represented but that of a boar. This motif corresponds with the heads that we shall see on the bridle-straps and crest (*Pl. 112*I).

The straps of the headstall are decked from top to bottom with leather cut-outs of three monsters (fig. 85 shows two of them). They occur in two variants, barely differing. The lower figure at the bifurcation of the cheek-straps is a feline animal in profile with a very long tail, curled at the end and terminating in a brush resembling a bird's head. Its narrow wings are lifted up, the tips pointing forward, and the carved wooden head is inserted. The claw-like paws, rendered conventionally, look like crab's pincers or a scorpion's tail. The figure is fixed on an individual, two-lobed base; comparison with its neighbour makes the idea evident. The figures arranged higher up are basically the same, but the wings are not lifted so high and are rather differently shaped. The front paw is not pincer-shaped but more like a feline claw, but the rear paw finishes in two broad projections, like that in the first figure. The two figures are joined by the profile head of a monster, cut out of leather, with round eye, large spatulate ear, snub nose and open mouth. Its lower jaw has a broad projection, like that at the extremity of the rear foot of the second figure.

The wooden insertable heads of these figures, carved in the round, are most

166

remarkable. They have short muzzles with boar's tusk and humped nose terminating in a characteristic pig's snout. The top raised lip is vertically puckered, the creases intersecting the snout. The eyes are round with tear ducts, while very long pointed ears of leather stick upwards, and the inserted horns are also cut out of leather. The heads were attached by thin thongs threaded through holes in the front and middle part of the neck.

The same kind of head, but twice the size, was fixed to the headstall above the horse's sinciput to serve as a crest (*Pl. 113*B, C). Again we see long, pointed, protruding ears of leather, and large leather horns, not antlers, but ring-shaped with disk terminals. One side of the disk was covered with red lacquer and the other pasted over with bronze circles covered externally with chipped ornament (fig. 86).

There were undecorated bridles in barrow 4 of which only the wooden cheek-pieces survived. One pair of cheek-pieces was like those with birds' heads described above, but the bird's ear was longer. An individual pair had a bird's head at the upper terminal with large eye, inserted leather ear (the socket survives) and large beak curving upward at the end (*Pl. 112*B). The lower terminals took a split, expanded shape, varying slightly, with excised triangles on their faces (*Pl. 112*C, D, F).

The sliders in barrow 4 differ from those in barrow 3. It is difficult to refer individual examples to particular bridles since they are all much the same. They are all made of antler, flat, with a small aperture in the upper part where the end of the rein was secured, and a large round opening for the sliding lead-rein. One of the large ones has been carefully made, the others carelessly, leaving the natural rugose surface of the antler (*Pl. 108*J–L).

As a result of the relatively good preservation of bridles and saddles from barrow 5 we can study them set by set, just as we did with barrow 1.

86. Decoration on a little copper disk from horse crest in barrow 4 ($\frac{1}{1}$).

In the first set the cheek-pieces are straight, with the shank sewn around with leather. The carved terminals bear eight grooves separated by arrises (*Pl. 113*A). Similar eight-sided figures, fixed to leather squares and rhombs reddened with lacquer, adorned the bridle-strap intersections, the middle of the noseband and the breast-strap. The small frontal plate took the shape of a half-horseshoe (fig. 62). The ends of the side-straps and noseband are intertwined, and at this point and the cheek-pieces there is an ornamental 'concertina' of thirteen folds (*Pl. 113*A).

The front saddle arches were sewn over with leather, covered by red lacquer and decorated with leather cut-outs covered with gold disks, and also by narrow unornamented wooden pendants. The straps holding the saddle cushions at back and front have pendants of the same scutiform shape at their ends (fig. 69B). Along the edges of the thick upper girth-strap (5·2 cm. wide) narrow ribbons of gold-leaf are pasted, between which are a series of rectangles (3 cm. by 3·4 cm.), cut from thin leather and alternately covered by gold-leaf and red lacquer. At the cushions semicircular plaques are attached to the same strap with holes for making fast the ends of the breast-straps (fig. 68A). To the back arch short straps are attached on the outside with wooden slides and the same pendants (fig. 70B) as on the saddle-strap ends. All the wooden plaques were covered with gold-leaf.

A great felt shabrack (58 cm. by 208 cm.) under this saddle was decorated along its lower edge by red woollen tassels fixed in wooden cups. The outer surface of this shabrack was covered by a very fine woollen cloth of dark cherry colour with a design of columns in squares, sewn on with separate pieces of cloth (*Pl. 177*B). The cloth is imported. The central field of the shabrack is covered by this cloth, but is bordered by another no less remarkable textile, pieces of which are sewn between two narrow bands of black colt's fur. The subject in the design on this cloth, reproduced in Gobelin technique, shows two pairs of women standing in front of a censer or altar within a toothed frame (fig. 139). The material had been cut up into pieces to make the border on the shabrack without any regard to the original pattern (*Pl. 177*C).

With this shabrack, as in all the others in barrow 5, besides the saddle breast-strap there was a special breast decoration consisting of a narrow felt band, on which was also sewn a strip of imported woollen cloth decorated in Gobelin technique. This showed a procession of lions one behind the other (*Pl. 177*A; fig. 140).

This shabrack, like all the rest from barrow 5, had a plain felt expanse (34 cm. wide) with no trimming under the saddle. In saddling the horse the lower girth-strap was passed through special slits made in both sides of the shabrack.

There were no complicated adornments in the second saddlery outfit in barrow 5.

The large straight cheek-pieces with carefully carved shanks have disk terminals, which have double concentric circles around a central protuberance (*Pl. 114*). The same motif has been applied on all the plaques fixed to the bridle and breast-strap intersections, the middle of the noseband and also the frontal plate. The bifurcation of the cheek-straps is covered by a wooden fork decorated with 'running waves'.

It is a plain saddle, the arches trimmed with red woollen cloth, in the middle of which are attached large low conical runners covered with gold-leaf. The saddle pendants are scutiform and decorated with stylized deer antlers, resembling a set of horn pendants that we have seen in barrow 3. The grooves were coloured red and the rest covered with gold. Two such small pendants had been fixed to the front saddle arches, two large ones at the end of the upper girth-strap and the remaining four on the end of the straps joining the saddle cushions (*Pl. 118*D, E)

The shabrack under the saddle is of fine white felt (measuring 70 cm. by 236 cm.). A comparatively narrow (24 cm.) band down the middle has been left un-decorated, the remainder of the upper face being covered with coloured (red, blue and grey) felt appliqué work (*Pl. 160*). Five deer antlers set in a circle are depicted in fine felt cut-outs; the figures are not sewn round the edge, as in the other appliqué work, but only in a circle in the centre, on which a four-petalled rosette is embroidered. So the edges are free to flutter. They are framed within a frieze of stylized antlers and a stylized lotus flower with the traditional notched triangle at its base. Separate antlers are shown on a stitched-on fringe. The pattern on the breast-band (9 cm. by 98 cm.) is the same. The frieze is sewn to the shabrack on the right side while on the left it is attached by a special thong.

In the third outfit the small S-shaped cheek-pieces have a profile cat's head on the upper terminal, and expand to a comma shape at the bottom (*Pl. 117*A). The feline head, with which we are already familiar, has a raised, puckered upper lip, narrow nose, large eye and wide round ear with a curl.

The bridle-strap junctions and breast-strap are decorated with sculptural feline heads (*Pl. 117*B), executed in the same style as the head on the cheek-pieces. The side-straps and noseband after intertwining are covered above the cheek-pieces by a wooden fork in the shape of a kind of profile wolf's head (*Pl. 117*A). In fact only the upper prong is a wolf's head, the lower jaw being shown plain with decoration only underneath. These are the characteristics of the head: long, narrow, puckered nose with a snub tip, low forehead, carefully carved eye and a large ear with curl. The frontal plate is half-horseshoe shaped.

The saddle is plain with the arches covered by red lacquer.

The felt shabrack under the saddle (64–68 cm. by 220 cm.), which expands at either end, is waisted in the middle. With the exception of the narrow (12 cm.)

strip in the middle it is covered by a coloured appliqué pattern. The basic colours are red, blue, orange and greenish, but since some parts of the original colouring have faded there are additional shades (*Pl. 161*). The edge is trimmed with a band of blue felt. The applied decoration is overlapping, with three similar repeated motifs following one after another, but because of the changing colours of the background the pattern becomes complicated. The motif consists of stylized deer antlers of two types. The ornamented field is framed by narrow (9 cm.) bands of ornament in the form of red stylized antlers on a background of greenish and orange circles. The breast-band, which bears the same pattern, measures 9 cm. by 104 cm. and is secured to the shabrack on both sides by thongs.

The basic theme of decoration on the fourth set is the head of a saiga antelope. The cheek-pieces (fig. 58) are straight with a saiga on the upper end and a comma on the lower (*Pl. 115*B). The antelope's mouth is half open, the hooked nose wrinkled, the eye round, with tear duct, the mandible ending in a curl, the ear broad and spatulate with twist at the bottom, and the horn shaped like a screw. The saiga heads decorating the strap intersections and breast-strap are sculptural representations mounted on red lacquered leather flakes and the ears and horns are leather inserts. The heads in the middle of the noseband and breast-strap do not have leather horns and ears, these being carved from one piece with the head (*Pl. 115*A). The bifurcation of the cheek-straps is covered by a wooden fork decorated with 'running waves', gentle or with toppling crests. The frontal plate is half-horseshoe shaped (fig. 58).

The bridle, breast- and crupper-straps are decorated outside, not only with saiga heads, but also by a series of grooved runner beads stitched on to them, as in one set in barrow 3. In this case the runners are all attached quite differently, by a thong passing through the strap and the runner perforation.

The saddle in this set is very carefully decorated (fig. 66). Its large arches are covered by facings of thick leather with horses' heads, back to back, excised, showing trimmed manes and large stylized ears. The background on which the horses' heads are depicted has been reddened (*Pl. 164*B). Thick leather bow-shaped facings, bearing incised ornament, cover the upper edges of the arches, which are partially coloured red or blue (*Pl. 164*A). In the wooden scutiform pendants, fixed on the front arches, and on the ends of the straps joining the saddle cushions, carved cats' heads of an original kind have been hung (*Pl. 115*C–E). These heads with slanting eyes are huge down to the ears, the upper lip is puckered, the large protruding ears have a curl at the bottom, the screw-shaped horns have knobs or curls at the end. Each one has been carved so individually that even in one head the work in one half does not always correspond with the other. On the upper girth-straps, next to the cushions, half-horseshoe-shaped plaques of thick leather have been sewn on, with holes for securing the breast-strap ends. On these plaques are excised pairs of heraldically

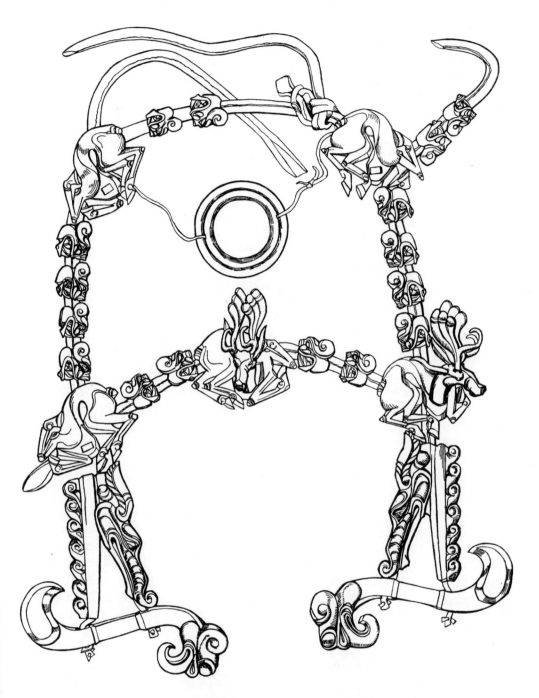

87. Bridle from barrow 5.

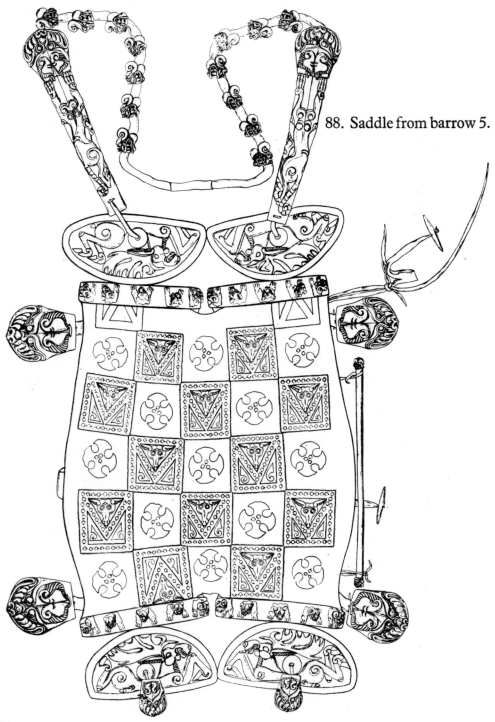

88. Saddle from barrow 5.

opposed, profile saiga heads (*Pl. 164*c). On the ends of the upper girth-strap thick leather facings of shield shape have been sewn with a hole in the bottom for passing the end of the lower girth-strap through. It also is decorated with incised ornament in the shape of stylized deer antlers (*Pl. 164*D). The background of all those excised leather patterns has been reddened.

There are very interesting decorations for the crupper-strap, expanded at one end and fixed to the back saddle-arch (*Pl. 115*F). The straps were covered by pairs of linked wooden plaques: a long one, bearing a series of repeating triangular figures notched at the bottom, and the other like the saddle pendants bearing representations of a horned feline head. Comparing these plaques with the similar ones from the next (the fifth) set in barrow 5 it can be inferred that originally the body of an animal was depicted on it, and that then the more complicated ornament, that we now see there, was substituted for it.

The upper face of the felt shabrack of this saddle (measuring 65 cm. by 233 cm.; undecorated strip in the middle 40 cm. wide) was covered by a pattern of polychrome felt (white, yellow, blue and red) (*Pl. 162*). Due to the intersecting strips bearing an ornament of triple teeth the main pattern is divided into rhombs, within each of which is a quatrefoil or rosette. Quatrefoils within circles decorate the band intersections. The border is decorated basically with griffins and three-petalled figures in triangles. On the lower edge from plaited woollen cords hang wooden pendants which bear representations of unopened buds with reddened petals. The breast-band bears the same decoration as the border of the shabrack itself.

The richest set of saddlery decoration occurred in the fifth outfit (figs. 87, 88). The solid S-shaped bridle cheek-pieces have a large-eared griffin head at the upper terminal with spatulate comma-shaped bottom terminal (*Pl. 116*A). The griffin has a big round eye, strongly curved, hooked eagle's beak with cere above and large round ear with a curl inside. The bridle-strap intersections with the breast-strap, the middle of the noseband and breast-strap are decorated with high-relief figures of deer with their cruppers twisted round and inserted sculptural heads (*Pl. 116*B). The deer is in a different attitude from any animals so far examined with crupper twisted round, and has both fore and rear legs retracted. The animal's body is portrayed in soft outline, the legs and hoofs being carefully carved. The deer's head on its long neck with expanding muzzle has been treated in a highly individual manner with which we shall become more closely acquainted in the deer's head on the horse's head-dress (*Pl. 121*D). Ears and antlers are leather inserts, the antlers being reddened with lacquer. The intervals between the deer on the bridle-straps, as well as the breast- and crupper-straps, were decked with profile feline heads sewn on (*Pl. 117*D, E). The heads show bared fangs, puckered upper lip, small blunt nose, large eyes with carved eyebrow, round ear with a curl inside and a lump under the chin.

173

The cheek-straps were covered by wooden forks taking the shape of a wolf's head (*Pl. 117c*), like those in the third set but worked with more care. The eye is very large, the muzzle long and narrow with a turned-up nose, the upper lip puckered and the ear with a curl at the bottom. The edge of the lower jaw is decorated with 'running waves' with toppling crests.

On the front and back saddle arches were thick leather facings bearing excised elk figures with twisted crupper against a reddened background (*Pl. 165A*). Leather bow-shaped facings on the edge of the saddle bore no decoration, but a series of sculptural feline heads was fixed to them by means of tenons (*Pl. 116D*). Little leather cut-outs showing a pair of paws were fixed below the head to give the impression of little animals looking straight ahead. These sculptural heads are executed in the same style as the profile feline heads.

In front, on the front saddle arch and on the ends of the straps joining the two saddle cushions, scutiform pendants of various sizes were attached, all bearing representations of a strongly stylized tiger or leopard head seen *en face* (*Pl. 116c, E*). These animals have a relatively narrow nose with winglike curls, large slanting eyes, large mouth reaching the ears with traditional puckering on the upper lip and large, extended, open ears with strokes and curls at the base.

The wooden facings attached to the back of the saddle for securing the crupper-straps were highly original (*Pl. 116F*); the two linked panels have the following composition. On the long panels the front part of a leopard with paws extended is shown seen from above with the rear part of the body seen in profile. The rear paws suggest a creeping or stalking animal. The long tail is twisted into a circle. On the short panels the animals' heads are exactly like those on the plaques and pendants of the same set.

All the saddle covers in barrow 5 were of plain, thin black felt with a red felt border, except the cover in this outfit which we shall discuss in the chapter on art when we describe the saddle covers from barrows 1 and 2.

The shabrack of this saddle (measuring 62 cm. by 226 cm.) is covered by Chinese silk of cream colour with an embroidered pattern (fig. 89). The material is a kind of tussore woven from raw silk, while the pattern, formed from multi-coloured silk threads, shows Wu T'ung trees with various kinds of pheasants (*Pl. 178*, figs. 90-2). The shabrack is trimmed with a narrow band of blue felt, within which is a strip of reddish-brown felt with tridenticulate leather cut-out decoration. The latter is pasted over with gold-leaf and tinfoil. Along the lower edge are three tassels of yak hair held by a leather collar. The breast-band (measuring 8 cm. by 107 cm.) has the same decoration as the border of the shabrack, with pendant figures cut out of felt in the middle. Besides the riding outfit a leather mask was found on the horse's head (*Pl. 121c, D*) bearing a crest in the shape of a large sculptural deer's head, carved from wood with inserted

89. Shabrack, decor-
ated with Chinese
embroidered silk,
from barrow 5 ($c. \frac{1}{6}$).

90. Detail of embroidered design on shabrack in fig. 89 ($\frac{1}{2}$).

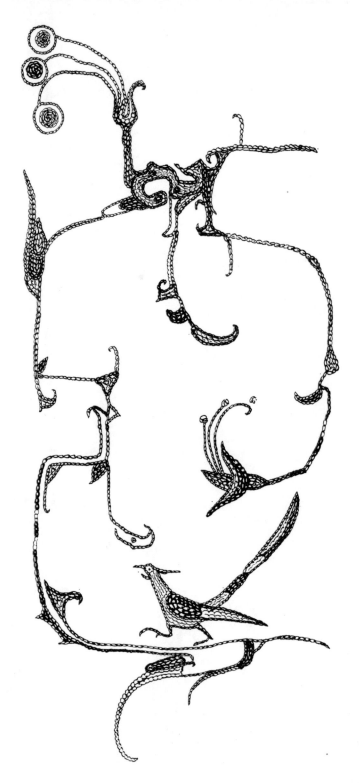

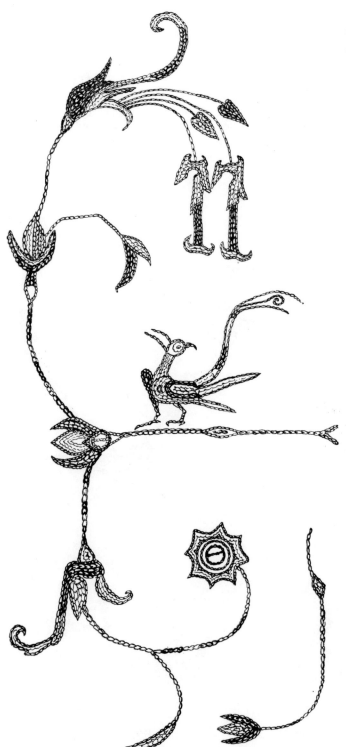

91. Detail of embroidered design on shabrack in fig. 89 ($\frac{1}{2}$).

92. Pheasants (phoenixes?) embroidered on shabrack in fig. 89 (*c.* $\frac{3}{5}$).

178

leather antlers and ears. The mane-cover found with the mask consisted of a simple piece of thick skin with a horsehair fringe, dyed red.

Four identical bridles from draught-horses in barrow 5 were very meagrely decorated. Their straight, elegant cheek-pieces terminate in half-spheres, and plaques of a similar shape decorated the strap junctions on the bridle (*Pl. 118*A, B). The wooden cheek-forks are decorated with 'running waves' (*Pl. 118*C).

A set of horn saddle facings and decorations from barrow 6 is of interest in that it precisely duplicated those found in barrows 3 and 4. On the high saddle arches were horn bow-shaped facings, resembling those from barrows 3 and 4 (fig. 93A).

Under the facings on the front arch were two pendants similar to those from the same barrows (fig. 93B), and at the back low conical runners (fig. 93C). The pendant plaques that were attached to the saddle cushions are also the same as in barrow 3 (fig. 93E), while the semicircular facings on the upper girth-strap with a hole for the breast-strap (fig. 93F) and the buckle plates on the ends of the upper girth-strap (fig. 93D) are also the same.

Consequently the saddles in barrow 6 were precisely the same as in barrows 3 and 4, and so all those barrows must be of the same date.

We can now turn to the so-called masks and mane-covers. The masks from barrow 1 have already been described more than once. Each mask consists of a kind of leather-covered felt sheath with large ears that was worn by the horse over its head. On one mask a pair of deer antlers of almost natural size are attached above it, and in front along the mask is pasted a schematic representation of a tiger, cut from fur, coloured blue and stuck over with gold disks (*Pl. 119*). Sewn up from thick leather the antlers are pasted over with fine leather in which the decoration has been excised. On the ends of the antler tines are tufts of horsehair dyed red.

On the second mask from this barrow, which is of exactly the same shape as the first one, a scene is depicted of a struggle between a horned and winged lion-griffin and a tiger (*Pl. 120*), the sculptural winged head of the griffin being over the horse's sinciput. Its body with retracted legs, like the deer's body in the first mask, is conventionalized and hangs in two flaps over either side of the horse's head. The griffin has seized the tiger with its front paws (*Pl. 122*A), the figure of which, as in the first mask, covers the whole of the horse's muzzle. The tiger has sunk its teeth into the chest, and its front claws into the trunk, of the griffin. The tiger's back legs are retracted. The griffin's horns end in knobs, its ears are long and pointed, its neck with a level comb is covered by characteristic pitting intended to represent a lion's mane; the pointed wings have their tips

179

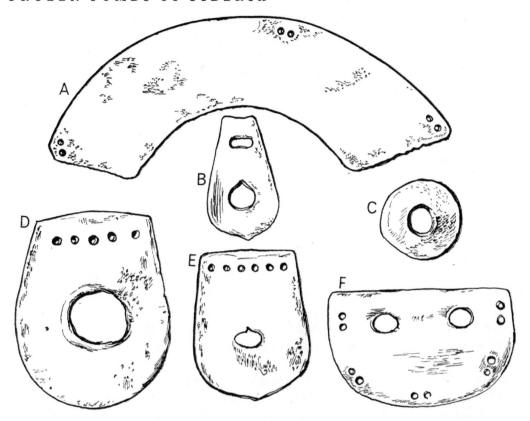

93. Set of horn saddle decorations from barrow 6: arch plate (A); pendant (B); runner (C); buckle (D); pendant plaque (E); semicircular plate (F) (*c.* $\frac{5}{8}$).

directed forwards. The now familiar half-horseshoes and commas on the body of the griffin deserve mention. Over the gold-leaf on the body the tiger's stripes were indicated by colouring and the front part of the muzzle was conventionally marked.

The manes on the horses which wore masks in barrow 1 were sewn to a band of stiff felt doubled over them, and over this were stretched fine leather mane-covers, fringed along the top with horsehair coloured red. On one of these (where the mask showed the struggle between griffin and tiger) was sewn a row of four cut-out leather cocks (*Pl. 123*A). These silhouette figures had schematic bodies covered by tinfoil, and heads, with large cock's comb covered by gold-leaf, twisted back. The second mane-cover similarly had four figures sewn on to it. Only by comparing it with the cocks on the first one can one say that cocks are also represented in this case, since conventionalization has reached the point

180

where in fact only the combs are shown, the head and body being converted into a single twist (*Pl. 123*B; fig. *122*).

In barrow 2 two horses also wore head decorations, which cannot be called masks but only mane-covers. The actual covers have not survived, but the trimmed manes on two horses are stitched through by strips of stiff felt doubled over them, as in barrow 1. One of the head-dresses was poorly preserved and so distorted that it is impossible to reconstruct its shape. All that was intact was a flat griffin's head made from red felt with applied thin leather (fig. 94). It has a sharply curved leathernose, large eye, and a horsehair comb dyed red with a blue border (*Pl. 167*B). This head without a doubt formed part of the crest of a horse's head-dress.

The second piece has survived comparatively well (fig. 95). It is formed from a single piece of soft white felt (*Pl. 122*B). Over the horse's eyes is a strongly projecting peak with flaps hanging down both sides that partially cover the neck. Long sheaths, also of felt, are sewn on for the ears, open at the front and not covered by felt or leather lattice-work, as was the case in the masks from barrow 1. On the crown between the ears was sewn a felt projection on to which could be fitted a goat's head. The outer surface of all of this part of the head-dress, as well as the attached figure, was covered by thin leather which was tucked under and ran all round the edge of the inside. Along the edge of the peak a pattern was fixed consisting of a series of uniform figures cut from gold-leaf. On the crown, as already mentioned, was sewn a goat's head with sharply turned-back horns to which rigidity was given by wooden pegs running from its ears to its muzzle tip. On the goat's neck near the horns stands a bird, also of felt pasted over with leather, with wings raised and cock-like tail distended. Its beak is also like a cock's. The wings, in addition to the leather, had gold-leaf pasted over them. The bird and tail are cut from single pieces of felt; the wings also are stitched to the body by fine thongs. The right wing has a smooth, the left a feathery, edge. In order to keep the wings raised little wooden stiffeners

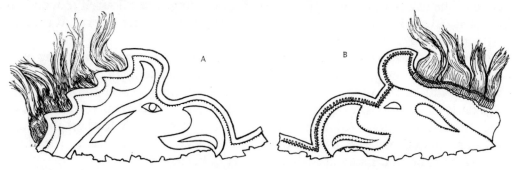

94. Griffin's head from horse crest in barrow 2, seen from right (A) and left side (B) (*c.* $\frac{1}{3}$).

95. Horse head-dress with crest from barrow 2.

have been set in them, as was also done with the legs. A toothed leather collar is attached to the bird's neck. The composition as a whole consists of a goat's head with a cock with outstretched wings sitting on its neck.

In barrow 3 no horses' masks were found, nor head-dress like that described, since in the horse burial of this barrow, except for articles of horn and wood, nothing else survived. Finials or crests were found, however, that had adorned some kind of horse's head or saddle decoration, resembling the bridle crest already described from barrow 4. They were carved out of wood and consisted of sculptural representations of birds' heads.

One of these, the head (*Pl. 121*B) of some fantastic bird, is fairly large, and was found in the north-eastern corner of the burial chamber. It is well executed with distinctly carved eyes with tear ducts and a very long beak. The tongue and powerful fangs are visible in the open mouth, and on the end of the beak is a large horn. The beak is broad and spatulate, like that of a goose or swan, and on the lower face of the beak are the carved, characteristic, 'under-tongue' grooves. The cavity of the mouth, the tongue and fangs are coloured red, and all the rest is covered with gold. The ears and horn were leather inserts. With this crest some leather bridle decorations were found.

Although the leather is extraordinarily badly preserved, careful working over the individual pieces has made it possible to reconstruct some of the decorations which are illustrated in fig. 96. These include an ear (A) and leather antlers (B–E), parts of a composite adornment of some kind (F) and, finally, the figure of some monster (fig. 97). All these pieces are cut from thick leather and bear additional incised ornament. It is possible that they all belonged to the side-straps of a bridle that had a crest like the one in barrow 4.

A second bird's head carved out of wood (broken into two) was found in the central part of the horse burial (*Pl. 121*A). It was rather smaller than that just

182

described. Again it is some kind of fantastic bird, although the shape of the head, the round eye and long narrow beak, especially its lower part, might allow it to be classified as a crane's head. On the other hand the end of the slightly open beak is hooked like that of an eagle. The leather insertable ears are covered with gold, and in the forehead is a deep socket in which evidently a leather horn had been inserted. In barrow 4, as we know, a horned boar's head acted as a crest (*Pl. 113*B, C).

In barrow 5, as mentioned, one of the horses had a leather head-dress and mane-cover. The head-dress was sewn together from thick leather covered with finely dressed thin leather and dyed dark red (*Pl. 121*C). Slits had been cut for eyes and nostrils, and the ears were covered by leather sheaths, open at the

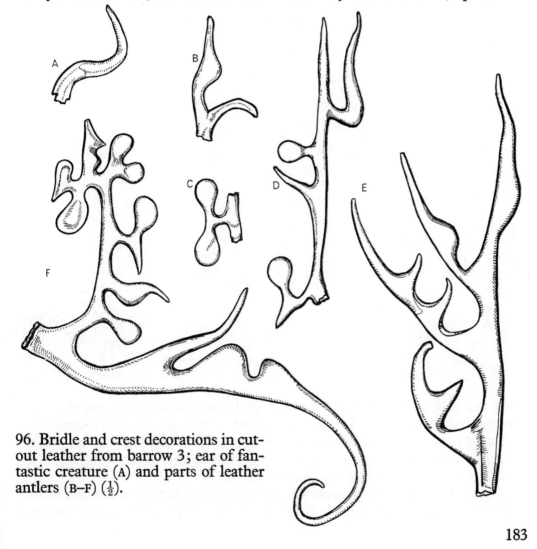

96. Bridle and crest decorations in cut-out leather from barrow 3; ear of fantastic creature (A) and parts of leather antlers (B–F) ($\frac{1}{2}$).

183

97. Leather cut-out
decorations of bridle
in barrow 3 ($\frac{1}{2}$).

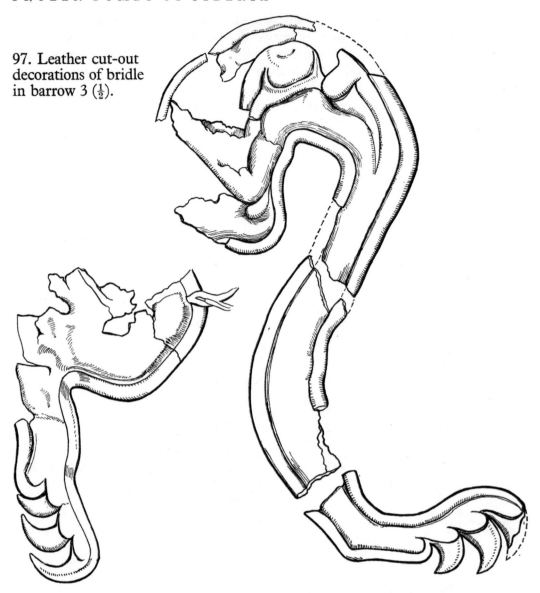

front, sewn on to the mask. The whole head was covered including the lower
jaw, and there was a special slit for the mouth. The head-dress was secured by
pairs of thongs (at the throat and under the lip). To the crown a carved wooden
sculptural head of a deer, which had insertable leather antlers and ears (the
latter now lost), was attached by thongs.

This head, which has been meticulously carved, has large eyes and ornamental
eyebrows, wide nostrils in relief and lower jaw with individual, artistically

executed curves. Under the chin are two knobs in relief circles and the under-mane is indicated by grooving (*Pl. 121*D). The spreading antlers are fixed to special spacer splints. Parts of the tines take the shape of birds' heads (*Pl. 118*F). The head and antlers have been dyed red with cinnabar.

Unlike the earlier examples in barrows 1 and 2 the mane-cover was not fixed by stitching the felt through the mane, but instead rested directly on the neck. It consists of a piece of thick leather bent double with a line of perforations along the fold through which have been threaded tufts of horsehair dyed red. This gave a fringe to both the inside and outside of the mane-cover. The cover and head-dress were joined together by a pair of thongs at their adjacent edges, and the former was in addition secured to the neck of the horse by two pairs of straps.

This head-dress had obviously not been especially prepared for the funeral, since it had undergone use for a considerable time. The solid base of the deer's head had been broken and part of its lower border lost, and the thick leather attachment had broken free.

Taking the head-dress of one of the horses to be a mask for a deer's head, N. Y. Marr saw it as a survival of the use of deer as a means of locomotion, preceding the use of the horse for this purpose.[1] He attempted thereby to find confirmation for his linguistic theories about 'stadial' changes of language.

I too at first assumed that we were dealing here with a religious survival of ancient deer-breeding that had preceded horse-breeding.[2] It is necessary there-fore to emphasize that subsequent excavations on the Pazyryk barrows showed this view to be erroneous. Of the eight head-crests found, only in one is there a deer's head and in a second antlers; all the rest made use of different motifs. So there could be no question of the general dressing up of horses as deer.

Up to the present there is too little material at our disposal to identify the origins of the group of horse-head decorations under discussion. I would only remark that mane-covers with crests of various kinds, but not representing animals, were a normal decoration of Assyrian riding-horses, not only for royalty but for servants. It should be noted, however, that in Assyria mane-cover and crest were a single piece, as can be seen on a series of bas-reliefs from Nine-veh.[3] I am far from seeing Assyrian influence in the Pazyryk horse-head decora-tions; it is very probable that this type of horse decoration had already made its appearance in the west Asian steppe and foothill areas in the first quarter of the last millennium B.C. In the seventh century B.C. it took one form in Assyria and another among the Altaian tribes; that is what we were looking at in the Pazyryk barrows.

Such horse adornment could not have been in everyday use in the Altai, since

[1] *Lectures to the Academy of Sciences of the U.S.S.R.* (1929), No. 17, pp. 324–5.

[2] Rudenko, A, 1931, p. 38.
[3] Weber, B, figs. 38 and 40.

185

98. Decoration on horses' tail-sheaths in barrow 1.

only single, selected horses in the graves wore it. It was probably intended for ceremonial, and not merely for funeral, use. The solid deer-head, the crest from barrow 5, had snapped at its base before the interment, as mentioned above, but had been specially mended with a thong.

Yet another detail has to be mentioned, found only on the horses with masks and mane-covers from barrow 1: their tails were fitted with special leather sheaths (*Pl. 124*A). These consist of long tubes, decorated below with a ribbon of blue fur, with a fringe of horsehair dyed red. They are stitched from leather cut-outs of two colours and decorated with the design illustrated in fig. 98.

In barrows 1, 2 and 4 there were single whips in the horse burials. In barrow 1 whip and handle survived, in the other two only the handles.

The handle of the whip from barrow 1 (*Pl. 124*B) was plain, pasted over with fine leather, the ends painted red. The fairly thick thong serving as lash was sewn over near the handle with a single layer of leather, and then a thong, which passed through three holes in the handle, secured it. The whip handle from barrow 2 was a bold design, representing a rushing horse on which a feline predator has sprung from behind (*Pl. 165*B). The horse's head at the front of the whip (carved in the round) is depicted extended, ears folded back and the mane trimmed. The forelegs are extended with the hoof at the head. The horse's crupper is twisted round and rear legs extended back. The butt end of the handle is rounded, terminating in the shape of a crouched cat, tail bent forward and curled at the end; the cat's body writhes like a snake around the handle but, alas, at the head the damaged handle has snapped off. Masterly and realistic in execution as are the horse's head and back part of the cat, the remainder is conventionalized. At the front under the horse's legs are two round openings for attaching the lash and at the back another for a loop. The whole handle has been coloured bright red with cinnabar.

A whip handle from barrow 4 (fig. 99), like that from barrow 2, has a horse-shaped figure at its fore end. Although badly damaged and deformed it is nevertheless possible to reconstruct it almost fully. Long and narrow, beautifully shaped in the round, the head has an extended neck and folded ears. The mane is evenly trimmed. The hoof of the front leg comes under the chin. The shoulder girdle is indicated by two ornamental curls, the ribs by a row of parallel strokes. At the butt end the handle is slightly thickened and rounded off. Under the horse's neck, as in the handle from barrow 1, there are three perforations in a row for attaching the lash, and a single one at the butt end for a loop. This handle, as in barrow 2, was coloured red with cinnabar. Finding whip handles in two barrows decorated with figures of a horse suggests that this motif was in fairly widespread use at that time for decorating these objects.

99. Whip handle from barrow 4 ($\frac{1}{2}$).

In the preceding account so much attention has been given to the saddlery for these reasons: first, horse-riding played such an enormous part in the life of the people of the High Altai; secondly, the objects yielded by the excavation have made possible an exhaustive study of the bridles and saddles; and, finally, the decoration borne by them was exceptionally rich and varied. Nevertheless the excavated barrows at Pazyryk have shown that, in spite of the mountainous terrain inhabited by their builders, 'cart' transport played an essential part in their means of locomotion.

In all the barrows except No. 4, where they had not survived, remains were found of primitive trolleys:[1] in barrow 1 the body and apparently parts of the yoke, in barrow 2 wheel and body, and in barrows 3 and 5 wheels, axles and body of two trolleys. All the wheels are made from a solid piece of larch trunk, 30–

[1] [Translator's note. The Russian word used is *telega*, a country cart, but the description shows vehicles so primitive, made only *ad hoc* at the time of the barrow construction, that it seemed wiser to translate as neither cart nor wagon, which have quite a different connotation in English, but instead by the vaguer word, *trolley*. M.W.T.]

47 cm. in diameter, 35–40 cm. thick, with central aperture 12–16 cm. in diameter, in some cases broadened by long use (*Pls. 126–8*). To judge by the surviving parts the body was as primitive as its wheels; it was made from thick larch trunks square in section. In barrow 3 the body of one trolley was made of larch trunks in such a way that the root that was left on stuck up at the front like the curves on sleigh-runners. The larch trunks were held together by a series of cross-struts fixed to them. At front and back thick axles (about 10 cm. in diameter) were fixed underneath the frame by large wooden pegs of rectangular section that passed right through axle and frame. The wheels were kept on the axle by wooden linchpins. In the front root part in the example from barrow 3 a transverse plank had evidently been set in a special slot. Lower down, almost at the bole, there had been haulage ropes or loops for shafts passing through slots, since these showed polishing from wear. The trolleys had sometimes been smeared with pitch, one wheel from barrow 2 being particularly liberally smeared.

The question is prompted: what was the purpose of these vehicles and why had they been buried in the barrows? Some of them, especially in barrow 3, that had been flung into the tomb, had seen long and heavy wear, and perhaps they had been employed on the barrow itself. The axles in some cases had been worn half-way through, and deep scouring from friction could be seen on the body itself. It would be difficult to admit that such a vehicle was used only for transporting the tree-trunk coffin and corpse during the funeral. Corpses could have been transported, as was done until quite recently by the Kazakhs and Kirgiz, on horseback with special equipment, or in the more sophisticated wagons with which we shall become acquainted below. The heavy tree-trunk coffins and rocks could have been hauled to the site on such trolleys.

Thus the hundreds of logs which occur in the shaft-filling of each barrow could have been brought by means of strap or hair drag-lines attached to a sled at one end and the saddles of riders at the other, a method used by the present-day Altaians. Special lug-holes are made in short and thick poles and beams for this purpose. Undoubtedly it would have been much more difficult to haul a vast quantity of stones to the barrow, some of which, as we saw, were boulders weighing several tons; this haulage of stone was evidently the purpose of these primitive trolleys. It is made the more likely by the fact that in barrow 5 many, more than a hundred, long thin sticks were found in large bundles, placed in the western and northern sectors—in the upper parts of the burial shaft. There could be no other possible interpretation except that they acted as a platform for trolleys discharging stones.

The question remains: if the trolleys were used for transporting stones why are they found buried in the burial shaft under earthen mound and cairn? In funerary cults there is a common belief about the necessity to leave in a tomb all the objects used in constructing it. If this is so we would naturally expect to find in it wedges, mallets, spades with which the shaft was scooped out, and trolleys for hauling the stones to the site. Hence one can suppose that just as the logs of the burial chamber had been hewn into shape beforehand elsewhere so, similarly, the stone had been carted to the site beforehand. The earthen mound and superincumbent cairn were heaped up by hand, the latter from material that had already previously been transported to the site as part of the funeral preparations.

A four-wheeled carriage or chariot found in barrow 5 is of exceptional interest. Here we are not dealing with primitive solid wheels cut from a tree trunk, but now, indeed, with multi-spoked wheels with nave and felloes.

The carriage, which is constructed almost entirely of birch, consists of the following parts: two axles with their wheels, joined by six horizontal boards, the body, a fretted surround, the canopy, draught-pole and yoke and terrets for reins (*Pls. 129, 131*). The great axles (310 cm. long) are rectangular in section in the central pillow (126 cm. long) with round arms 92 cm. long at either end. The working part of an axle extends over 70 cm. After the wheels had been fitted the two axles on each side were joined together by horizontal rods, each 178 cm. long, thickened at the end and fixed with wooden linchpins driven through openings in the axle ends. These rods had the very practical function of preventing friction between the wheel and the linchpin. The wheels were about 160 cm. in diameter and consisted of spokes, felloes and naves. The naves were about 66 cm. long and irregularly cylindrical in shape: their external diameter was on average about 12 cm., and in the middle at the junction with the spokes about 24 cm. The diameter of the conical aperture at the inner end was 11 cm. and at the outer 7–7·5 cm., and consequently when in motion a wheel pushed and heaved against the lateral rod joining the axles and not against the pillow of the axle.

Each of the two felloes consisted of a bent piece of wood 7 cm. wide, 5·6 cm. thick (in the worn part) and about 290 cm. long. The ends of the felloes overlapped one another for 30–40 cm., and were fixed with wooden pegs and lashed with straps. The sockets for the spokes were 5 cm. long and 1 cm. wide, chiselled through the wood. The apertures for the spokes in the naves had been chiselled to the same dimensions.

Each wheel had thirty-four spokes 70–71 cm. long, such a large number being required for rigidity and on account of the large diameter of the wheel.[1] It should be noted that although round in section the flattened ends of each spoke [1] are at right angles to each other and so contrived that the greatest width of the spoke [1] is parallel to the long axis of the nave at the nave, and to the axis of the felloe at the felloe. It may be noticed that all the spokes were bound with thin

[1] [Translator's note. Author has written nave in his typescript. M.W.T.]

birch bark stuck with glue at their seating in the nave. The thicker parts of both nave and spokes also were pasted with bark. This not only reinforced the wheel but also reduced the tendency to cracking. The axles had not been greased.

Due to the great size of the wheels and the slight length of the body of the carriage the gap between front and rear wheels was barely 6 cm. In the front axle pillow three horizontal apertures had been chiselled out for the attachment of the draught-pole.

The body of the carriage was of fairly complicated construction. It consisted of two frames, a lower measuring 128 cm. by 238 cm. and an upper 128 cm. by 206 cm., united by a series of twenty-one carved balusters 27 cm. high (overall height of a baluster with tenons 40 cm.), and lashed together by straps.

The lower frame was secured by four transverse rods fitted into the longitudinal bars, three in the front and one in the back. In the upper frame six transverse bars were similarly fixed, two in the front part above the second and third of the lower frame and the others at equal distances from each other.

The balusters were set between the longitudinal bars of the frames and between the back, first and second bars of the upper frame in front and the second and third bars of the lower frame below. In the gaps between the balusters, as mentioned above, there were strap ties.

Between the front transverse rods of the lower frame three longitudinal rods 22 cm. long (without tenons) were set at equal distances and on them was a platform of sixteen carefully whittled sticks about 1 cm. in diameter, tied together by thongs intertwined at several places. Just such a staging 27 cm. wide occurs on the upper frame between the front two rods. The remaining area of the upper frame is covered by a platform of the same whittled withies connected by a thong and laid longitudinally on the three transverse rods. The coachman probably sat on the upper level of intertwined twigs with his legs resting on the lower one.

Over the area of the upper frame behind the coachman was a skeleton frame, rectangular with rounded corners, consisting of fourteen uprights for a canopy. Within the uprights was a trellis, the carriage rail, made of several rows of round, bent sticks, 3·5 cm. in diameter, joined together by thin rods (diameter 6–7 mm.) held in the bent sticks by means of holes bored through them at intervals of 4–4·5 cm. The sticks are composite, made up of short rods, the ends of which are scarfed together and bound round with bast. The whole trellis was painted red. The canopy, as also the place where the driver sat and where he put his feet, were covered by hewn planks about 1 cm. thick, firmly lashed by thongs passed through apertures along their edges.

The draught-pole, 320 cm. long and 6·5 cm. by 8 cm. in section, which thickened at the front, was fixed to the middle, the pillow, of the front axle, not directly but by means of a special bow. This bow was lashed at its ends to the

190

front axle, and at about 1 m. from its back end in the middle the pole was lashed by straps passed through holes in its arms. At its front, thicker, end a pair of holes had been bored through the draught-pole for attaching the yoke. In the middle of the yoke on top a small socket had been bored into which a little peg had been fitted. Straps were looped over this, passed through the holes on the end of the draught-pole to which the yoke was firmly lashed. The yoke, which is 164 cm. long, has a slightly bent shape, and at 30 cm. from the draught-pole on either side a pair of horizontal openings through which the straps passed that held the forks to the yoke.[1] There were four holes in these, two in the upper parts of the rods and one on the fork ends. Straps passed through the upper holes attached the forks to the yoke, while straps through the lower ends of the forks passed under the horses' necks. At 12 cm. from the ends of the yoke there were holes, probably used for attaching the reins of supplementary horses.

Two terrets 44 cm. long and 4·5 cm. in diameter have elongated openings at their thickened ends, in which fragments of thick leather reins have survived, knotted at the ends and held in massive carved horn runners shaped like horses' hoofs.

The carriage had been hauled like a quadriga with four horses, which had been buried with it. One pair of horses were harnessed to the pole in the forks, primitive horse collars (*khamuty*) lying on the animals' necks. The second pair of horses outside the yoke hauled on traces, but whether the horses wore bands or the traces were attached to the saddle we do not know.

Since the front axle was firmly fixed to the body of the carriage, in order to turn the vehicle had to describe a wide arc. The attachment of the draught-pole indirectly to the axle by means of a bow served a very practical purpose, since otherwise, with direct attachment, turning would unavoidably have caused the vehicle to break up.

The carriage was either a wedding present or designed for ceremonial journeys. It is quite probable that the corpses buried in barrow 5 were brought to the site on it, but it had had long use before the burial, as is indicated by heavy wear on the felloes, the abrasion of axles and wheel sockets as well as on the holes in the yoke ends for harnessing additional horses.

The presence of such a carriage of light but intricate construction with multi-spoked wheels indicates the advanced stage reached in the use of carts, at least in the steppes adjoining the High Altai, since the mountains themselves were unsuited to wheeled transport.

If the carriage was a wedding present, then the woman buried in barrow 5 with the tribal chief, presumably a secondary wife, could have been a Chinese princess. Two-wheeled carriages of analogous construction have been found in

[1] [Translator's note. For a fuller description of these objects ('yoke-saddles') and their method of operation, see *Antiquity*, vol. xlii (1968), pp. 27–31, particularly fig. 2. M.W.T.]

China in researches on antiquities of the period of the warlords.[1] The wheels of these vehicles are multi-spoked, with twenty to thirty spokes on each wheel, with naves just as in the Pazyryk carriage and with untyred felloes. The draught-pole with forks at the yoke for a pair of horses is also of the same type. In addition, the bridles of the draught-horses with bronze, two-piece bits and antler cheek-pieces with a pair of holes are similar to those found in Pazyryk barrows 3 and 4.

Chinese chariots drawn by four horses are referred to in the description of a campaign of the Emperor Syuan (ninth century B.C.) against the Huns, and also subsequent Chinese records that enumerate gifts from the Chinese court to chiefs of the Huns and other horse-breeding tribes mention them.

The canopy of the Pazyryk carriage was covered with black felt, and was decorated by four sculptural felt figures of swans (*Pl. 166*).

Among the logs filling the upper part of the shaft of barrow 1 two wooden stakes were found with two pairs of holes at the ends and one in the middle, which, to judge by their working, can be regarded as part of a yoke. If so, then not only horses but also oxen were employed as draught animals.

In barrow 5, in the upper part of the burial shaft, together with numerous thin sticks, was a shaft of birch wood 3·35 m. long (*Pl. 130*). The bent shape of the flattened part, the small size (6 cm. by 6 cm.) of the hole at its end and the presence of two holes 60 cm. and 127 cm. from the back end and the polishing on its lower surface suggest that we are dealing not with a cart shaft but with a much more primitive device for moving loads, a sled (*volokush*). This indicates that besides draught-pole haulage sled haulage was also practised.

The recovery of the trolleys and carriage in a fragmentary state has prevented a total reconstruction. Nevertheless they are extraordinarily important since they reveal the existence of varied cart transport at the time under discussion. In the High Altai, I repeat, the mountainous conditions were very unfavourable for the use of wheeled transport, but nevertheless (besides the sled and later the sledge) primitive wagons or trolleys were widely employed, and also light wagons of highly sophisticated, albeit individual, construction. They lacked the iron tyres which were by that time used in Scythia, but iron was rare then in the Altai and it was too dear to be used on carts. Harnessing, as we have seen, was to a draught-pole (horses and oxen) and to a sled.

The existence in the Ulagan district of a vehicle of such sophisticated construction as that found in barrow 5 can be explained only by direct links between the inhabitants of the Ulagan plateau with the steppe regions of the south and east.[2] In the Ulagan district, which is quite roadless, such a carriage could have

---

[1] *Report on Excavations in 1956.*

[2] [Translator's note. The author has written south and east, but this might be a slip. M.W.T.]

had only an extremely limited use. We have already discussed possible reasons for its presence, including the possibility that it was of Chinese origin, reaching the Altai as part of the dowry of a Chinese princess, since carriages pulled by four horses forming part of a dowry are recorded in the Chinese sources.[1]

[1] Bichurin, A, pt iii, pp. 192, 204. [Translator's note. This last sentence has been modified in order to bring it into line with the new typescript material provided by the author. M.W.T.]

7. TECHNIQUES EMPLOYED IN WORKING THE DIFFERENT MATERIALS

A PEOPLE inhabiting patches of steppe amongst virgin woods naturally used timber not only for building but also for every type of article. Park-like larch clumps, just as today, were the prevailing form of tree growth, the timber of which was available for building. It is no accident that for all the burial chambers hewn larch wood was used, and in the log fillings of the shaft larch predominated. The coffins were hollowed out of larch trunks, as well as their lids, and larch was also used for the wheels and platforms of the massive trolleys. Ladders, wedges, mallets, shovels, stools and many other articles were all made of larch. Larch bark, which was extensively used as a cut-out material, occurred in almost all the burials. Firs that grow either in the deep ravines on the river banks, or more commonly on the north-facing slopes, were little used; fir logs were rarely found in the shaft fillings. The bows of saddle arches were bent fir splinters, and they were also used for shields, axe-handles and other small articles. The very homogeneous and soft but brittle wood of cedar was employed for objects decorated by incising and sculpture; almost all the incised, gold-covered, wooden saddlery decorations were of cedar, which was also used for some carved table legs.

Birch was highly valued for certain articles. In the Great Ulagan valley, particularly around the Pazyryk barrows, birch today does not grow, its upper limit of altitude in this area being 1,500 metres above sea level. Birch is only encountered here and there in the lower parts of the valleys of the Bashkaus and Chulyshman, where poplar is also found. However, in the barrows we found various articles of birch, some of large dimensions. The dish table-tops and often their legs, as well as wooden vessels, were made of birch wood. The carriage from barrow 5 was made basically of birch; its great wheels (felloes, spokes and naves), the rods of the platform and the balusters. The tomb cover was of birch bark in all the barrows, peeled from large trees up to 20–25 cm. in diameter. The people of the Ulagan Mountains, leading a similar life to the folk of the central Altai district (where on account of a milder climate birch was more

195

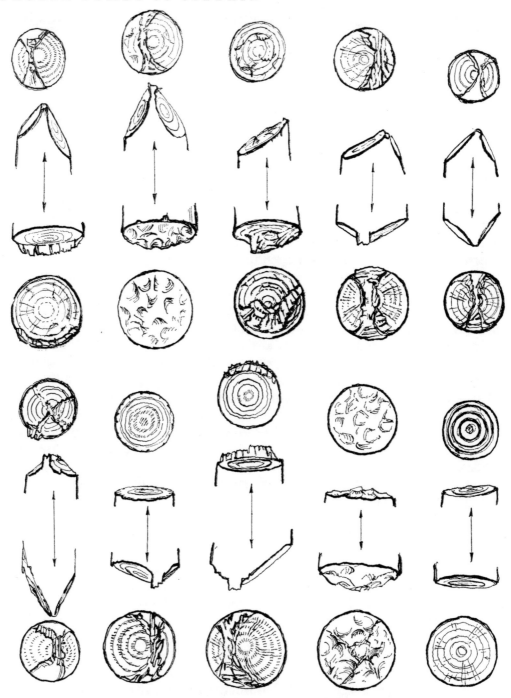

100. Traces of chopping on the ends of logs.

widespread), could have obtained articles made of this wood from them, probably indeed from the Chulyshman and Bashkaus valleys. At all events the habit of covering the tomb with birch bark had not been formed in the Ulagan valley, not at Pazyryk, but in areas with a milder climate, such as the basin of the River Ursul. Juniper was utilized only for bedding in the horse burial in barrow 2. The shrub 'smoky tea' generally covered the tomb, and probably was also used on real dwellings. Objects of poplar have not yet been found, although in the deep gorges of the High Altai poplar occurs everywhere. For stitching the sheets of birch bark, willow bark had been used.

Of fibrous vegetable matter only the fibres of hemp and kendyr seem to have been used. Sedge and stalks of some grasses were employed for stuffing saddle cushions.

The logs of the burial chambers and those filling the shafts were not thick, diameters at the root end varying from 16 cm. to 25 cm. Thicker trees, the diameters of which reached 50 cm., had to be cut, e.g. for the uprights and beams bearing the load of logs and stones over the burial chamber. Thickest of all were the tree trunks used for coffins, which were as much as 1 m. in diameter.

In view of the toughness of larch, working it with small, light axe-celts was not easy. Detailed examination of several dozen chopped logs has shown that there were no rigid, fixed methods of chopping and felling the trees. Usually, as is done today, the tree was hewn from opposite sides, one side slightly deeper than the other, although logs with two uniform grooves are found. The unchopped part usually had an X-shape, caused by breaking when the tree fell. Less often the tree was hewn from one side only. Logs are found that have been hewn from three sides in which a broken-off three-sided pyramidal stump remained. In exceptional cases the trunk has been chopped from four sides or even all the way round, in which case the stump at the root end has a very flattened conical or even spherical shape. It may be observed that the thicker the tree trunk the greater the number of directions from which it was chopped; for this reason the upper end of the trunk had more often been chopped only from two sides, although the majority of the upper ends have a straight chop (fig. 100).

The bark had been peeled off the lower parts of some of the trees before felling. The stripping was effected in just the same way as is done by modern Altaians. A ring was chopped round the trunk and then a longitudinal groove chopped through the bark above, the bark being chopped off by side blows with an axe. The stripping off was done with a wooden spatula. The lower and side edges of the bark are smooth but the top ragged. Knots in the wood were cut round from behind the bark or pared off from the surface of the trunk with the bark.

Logs intended for building underwent careful working. Knots and other projections were chopped off and the whole surface of the wood made even and

197

smooth. In the box tomb the logs were so trimmed that they fitted tightly without the slightest gap.

For lack of saws, planks and boards had been dressed with axe and adze. In making spars and thick planks from logs the superfluous part was split off and then the surface and edges carefully trimmed. When it was necessary to make thin planks, a centimetre or less thick, the wood was split into pieces of corre-

101. Iron knife with wooden sheath, from barrow 2 ($\frac{1}{2}$).

sponding size, and the unevennesses trimmed off, leaving parts of the original split surface visible in places.

Neither axes nor adzes were found in the excavation and we can only judge their character by the traces left by working on the wooden objects (*Pl. 125*D). The axes and adzes were light and narrow, their slightly curved blades 35–55 mm. wide. Judging by the handle found in barrow 1 (*Pl. 125*A, B) the axes were wielded from the shoulder. The adzes differed from axes not only in the method of hafting but in the asymmetry of the blade edge. Adzes had been employed in hollowing out the huge tree-trunk coffins and their lids.

Numerous wooden articles, particularly of an artistic character, had been carved with metal knives with a straight blade. A metal knife and two wooden knife sheaths were found in barrow 2 (fig. 101). The knife, which is flat, has a long handle (12·5 cm.), a comparatively short blade (7·5 cm. with a broken end) and a small hole at the slightly expanded end of the handle. It is 1·4 cm. wide in the middle, the thick back is 0·6 cm. across and the handle on the cutting side is 0·3 cm. thick. The upper part of the handle is faced with gold plates. Similar knives are a usual occurrence in the early Iron Age, but these were the first wooden sheaths or cases of such knives to be found. They have been made from a single piece of wood with a deep groove for the knife cut in one side leaving part of the handle projecting. In the lower rounded end was a hole through which was threaded a thong knotted at the end. The knife was probably worn at the belt secured by a thong passed through a lug in the handle, and the sheath would have been secured to the belt by another thong fixed to its lower end.

Plain bronze knives were in use at the same time, two of which were found in

Aragol barrow 1 (*Pl. 125*E, F). Both were flat, broad-bladed, thick-backed, expanding slightly at the upper rounded end, where there were perforations for a thong. The larger was 13 cm. long but broken, the smaller 11·5 cm.

The wooden vessels had been worked on the outside with a straight-bladed knife, but on the inside with a curved twisted blade.

In barrow 4 a massive chisel (*Pl. 125*H) of maral antler was found, consisting of two parts, a clip handle and the chisel blade set in it. The handle had been made of a lump of antler chopped from the shaft with an axe with a very jagged blade edge. The axe had probably been made of iron and the profile of its blade constantly changed during the work, so that there were no two traces of blows showing the same jagged marks. By scooping out the inner spongy matter a socket (3·5 cm. diameter) was made in the handle in which the chisel was fitted. For this a maral antler tine, almost straight, but requiring slight straightening during manufacture, was used. The upper end, set in the handle, was pointed, but the lower end was wedge-shaped. The working part of the tool was strongly polished and worn as a result of prolonged use. In addition metal chisels had been used, a clue to the size of which is given by the elongated openings in the wooden articles. Although the wide openings, like lug-holes in logs, had been made from both sides, small perforations had been made with chisels with blades of varying width, on the average 12 mm. Circular holes were made with a gimlet or drill, the bits of the latter varying usually between 6 mm. and 10 mm. in diameter. Small holes, especially on wooden decorations of saddlery, were made with an awl.

The Altaians of that period were probably familiar with the lathe, since the legs of one of the little tables in barrow 2, as we have seen, had undoubtedly been turned on a lathe.[1]

Among fibrous vegetable materials, as just mentioned, hemp and kendyr were evidently used. Rough thread was twisted from the fibres, but a finer thread was also spun, using spindle whorls, suitable for spinning yarn. A clay spindle whorl was found by me while excavating a cemetery at Biysk contemporary with the Pazyryk barrows (*Pl. 125*C). In studying the physical properties of the threads of vegetable origin in the cloth from barrow 2 it should be observed that the maximum thickness of the fibres used was 25 μ. The original fibres in flax have a maximum thickness of 17 μ, hemp 28 μ, Chinese nettle 30–40 μ, but there are no grounds for considering the fibres of the cloth under discussion as belonging to one of these plants. Microscopic study of them has not revealed the existence of any of the anatomical peculiarities characteristic of these three plants (knotty

[1] [Translator's note. Rudenko has since expressed himself as quite definite on this point. Rudenko, A, 1960, p. 215. M.W.T.]

swellings, thickenings, transverse faults). Their thickness most closely resembles that of kendyr, which has an average thickness of 20–25 μ.

The weave in this cloth was plain linen, also called *gradenaplevy* or taffeta weave; the threads in both directions in a centimetre square averaged 23 by 23 (*Pl. 133*A).

The treatment of animal products, given their wide range, was extremely varied and in many cases highly skilled.

The working of horn and antler deserves attention, and first the use of maral antler. It furnished material for mattocks, for such tools as chisels and mallets, for buckles and slider blocks and, most important, for all kinds of artistically carved objects. Parts of the beam or the tines were chopped round with a metal axe and then broken along the line of the cuts. Plaques were carved with a knife in the same way as the wooden ones. Round holes were drilled through them with drill bits of diameters varying from 2 mm. to 5 mm. When an object like a strap slide with a narrow but deep slot had to be made, first a line of holes was bored and then the intervening material worked out with a knife. Besides maral antler large flat objects were made from what was evidently elk antler.

Dry antler, particularly the outside part which is most valuable for use, is very tough, and can only be worked with difficulty with a metal knife. So it can be assumed that before working the antler was soaked in warm or hot water, as was widely practised by the aboriginal people of Siberia until recently. Undoubtedly the horns of domestic cattle also were stewed when such objects as the one-sided, goblet-shaped drums were made. We may observe that such drums consisted of two perfectly uniform halves lashed together by a line threaded through a series of drilled holes, the diameters of which did not exceed 1 mm.

The whole of a goat's or ram's horn, its base cut away, was used as a special type of vessel without further treatment.

The fur of all the domestic animals was used; we have actual examples in the case of sheep, goat and horse (colt). The fur of elk, deer, mountain goat or ram because of its poor quality was not used, but there are examples of leopard, otter, steppe cat, squirrel, sable and ermine fur.

It is still hard to say how such furs were treated. Sheep and goat skins would undoubtedly have been treated with sour milk and curds and then softened by hand, since the specimens are soft and white just like modern skins treated in this way. Skins of small animals (sable, squirrel and ermine), after cleaning off the fat, would be merely kneaded between the hands without the application of any chemical agent.

The people of the High Altai joined the pelts of small animals with great skill. The fine stitching with thin twisted sinew threads along the underside of the skin deserves attention (*Pl. 132c*). As already observed in describing the dress, in spite of the very thin skin of animals such as squirrel or sable, the stitching passed only through the surface and did not penetrate to the fur side of the skin. If one considers that in 1 cm. there were up to sixteen stitches one can appreciate with what fine needles the work must have been executed. In making up the pelts into a whole, damaged places were patched, but in such a way that they fitted wherever possible into the general pattern on the outside face of the fur. In addition to uniformly made-up furs quite commonly small pieces of fur were sewn together to produce a mosaic (*Pl. 132E*), this being a device used on clothing and pouch covers. Fur mosaics, analogous to incrustated decoration, were made by sewing together polychrome, often dyed, pieces of fur or sometimes fur with leather insets. We may recall the costume from Katanda barrow, and the leather bags from barrows 1 and 2 at Pazyryk (*Pl. 150A, B*).

The different leather articles and straps were very varied in material, treatment and quality. How the leather was tanned and the straps produced we cannot with certainty say, although undoubtedly with the thick skins, like that of horse or ox, the hair was scraped off and mallets were used in rendering the skin elastic.

So far as I know there is only one observation by Herodotus about leather-making among the pastoral tribes: first they remove the flesh with an ox rib and then soften it by rubbing with their hands.[1]

In barrow 2 a massive mallet made of a section of maral antler was found (*Pl. 125G*). The striking surface was at the base of the velvet, and the beam had been chopped off slightly higher up, leaving the brow tine as a handle. The mallet can reasonably be supposed to have been used in working leather; such a method of softening thick skin by repeated blows with an antler mallet or the butt-end of an axe is widely employed today by the aboriginal inhabitants of Siberia.

Apart from cutting out straps from it, thick leather was used also for making vessels in which cheese, and possibly fluids, were kept. This leather had also to be tanned, which was probably done by smoking.

A remarkable feature of the culture being studied was the widespread use of thick leather for artistic carving comparable to that on wood or bone, and even for sculpture. We have already met examples of this more than once. Also widely used for decoration was thin, finely dressed leather (sheep's or goat's hide), from which every kind of silhouette shape was cut out and which was used to trim the rough bridle- and saddle-straps. Leather was invariably sewn with sinew thread, regardless of whether it was for bridle-straps or delicate appliqué work. The sinew threads were used thick and twisted or thin and fully twined according to need.

[1] Herodotus, A, bk iv, 64. [Translator's note. Herodotus is here referring to human scalps, not normal leather-work. M.W.T.]

Hair was widely and variously used. Plucked deer hair seems to have been used only as stuffing. The saddle cushions in all the Pazyryk barrows were stuffed with it, as well as various small cushions of uncertain use and the felt figures of swans from barrow 5. The wool and down of domestic goats, and more especially sheep, had multifarious uses.

The technique of rolling felt of different sorts and qualities was highly developed. Coarse, heavy felts do not occur, due no doubt to the fact that among the rich families of tribal chiefs whose tombs were excavated it would be predominantly fine-fleeced sheep that were reared. The felts in the mane-covers from barrows 1 and 2 were relatively thick and rough. The felt that covered the tomb walls in barrows 1 and 2 and the floor of barrow 2 was thick but soft, as also were the sweat-cloths for the majority of saddles. Thinner and softer felt was used in the stockings. The black or white colour of the felt reflects the colour of the sheep; its yellow colour is due to discoloration produced by its prolonged stay in the damp ground.

The best make of felt scarcely differs from contemporary fine felt, but is not so roughly pressed. The raw material, exclusively sheep's down, has been cleaned of extraneous matter and washed out. The uniformity of thickness, varying from 2 mm. to 3 mm., over quite large areas is noticeable. The uses of such thin felt were very varied: in dress for caftans and stockings, the base for leather head decorations, ornament on wall hangings in the house, the covers of saddle cushions, shabracks and so on. In some cases, as for example in the saddle covers, the felt had been dyed red or blue. Pieces of fine felt dyed various colours were cut in different shapes for making up composite figures, or even pictures.

Woollen threads, twisted from two pieces of yarn, were generally used only in felt appliqué work and in general on objects of fine felt. When dyed various colours they were also used in intricate embroidered patterns of tambour stitching.

Woollen cords were of two kinds: two or four threads twisted or plaited. A great mastery in plaiting various kinds of braid had been achieved. Plaiting three or five tresses in a horse's tail was not difficult, but it was incomparably more difficult to plait the thick, square-in-section braids (*Pl. 66B, top*), 1–1·5 cm. wide, with a pattern of very delicate design. Besides simple plaiting lace weave was made, an example being the plaited pigtail covers from barrow 2. In the photo-projection (positive) one can see the pattern of the inner cover in a less intricate plaiting (*Pl. 133E*) than the more complicated work on the outside (*Pl. 133F*).

Woollen cloths found in the Pazyryk barrows are both of local manufacture and imported. We will first study the local cloths. The fibres of the yarn of these are of wool, all the signs indicating sheep's wool, exclusively down. The plucked hair with down (coarse wool) is found only in the warp of imported carpet textiles. Microscopic examination of the fibres of warp and weft yarn was made of all types of cloth. Only down was found with maximum thickness that rarely reached 50 μ. The great mass consists of fibres of 12–27 μ, and in several cases the wool threads do not exceed 14 μ.[1]

Thus the wool used in the cloth consisted only of down. The slight diameter of the fibres, their scaly make-up, the skin attached and the way they lay on each other—these all have analogies in the down of the best breeds of sheep that yield fine wool with fibre thicknesses of 11–26 μ. Study of the fleeces in barrows 2 and 5 has revealed that the sheep bred locally at that time bore just such wool.

In barrows 1 and 2 pieces of red woollen cloth of plain linen weave were found in which the threads in a centimetre square averaged 11 by 17. The photo-projection in the positive (*Pl. 133*D) is at double size.

In all the barrows red woollen cloth was found of completely identical weave. The warp and weft are woven in a serge (twill) two-way weave with a diagonal pattern. Although their method of manufacture is the same the cloths differ in the density of warp and weft threads. Thus, in some examples, in one square centimetre there are 15 warp threads against 28 weft, in others 20 warp and 30–35 weft. Moreover in some cloth the weft threads have been pushed so close together that the warp threads are hidden, except where there are spaces between them. Such a disposition gives an individual appearance, an example of which with diagonal pattern is shown enlarged to double size in *Pl. 133*C. In barrow 2 cloth of this type was found but more rarely, dyed green and with a thread count of 18 by 19 in a centimetre square.

An extraordinarily dense red woollen cloth was found in barrows 2 and 3. In the former, two strips 15 cm. wide, one 2·7 m. and the other 2·5 m. long, were found in the burial chamber. The ends of the strips were hemmed with woollen thread. In barrow 3 small pieces of this cloth were found. A serge weave had

[1] The analysis of textiles at Pazyryk was carried out by V. N. Kononov, and the analysis of the weaves by A. S. Verkhovskaya.

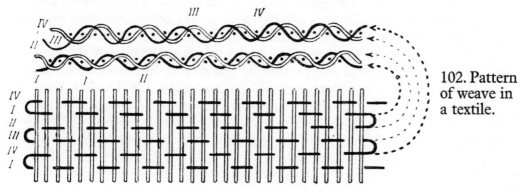

102. Pattern of weave in a textile.

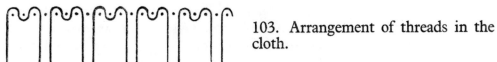

103. Arrangement of threads in the cloth.

been used in the cloth, as illustrated in fig. 102, where the warp threads are white and the weft black. The pattern on the cloth is diagonal ribs of four weft threads, marked in the figure by roman numerals. In the transverse section through the cloth in the figure the warp threads are shown by black dots. The cloth is double-faced. In a centimetre square there are over 60 threads of weft to 15 warp threads, the former being so tightly pushed together that the latter are entirely hidden and a very dense cloth is produced. On *Pl. 133*B the cloth has been enlarged to double size.

In barrow 2 a dark brown woollen cloth with a nap of two types was found, with whole (*Pl. 134*C) and with cut pile loops. Pieces of the same kind of cloth with whole loops were found in barrow 3. The cloth was normally in strips 42 cm. wide sewn together for covers or coverlets, which had a width of not less than 82 cm. and a length in the surviving tatter of 120 cm. It had a plain linen weave in which the weft threads, forming the nap, stuck out as loops, and were then either cut off or left uncut. In fig. 103 the weave is shown in transverse section with the warp threads shown as dots. Between the nap threads there are thin weft threads at intervals, up to 30 per centimetre.

The types just enumerated exhaust the unquestionably native, and evidently widely used, cloths, which were predominantly serges.

I now turn to consider woollens of which either the local origin is doubtful or that were certainly imported.

The long strips of red cloth from barrow 2, described above, were trimmed with comparatively narrow (9·5 cm.) ribbons of woollen cloth with a polychrome, ornamental, rhythmic pattern in two variants, a relatively small and a larger pattern. The cloth evidently caught the attention of the looters, who left the red cloth but carefully tore off the polychrome, of which only relatively small tatters remained. The weave in the latter is plain linen, 11 threads of warp to 54–56 of weft per centimetre. Due to the varying thickness of the weft and irregular pressing down the density varied. The pattern had been woven in with yarn of different colours (white, yellow, red, violet-red and blue) in the weft, covering the warp on both sides, forming the pattern both inside and outside.

The yarn of the warp consisted of thick, undyed wool, made up of hair and down, well spun in several series. The weft threads were finer, more sloping and closer than the warp, and because of their relative thinness and closeness (although a normal linen weave had been used) grooves running parallel to the warp had been produced. This kind of weave, it may be recalled, is called weft ripple. A distinctive feature of ancient hand textile and carpet work was decorative patterns leaving voids or splits in the material, running parallel to the warp and separating one colour from another. These were caused by the weft threads of various colours not joining up on the long sides of the loom, but running back and not interweaving with the neighbouring thread. Due to this, on each side of the coloured field edges were formed between which there was a void. Such a method of joining warp and weft is known as the 'Kilim' or 'Palas' technique; it has been used for the pattern and has caused the graduated surface lines in the materials illustrated in *Pl. 157*A, B.

The pattern of interweaving of the weft thread produced by this technique is shown in fig. 104. So far there are about a dozen barrows which have yielded different types of the cloth just described. It was exclusively of the kind about which we have just spoken. It is possible that it was not local but originated on the frontiers of the western or south-western steppes, where 'Palas' technique remained in use almost until our own times.

In order to identify the original dye a special study was carried out which gave the following results: white—natural undyed wool; yellow—changed into dark grey; blue—a kind of indigo; green—has lost its sharpness, the original dye with chemical composition resembling indigo; red—purpurin and alizarin.

The cloth from Hither Asia used to decorate one of the shabracks in barrow 5 is technically very accomplished, especially the pieces showing the women in front of the censer and the lions (*Pl. 177*A, C). The density of the warp is 20–24 threads and of the weft over 100 threads per centimetre. In making the patterns,

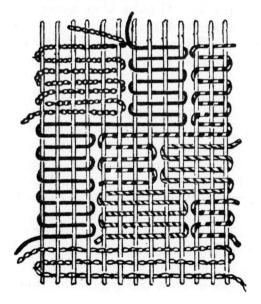

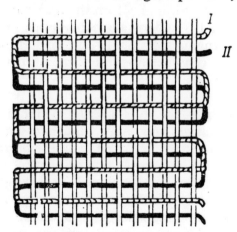

104. The weave in 'Palas' type of cloth.
105. Weave with one warp and two weft threads.

part or the whole extent of the web has been drawn on canvas paper (the so-called 'rapport') with precise allowance for thickness of warp and weft, in order to work out the exact form of web necessary. In our looms the pattern is worked out without translating it on to a check paper; the shape of the pattern runs parallel to the weft. When vertical lines predominated, as in human figures, buildings with columns and so on, the horizontal position of the web caused elongation of those parts of the picture, because the different coloured threads had to be put on one after another. This was the method employed on our Achaemenid textiles, on Coptic textiles of the fourth to sixth centuries A.D. and in recent Spalier and Gobelin work of the seventeenth to eighteenth centuries. The textiles being studied therefore constitute one of the most ancient and most accomplished examples of Gobelin work.

Several examples of Chinese silks were found in barrows 3 and 5 (they would not have survived in barrow 4; in barrows 1 and 2 none came to light). Plain silk with linen weave of fairly fine work occurred, for example, in a pouch which gave a thread count of 30 by 50 in each centimetre square (*Pl. 134*B). The yarn was unspun silk. A kind of tussore used for covering a shabrack in barrow 5 had the same weave; the piece was 44 cm. wide and gave a thread count of 40 by 52 per centimetre square.

In barrow 3 a more complicated patterned silk was found, which had been woven on a loom with one warp and two wefts. The relationship of wefts was 1 : 1 and a serge weave 1/3 or 3/1 had been employed, which is illustrated in fig. 105. A grey weft I is interwoven with a warp in serge weave 1/3, giving a serge weave of 3/1 on the underside. A greenish weft II has a serge weave 3/1 and 1/3 underneath. Alterations in the interweave took place according to the changing sequence of pattern and background, which are shown in *Pl. 134*A. In one centimetre square there are twenty-four longitudinal to eighteen transverse threads.

Besides the dyes already mentioned mineral colouring, particularly ochre and cinnabar, was used. Cinnabar, which was evidently highly prized as a paint, was widely employed in all the barrows for colouring not only wooden but also leather objects. It is possible that mixed with resin, which was used as glue, cinnabar was employed in making lacquer. The cinnabar was undoubtedly obtained locally because outcrops are known 30–40 km. south of the Pazyryk barrows, and since it occurs at the surface it was easy to work.

A by no means insignificant part in the life of the population was played by the extraction of minerals (stone, clay) and various metals. The stone lamp made of hard sandstone found in barrow 2, like others of a similar kind discussed in the chapter on economy, required practice in the working and grinding of stone for its manufacture. In order to carve out the tall feet a metal file would be the basic tool needed. This lamp is indeed made only of a hard sandstone, but in the Provincial Museum there are just such lamps made of hard materials like diorite (from Multa valley). The skill reached in grinding and boring holes in stone can be judged by the sculptured stone figure of a boar preserved in that museum (fig. 118). The provenance of this figure is uncertain, but its method of working makes it probable that it belongs to the culture that we are discussing.

Given the existence of wooden, leather and metal vessels, earthenware ones would only have had secondary significance, and so their manufacture had not achieved a very high level of skill. Nevertheless, since earthenware bottles were found in all the barrows, they were extensively used. They have already been described and I will merely recall that these narrow-necked bottles were hand made from a paste with grits of sand and fine gravel. Their firing, which had been carried out on an open fire, was uneven.

Incomparably more complicated and varied were the techniques, in all probability of native Altaian origin, employed in metal-working.

Nothing as yet can be said about the smelting of iron or where this was done. It is possible that iron bits, knives and swords were manufactured outside the Altai and then obtained by trade. With regard to techniques used in their manufacture, it need only be said that they are all forged and that the handles of knives and swords were usually encrusted with gold.

In many districts of the High Altai not only the local outcrops of gold ores, with some mixture of silver, but also the deeper veins were worked, as well as outcrops of copper and tin.

In spite of the existence in this province of ancient workings for different metals, it can hardly be conceded that mining for metals was one of the basic occupations of the population of the High Altai in the relevant time, although the matter has not been fully studied. There can be no doubt that gold, cinnabar and pyrites crystals were obtained locally, but probably only certain families were concerned with their extraction. Pure tin, which was evidently prized since it was used like gold-leaf for covering various articles, could be obtained in the Pazyryk district on the south-western borders of the High Altai, where the copper also was probably worked.

A relatively small number of the metal objects from Pazyryk have been submitted to compositional analysis,[1] but all the same the analyses have yielded interesting results. It emerged that for many articles almost pure copper was

[1] The composition of the metal objects from Pazyryk was determined by spectral analysis employing a direct current on carbon electrodes on a quartzite spectrograph of medium dispersion, ISI–22. A sample of several milligrammes was put in the hollow of a low electrode and burnt to complete evaporation with a 9-ampère current. Determinations of all the metals were made by the 'last line'.

used; vessels, bits and nails were cast from it and all kinds of decoration hammered from it. As bronze objects, which contained significant quantities of tin, we can cite only one of the mirrors and the torque from barrow 2. Copper ore from which individual objects in the barrows have been made came from different outcrops, it seems. Some of the copper objects are distinguished by the presence of bismuth, and in some there are appreciable amounts of silver. Varying quantities of antimony in the bronze objects indicate different places of origin. It follows therefore that the copper and bronze objects from the barrows were not prepared locally, but came there as a result of intertribal trade from different places of manufacture in the Altai.

The gold is uniform, which points to a single source. Analysis of the gold showed that it is all white gold (electrum), an alloy of gold and silver (up to 20 per cent) with a significant admixture of copper. The technique used in producing gold-leaf was probably the same as that of the contemporary goldsmith. The only difference is that nowadays gold-leaf can be produced thinner than $0·1 \mu$, after which it becomes translucent and shows a green light. At Pazyryk the gold-leaf was considerably thicker: in the earlier barrows it varied from 15μ to 30μ and in one case about 10μ, and in the later barrows it fluctuated between 8 and 17μ. Certain pieces of gold-leaf were up to as much as 200 sq. cm. in area or more. The tinfoil was appreciably thinner.

The technique of stamping decoration on thin sheets of copper was well known since, as we have seen, examples of it occurred, especially in barrow 2.

Cast metal objects were scarce, partly due perhaps to the majority having been taken by the looters. Those that there were indicated a far from uniform level of skill employed on the different objects. The silver adornments, belt plates and pendants are the work of great craftsmen; the copper bits are not bad, but this could hardly be said of the copper vessels.

There can scarcely be grounds for doubting that the belt plates bearing a picture of a lion attacking a goat, as well as the silver pendants depicting horses, are native Altaian work; their style of execution down to the minutest detail is exactly the same as in the mass of objects carved in wood.

The copper nails have been cast in two-valve clay moulds, which were broken up after each casting. In some cases, if not always, the nail heads have been cast separately from the shank and then welded on. The copper bits were cast in the way reconstructed by Radlov and described in detail by him.[1]

The casting of the two censers, the rectangular one on four feet and the second in the shape of a 'Scythian cauldron' (*Pl. 62*A, B), as already remarked, was poor. The rectangular one had an irregular shape. The molten metal had been poured into a two-valve mould, the joint between the valves showing at about 1 cm. from the bottom. The handles, feet and lugs were cast separately

[1] *Materials for the Archaeology of Russia*, 15 (1894), pp. 119–21.

and then welded on. In the bottom was a patch over a hole caused by a defect in the casting operation. The other censer was spherical with a pedestal foot, the body, pedestal and handles of which had been cast separately and then welded together. After casting, six holes appeared in the vessel, five of which were patched, but the other plugged with a wooden bung.

The extent to which fine tools were employed in metal-working can be judged by the holes drilled in the pyrites crystals. In the description of costume it was noted that the soles of one pair of shoes were decorated with fifty-four sewn-on gilded cubical pyrites crystals (iron sulphides). This is one of the commonest of iron ores, encountered everywhere in the Altai, sometimes with gold in the quartzite veins, sometimes without it. The crystals therefore could be obtained locally either as a by-product in extracting gold, or independently. The only surprising point is the skill with which the crystals were drilled to produce minute holes, no more than a millimetre across, by means of which they were attached to the sole. Pyrites is fairly hard (6–6·3 on Mohs' scale) and with an iron bit it would scarcely be possible to make such an opening. What made it more difficult was that the material is very brittle and the opening has to be drilled not in the middle but on an edge at the side. On each crystal there are two holes drilled down at obtuse angles from either side until they met.

The gold earrings from barrow 2 have already been sufficiently described as examples of adornment in the chapter devoted to that subject.

8. SOME EVIDENCE ABOUT THE SOCIAL STRUCTURE

WE HAVE NO direct documentary evidence about the social structure of the ancient inhabitants of the High Altai at the period under discussion, but burials throw indirect light on this matter. A valuable additional source is the reports of Greek historians and Chinese chroniclers about the nature of the social structure of the numerous pastoral tribes inhabiting the steppes and mountain valleys of eastern Europe and Asia, that resembled one another and the Altai tribes in their way of life and culture. In a number of cases also ethnographic data can be drawn upon for analogies.

In the study of this important question we will try to make use of all the facts, however small and fragmentary, which are available to us.

We have already seen that the basic occupation of the population of the High Altai in the last millennium B.C. was stock-breeding. It follows that as stock-rearing is a man's affair so he must have been the head of the family, which would therefore have been patriarchal. To judge by written sources such was the case among the other tribes of eastern Europe and Asia. A number of references which imply this will be cited.

In patriarchal society the descent from father to son, particularly the youngest son, is naturally the rule. That such an arrangement existed among the Scyths is indicated by the legend about the sacred gold descended from heaven and obtained by the youngest brother.[1] Just as characteristic in patriarchal society was the custom of marriage with stepmothers and sisters-in-law, both to continue the clan and because exogamy required the redemption of the bride from a second clan. Chinese chroniclers recorded of pastoral tribes closest to Pazyryk (the Wu-sun and Huns) that 'on the death of his father a man marries his stepmother; on the death of his brother he marries his sisters-in-law', and go on to cite actual cases.[2] Herodotus records the story of a Scythian king, Scylas, who married the widow of his father.[3]

[1] Herodotus, A, bk iv, 5.
[2] Bichurin, A, pt i, pp. 40, 52, 143.
[3] Herodotus, A, bk iv, 78.

In spite of the prevailing patriarchal form of society and the firm evidence for patrilineal descent among them,[1] some of the stock-breeding tribes of *c.* 500 B.C., in particular the Massagetae, still retained traces of matriarchy. With the Issedones women enjoyed a status equal to that of men.[2] Chinese chroniclers record that among the Wu-huan on every matter 'they consult the women, who sometimes even make decisions on matters of war'.[3] Among a number of tribes the women played an equal part with men in war; Herodotus reported of the Sauromatae that 'the women ride hunting and to war with the men and that they dress in just the same way as the men'.[4] Ctesias recorded a legend that in the reign of the Median king Astibar there was a prolonged and bloody war between the Sacae and the Medes. 'At this time the leader of the Sacae was called Zarina, a female warrior far exceeding in courage and skill the other women of the Sacae. Among the people in general women are courageous and help the men in the dangers of war.'[5] At a later date when the supreme chief of the Sacae, Amorg, had been captured by the Persian king Cyrus, his wife, Sparetra, according to legend, gathered an army of 300,000 men and 200,000 women which inflicted a defeat on Cyrus.

According to Herodotus, when the Persians made war on the Massagetae the leader of the army of the latter was Tomyris, widow of their king.[6]

Bearing in mind the references just cited to the position of women, mainly no doubt applying to people at a higher social level than the Altaians, it must be supposed that the women buried with the chiefs at Pazyryk could hardly have been their wives, or at all events their senior wives. Perhaps they were junior wives taken from another tribe 'as a sign of peace and kinship'. We may recall the report of Herodotus that together with the corpse of a supreme chief was buried one of his concubines, who had been strangled.[7]

An unmistakable trace of the patriarchal-clan structure of society among the pastoral tribes, in contrast to the earlier matriarchal form, is the family ownership of property, in the first place livestock.

Livestock, the main possession of pastoral folk, as F. Engels[8] assumed, belonged originally to the clan, that is, it was social property. Very early, however, from common ownership of the tribe or clan it was transferred to the particular ownership of heads of families. Within a pastoral family individuals could obviously privately own such things as certain riding-horses and the like. Various written sources record family and individual ownership of cattle amongst the ancient stock-breeding tribes of eastern Europe and Asia. A

[1] Artamanov, A, 1947, p. 71.
[2] Herodotus, A, bk i, 216; bk iv, 26.
[3] Bichurin, A, pt i, p. 143.
[4] Herodotus, A, bk iv, 116.
[5] Ctesias, A, pp. 42 and 43.
[6] Herodotus, A, bk i, 214.
[7] *Idem*, bk. iv, 71.
[8] Marx and Engels, A, vol. xvi, pt i, pp. 37 and 38.

Chinese chronicle recorded that among the Huns 'he who kills in battle receives all that belonged to the dead man'.[1]

A Chinese writer reported of the Wu-huan tribes that at a funeral 'they take the horse the dead man rode, his clothes and all his possessions and burn them'.[2] At a death the cattle, as with the Black Sea Scyths and the Issedones, were inherited not by the tribe or clan but by the relatives or friends of the dead man.[3] In addition, according to Herodotus, the property of a Scyth executed for oath-breaking was shared among the soothsayers who testified to his for-swearing.[4] Direct confirmation of the private ownership of riding-horses among the Sacae of central Asia is provided by a curious half-legendary story told us by Xenophon. In the equestrian contests arranged by Cyrus on the capture of Babylon, a Sacian, a simple rider, left the other competitors almost half the length of the hippodrome behind him. Then the Sacian presented the horse to one of the friends of Cyrus, Fevral.[5] This would only have been possible if the young man owned the horse himself.

The stock-rearing tribes of the High Altai were no exception to this. In all the tombs of the period, whether of a male or female, rich or poor, horses were buried with the other private possessions of the deceased. The right of private property in animals finds confirmation in the presence of family, but not clan, marks on the ears of the horses buried in the barrows at Pazyryk. Since the horses were riding-animals they were the property of the individuals with whom they were buried, not gifts to the deceased chief from his subordinates, as M. P. Gryaznov described them.[6]

A number of essential differences in grave-goods and in details of burial rite observed by us in the barrows of the High Altai suggest this region was occupied during Scythian times not by a single tribe but by several, closely akin cul-turally. Each tribe would naturally have its own definite territory where it would not brook interference, but the territory itself would be owned in common. K. Marx wrote of land among the pastoral tribes in the Asian steppes and plateaux: 'They use it for pasture and the like on which to feed their flocks, which in turn makes it possible for the pastoral peoples to exist. They treat the land as if it were their property although they never divide it up into private property.'[7]

The significance attached to control over territory by pastoral tribes in antiquity can be appreciated from the following record of a Chinese chronicler. Receiving information that Mao-Tun had made himself shan-yu of the Huns, the neighbouring tribe of the Dung-hu wanted first to obtain from him a thousand-li horse (one that could cover a thousand li in a day), then one of his wives, and,

[1] Bichurin, A, pt i, p. 50.
[2] Ibid., p. 144.
[3] Herodotus, A, bk iv, 26, 73.
[4] Ibid., 68.

[5] Xenophon, A, *Cyropaedia*, bk viii, 3, 25–6.
[6] Gryaznov, A, 1950, p. 70.
[7] Marx, A, 1940, p. 23.

finally, that between the domains of the Huns and Dung-hu a strip a thousand li wide should be left uninhabited. In spite of the advice of the elders not to give up a horse or a wife Mao-Tun did not mind losing a wife or a thousand-li horse to preserve a good-neighbourly relationship with the Dung-hu. When the elders told him that the ground wanted by the Dung-hu was useless (for raising stock), so 'you can give, without giving anything', Mao-Tun said in an extra-ordinary fury: 'Land is the foundation of power; how can I give it away? Cut off the heads of all those who advised giving away land.' [1]

Under the unchanging conditions of the thorough-going pastoral economy of the steppes, tribes retain their ancient social arrangements: 'The more deeply the methods of production are rooted in ancient tradition . . . then the less change is undergone in the process of appropriation, the more unyielding the old forms of ownership and consequently of collective society in general,' wrote Marx.[2] This justifies us in turning to ethnography, to the surviving character of the social organization of Kirgiz and Kazakhs in the last century, which can help us to understand more fully the life of the ancient Altaians.

The Kirgiz and Kazakhs were divided in the nineteenth century into great clans (tribes) and their branches, small clans. Among the Kazakhs, for example, each tribe and each clan owned its own definite territory, and even each family had its own precise winter quarters. The boundaries of these portions were well known to all the members of a clan and their neighbours and were safeguarded by the clan. While the winter quarters were divided between families, or more precisely heads of families, the summer stations were common clan property.

In spite of the absence of private property in land the rich, having a larger number of cattle, made more use of the best pastures, which tended to increase the inequality. Something similar must have taken place amongst the ancient stock-rearing tribes.

The presence of poor and rich families was accompanied undoubtedly by the employment of some alien labour by the rich stock-rearers. Among the latter there were perhaps slaves, although it would be easy to exaggerate the part played by the work of the latter; the extent of the use of slave labour in a pastoral economy was extremely limited. Even the Black Sea Scyths, among whom at this period primitive society was in the process of dissolution, and among whom slavery went further than in the Altai, employed slaves for only a limited range of domestic tasks (like making koumiss) and then only after blinding them.[3]

A Chinese chronicle reports of the Wu-huan tribes: 'From the elders down to the lowest menial each pastures his own cattle and looks after his own property, not using others in his service.' [4]

[1] Bichurin, A, pt i, 47–8.
[2] Marx, A, 1940, p. 28.
[3] Herodotus, A, bk iv, 2.
[4] Bichurin, A, pt i, p. 143.

With regard to the Altai region there is in general no evidence for the existence of slavery or, at all events, no case of the burial of slaves occurred in the excavated barrows. The most one can assume is the existence of domestic slavery. It is more than likely that there was patriarchal exploitation of kinsmen in the form of *saun*, the giving up of cattle under guise of mutual assistance in the clan. Naturally the differences of property between rich and poor families, normal in patriarchal society, which revealed themselves in sharp distinctions in social position, must not be underestimated. The existence of private family ownership of livestock, and its inheritance on the paternal side, was all conducive, as Engels showed, to the accumulation in pastoral tribes of riches within the family and increased its importance as against the clan; also to be taken into account is the influence on the social system of the growth of a rudimentary royal court.[1]

This property and social stratification within the Altaian tribes found a clear reflection in the burial structures. Besides a vast number of small (8–10 m. diameter) barrow-cairns there are others of medium size, and, of course, large ones up to 50 m. in diameter. The largest that I have seen in the central Altai were in the valley of the River Ursul and its tributaries, where there are groups containing single examples 75–80 m. in diameter and correspondingly high.

The small barrows, which constitute the great mass of monuments of the period, were the graves of the ordinary herdsmen buried with one or two horses and a few, absolutely necessary, grave-goods. In a single large barrow of the Pazyryk type a member of the tribal nobility was buried in rich clothes with rich gold adornments and foreign textiles and a dozen or so horses. The very dimensions of these barrows show that they were beyond the ability of a single family to construct, and, if not a whole tribe, at least a whole clan must have taken part in the funeral. It follows therefore that the individuals buried in them were not only rich but also exercised great authority; they must have been either tribal chiefs or members of a clan nobility. The home of the supreme chiefs was in all probability in the central Altai, in the Ursul valley, but their graves have not yet been investigated.

The written sources dealing with the pastoral tribes contemporary with the Altaian ones paint a picture like this. At the head of the Asian pastoral tribes, e.g. the Wu-sun, the Huns, the Yue-chi and the Wu-huan, were chiefs of tribes or tribal unions, who were called *shan-yu, gunmo* and so on. In some tribes, e.g. among the Huns, besides the shan-yu, who was chief of a tribal union, there were war leaders subordinate to him, *dugi,* who were usually his sons or relatives. In each tribe there were elders as well as war leaders.

[1] Marx and Engels, A, vol. xvi, pt i, pp. 38, 86.

215

According to Greek historians the Scythian tribes were also led by a chief of tribes or tribal unions; it was the same among the Sacae, whose chiefs are referred to in the Bisutun inscription. Among both Scyths and Sacae, in addition to clan or tribal chiefs, there existed supreme chiefs, 'kings'. According to Herodotus the wife of a Sacian king, Sparetra, assembled an army half a million strong to fight Cyrus, as just mentioned.[1] An army of this size could only have been produced by a great confederacy of Sacian tribes.

Among the Black Sea tribes the office of chief seemed to have passed hereditarily from father to son or other relative, as is testified by Herodotus in the story of Scylas inheriting power and his wife from his father.

Precisely the same arrangement of inheritance of the office of chief existed then and later among a number of tribes in central Asia. Something similar could have existed in the High Altai, although it is more likely that there the chief's office was elective.

One of the characteristic features of clan and tribal organization is the existence of a communal place of burial, in which family burials are distinguishable; in the Altai these consist of a row of graves extended in a straight line like a chain. Close examination of cemeteries with large barrows of important people reveals that they occur four or five together in an extended row. Some cemeteries contain only two or three large barrows, some only one. Where the barrows are arranged in a definite alignment we can with justice assume that we are dealing with burials of chiefs from the same noble family who consecutively enjoyed hereditary power. At Pazyryk the case was different; there were five burials of important members of a clan or tribe, but belonging to three different families, since they are not in a row. As we know, barrows 1 and 2 occupy a special position, then 3 and 4, and, finally, 5 in quite separate positions.

It is noticeable too that all the men buried in the large Altaian barrow-cairns, including Pazyryk, as already mentioned in the chapter about the physical type of the population, were distinguished by their stature and physique. On this point it is worth recalling the report of a Chinese chronicler about the Wu-huan: 'Those who are brave and strong and can skilfully settle disputes are appointed as elders; there is no hereditary succession among them.'[2] We may add that to judge by the excavation results, in the Altai tribes high social position as elder or chief was retained by men to an advanced age.

From what has been said it can be seen that at this time in the Altai a decisive role in appointment to office could still have been played by a tribal council of elders.

It is interesting that even among the Black Sea Scyths King Scylas, 'who did not like the Scythian way of life', after due investigation of his actions by the elders was deposed and replaced by Octamasadas.[3]

[1] Ctesias, A, pp. 42–3.   [3] Herodotus, A, bk iv, 78–80.
[2] Bichurin, A, pt i, p. 142.

The chiefs had an enhanced importance during war, either when tribes or clans made successful raids, capturing the best pastures or obtaining war booty, or when under the chief's leadership they were able to resist enemies and keep their property inviolate.

During peace the bonds between clans slackened and so correspondingly did the power of the chiefs. However, any threat of war always produced a rapid combination of tribes into such confederacies as the situation might require. Then of course the authority of the chiefs increased again.

One of the causes of fighting between pastoral tribes was either drought or the so-called 'jut' (murrain) among the cattle, produced by exceptionally heavy snow or spring freezing after thaw that prevented the animals from getting their food.

In these circumstances Kazakhs or Kirgiz in the nineteenth century, for example, would abandon their pastures and go into their neighbour's territory and keep on going until they reached a point where the cattle could feed. If they were lucky and the weather changed they returned to their normal sites with their remaining stock; if their cattle died they had no other recourse but to attack rich neighbours and carry off part of their cattle. Such an operation depended for its success on an organization commanded by a clan or tribal chief. Driving off cattle was not regarded as a felony and rustling was considered to be a special kind of profession.

Chinese chronicles draw an analogous picture in the descriptions of Huns and other pastoral tribes of central Asia: 'The cattle eat grass and drink water; according to the season the people move from place to place; in bad times they practise on horseback with bow and arrow, and in the good times they enjoy themselves and do not care about anything.' [1] Another reference says: 'In good times they are accustomed to following their cattle, enjoying field sports and getting drunk; in bad times everyone prepares for war in order to make raids.' [2]

In this connection the remains of arms or objects related to war in the Pazyryk barrows are of great interest. It is a pity, however, that insufficient weapons remained in them to offer anything like a full picture. The basic weapon was the short, composite bow of Scythian type.

Evidence about this is afforded by the riding warrior depicted on the great felt carpet from barrow 5 wearing his gorytus (bow-case and quiver) after Scythian fashion on his left side. No remains of an actual bow have survived; all that was vouchsafed us were bone arrow-heads from barrow 2 and arrow-shafts from barrow 3 (*Pl. 143*B, C).

The arrow-heads are of bone, or more exactly of antler, and of typical Scythian pyramidal shape with concealed socket. Two arrow-heads were all that

[1] Bichurin, A, pt i, 58.   [2] Ibid., p. 40.

were found (*Pl. 143*B). Both have equilateral triangular sides with the maximum breadth in the upper third of the head. To judge by the dimensions of the socket (diameter about 4 mm. and 8 mm. deep) the shafts would have been just like those found in barrow 3. Precisely similar arrow-heads, but made of bronze, were found by S. V. Kiselev in barrows 6 and 11 at Tuekta in the Ursul valley.[1]

The broken arrow-shafts lay on the floor of the chamber of barrow 3 beside the corpse thrown out of its coffin. To judge by the surviving back ends there had originally been twenty-four arrows, and from the different parts of two shafts one which could be fully reconstructed was 80 cm. long. The forepart of the shaft in most cases had been broken off and taken with the head by the robbers,[2] but nevertheless from these foreparts we can conclude that the socket on the head was up to 15 mm. deep and up to 5 mm. in diameter. The shafts were circular in section, 6–7 mm. in diameter, thinning a little in the front and then thickening up to 9 mm. at the back. To judge by the size of the nock the bowstring would have been 5 mm. in diameter, and the arrows had probably been plumed, since some sinew lashing survived at the back end of one shaft.

The painting on the arrow-shafts deserves special mention. They all bore painted designs, some along their whole length, others on the back third of the shaft; black and red paint was used for the pattern which, darkened by time, had become difficult to distinguish. It is only due to the fact that drawings were made at the site, directly after the removal of the objects from the burial chamber, when the pattern was at its clearest, that it has been possible to draw all the elements of the decoration. Studying *Pls. 179* and *180* it can be seen that although the range of motifs is narrow, by altering the combinations and colours a considerable variety of patterns were displayed.

The basic motifs are transverse curved lines, continuous or diagonal strokes like a cord pattern; longitudinal, curved, bent lines, plain or with rows of teeth or hooks; and bent S-shaped lines of plain or composite hooks. Besides the various combinations in which these motifs are used, variety was also achieved, as was mentioned, by altering the colour. Some of the shafts are painted exclusively red, some exclusively black, but the majority are red and black together.

It is worth observing that the bow and arrow was an extremely effective instrument of war, especially if one bears in mind the widespread habit of

[1] Kiselev, A, 1947, p. 164, fig. 3, a and b.

[2] Kiselev has explained the absence of arrow-heads as due to their deliberate removal for fear of their use as weapons, with which the spirits of the dead could do harm to the living. (*Idem*, 1949, p. 266.) Such an interpretation seems contrived and is contradicted by the finds of arrow-heads in unrobbed graves.

106. Dagger from Aragol barrow ($\frac{2}{3}$).

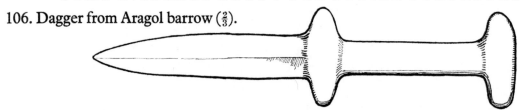

practice shooting; the preparation by the Scyths of the target for this is, for example, described in detail by Aristotle and Theophrastus.[1]

A short iron sword—acinaces—and a dagger also formed part of the weapons used. Acinaces with typical winged hilts have been found at the Tuekta barrows mentioned, Shibe and Berel. A copper dagger of medium size (17 cm. long) with cross-hilt and cross-pommel, ground on the four faces, was found in Aragol barrow 1 (fig. 106).

Battle-axes were also wielded as weapons, to judge by the marks of this weapon left on the skull of the slain warrior in barrow 2 and the same kind of trace on the skulls of the horses in all the barrows, which were 16–18 mm. in diameter. In section the battle-axe was not round but oval (11 mm. by 16 mm.), the striking, pointed end being round or, more often, rhomboidal in section.

Of defensive weapons only shields were found, which were of two types of identical construction. A small rectangular shield (28 cm. by 36 cm. in the middle) consisted of thirty-four to thirty-five round sticks, carefully whittled into shape, pleated through thin leather. The slits for the sticks had been cut through the leather in such a way that they produced an ornamental pattern on both sides, the basic motif of which is a rhomb (*Pl. 144*). Along the edge the leather was turned over and secured at the back of the shield. Behind in the middle is the broad loop or strap inserted from the front face. Shields of this type were found in barrows 1, 2 and 4 at Pazyryk. Where it was possible to determine, they had been secured at the right-hand side of the saddle.

Another type of shield was represented in barrow 3, where three shields were found as in barrow 1 (in barrows 2 and 4 there were only two). They were large (53 cm. by 69 cm.) with a convex upper edge (fig. 107). As in the other barrows they were made of carefully whittled wooden sticks about a centimetre in diameter, threaded through a piece of leather, in addition to which there were two transverse sticks (one 1 cm. above the bottom, another 3·5 cm. below the convex top, the curve of which it followed). Such a shield of sticks plaited through a piece of leather was a typical Scythian defensive weapon; we can see them in the hands of the fighting Scyths on the well-known gold comb of Greek workmanship from the barrow at Solokha.

By comparing the dimensions of the shields in the representation of Scythian warriors with the Pazyryk examples it can be seen that only the shields from

[1] Tevyashov, A.

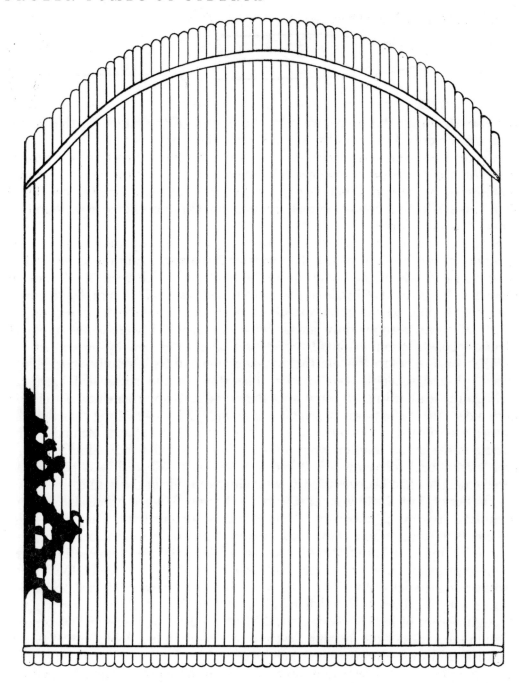

107. Shield from barrow 3 (*c.* $\frac{1}{4}$).

barrow 3 correspond in size; the others are too small. All the same, their complete uniformity in size and construction in the three barrows indicates that a widely employed form of defensive weapon is being dealt with.

An unexpectedly clear trace of war customs in the High Altai during the relevant period was found in barrow 2, where the head of the chieftain's corpse bore marks of having been scalped. The skin above the forehead had been cut through from ear to ear through a forelock of hair and then torn off backwards, baring the skull as far as the neck.

This tallies exactly with the method described by Herodotus used by a Scyth to remove the scalp from the head of a slain enemy: 'He makes a groove around the head near the ears; then he holds the head in his hands and pulls off the skin; then he scrapes off the fat with an ox rib and works it in his hands to make it soft; now he can use it as a duster and hangs it from the bridle of the horse he rides; he is then very proud of himself.'[1]

This prompts us to reflect on other barbaric war customs of the pastoral tribes of eastern Europe and Asia referred to in written sources and those which, to judge by the Pazyryk finds, were actually practised in the High Altai in the middle of the last millennium B.C.

Scyths, according to Herodotus, drank the blood of the first enemy that they slew and only those that produced the head of a dead man received part of the booty. The tribal elders at the time of the annual feast offered wine only to those Scyths who had killed an enemy, and those who had not achieved this tasted no wine and sat ashamed at one side.[2] Equally the Chinese chroniclers record that the Huns who chopped off the head of an enemy in battle received a goblet of wine as reward.[3]

We learn from Herodotus also that the skulls of especially detested enemies were made by the Scyths into drinking cups. They did the same thing with the skulls of relatives over whom they had triumphed in a dispute: 'When they wish to show special respect to a certain guest he displays these skulls, pointing out that they belonged to relatives whom he fought and beat. They regard this as a heroic deed.'[4]

The pastoral tribes of central Asia had an analogous custom: the Chinese chronicles record that after concluding a treaty the Chinese envoys and Hunnish shan-yu 'drank wine to seal the agreement from the skull of a Yue-chi ruler who had been killed by the shan-yu'.[5]

Even allowing that conflicts over pastures were as much a habitual part of pastoral life (especially among nomadic tribes) as were raids on settled agricultural tribes actuated by the desire for plunder, still the significance of war in

[1] Herodotus, A, bk iv, 64.
[2] Ibid., 64, 66.
[3] Bichurin, A, pt i, p. 50.
[4] Herodotus, *op. cit.*, 65.
[5] Bichurin, *op. cit.*, 92.

their social life ought not to be exaggerated, as has been done by M. I. Artamanov and a number of other scholars. The former writer in particular has
written that 'given the ill-developed state of trade a specialized pastoral economy
could not effect exchange without war as a substitute for barter. An increase of
private property, furthermore, aroused a thirst for enrichment which in the
undeveloped form of exploitation of fellow tribesmen and slaves could only be
quenched by the military plundering of neighbours'. [1] He went further than
that: 'With the creation in the steppes of a nomadic pastoral society belligerent
hordes came into existence for which uniting for war with the object of plunder
became a form of production.' [2]

One cannot agree with the estimate of an essentially primitive society of
herdsmen as a specialized economy, nor with the statement about the ill-
developed exploitation of fellow tribesmen, nor, finally, with the description of
war as 'production', even when qualified by 'a form of'.

Let us pause therefore to look at other kinds of relationship between the
mountain folk and the inhabitants of other regions and countries. The first
important form of relationship was undoubtedly trade.

F. Engels, in examining the question of the first considerable division of
labour, especially remarked that the appearance of pastoralism and then the
transfer of cattle to private ownership of different individuals in the tribe made
possible regular intertribal (and not just internal as hitherto) trade in livestock and pastoral goods.[3] Livestock became not only a commodity but, even
at this time, began to be used as money by becoming a common standard
against which the value of all others could be measured. The original middlemen between tribes were the chiefs and elders.

From numerous references in Chinese sources it is known that the tribes of
central Asia and Dunbei (Manchuria) from a comparatively early period of
their history traded with China by means of their elders. The basic form of
livestock which was sent for barter to the Chinese border was horses 'of the
best breeds'. The Chinese Government in order to regularize the trade at a
certain time of the year opened on its border the so-called 'horse fairs' at
which the products of agriculture and workshops were swapped for horses.
Thus it was not any livestock that became money, but more exactly the horse.
Judging by the thoroughbred horses found in the Pazyryk barrows it can be
supposed that this animal played just the same part here in barter with settled
neighbours, but other articles, notably textiles and artistic objects (for adornment), also were the object of exchange, buying and selling.

The intensity of this type of exchange may be judged by the case of barrow 1,

[1] Artamanov, A, 1950, pp. 27, 28.
[2] Ibid., p. 28.

[3] Marx and Engels, A, 1937, vol. xvi, pt i, p. 136.

in which ten horses had originally belonged to at least seven owners before they had become the property of the buried chief.

It is important to recognize the fairly high technical level of working in various materials which must have needed the skill of leather-workers, farriers, turners, weavers, wood and horn carvers and metal-casters. A certain type of craftsman, already referred to, had not yet emerged in local conditions from the general community, as was the case among the southern Sacae with an urban population. The common finds of foreign textiles and of a Chinese mirror bear witness to this. When considering the trade links of the High Altai with distant areas the following circumstance has to be borne in mind; as opposed to their neighbours of the steppe and semi-desert steppe massive stock-breeding for the peoples of the mountains was not possible. Furthermore the regions with a settled peasant population requiring livestock were remote from the Altai, the requirements of which could more easily be met by pastoral districts closer to hand. The probability is that furs and gold, rather than livestock, were the predominant exports from the Altai, which would have been exchanged for southern and eastern imports of valuable cloths and the other objects of luxury already mentioned. Excavations, not only at Pazyryk but also in other barrows, have shown that sable, for example, was obtained in considerable quantities. One has to remember the hunting tribes of the adjoining taiga regions who could hardly have had any opportunity for direct links with distant countries; it is more likely that they swapped valuable furs for livestock and pastoral products from the Altaians, and the latter played the role of middlemen, to their advantage, in the exchange of furs.

The pastoral tribes of eastern Europe and Asia, both in the last millennium B.C. and later, maintained close links with one another by the barter of goods as well as by blood relationships. Confirmation of this is furnished not only by the homogeneity of their material culture but by their customs. Exogamy contributed to maintain links, and treaties of union were cemented by marriages of chiefs of different tribes. In Chinese sources, such treaties are given the title of 'peace and kinship', and they refer to them as regular occurrences. Treaties founded on 'peace and kinship' were cemented by the Chinese emperor with the marriage of a princess to a powerful chieftain, whose friendship or enmity was important, whether he were Hun, Wu-sun or of another tribe.[1] The same custom prevailed at the conclusion of a treaty among other tribes. There is a curious record that one Wu-sun gunmo, taking the daughter of a Hunnish shan-yu and Chinese princess in marriage after such a treaty of 'peace and kinship', first of all set himself up with senior and junior wives.[2]

A special point of interest for us about these marriages is that an exchange was

---

[1] Bichurin, A, pt i, pp. 51, 57, 69, 83.   [2] Ibid., pt iii, p. 192.

obligatory at the same time; the Chinese court sent with the princess, and had to do so each year, gifts in the form of silks, cotton cloths and various edible delicacies,[1] and in return the nomad chiefs gave mainly horses.[2] The traditional gift which the Chinese emperor gave to nomadic tribes was a carriage drawn by a quadriga of horses, which would be granted to the princess upon her marriage by the Wu-sun and Hunnish tribes.

The discovery in barrow 5 of a carriage pulled by four horses, and also of precious Chinese silks, has prompted the suggestion that the tribes of the High Altai were in close relationship with China in Scythian times through the medium of their neighbours, the powerful steppe tribes of central Asia, with whom they might also have been connected by a treaty of 'peace and kinship'.

It is very important furthermore, in the light of what has been said, for us to recall the major events of this period in the history of the Orient and the agricultural parts of central Asia, and the part played in them by the south-western neighbours of the Altaian tribes, the Massagetae and Sacae of central Asia. I give as examples, albeit only the most important, the more reliable facts accorded us in this matter by ancient writers.

The first historical information about the Sacae and their intrusion into Hither Asia, as is well known, belongs to the seventh century B.C. (about 630), when they conquered Media and ruled there for twenty-eight years. Later on, while Cyaxares was still ruling Media, part of the Sacae as a result of a civil war went into Median territory and settled there for some time, at the request of Cyaxares teaching the youths their language and how to shoot the bow.[3] According to Ctesias the Sacae appeared on the historical scene in the reign of the Median king Astibar when the Parthians, hitherto subject to the Medians, broke away from them and freely placed themselves under the authority of the Sacae, which led to a bloody war of many years' duration breaking out between Medians and Sacae. Ctesias reports that Zarina, queen of the Sacae at this time, after the death of her first husband and brother Kydreias, king of the Sacae, married the Parthian prince, Mermer.[4] This marriage could signify the political union of the powers directed against the Medians, causing the division between the latter and the Parthians. For us the fact of union, albeit ephemeral, of Parthians and Medians under one supreme ruler is important. Such accidental unions of Sacian and Scythian tribes or other tribes of central and Hither Asia as a result of dynastic marriages which produced a single supreme ruler were not rare it seems.

Herodotus records that while Tomyris, widow of a former king of the Massagetae, was queen, 'Cyrus through his agents tried to make it look as if he wanted to get married and that it was she that he wanted as a wife. Tomyris, however,

---

[1] Bichurin, A, pt i, p. 69; pt iii, p. 192.
[2] Ibid., pt iii, p. 192.
[3] Herodotus, A, bk i, 73.
[4] Ctesias, A, pp. 42 and 44.

understood that he was not really proposing marriage to her but to the kingdom of the Massagetae and she refused his overtures'.[1]

Reports are especially numerous about the participation of the Sacae as allies on this or that side in the wars that took place in the sixth to fifth centuries B.C. in central Asia and Asia Minor. Ctesias recorded that in his war against Croesus, the Lydian, Cyrus was assisted by the Sacian king Amorg and later when Cyrus was wounded fighting insurgents Amorg hurried to his assistance with twenty thousand cavalrymen.[2] Xenophon recorded that the Sacae assisted Cyrus in his war with the Assyrians, finding ten thousand foot and one thousand mounted archers,[3] and took part in the ceremonial entry into Babylon.[4]

Later still, during the war of Xerxes, there were Sacian soldiers in all the boats with Medes and Persians.[5] In the battle of Plataea Herodotus recorded that the Sacian cavalry and Persian infantry distinguished themselves by their valour.[6] Similarly Diodorus Siculus referred to the Sacae, together with the Kassites, as especially distinguished by their valour at Thermopylae.[7]

In addition to their military activities the Sacae evidently played a certain part in the peaceful life of the peoples of Hither Asia. We may recall how they taught the Median youth to speak their language and shoot from the bow.[8] Xenophon described in detail the honoured position held at the court of the Median king, Astiag, by his Sacian steward.[9]

Thus, given the interrelationships which existed in the sixth and fifth centuries B.C., and as we know existed later on between the Sacae and their neighbours in Hither Asia, the exchange of goods was quite natural. It was indeed so intensive that it extended through the Massagetae and Sacae far to the north, right up to the High Altai.

In return for precious textiles, carpets and other objects of luxury, leopard skins and seeds of cultivated coriander imported from the south, from the Altai there were sent back to the south probably furs and gold, possibly livestock and pastoral products.

All the same, it must be borne in mind that the level of social and cultural development of the Altai mountain tribes was below that of their western neighbours.

A sketch of the correspondence in social structure between the Altai tribes and the steppe and piedmont pastoralists from north of the Black Sea to north China has been made above. Yet in order to study more deeply the problem of

---

[1] Herodotus, A, bk i, 205.
[2] Ctesias, A, pp. 46 and 47.
[3] Xenophon, A, *Cyropaedia*, bk v, 3, 24.
[4] Ibid., bk viii, 3, 18.
[5] Herodotus, A, bk vii, 96.
[6] Ibid., bk ix, 71.
[7] Diodorus Siculus, A, bk xi, 7.
[8] Herodotus, A, bk i, 73.
[9] Xenophon, A, *Cyropaedia*, bk i, 3, 8 ff.; 4, 6.

the social structure of the Altai tribes of the second half of the last millennium B.C. it is necessary to consider the differences, where they can be traced, and then conclude with which of the repeatedly mentioned tribes their social structure had its closest analogies. In the first place, sharp ethnic distinctions between the pastoral tribes have to be recognized, as the fact that they spoke several mutually unintelligible languages shows. Referring to one of the tribes (the Argippaei) living not far from the Altai, Herodotus wrote: '. . . anyone from the Scyths who visits them makes use of seven interpreters speaking seven languages to conduct his business.' [1]

I. V. Stalin stated that the development of language follows the course: 'evolution of clan languages to a tribal language, tribal languages to the language of a folk and from that of a folk to that of a nationality.' [2] It must be assumed that languages spoken by these tribes had not yet passed beyond the second stage defined by Stalin in the evolution of language, that is, tribal languages. Secondly there can be no doubt that the economic and social development of the tribes over this huge area at the relevant time was uneven. Among the Sacae there were already in existence more or less stable tribal unions with highly stratified society, possessing not only towns but also 'capitals'.[3]

Among the Black Sea Scyths, as among the Huns, large tribal confederacies had already come into existence. A tribal aristocracy, already distinguishable from the rest of the community, had concentrated in its hands the riches derived not only from trade in livestock but to some degree from wars of plunder. This noble class, who had seized power, kept it among a few aristocratic families who transferred it after their own lifetime by hereditary succession.

Evidence of a high degree of social differentiation, and consequently of a relatively high level of social development for that period, is furnished by the archaeological remains: in the Black Sea district large barrows are known in which a corpse was interred with more than four hundred horses. The written sources are indeed eloquent enough on this point. According to Herodotus a Scythian king was buried with horses, all types of livestock and gold cups, but his authority was so great that with him, in addition to concubines, they buried a steward, a cook, a servant and a herald and furthermore, in the following year, a further fifty young attendants were slain at the tomb.[4] According to the Chinese sources, at the burial of a Hunnish shan-yu the 'companions in death', attendants and concubines, numbered several hundred individuals. With regard to the Altaian barrows one can see a uniformity in the grave-goods in

[1] Herodotus, A, bk iv, 24.
[2] Stalin, A, 1950, p. 10.

[3] Nicholas of Damascus (*World History*) referred to the town of Roxanaka, capital of the Sacian kingdom, in which Queen Zarina, just mentioned, lived.
[4] Herodotus, A, bk iv, 71 and 72.

small and large barrows alike, distinguished only by quantity and size of the burial structure. The fact that the buried chiefs belonged to different families, discussed above, speaks of a tradition of elective appointment. The small number of horses and only one concubine (or junior wife) buried with the corpse indicate that the tribes of the High Altai stood closest in their social structure to the Wu-huan, among whom the separation of the more prosperous families from the rest of the tribe had not begun. Wealth alone was still not the decisive factor in the selection of a chief; other personal qualities remained important, notably courage and skill in resolving disputes.

Thus at the time under discussion the population of the High Altai had a social structure not yet far removed from that of primitive society. For even at the October Revolution the population of this region in no way differed from tribes and folk who, as Comrade Stalin has shown, 'retained in the majority of cases a pastoral economy and patriarchal clan way of life (Kirgizia, Bashkiria, North Caucasus)'.[1]

[1] Stalin, A, 1947, v, p. 25.

THE PAZYRYK barrows have yielded a quantity of varied objects of art of the pastoral tribes of that period never seen before; so filled were they with manifestations of art that even the most commonplace carved objects, appliqué work, ornament and sculpture constitute examples. In the preceding account of each group of finds much has been said already about their aesthetic qualities.

In the present chapter attention is particularly devoted to those examples of art which have not been given due notice in the preceding chapters, and to those objects which markedly display the main individual qualities of the tribes of the High Altai in the relevant period. Foremost among these are the designs on the saddle-covers.

Various artistic compositions are especially characteristic of the fine felt saddle-covers of barrows 1 and 2. In barrow 1 they all bore applied decoration of one kind or another, but in barrow 2, so far as could be established, only one out of the seven bore any decoration at all. In barrows 3 and 4 saddle-covers did not survive and in barrow 5 of the five saddles only one had a decorated cover, the remainder being of plain, thin, black, undecorated felt. Perhaps this should be attributed to the presence of decorated shabracks in barrow 5.

The most widespread motif used on the covers is the attack of a carnivore on an ungulate or a struggle between beasts, represented by whole animals or their heads. The technique employed is appliqué, or pasted-on silhouettes (cut from leather and partly coloured and covered by gold-leaf or tinfoil) or composite figures of polychrome pieces of felt sewn on to the cover.

On a blue cover from a saddle in barrow 1 a cut-out of thin leather representing a tiger seizing an elk has been pasted on (fig. 108). The tiger was painted yellow with some details of the skin indicated by brown colour; the elk was covered by tinfoil. The elk, under the attack of the tiger, which is biting into its back, has sagged on all four legs. The snout of the elk's head, its short beard, long ear and stylized palmating antler are finely rendered. In the powerful predator with contracted stomach the broad forehead and short, cat-like ears

229

108. Decoration on saddle-cover from barrow 1; a tiger falls upon an elk (*c*. $\frac{1}{5}$).

are well caught, as also is the curvature of the body. On the elk's body are the traditional commas and stops.

Another scene of a tiger falling upon an elk comes from barrow 2 (fig. 109), made from a thin leather cut-out pasted on to a red saddle-cover. The tiger, with its characteristic twist of body and neck, tail curved into a curl at end, with soft but clawed paws, bites into the elk, which has its head raised and back twisted round. The figure of the tiger is covered with bright yellow paint with dark spots and streaks on its body. Details are indicated on the body of the elk by cuts through which the light red of the saddle-cloth is visible; the slashes, which are of stop, comma and half-horseshoe shape, emphasize parts of the body.

An unusual composition is a leather cut-out of a tiger tearing at a deer (fig. 110). Both tiger and deer have their backs twisted round. The curved figure of the tiger is shown with smooth lines; the deer in spite of the schematism is realistically portrayed. Its well-proportioned head with small ears is crowned with typically cervid antlers; the body has a short tail and legs shorter than those of an elk. The blue saddle-cloth serves as a background to the scene. The tiger is coloured orange-yellow with brown lines for details; the head and hoofs of the deer are covered by gold-leaf, the body by tinfoil.

Two remarkable scenes of a tiger or leopard seizing a mountain ram were found in barrows 1 and 2; fig. 111 illustrates the leather cut-out of one example, which is badly decayed. Only the fact that the parts of the picture destroyed on one cover survived on the other made it possible to make a full reconstruction. The ram, with large, strongly twisted horns and projecting tongue, has fallen on its forelegs while the back ones on the twisted crupper are thrown back and up. Its crupper bears the traditional stop and half-horseshoe, and the body ornamental slashes; the undermane is exquisitely indicated by slashing. The horn, tongue, stop and half-horseshoe are coloured in red. The tiger, with

230

typical feline tail, is biting into the withers of the ram, on the body of which it stands with all four paws, while it touches it with the twisted tip of its tail. The tiger is coloured yellow.

Rather different is a leather cut-out scene of a tiger attacking a mountain ram in barrow 1 (fig. 112). The ram is again shown fallen forward on its forelegs with its crupper twisted round. The tiger stands with all four paws on the ram but it is biting not into its withers but at its throat. The tiger is treated as a simple shape with supple body, clawed paws and long tail curled at the end. This silhouette scene is lent an air of open-work by the slashing on the body for stops, commas and half-horseshoes. The figure of the ram was covered by tinfoil, the horn coloured yellow and the undermane and circle in the horn in red. The tiger is yellow with dark-brown stripes.

A unique composition in leather cut-out from barrow 1 is that of an elk in the talons of a big-eared griffin (fig. 113). The heavy-muzzled head of the elk with large ears and typical palmating antlers is a particularly lively piece of work, and the whole group has been dealt with in a masterly way, simply and yet comprehensively. The strong body has a twisted crupper, slender legs and short tail, and the trunk is slashed with stops, commas and half-horseshoes. The griffin, with big ears and a comb, extended wings and a distended tail, grips the elk in its claws. The piece was pasted to a red saddle-cloth and covered with tinfoil.

An elk is represented in an individual way on a white saddle-cover from barrow 2, done with multicoloured thin felt and stitched on to the cover (*Pl. 168*A). The animal is shown with head raised and thrown-back horns, front legs stretched out and back legs retracted: on the body are the same conventional

109. Decoration on saddle-cover from barrow 2; a tiger falls upon an elk ($\frac{1}{3}$).

231

110. Decoration on saddle-cover from barrow 1; a tiger seizes a deer ($\frac{1}{4}$).

111. Decoration on saddle-cover from barrow 2; a tiger falls upon a mountain ram ($\frac{1}{3}$).

232

112. Decoration on saddle-cover from barrow 1; a tiger falls upon a mountain ram (*c.* $\frac{1}{3}$).

signs; the eyes and snout have detail picked out in woollen chain-stitch embroidery. In the same barrow was part of a saddle on the cover of which the same technique had been employed in a scene of some kind of predator seizing an elk (*Pl. 169*B).

The bright red felt cover of one of the saddles of barrow 1 had leather cut-outs stuck on it covered with tinfoil of silhouette lions (fig. 114). The thickset and powerful shape is characteristic of the beast, and the open jaws in the great head are fanged. The large ears pointing forward are out of proportion; the long tail is exaggerated and has an unnatural twist (often used in representations of lions in order to give counterbalance to the figure), and finishes in a typical brush. The ribs, musculature of the shoulder girdle and crupper have been treated in a manner with which we are now familiar. Taken as a whole the figure has a static monumental air; the vivacity and dynamism of the tigers and leopards attacking ungulates are quite lacking.

In all the saddle-covers so far discussed we have been dealing with real creatures and realistic treatment, save for a few conventionalizations in the big-eared griffin attacking the elk. However, fantastic beasts, eagle- and lion-griffins, motifs from Hither Asia, yet with individual Altaian treatment, do occur on the saddle-covers.

On a white cover, yellowed by time, from a saddle in barrow 2 is an eagle-griffin of applied polychrome felt (*Pl. 168*B). The figure is unrelated to any other animal, and is not part of a scene, which has caused the craftsman to concentrate all his attention on showing the characteristics peculiar to the monster. A special effort has been put into the griffin's head, with jagged comb, ruff, powerful beak and sharp eye. The wings have been done carelessly, conventionally rendered with ends pointed forward; the extended trunk carries the full range of stops, half-horseshoes, commas and triangles.

The same technique has been employed in the quite remarkable scene of a lion-griffin falling upon a mountain goat on a saddle-cover from barrow 1, a precise analogy for which I have not been able to find (*Pl. 169*A). The griffin has sunk the talons of its right foreclaw into the goat's withers and with its left seized the extended rear leg of the victim, which is making a frantic movement trying to tear itself away. The figure of the lion-griffin has an imperturbable monumental air: the open jaws, large ears, comb and horns recall the tiled frieze at Susa or on some stone plaque of the Achaemenian period. The wings are conventionalized and bent up and the tail has a bird's head terminal, while the body is again highly conventionalized.

The same appliqué technique has been used on another red saddle-cover from barrow 1 for a scene of an eagle-griffin falling upon a mountain goat (*Pl. 170*). The wretched creature is in a familiar attitude, thrown forward on its forelegs, rear legs extended on its twisted crupper and head turned back. The eagle-griffin standing on the goat has seized its horn in its beak. The griffin's head has a powerful eagle's beak, large ears and a topknot; the comb on its neck and its wings are represented quite differently from those on the lion-griffin. The trunks of both animals bear the conventional stops and commas.

An intensely interesting subject is treated in a leather cut-out silhouette on a blue saddle-cover from barrow 1 which shows a fight between an eagle-griffin and a lion-griffin (fig. 115). The piece is unfortunately badly preserved, but an eagle-griffin with comb biting into the neck of a lion-griffin with its beak can be clearly distinguished. Both beasts are winged and the lion-griffin is horned. The back leonine half of the trunks of the griffins is differently treated in the two cases.

On a red felt saddle-cover from barrow 1 representations of lions' heads, cut from thin leather and covered by tinfoil, are glued in pairs on either side (fig. 116). These profile lions' heads stylistically resemble those which we have already met on the frieze of the felt wall-hanging from the same barrow (fig. 12). The open jaws with bared teeth and conspicuous fangs are the same, so is the way the eyes are formed, and the mane has the same curls. They differ in that the heads on the

113. Decoration on saddle-cover from barrow 1; an elk in the talons of a griffin ($\frac{1}{3}$).
114. A lion decorating a saddle-cover in barrow 1 ($\frac{1}{3}$).

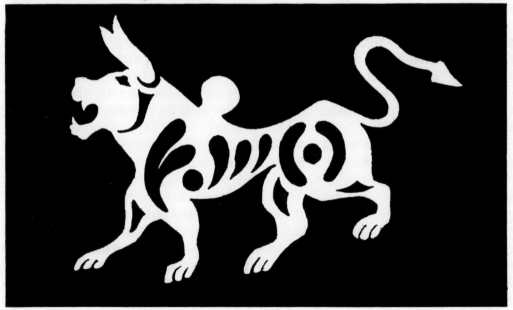

115. Struggling griffins decorating a saddle-cover from barrow 1 (*c.* $\frac{1}{3}$).

saddle-cover are horned and have the ear in its natural position, not on the crown as in the wall-hanging, and the forming of the head is more elaborated, more worked out in detail. The treatment of these leather lions' heads is the same as that of the winged lion-griffin just described (fig. 115).

Finally, another saddle-cover from barrow 1 bears four representations of profile rams' heads with protruding tongue, cut from leather and covered by tinfoil, glued on either side (fig. 117). These silhouettes with circular eye and brow and sharply curved horn are very expressive, and their realism is only disturbed by the ornamental branching of the horns, and by the apparent turning-up of the undermane, resembling the curls on the manes of the lions' heads.

The saddle-covers from barrow 5, with the single exception mentioned, were made of plain thin black felt, trimmed with a strip of red felt. The decorated example, finer than the others, was highly original (fig. 88). It is made up of square pieces of brick-red woollen cloth and fine leather arranged in a chequer pattern. In the centres of the cloth squares were fixed little crosses cut from fine yellow silk attached to the cover only at the centre, and there were three disks of gold-leaf stuck on to disks of thin copper. On the leather squares black colt's fur was sewn with three triangular slashes in it. The leather under the large triangles was lacquered in red over which were pasted facing relief elks' heads cut from gold-leaf. In the small triangular slashes fur dyed a blue colour had been

236

116. A lion's head decorating a saddle-cover from barrow 1 ($\frac{1}{4}$).

117. A ram's head decorating a saddle-cover from barrow 1 ($\frac{1}{2}$).

stitched on, over which were pasted stylized ox-horn shapes in gold. On the edge of the colt's fur and on the inner triangle, as also in the centre of the little crosses, thick little gold disks were fixed (*Pl. 167A*). The majority of disks and elks' heads had been lost, but all the same it was possible to reconstruct the original appearance of the cover.

The head of the elk set in the triangle had round eyes and characteristic ears with curl at the base, stylistically similar to the facing elk's head on the wooden belt-plate from the Katanda barrow (*Pl. 140B*).

Besides the covers discussed above six saddles from barrow 1 were decorated with various pendants representing rams' heads, lions, fish and human heads (masks).

Rams' heads were used as pendants, four on each side, to decorate the same saddle as that which bore the ram's head shown in fig. 117 on its cover. These pendants were made from layers of coloured leather sewn together, trimmed with fur dyed blue and with a horsehair fringe dyed red (*Pl. 167C*). A leather cut-out sewn on the outside was covered with tinfoil, which represented a ram's head similar to that in fig. 117 but with mouth nearly shut, elongated (not round) eye and pointed ear. The framing of the head—possibly the same under-mane was intended—has been executed in quite another style from that in fig. 117.

Another saddle had three very interesting profile rams' heads hanging from

237

either side (*Pl. 135*). They are sewn up from polychrome felt and are also trimmed with blue fur with a fringe of red horsehair (*Pl. 171*). The heads, rosettes within the horns and the framing of the horns are of red felt, the horns of blue felt. The eyes, lips, ear and banding on the horn are covered by cut-out leather shapes pasted over with tinfoil. The muzzle of the ram is pressed between two profile horned lions' heads, made of blue felt, ears of red, neck, comb and horns of yellow felt. The eyes are gold plates; the horns, neck and part of the lower jaw are covered by thin leather stuck over with tinfoil. Stylistically the rams' heads are similar to those described above, and the lions' heads like that of the lion-griffin in fig. 115.

Two pairs of long flaps, over 1 m. long, hung from either side of the saddle-cover, the lions on which have been discussed, and terminated as horned lions (*Pl. 48*). They are sewn up from red felt on a leather backing (*Pl. 172*). The lion is shown with forepaws extended touching the chin and it has a horsehair mane dyed red. The eyes, ears, mouth, puckering on upper lip, ribs and details of the body are indicated by excisions on the leather covered by tinfoil of corresponding shape pasted on to the lion's body.

From two of the saddles hung pendants shaped like fish, six on either side in one example and two in the other. The fish in the case of the first saddle (*Pl. 167*D) was shown very schematically and conventionally with a bifurcating tail fin and two fins on the back and belly. The figures are cut out of thick leather and partially covered by blue fur and strips of tinfoil, and a tuft of horsehair dyed red was attached to the tail.

The large pendants of the second saddle consist of figures of fish with heads of rams in their mouths (*Pl. 47*). They are cut from thick felt and covered by thin leather. In this cool, balanced composition the silhouette, profile ram's head is made up of two colours (the head itself a gold plate, the horns of coloured leather). The fish's body twists round the head. On the schematically shown head of the fish are two little gold disks (the eyes); the tail fin bifurcation is typically fishlike, but the other fins are shown unnaturally in a continuous row from head to tail. There are little gold disks along a narrow strip of leather on the backbone.

The most interesting pendants, on account of both motif and shape, as human heads, hung six a side on one of the saddles from barrow 1 (*Pl. 138*F). These masks are made from two pieces of leather, one, the base from which the details were excised, and the other acting as backing, visible only through the excisions. A fringe of horsehair dyed red was stitched on them at the back. The formation of the upper part of the head into lotus ornament and the three-petalled design on each side are extraordinarily interesting.

Since the basic function of the art being discussed was the decoration of a

238

variety of utilitarian objects, regardless of the material from which they were made, a modern classification by forms is not feasible. An attempt to divide the art into groups according to the techniques and methods employed in its execution—sculpture in the round, relief, painting or graphic art—is doomed to failure in as much as in the execution of one and the same piece several methods were often made use of at the same time. Consequently, after discussion of the various technical methods of execution, we shall concentrate our main attention on the motifs and style of this art. As we go along we shall attempt to explain the origin of a part of these motifs, and we shall examine the purpose of some of them in the next chapter dealing with the religious ideas of the people.

Artistic objects sculptured in the round, by comparison with those in relief, are not numerous, but still there were more than forty. The materials employed were wood, horn, leather, felt and metal. We may recall the table-legs carved as tigers from barrow 2 (*Pl. 50*), numerous carved feline figures and heads (*Pl. 111*), a deer's head (*Pl. 121*D) and birds' heads (*Pl. 121*A, B), the crests of horses' head-dress in barrows 3 and 5, and much else. From leather were carved sculptural heads of goats (*Pl. 137*C, D) and a griffin (*Pl. 81*B) from barrow 1 and cocks from barrow 2 (*Pl. 65*B). Also sculptured in the round are the remarkable felt swans from barrow 5, the cock and goat's head from barrow 2 (*Pl. 122*A) and the horned head of the lion-griffin from the horse-mask in barrow 1 (*Pl. 120*).

In the eastern part of the tree-trunk coffin in the chamber of barrow 2 sculptural figures of deer and griffins carved from wood were found (*Pl. 137*A, B, G, H). I had originally thought that together with the horned head of the lion-griffin they could have belonged to a diadem. Now the lion-griffins have been explained as part of a torque, but the question of the use of the deer and griffins remains open, although their artistic value is indisputable.

The figures of deer carved from single pieces of wood standing on a ball support are fine sculptural work (*Pl. 137*G, H); these beautiful realistic figures have been executed with quite exceptional skill. The proportions of the body are severely restrained, except the inserted leather ears and more particularly the branching antlers, which were deliberately exaggerated. Four such figures were found, but to judge by the quantity of antlers there must originally have been six. Since each figure was carved separately they all differ from one another in detail. In the sockets of the spherical bases were small iron rods showing that originally the figures had been hafted in some way. The figures as a whole, including stands, ears and antlers, were covered by gold-leaf. During manufacture a leg of one of the deer had snapped off, but the craftsman had carefully bound the break with very fine sinew thread and then pasted it over with gold.

With the deer were found wooden figures of griffins with small schematic bodies, disproportionately large head, typical eagle's beak and marked cere, pointed topknot, large leather ears and inserted leather wings raised up (*Pl.*

137A, B). Below were sockets for hafting the figures. Two methods of fixing the leather wings were employed: either they were fixed by means of a wooden pin, as was the case in the example illustrated in *Pl. 137B*, or they were inserted into special slits on the back, as can be seen in *Pl. 137A*, where wings and ears have been taken off. A slit is visible at the back of both figures, probably for an inserted leather tail.

Carved, wooden, sculptured heads of griffins with big ears and comb (*Pl. 136H, I*) and an elk (*Pl. 136G, J*), forming pendants of some part of a composite object, were found in the central part of the chamber of barrow 2, where they had been thrown out of the coffin by the plunderers. There were two griffins' heads. Except for the lost leather comb, the fixing for which is indicated by a long, deep slot in the neck, one head survived beautifully, but the other was badly decayed. The griffin with long neck is done in a conventional manner, but skilfully and very expressively, with strong, sharply curved-down beak painted red, like the mouth. The cere and ruff are deeply ribbed; the large watching eyes and eyebrows have been deliberately emphasized; the inserted leather ears are long. For suspension or fixing to some kind of base there was a special peg at the neck with holes through it in which straps still remained.

The elk's head had a precisely similar device for securing to some sort of object. It is a pity that the front part of the muzzle of this beautiful sculpture is broken off. In style and quality it resembles the griffin's head and was probably made by the same craftsman. It has the same carved eyes with tear ducts and brows, deep grooves running from brow to nose and well-shaped projection of the mandible; the beard of a male elk is indicated and the undermane is shown by ribbing. There are little holes for inserting leather ears and antlers; the ears have been lost, but the antlers, which partially survive, are shown together with head in *Pl. 136G*.

Isolated and independent of everything else was the carved wooden figure of a bird in the middle of the horse-burial in barrow 3 (*Pl. 49*). It is difficult to identify the species. To judge by the round eye it was not a predatory bird, and taking into consideration its relative proportions and shape of beak it might be considered that a pelican was intended. The body is represented very schematically, and the holes bored in it indicate that it had leather inserted ears and wings, remains of which survived in the holes in the back. There had evidently also been an inserted tail since a deep socket had been bored at that end. On the bird's stomach there were two long, deep slots evidently for legs on which it could stand. The whole figure is coloured red except the head, which is covered by gold-leaf.

Artistic objects carved in the round from horn were not found at Pazyryk, but two lions' or tigers' heads are known from ordinary graves of this period (my excavations at Katanda and near Biysk). The miniature head (2·1 cm. long) from

240

Katanda is of exceptionally fine and beautiful workmanship (*Pl. 136A*), and resembles a wooden head from barrow 3 at Pazyryk, described below, which was hafted to a rod. For this purpose a socket had been driven right through, and a hole drilled under the lower jaw for fixing with a peg. In this head the eyes of the predator are neatly carved, the mouth with upper lip puckered, stylishly shaped, the nose is small and the ears round. At the base of the head is a ring-like ridge.

Of incomparably more simple shape is the sculptured wooden feline head with socket, fixed on a wooden rod, from barrow 3 (*Pl. 136E*). It has a broad muzzle, narrow nose and ears with a curl at the base, while the corners of the lower jaw are marked by hemispherical protuberances. Under the chin in the socket is a tiny conical hole for the peg fixing the head to the rod. The head was found with one of the saddles in barrow 3; another wooden rod with a sculptural feline head terminal, as we know, was found with one of the saddles of barrow 5 (fig. 88; *Pl. 136F*).

The tiger's or leopard's head carved on a horn runner from the barrow near Biysk had been executed in quite another style (*Pl. 136D*). Its teeth and fangs are visible in its open jaws; the eyes and outline of the muzzle were only indicated, not completed.

There was very little cast-metal sculpture, perhaps because the metal objects had been stolen. However, to judge by the articles in the collection of Peter the Great, the techniques of artistic casting, including round relief, were fairly accomplished at that period. So far we have only four cast bronze figures of griffins with big ears and topknot found in the four corners of the tree-trunk coffin in Berel barrow (*Pl. 143D*). In spite of the rough casting these figures with exaggeratedly large heads, characteristic eagle's beak and large protruding ears are reasonably expressive. Disproportionately small relative to the head, the trunk, opened wings and raised tail give an individual air to this short-legged

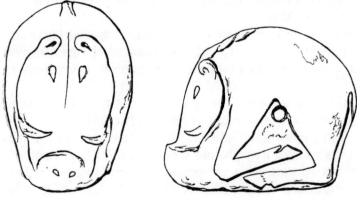

118. Figurine of a wild boar ($\frac{1}{3}$).

241

griffin. In their shape they have much in common with the small wooden sculptured griffins from barrow 2 at Pazyryk. It is particularly noticeable that the figures originally served as crests, since the lower surface of their wings is more carefully treated than the upper and the character of the plumage altered. Consequently they will be discussed below.

The single sculptured object in stone, already referred to in the chapter on techniques, a figure of a boar (fig. 118), was a chance find which may with a reasonable degree of probability be referred to this period. This is rendered the more likely by the similar carved representations of boars found in my excavations in 1950 on the lid of one of the tree-trunk coffins in a barrow in the Karakol valley.

The number of animals carved in medium or high relief is not great; some of them are in open-work, some have a sculptured head. Among them, and carved in wood, can be counted the whole figures of cats (*Pl. 111*E, G) and birds' heads (*Pl. 112*G, H) from barrow 4 and, with inserted, sculptured head, deer, elk and griffins from barrow 1 (*Pls. 86*A, B; *89*B) and deer from barrow 5 (*Pl. 116*B). We know of a leather cut-out, relief representation of a bird with inserted sculptured leather head (*Pl. 81*B, C), and even some that have a leather body and inserted carved wooden head (monsters from barrow 4, fig. 85).

The overwhelming preponderance of the very varied decoration consists of shallow relief work, carved from wood, horn and leather, in the same technique as was used to carve wood, and finally stamped and cast objects. The latter are comparatively few. Among those deserving attention are the goat in an open-work bronze belt plate-clip from the barrow near Biysk (*Pl. 67*C) and a deer, attacked by a winged lion-griffin, on another open-work bronze buckle from a barrow near Biysk (*Pl. 136*B). The last composition is identical with the one we have seen on a leather coverlet from barrow 2 (fig. 28).

All the silhouette figures are cut out from leather. These consist of figures of cocks or deer, or scenes of animals fighting. When it was necessary to obtain symmetrical, heraldically opposed figures the leather was bent over double and two figures cut from it at the same time.

Drawing held a very small place in representational art. It was an auxiliary device used in colouring on leather cut-outs, and it is found in the painting on arrow-shafts (*Pls. 179, 180*). Independent graphic representation is seen only in tattooing.

There was a very general use of appliqué for figures cut out from leather and multicoloured felt, and incrustations or mosaics of leather, fur and felt.

Silhouette leather cut-outs, mentioned above, were usually stuck on. In leather appliqué work the shapes and background would be of different colours and in this way very complicated patterns were created. As examples of artistic work executed in this technique the flasks (*Pls. 61*C, *152*B), the leather coverlet

242

(fig. 28) from barrow 2 or the apron (*Pl. 156*) from the same barrow may be cited. In the case of the last the applied ornament consists of two parts, done separately: convex along the edge, and straight, hanging down in the middle of the apron. Both parts consisted of two pieces of leather each. After the necessary ornament had been cut for the two upper pieces, they were laid on two others (of different colour for the base) of the same shape and stitched on to them around the edge of the figure with thin sinew thread. Then when these applied patterns were ready the leather cut-outs of rams' heads, covered by gold-leaf sewn to squirrel fur, were sewn on to the corresponding places.

In appliqué work making use of coloured felt applied to monochrome felt, pieces of different colours of the right shape were stitched on with fine sinew or woollen thread. Such work would be completed by plain embroidery with coloured woollen threads. Sometimes slits were made in a strip of felt, and felt of another colour sewn in behind for a background.

When a mosaic pattern was desired, e.g. on a pouch or shabrack, two or more pieces of fine felt or fur of different colours were applied one on top of the other from which at the same time the shapes had been cut out. If two pieces were used the cut figures were swapped in places and then stitched together, from which two identical patterns of different colours were obtained. The technique of producing three-colour patterns was a little more complicated, in the case, for instance, where two shades of fur and leather were used.

Embroidery, as already remarked, was not employed for a whole design, and its function in felt appliqué work was as an auxiliary one. The 'pseudo-glass-bead' technique of making a pattern, when sinew thread was bound spirally round a narrow strip of tin or gold, we have already met in the description of the belts and shoes from barrow 2.

One of the distinctive features of the appliqué art under discussion was the use of different materials in the creation of a single object. In cutting out an object, let us say of wood or horn, it was rarely left without a partial or complete covering of gold-leaf or colouring. In making the patterns, e.g. on shabracks, multicoloured textiles, fur and leather, covered by gold-leaf or tinfoil, would all be used at the same time. In saddle pendants and horse head-dress felt, leather, fur, horsehair and gold-leaf were all used together.

No less varied than the materials and techniques employed in making the objects were the motifs reproduced. Geometric shapes—squares, rhombs, triangles, circles, spheres, pyramids—held a secondary place in the art of the Altai at this time. Some shapes like squares and rhombs arose mechanically, in plaiting the sticks through a piece of leather in the shields, for example (*Pl. 144*). Rhombs were formed as the result of crossing strips over an ornamental field, as we saw on a fur bag in barrow 1 or on the shabrack from barrow 5. In some cases the

243

119. Schematic representation of a griffin decorating a breast-strap in barrow 1.

rhombs constitute an independent ornamental motif, as, for example, on the soles of the shoes from barrow 2 (*Pl. 64*A), sometimes with an additional figure inscribed inside, as we saw in the head-dress from the same barrow (*Pl. 65*C). The triangle is the geometric shape most frequently encountered, usually excised on wooden and horn articles (cheek-pieces, slides) or in leather appliqué work. Triangles usually have an irregular shape, often with the sides curved, because triangular voids often fill free space between the basic ornamental motifs, and their sides are formed by repeating the main lines. A very widespread ornamental motif is a triangle with a circular notch in one of its sides, which is encountered in all the barrows. A circle was used fairly often, particularly on the round frontal plates of the bridles, with a hemispherical or shallower protuberance in the middle, sometimes within concentric rings in relief. Spherical decorations in the form of pyramids of four balls have been met only in barrow 2 in the earrings (fig. 49) and from barrow 3 in the decoration of one of the bridles (fig. 65). The frontal bridle plates of semi-lunate or half-horseshoe shape can be conditionally referred to this category of motifs.

The ornament consisting of a system of spiral lines, or of grooves cut into objects, occupies a special position. The former are often seen as running waves, sometimes with toppling crests, in the wooden forks covering the branching of the bridle-straps at the cheek-piece and in the leather on the saddle arches. The latter occur on the drop-shaped or starlike shapes decorating the bridles.

A fair range of plant motifs were used, including multi-petalled flowers, rosettes, palmettes and, especially richly represented, lotus flowers. We have seen three-petalled ornament on a leather purse (fig. 26), buds and flowers decorating the

244

saddlery from barrow 1, multi-petalled flowers or rosettes on cheek-pieces and bridle decoration from barrows 1 and 3.

An interesting motif is one that can be conveniently called a little palmette. Three- and four-petalled palmettes like this were used as part of a more or less composite artistic composition, as in the deer in profile (*Pl. 89*c) or in the shape of a bird's tail from barrow 1 (fig. 119), or independently. They are especially varied in the cheek-pieces and other decoration on the saddlery in barrows 1 and 2.

To this same category of plant motifs can be referred the frequently found heart-shaped figures and garlands of intercoiling plants, which we have seen on one of the belts from barrow 2 (*Pl. 67*F).

The lotus motif has exceptional interest, unexpectedly richly represented and commonly in a very developed and complex form. The silhouette, fine leather cut-outs of the flower from barrow 2 are remarkable for their simplicity of execution (fig. 120), while it occurred in a more developed, intricate form combined with other flowers on two polychrome felt applied borders in the same barrow.

One border of fine white felt, browned by age, has a sewn-on pattern of even thinner polychrome felt (*Pl. 148*c). The appliqué work is strengthened by polychrome twisted woollen threads outlining the various figures in the design, and in places detail is embroidered in. A plain double stitch or chain-stitch was used. The large central figures of the band are lotus flowers cupped with leaves and small petals; the intervening figures are lilies and their buds. Above in between these figures are buds, and below a plain monochrome border. The distinctive elements in common in this composite ornament are the various flowers succeeding one another. Given the range of colour in the pattern the shapes have been so ordered that two of the same colour are never juxtaposed either horizontally or vertically.

120. A lotus flower from barrow 2 ($\frac{1}{2}$).

245

The design in a second border (*Pl. 148*B) basically consists of the same elements as the first, but the lotus flowers are not shown on stands but in, as it were, baskets joined to one another by a continuous garland. There is not such a variety of colour in the appliqué work, which is orange and red on a white background, the pattern outlined by twisted woollen thread of yellow colour.

The same lotus pattern was seen on the soles of the bootees (*Pl. 152*C), in the appliqué work on the pouch and flask (*Pls. 151*A; *152*B), in the circular horn decorations of a bridle (*Pl. 159*B, C), on the skin parts of the woman's bootees and on the apron from barrow 2 (fig. 39; *Pl. 156*). The lotus pattern received special treatment in the intricate and exquisite composition on the bootees and apron.

The lotus was used not only independently but also as an auxiliary motif. We have already seen, for example, that one of the human masks on a saddle pendant from barrow 1 (*Pl. 138*F) takes the shape in its upper part of a lotus flower.

Geometric figures, just discussed, are too rudimentary to raise the question of what might be the relationship of Altaian art with other contemporary cultures. The same can be said about the classical palmette and the Persian rosette, both of which occur, as we have seen, amongst the Altaian ornamental motifs. The case of the lotus is quite different.

The lotus, a sacred plant for the ancient peoples of the Nile and Ganges valleys, was widely employed as an ornamental motif in Egypt.[1] Later we find it in Assyria,[2] whence it was adopted by the Persians.[3] Lotus ornament is well known in Persia from numerous examples in Persepolis, Susa and at Naqsh-i-Rustam in the tomb of Darius. With other Hither Asian motifs the lotus penetrated to the Scyths, where it is found not only on objects of Iranic origin, as, for example, on the silver rhyton from Seven Brothers barrow,[4] on the sword hilt from Chertomlyk,[5] but as a detail in articles of native manufacture. A very important factor in this matter is the following circumstance: in all examples cited, from Egypt, Assyria, Persia and Scythia, the lotus is plain, as in the shape in the human mask from barrow 1. Yet in a number of occurrences of lotus ornament in the Altaian barrows we see examples of a subsequently developed form not found so far in the countries just enumerated; there can be no question of the Hither Asian lotus being merely borrowed. The population of the High Altai in the period under discussion belonged to a cultural environment, in which this motif, borrowed at some former time (probably in the eighth to seventh centuries B.C.) from Hither Asia or India, underwent further brilliant

---

[1] Dieulafoy, B, 1885, pt iii, fig. 78 for Egyptian lotus; figs. 81 and 82 for Assyrian lotus.

[2] Perrot and Chipiez, B, vol. ii, figs. 8, 81, 90, 135 ff.

[3] Herzfeld, B, Pls. 63 and 84.

[4] *Report of the Imperial Archaeological Commission* (1877), Atlas, Pl. I, fig. 5.

[5] Tolstoy and Kondakov, A, vol. ii, p. 145, fig. 122.

and independent development, the finished forms of which were found in barrow 2 at Pazyryk.

Amongst ornamental motifs persistently occurring in significant numbers may be numbered stylized animal horns. There are two basic forms: one which we can call ox or ram's horn, and the other, deer's antlers. In its simplest form the ox horn can be seen on various decorations on saddlery and costume, and in its complicated form predominantly on saddlery decoration. Antlers are especially fully represented in the saddlery decoration in barrows 3 and 5, both simple (*Pl. 102*A–C) and very intricate (*Pl. 101*B, C) forms.

It should be noticed that the ox-horn motif had especially widespread use in the High Altai. Besides the Pazyryk barrows it is also found on the saddle plates, pendants and arches from Shibe barrow (*Pl. 139*A, B, D), on the saddle facing in the Pogodin collection (*Pl. 143*A) in the Historical Museum and also on artistic objects from barrow 2 at Bash-Adar (fig. 136) and barrow 1 at Tuekta (fig. 137).

In spite of the remarkable variety of motifs just recited, those drawn from the animal world still predominate over all the rest. Among them are representations of fish, birds, two- and one-toed ungulates, rodents, carnivores and all kinds of fantastic animals.

There were few representations of fish. In the tattooing on the right leg of the chieftain from barrow 2 (figs. 51, 121) the fish is represented by a simple graphic schema. The eyes are shown by little disks and the branchiate scales, the tail bifurcation and three pairs of side fins are indicated. Judging by the general outline of body and head, by the shape of the tail fin and, more important, by the presence of three barbels (one in the middle of the chin and two at the front nostrils) it must be supposed that a burbot was intended. This fish is shown in the same manner on the saddle-pendants from barrow 1 discussed above (*Pl. 167*D).

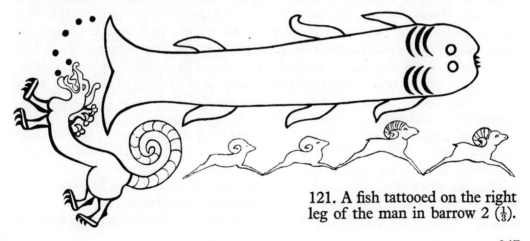

121. A fish tattooed on the right leg of the man in barrow 2 ($\frac{1}{3}$).

247

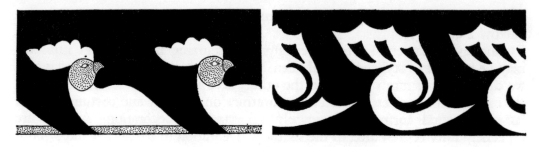

122. Cocks on mane-covers from barrow 1 ($c. \frac{1}{4}$).

Representations of birds are incomparably more numerous, amongst which figure blackcock (the cock bird), goose, swan, pelican, domestic cock and others. The two figures of blackcock occurred in barrow 2. One small figure, cut from thick leather, is shown in a schematic profile with a large raised head and typical 'scythe-shaped' tail (*Pl. 137*F). A second, already met in the composition with a griffin (appliqué on the leather flask), reveals the peculiarities of the species more clearly (*Pl. 61*C). Representations of geese are numerous: from barrow 2 there are miniature copper geese, covered with gold, their wings raised and head turned back (fig. 25); there is another on a bridle frontal plate (*Pl. 159*A); on a crest (*Pl. 141*D), which will be studied more closely later; and there are cheek-pieces with goose-head terminals (*Pl. 94*B). A sleeping goose in profile on a wooden saddlery pendant in the Pogodin collection, its feet retracted and head resting on its back, is very interesting. All these representations are completely realistic and depict the characteristics of the bird, although the attitudes in which it is shown, as well as the material, vary.

An individual work in the Pogodin collection (*Pl. 140*H) shows three swans in a wooden disk. In the space between two concentric circles (one on the edge, one towards the middle of the disk) three swans are arranged with long extended necks, their beaks directed towards the inner ring, the disposition of the figures successfully filling the space between the rings. The details of the species are rendered conventionally: shape of tail, wings, head or long neck with a broad beak. Each figure is individual, differing slightly from the rest. Schematic sculptural renderings of swans decorate a bridle from barrow 3 (*Pl. 97*A). Sculptural renderings of swans in felt, found with the carriage in barrow 5, on the other hand express the individual traits of these birds with great precision, and reveal an exquisite style in their shape (*Pl. 166*).

They are sewn up from fine felt and stuffed with deer hair. The trunks are well modelled, the necks long; the beak with cere and lower jaw is sewn over with fine black felt; the eyes are black and round. The fan-shaped tail is yellow

248

and rose with rose disks sewn along the edge of its upper surface and black ones underneath. The feathering of the tail is indicated on the upper surface by long lines of woollen thread. The freely hanging wings in their upper part are white, in their lower (the wing feathers) black. Within the yellow-rose or greenish legs wooden rods have been fixed to keep the figures upright. In *Pl. 166* the wing of one swan has been slightly pushed forward in order to show the formation of the upper part of the legs. The swans were tied by the legs with special straps to an angle of the trellis-work rail of the carriage.

Not linked with any other figure was that of the pelican already described (*Pl. 49*).

The numerous representations of the domestic cock from barrows 1 and 2 are very varied and characteristic, the great mass of them being cut-out leather silhouettes. They are quite realistic (in spite of a certain conventionalization in the reproduction), as we have seen on the bottle (fig. 22), strap (fig. 42) and head-dress (*Pl. 65*B) from barrow 2, and single and heraldically opposed profile examples from the log coffin of barrow 1 (fig. 10). The sculptural figure of a cock in felt and leather forming the crest of a horse head-dress from barrow 2 (*Pl. 122*A) holds a special position. Cocks are rendered schematically and conventionally on the horse mane-covers from barrow 1 (fig. 122; *Pl. 123*A, B). In all the figures of cocks special attention is given to the reproduction of the comb, which in one of the mane-covers just mentioned is converted into an ornamental motif, and on the woman's costume from barrow 2 it constitutes indeed one of the basic ornamental patterns (*Pl. 152*A).

Stylization of the bird's head is carried to its limits in the pendant decorations of the bridles of barrow 3 (*Pl. 98*H, I).

There is a very original representation of a bird in coloured appliqué felt on the wall-hanging from barrow 5, although unfortunately it has not survived intact (*Pl. 149*A). Its pointed tail terminates with luxuriant plumage, stylized, as with all its feathers. The wing with pointed feathers is raised. The figure is basically red, but the legs, bottom of the wings and some of the tail feathers are light blue, the claws orange-brown and the ends of the wing feathers black. The feathering at the base of the tail is indicated by unusual scaly decoration, embroidered with woollen thread.

The most richly represented among mammals in the art of the High Altai are ungulates, in the first place deer and elk.

There is no need, it seems to me, to discuss whether it was intended to portray a reindeer or red deer, that is, maral; both would have been well known to the population. Maral antlers or articles made of them were found in all the barrows, and almost all the saddle cushions were stuffed with reindeer hair. In some cases it can be seen from the shape of the antlers which deer was intended, but in the majority of examples this is not possible, and it must be supposed that the craftsman wanted to represent a deer without attempting to define whether it was a red deer or a reindeer.

The superb deer, upright on four legs, on the spherical stands from barrow 2 are work of high artistic quality (*Pl. 137*G, H). Thence also came the running silhouette figures of deer (fig. 11). The cheek-pieces from barrow 1 in the shape of a springing deer (*Pl. 88*B) and the profile pairs (*Pl. 89*B) are characteristic. Also a very expressive piece, with the deer's forelegs extended forward, is the scene where the tiger tears at the animal (fig. 110). A deer with twisted crupper and inserted head is a skilful piece of work (*Pl. 116*B); it is a saddlery decoration from barrow 5. A sculptural deer's head of very fine workmanship adorns the horse crest from barrow 5 (*Pl. 118*G), and there is another in the griffin's beak from barrow 2 (*Pl. 141*B). A simpler example is a wooden decoration from the saddlery of the Berel barrow (*Pl. 142*C).

Representations of elk are even more numerous and varied. In the first place amongst these the silhouettes deserve attention, showing the animal being attacked by predators, two with twisted crupper (figs. 109, 113) and head turned back, and in a third, the animal in flight, and as the enemy falls upon him his legs sag (fig. 108). A remarkably expressive figure cut from thick felt comes from barrow 2; a male elk clambers out of water or deep snow and only the body and head with one foreleg bent at the knee are shown (*Pl. 137*E). It is a typical bent-muzzled head with large palmating antlers, big ear and under-mane. The eyes, mouth, mandible, mane and shoulder are rendered in relief carving on the leather. The exaggeratedly large head and especially the antlers catch the essential traits of the animal. An individual example is that in polychrome felt appliqué on the saddle-cover from the same barrow (*Pl. 168*A).

A thick felt cut-out elk with twisted crupper decorating a saddle arch in barrow 5 is especially interesting (*Pl. 165*A). The wooden plaque bearing the representation of an elk in the Frolov collection (*Pl. 139*K) has earned wide fame. The animal, which is shown recumbent with legs retracted and its huge antlers extended along its back, has been skilfully fitted into the restricted space of the plaque. The disproportionately large head, the huge palmated antlers and the powerful musculature reveal a male elk, the sexual organ in this case being shown, which is extremely rare. The purpose of this plaque was not known before the Pazyryk excavations, but now we know that it was one of the four plates decorating the arches of a saddle like those in barrow 5.

Wooden open-work figures of elk, split sectionally as it were, with an inserted head, have been met in the saddlery decoration from barrow 1 (*Pl. 80*A).

A very popular motif was the elk's head in profile or facing. A well-known wooden plaque decorating a belt from Katanda barrow has an elk's head carved on it (*Pl. 140*B). The muzzle is marked in relief by planes meeting at an obtuse angle with disproportionately large eyes, exaggerated and widely spaced ears

123. Mountain ram tattooed on right arm of man in barrow 2 (*c.* $\frac{3}{4}$).

above which antlers are conventionally shown. Similar carved leather facing elk-heads covered with gold-leaf decorate one of the saddle-covers of barrow 5 (*Pl. 167*A). We have seen sculptural elk-heads on cheek-pieces and bridle pendants in one of the sets in barrow 3 (*Pl. 100*A–C).

The profile heads of elk vary a great deal. Heraldically arranged pairs of such heads are carved on horn and wooden facings from saddles in barrow 3 (*Pls. 96*A, *101*A). A piece of a similar horn saddle-facing bearing a schematic elk's head in the Frolov collection has been published more than once (*Pl. 139*E), but since the Pazyryk excavations we have been able to identify its purpose. Also now intelligible are two horn pendants bearing elks' heads from the same collection and evidently belonging to the same set of saddle decoration. I refer to a narrow pendant from a front saddle arch showing two confronted elks' heads with a heart-shaped opening between them (*Pl. 139*H). In this beautiful pendant the single S-shaped figure used to indicate ear and corner of mandible may be

251

noticed. Another large horn pendant, also showing two confronted elks' heads, was one of those that are fixed to the ends of the front and back straps that join the two saddle cushions (*Pl. 139*I). The shape of these heads is extraordinarily close to those we have seen in the facings to the saddle arches in barrow 3.

Fairly common motifs were the mountain ram and billy-goat; it is by no means always possible to say with which we are dealing. Only by the more markedly curved horn can a ram be distinguished from a billy-goat.

The most remarkable for its decorative quality is the mountain ram tattooed on the right arm of the chieftain from barrow 2 (fig. 123). The person who did the tattooing concentrated his attention on the front part of the animal—head, chest and forelegs. The back half with twisted crupper is represented schematically, probably because this was on the inner surface of the arm. The typical, twisted, annulated horn is rendered simply but masterfully, the thick, long under-mane hanging in wisps and special curls emphasizes the muscular neck. On the inner side of the right leg of the chief four running rams or goats with front and back legs extended are depicted in a row (fig. 121). The figures, which touch each other, constitute one single dynamic composition, and they are not rendered at all schematically but quite realistically, with no conventionalization. Their structural features are depicted in skilful but simple outline, as is the effort of their running. On the two front animals the annulations on the horns are represented, but on the two back ones just the general shape.

On the saddle-covers of barrows 1 and 2 there are two characteristic silhouette mountain rams with twisted cruppers (in the scenes where tigers or leopards attack them, figs. 111, 112). The mountain ram with twisted crupper with back leg touching its head is an original design among saddlery decoration from barrow 3 (*Pl. 99*C). The ram on the cheek-pieces from barrow 1 (*Pl. 82*B) has been executed with great skill. There is a ram, shown in a facing position, in a composition without parallel, in pendants from one of the sets of saddlery decoration from barrow 1 (*Pl. 83*E, F). There are numerous rams' heads, facing, but more particularly in profile, in the various saddlery adornments from barrows 1 and 2 and in the decorations of costume from barrow 2.

The mountain goat occurs appreciably less commonly. The animal is represented by three examples in different styles in barrows 1 and 2. In barrow 1 it appears on saddle-covers as the victim of griffins' attacks (*Pls. 169*A; *170*), and in barrow 2 in the silver belt-plates in a scene of a lion falling upon a mountain goat (*Pl. 67*A, B).

In the scene of an eagle-griffin falling upon a goat (*Pl. 170*) the latter is shown in the normal attitude for such scenes, forelegs bent under, rear legs extended, twisted crupper and head twisted back, but in the case of a lion-griffin's attack the attitude and stylistic design are quite different (*Pl. 169*A). In this case there is a series of elements in the reproduction of details that has analogies in central

124. Donkey tattooed on right arm of man in barrow 2 (*c.* ½).

and Hither Asian art. To a certain degree the same can be said of the mountain goat on the silver belt-plates (*Pl. 67*A, B).

The clasping goats (fig. 45) on a copper plate from barrow 2 occupy a special position because of the similarity of the composition to that on ancient cylinder seals from Hither Asia.

Goats' heads were only once employed as an ornamental motif for saddlery adornment, in barrow 1 (*Pl. 81*D), and in the same barrow similar cut-out sculptural leather goats' heads were found in the burial chamber (*Pl. 137*C, D).

The steppe or saiga antelope, especially its head, adorned bridles found in barrows 3 and 5 (*Pls. 103*B, C; *115*A). The identical manner of reproduction of the head in the two barrows deserves our attention. There is an interesting case of a saiga on a horn plaque on a saddle arch from the Uvarov collection (*Pl. 140*A). A massive, disproportionately large head with humped snout is shown with mouth half open and typical saiga's horns. The trunk with twisted crupper is furnished with the conventional system of curls and triangles, while the forelegs are retracted and the rear legs extended. The whole figure has been skilfully fitted into a narrow plaque.

There are only two representations of roebuck, of just the head. One, in the jaws of a wolf, is on a bridle pendant from barrow 4 (*Pl. 110*F); the other is from Berel barrow (*Pl. 142*B). The identification of the latter depends on its similarity with the former. The Berel example is interesting in that there is an attempt to represent the body, albeit only in the form of three twirls.

The single-toed mammals are represented by the onager and horse. A single representation of an onager or a donkey occurred in the tattooing of the chief's right arm in barrow 2 (fig. 124), the animal being shown with bent front legs and flexed back ones, and twisted crupper. It is a schematic sketch, only the shape of the hoof, the long ears and the tail allowing us to identify it. The horse is represented by many examples. From barrow 2 there are beautiful profile horses as silver pendants (*Pl. 67*D, E). The front parts of the whip handles from barrows 2 and 4 have also been worked into the shape of a horse (*Pl. 165*B; fig. 99). For all these horses a characteristic attitude is head stretched forward with ears retracted, trimmed mane and the hooves of the forelegs under the lower jaw. In a different rendering the mane is also clipped but the stylized ears are raised, as in the saddle arch facings of barrow 5 (*Pl. 164*B).

Rodents are represented only by typical figures of hares [1] (*Pl. 102*I, J) with twisted crupper in one of the sets of saddlery from barrow 3.

Carnivores are represented by wolf, cat, leopard or tiger and lion.

Beautiful, exact representations of wolves are seen in one of the sets of bridle decoration from barrow 4 (*Pl. 110*B), and the jaws holding the roebuck's head from the same barrow (*Pl. 110*F) undoubtedly belong to a wolf. In all probability the case is the same with the profile head from the Frolov collection (*Pl. 138*B), shown with open mouth and bared teeth. The general style of the muzzle, lower jaw, shape of eyes, ear with curl and puckered upper lip, all bring it close to the wolves' heads from Pazyryk.

There is a whole series of carnivores' heads with tip of the nose turned up, all in profile. One of them from the Pogodin collection (*Pl. 138*C) with fanged mouth, upper lip puckered and nose bent up in a curl can be distinguished from the others. A similar head from Katanda was treated differently; it has a long muzzle, the jaws closed but teeth bared, puckered upper lip and nose ending in a curl (*Pl. 140*C). Similar narrow-snouted, elongated heads with the tip of the nose curled up occur on the forking straps at the cheek-piece in barrow 5 (*Pl. 117*A, C). The combination of traits just enumerated allows these heads to be regarded as belonging to wolves.

A very large quantity of representations of cats, particularly their heads, occurred. It is still not known whether there were domestic cats at this time in the High Altai, but the inhabitants were undoubtedly acquainted with the steppe cat; in barrow 2 a sheath was found made of its skin. That they were familiar with cats and kittens is demonstrated by the fine representations of them by the local craftsman. They were also well acquainted with the snow leopards (*bars*) or *irbis*, and tiger, but it is by no means always easy to decide whether we are dealing with the head of a cat or a tiger, particularly in stylized representations.

Cats' heads are represented by two superb reproductions on bridle decorations from barrows 2 (*Pl. 93*A, B) and 4 (*Pl. 111*E, G). All the Pazyryk barrows contained sculptural cats' heads: from barrow 1 an example with a boar tusk in its mouth (*Pl. 90*A–C); from barrows 2, 3 and 5 on the ends of wooden rods in the pouch or saddles (*Pl. 136*C, E, F); from barrows 3 and 5 as decoration on the border of the front saddle arches (*Pls. 102*E–G; *116*F); from barrow 5 as decoration on bridles (*Pl. 117*B). Relief representations of cats' heads, facing and in profile, occur on bridle decorations from the Shibe barrow (*Pl. 139*J), in saddlery

---

[1] [Translator's note. Since the author wrote this, hares have been reclassified in the Order Lagomorpha; thus no rodents, strictly speaking, are represented. M.W.T.]

decoration from barrows 4 (*Pl. 111*D, F) and 5 (*Pl. 117*D, E), on cheek-pieces from all the barrows except barrow 1, and in the Frolov collection (*Pls. 138*D, E; *139*F). The heads from the last collection are interesting on account of the extremely exaggerated puckering of the upper lip, the typical shape of the hooked nose and the round ear with a curl in it.

The cats' heads *en face* with slanting eyes and large mouth deserve special attention. We see a similar representation on one of the bridle pendant plates from the Frolov collection (*Pl. 138*A), where a typical feline head with large mouth and ears in the form of curls is shown in a medallion of astragals. A similar cat's head is represented in horn saddle plates from barrow 3 (*Pl. 96*B). Similar but slightly different was a cat's head on a horn plaque in the Frolov collection (*Pl. 138*D). The slanting eyes with huge brows are shown just as on the horned carnivore's head on a frontal plate from barrow 2 (*Pl. 159*A), with puckered upper lip and large toothed and fanged mouth.

On a hemispherical pendant from the Katanda barrow in which two carnivores are interlocked in combat (*Pl. 140*G) there is just such a feline muzzle with slanting eyes, broad nose and large mouth.

Cats' heads adorned not only saddlery but also costume. A very interesting leather cut-out, covered with gold-leaf, which was found in barrow 2, has a facing cat's head drawn in a circle in the middle (fig. 125). The slanting eyes, wide nose, deeply puckered lip above a large mouth and the individual brows are all executed in a style now familiar to us. The shaping of the ears with a curl below is highly original; they are set on the head just as on the horned head of the carnivore holding geese in its teeth, which also came from barrow 2 (*Pl. 159*A). Since there are two holes on this plaque we may suppose that it had been sewn on to some kind of dress.

As already remarked it is not always possible to say whether a leopard or a tiger was intended; both animals would have been known in the Altai. In some cases on silhouette leather cut-outs additional colouring was used on the figure to represent stripes or spots, but sometimes stripes and spots were both stuck on the figure. From now on I will speak of these representations conditionally as leopards.

There are remarkable reproductions of this animal in the scenes of a tiger attacking an ungulate from barrow 1 (figs. 108, 110) and 2 (figs. 109, 111),

125. Feline head from barrow 2 (*c.* $\frac{3}{4}$).

where it is rendered with very varied foreshortenings and with a fine knowledge of the animal's habits. The legs of the little table from barrow 2 took the shape of leopards or tigers to judge by the shape of the tail (*Pl. 51*G–J). We know of nothing to equal the tigers or leopards in the horse accoutrements of barrow 5 for expressiveness and stylistic candour (*Pl. 116*F).

The feline heads with horns occupy a special position because of the link with the lion-griffins. The little head from barrow 2 in the jaws of which are two geese (*Pl. 159*A) may especially be recalled. We have seen horned feline heads, always with a knob or twist on the end of the horns, in the sets of saddlery decoration from barrows 3 (*Pl. 104*A–D, F, G), 4 (*Pl. 111*B, D, F) and 5 (*Pl. 115*C–E) treated in a variety of ways. To them may be referred a pair of horned (lions' rather than cats') on pendants from barrow 1 (*Pl. 171*).

Representations of lions are few. The salient features, apart from the general make-up of the body, by which one distinguishes, say, a tiger from a lion, are the brush on the end of the tail and the mane. The latter is not, however, essential since in Hither Asia there were lions it seems without manes, and besides in some cases lionesses could have been intended.

In the scene depicting a lion falling upon a mountain goat on the silver belt-plate from barrow 2 (*Pl. 67*A, B) we are justified in seeing a lion by analogy, as already remarked, with the similar representation of a lion-griffin on one of the gold plaques from the Oxus treasure.[1] We have seen lions on the saddle-covers (fig. 114) and in saddle-pendants from barrow 1 (*Pl. 172*). Lions' heads are represented on the border of a felt wall-hanging from barrow 1 (fig. 12) and on the saddle-covers from the same barrow (fig. 116); horned lions' heads cut out of leather exist among the bridle decorations of barrow 2 (fig. 75). At all events besides the typical leonine structure of the head it is very characteristic to represent the mane by individual curls. The mane is represented in just this way on the lions' heads in the Karakol barrow,[2] in the well-known Berkkarinsk buckle,[3] in the gold plate from the Kul-Oba scabbard[4] and earlier in Assyrian representations of lions.[5]

Although the leopards or tigers and cats are lively and faithful representations, full of movement, those of lions are wooden and the heads just copies. The artists had never seen them in nature and were probably copying a foreign piece, most likely a Hither Asian one, which, as we know, would be to hand (*Pl. 177*A).

In the period being discussed lion- and eagle-griffins were also depicted, not very many in general and found exclusively in barrows 1 and 2. There are lion-griffins from barrow 1 in the crests on the horse head-dresses (*Pl. 120*) and on

---

[1] Dalton, B, Pl. XI, 28.
[2] Kiselev, A, 1935, p. 102, fig. 16.
[3] Bernshtam, A, p. 9.

[4] Tolstoy and Kondakov, A, vol. ii, p. 148, fig. 125.
[5] de Morgan, B, fig. 74.

two saddle-covers (*Pl. 169*A; fig. 115); from barrow 2 on a copper pendant (fig. 43A), on the torque (*Pl. 68*E) and on a leather cover (fig. 28). Eagle-griffins occurred in barrow 1 on two saddle-covers (*Pl. 170*; fig. 115) and in barrow 2 on a saddle-cover (*Pl. 168*B) and in copper plates adorning dress (fig. 46).

The horned and winged lion-griffins in spite of varying attitudes are of one type: all have a lion's body, horns usually with knobs on the end, tail with brush obligatorily lifted up and wings with their tips directed forward. A distinctive peculiarity of the lion-griffins is their static posture, even when they are falling upon a goat or an elk; in marked contrast are the sharp and lively leopards or tigers when they fall upon an ungulate. Depending on function and material from which they were made the individual lion-griffins varied, but all unchangingly repeat the basic peculiarities of these monstrous creatures. Only the griffin falling upon a mountain goat occupied a special position, since, as already remarked, its horns have a special serpentine form, the wing is schematically rendered and instead of a brush on the end of the tail there is a bird's head.

Eagle-griffins as a rule have a lion's, or more precisely a tiger's or leopard's, body with a large-eared griffin's head and, it goes without saying, wings. Like the lion-griffin the eagle-griffin is represented as if stencilled and more conventionalized than the griffins to be discussed below. The clasping eagle-griffins on copper plates from barrow 2 are a special case; their back part is that of a tiger, their front an eagle's without wings.

The griffin is without any doubt a motif derived from Hither Asia, the horned lion-griffin being known only to Persian art. We may recall the capitals from Persepolis,[1] the tile friezes in Susa [2] and the cylinders showing a lion-griffin of Achaemenian times.[3] The griffin is known to have been borrowed by the Persians from Assyria and Babylon, although the creature we see in the majority of cases at Pazyryk is especially Persian. Babylon knew a winged lion with long, pointed ears, eagle's claws and tail; in Assyria an eagle's head with a comb was sometimes substituted for a lion's head. The Persians made use of both variants and gave the griffin new features, adding horns and sometimes replacing its short bird's tail with a scorpion's tail.

A series of details in our griffins relate them to the Persian representations of these monsters, in particular the horns with knobs on the end, the indication of musculature and shape of body by stops, commas and half-horseshoes. However, this motif originally penetrated into central Asia and the High Altai long before Persian rule in Hither Asia. Persian lion-griffins are depicted with rear legs as eagles' claws, which does not occur in Altaian examples. A bird's head instead of a brush on a lion's tail is an ancient motif occurring in Hittite sculpture but not known in Persia. Eagle-griffins with a lion's body are also an Assyrian motif.

[1] Herzfeld, B, Pl. 58.
[2] Dieulafoy, B, 1892, pt iii, Pl. 11.
[3] Furtwängler, B, Pl. 11, fig. 19.

Unquestionably the clasping eagle-griffins on the copper plates from barrow 2 are a very ancient motif, well known on cylinders and seals of Hither Asia. Thus the griffins disclose ancient cultural links (albeit slight) between the High Altai and the cultural world of Hither Asia.

Now let us consider large-eared griffins with combs on their necks, a motif that is extraordinarily richly represented in the Altai in spite of the complete absence of any real eagles in the art.

A big-eared griffin with extended wings of marked decorative quality, with distended tail and turned-back head, can be seen falling upon an elk in a saddle-cover from barrow 1 (fig. 113). In a different attitude, profile instead of facing, is another griffin, equally remarkable, which is tearing at a black grouse, depicted on the leather flask in barrow 2 (*Pl. 61*C). A simpler leather cut-out figure erved as a pendant to a breast-strap in barrow 1, the monster being shown facing with outstretched wings and a sculptural head (fig. 119). No less interesting are the wooden open-work plates showing the same griffin with inserted head decorating the bridle in barrow 1 (*Pl. 86*A, B). Large-eared griffins with top-knot reveal the same motif carried out in round relief: small examples carved in wood in barrow 2 (*Pl. 137*A, B) and large copper examples from Berel barrow (*Pl. 143*D). The horned griffins on a frontal plate from Tuekta, barrow 1, are very interesting compositionally (*Pl. 143*E).

The griffins' heads with deer's heads in their mouths from barrow 2, the function of which is still unexplained, are of especial interest (*Pls. 141*A, *142*D).

The first one (*Pl. 141*A), evidently some kind of crest or finial, was found in the coffin at the head end; it is an exceptionally original piece, bold in conception and fulfilment. In it there are two independent motifs both signifying the same thing: a deer, more particularly its head, in the beak of a griffin and a goose in the claws of a griffin, a double representation of the same subject engraved on both sides.

The basic figure is the griffin's head on a long neck with the deer's head in its beak. The griffin's head with powerful beak, carved in wood, is conventional but expressive; it is painted red with large, emphasized cere and ruff painted yellow, and has large protruding eyes. The comb runs from the sinciput all the way down the neck, and the ears are leather. The sculptural rendering of the deer's head is finely done. The brows are coloured red; its ears and spatulate antlers are of leather.

On the flat neck at the base of the head of the griffin the same scene is engraved on both sides, a goose in the claws of the griffin. The superb goose quite realistically displays the characteristics of its kind: short head and markedly goose-like beak with high cere, large eyes, long neck, typical body with folded wings and broad, goose-like feet. The griffins as usual are conventional with flat body only outlined; the tails are schematic but, as always, fan-shaped; the legs are more carefully worked, with typical feathery 'breeches' on the upper part of the knee; the claws grip the goose behind the head and on the neck. The inserted heads of the griffins are even more carefully and curiously shaped; sculptured in the round they project symmetrically to left and right from the upper part of the base of the main griffin lending a special air to the whole composition. They look down on their victim. The two subsidiary griffins' heads like the main one have strongly curved eagles' beaks painted red, and yellow ceres and ruffs. Above sharp eyes are red brows, while the large, long combs are coloured red. The ears were leather inserts, as also were the wings, cut from thick leather. The whole work, except the griffins' heads, was covered by gold-leaf.

The second carved wooden sculpture (*Pl. 142*D), to judge by the thong fixed to the griffin's neck, was intended to be attached in some way. The griffin has a very short neck with a deer's head in its beak. The large comb and ears of the griffin are of leather; the wings cut from thick leather are fixed on the neck near the beak; the ears and antlers of the deer were also of leather. The antlers are of highly original form: they were cut from thick leather in a very schematized way since the tines consist of cocks' heads on long necks. The eye, beak and comb of the cocks are indicated only on the external side by grooving, the inside face being left smooth. The cocks on the brow tines looked up, all the rest down. Of the gold which covered the whole work originally, especially the wings, only traces remained.

In the burial chamber of barrow 2 two pieces of thick leather survived by chance on which was engraved an interesting scene of a goat in the talons of a griffin (*Pl. 139*L). One piece shows a claw and part of a wing, the other a goat with forelegs extended forward and bent at the knees into both of which the griffin has plunged its talons. It can be inferred that this is exactly the same composition, engraved on leather, as that in the well-known gold decoration in the collection of Peter the Great, showing a mountain goat in the claws of a griffin.[1] The goat there is in the same attitude, with its forelegs doubled up since the griffin has plunged its great talons into its back.

There are a large number of griffins' heads on the pendants and particularly on bridle cheek-pieces. Amongst those worthy of attention are the big-eared heads with combs from barrow 2 (*Pl. 136*H, I), stylistically remarkably akin to those on the crests just discussed. Big-eared griffins' heads with combs and top-knots we saw in barrow 1 (*Pls. 86*C, D; *87*B). On the cheek-pieces of barrows 3 (*Pl. 104*A) and 5 (*Pl. 116*A) another style is used, generalized griffins' heads, big-eared but without a comb. They have a large round eye, a huge hooked eagle's beak and a large curled ear. This most curious of ornamental motifs occurred on costume and leather pouches from barrow 2, on one of the shabracks from

[1] Rudenko, A, 1962b, Pl. XIX, 1 and 2.

△
126. Fantastic monster tattooed on right arm of man in barrow 2 (*c.* $\frac{1}{1}$).

127. Fantastic monster tattooed on chest and back of man in barrow 2 (*c.* $\frac{1}{3}$).

128. Winged monster tattooed on right arm of man in barrow 2 ($\frac{2}{3}$).
▽

barrow 5, on the tips of antler tines (*Pl. 118*F) and especially in the tattooing (figs. 126–31).

The motif of a big-eared griffin with comb, unchangingly repeated in all the representations of eagle-griffins, had very widespread use in the High Altai; the methods of its reproduction were very persistent. The toothed comb running along the whole neck of the griffin especially deserves to be noticed, for it is a very ancient form found in Assyria, where the genie with an eagle's head and eagle-griffins are always represented with a great toothed comb of feathers.[1] Eagle-griffins were always represented with a comb in Achaemenid Persia,[2] but there the combs were not tall but little short ones, trimmed, running along the neckline, like the horned lion-griffin on one of the horse head-dresses from barrow 1 (*Pl. 120*). The griffins of the High Altai are distinguishable from those of Hither Asia by their long ears, and by a much greater range of variation in their treatment by the native craftsmen.

Apart from the fantastic animals just described, the Hither Asian origin of which is hardly disputable, there is a series of creatures, also mythical, containing features drawn from a range of different animals, the local origin of which cannot be doubted, as we shall see.

On the cheek-pieces from barrow 4 there is a series of birds' heads with ears that clearly belong to carnivores (*Pl. 112*B, E); in this barrow stylized birds with feline ears served as pendants on one of the bridles (*Pl. 112*G, H). One of the crests of a horse head-dress from barrow 3 consists of the head of a fantastic bird with inserted leather ears and a horn on its forehead (*Pl. 121*A). Another crest from the same barrow also takes the shape of a bird's head but fanged and with a horn on its nose and inserted leather ears and horns (*Pl. 121*B). From the Katanda barrow the figure of a recumbent deer with long bird's beak is known to us (*Pl. 140*F). In barrow 4 a large-eared griffin's head with a deer's antler cut from thick leather was found, the tines of which terminate in heart shapes (*Pl. 142*A). In a bridle decoration from the same barrow we have seen winged animals with boars' heads surmounted by horns (fig. 85).

The fantastic beasts represented in the tattooing on the man from barrow 2 are extraordinarily interesting. Amongst other figures on the right arm we can see a carnivore of clearly feline type with large head and gaping fanged jaws, the upper part of which is shaped like a bird's beak (fig. 126). The animal has small ears. It stands on four clawed feet, the annulated tail terminating in a bird's head, although it takes a different shape from the majority of those in the tattooing. There is a bird's head also at the foot of the neck. The trunk is represented schematically.

In the representation of a second animal in the tattooing (fig. 127), whose

[1] Layard, B, 1867b, p. 47; 1849, Pls. 6, 43 and 48.   [2] Herzfeld, B, Pl. 65.

head has not survived, the shape of the back claws, the tail which terminates in a bird's head, and the bird's head at the base of the neck deserve mention. The general figure is conventional, in particular the back feet. The strong, sharp nails of the beast are finely shown, the soles indicated by a special curl, while triangular marks emphasize the musculature of the limbs. This habit of portraying a carnivore with pointed, sharply projecting nails is, as we shall see below, characteristic of all the carnivores in the tattooing. We may recall that the carnivores' claws are portrayed in precisely the same way in the well-known gold plates in the collection of Peter the Great.[1]

One fantastic winged carnivore is extremely interesting (fig. 128). Its head has open, toothed jaws and a nose turned up at the end, a device we have seen used on wolves; the trunk is typically feline, as is the turned-up, annulated tail. The musculature of the paws, especially the back ones, is simply indicated by ornamental curls. The wings with tips twisted forwards are an individual feature, rather like what we have seen in lion-griffins, although in this case the decoration blends into that on the chest, neck and ears and even the legs.

Another monster, with a feline tail, and in this instance horned, had been tattooed on the right leg (fig. 129). The tip of the nose is turned up more markedly than on the preceding example. Its toothed and fanged jaws are open; there is a knob on the end of the horn; the paws are strongly clawed; the annulated and raised tail is twisted into a spiral; and there are three birds' heads on the base of the neck.

129. Horned monster tattooed on right leg of man in barrow 2 ($\frac{3}{5}$).

---

[1] Rudenko, A, 1962b, Pl. II, 5, 9; III, 5; V, 3, 5; VI, 3, 4; IX, 6; XII, 4, 5.

130. Fantastic monster tattooed on right arm of man in barrow 2 ($\frac{1}{3}$).

131. Fantastic monster tattooed on left arm of man in barrow 2 ($\frac{1}{3}$).

Another monster, a deer with the beak of an eagle and the tail of a cat, is tattooed on the right arm. It is illustrated in fig. 130, where besides its twisted crupper other peculiarities can be seen: deer's antlers with tines terminating in birds' heads, the muzzle with large sharply hooked eagle's beak and the feline tail terminating in a bird's head.

A second representation of the same beast occurred on the left arm (fig. 131). The deer's muzzle turns into an eagle's beak; the antler tines terminate in birds' heads as previously; the antlers are conventionalized into a series of segments; three birds' heads are set on one of the tines above the neck; the tail is long and decidedly feline; the chest and neck are drawn over with wavy and spiral lines; the forelegs are bent as in running but due to the twisted crupper the rear legs are in the air. In this, as in the deer just described, individual features of deer, eagle and feline carnivore are mingled together.

There are in addition three similar but only partially preserved figures: one tattooed on the right arm and two on the left. On the right shoulder (fig. 132) a deer is depicted with twisted crupper and feline tail with a bird on the end; its head survives badly. On the left arm was a figure (fig. 133) of a deer with bent forelegs, rear legs on a twisted crupper thrown up in the air, the same kind of tail terminating in a bird's head, and antlers schematized into segments. A second animal with retracted forelegs (fig. 134) was, to judge by its horns and under-mane, a mountain ram.

A similar fantastic monster occurs on a well-known wooden plaque from

263

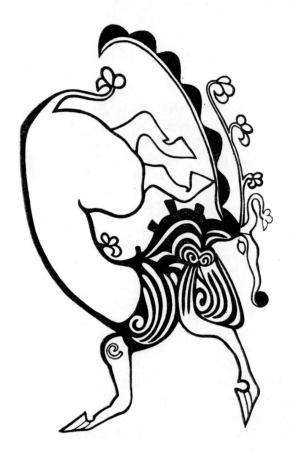

132. Fantastic monster tattooed on right arm of man in barrow 2 ($\frac{1}{3}$).

Katanda barrow (*Pl. 140*E), which has a lion's body, a deer's (or elk's) muzzle terminating in an eagle's beak and bird's-head tips to its antler tines and tail.

Arising from the figures just discussed the following details deserve closer attention: the bird's-head terminals of the antler tines and tails and those on the neck, the twisted crupper and the scenes of fighting animals.

Snake's- or bird's-head terminals in representations of monsters had been familiar in Hither Asia since at least 2000 B.C. From Mesopotamia this and other artistic details reached the Hittites; it occurs in sculptures and bas-reliefs in ancient Hittite towns by the fourteenth century B.C.[1] In the griffins of Achaemenid Persia, as in Assyria, such a tail was sometimes replaced by that of a scorpion.[2] The same can be seen on the monsters from Lity barrow in Scythia.[3] Nevertheless in the middle of the last millennium B.C. nowhere was it so widespread as among the Scythian and High Altai tribes, not merely as a little bird's head but as the head of a long-eared griffin, however schematically reproduced.

[1] Pottier, B, figs. 27, 29, 67, 68, 73.　　　　[3] Pridik, A, Pl. 3.
[2] Herzfeld, B, Pl. 65.

264

Outside the Altai not a few examples can be cited among the Black Sea Scyths of griffins' heads on the tips of antler tines and lions' tails.[1] While insufficient evidence prevents a decision on the date of the first appearance of this motif in the High Altai, it can be confidently stated that both it and the big-eared griffin enjoyed widespread use long before the Persian Achaemenid dynasty had assumed power.

Another curious device employed in the Altai in the period under discussion was the representation of an animal (as a rule an ungulate, rarely a carnivore) with its crupper twisted right round, usually in the position of victim of attack by a stronger animal. It was very suitable when the animal had to be fitted into the limits of a circular plaque, but this was not a decisive factor since, as we have seen, the Altaian craftsman knew how to fit his figures into any geometrical shape.

The back half of an animal's body twisted round to face upwards was a very ancient Sumerian device, although in Hither Asia such representations occur extremely rarely.[2] We meet them in great numbers on ancient Greek gems, in particular Mycenaean ones.[3] The device was employed among the central Asian Sacae;[4] in the Altai itself, as we have seen, it was extraordinarily widespread. Apart from our finds, this way of showing victims with a twisted crupper can be seen in the gold collection of Peter the Great, in those examples where a griffin has seized a mountain goat in its claws, or a horned and winged carnivore falls upon a horse, and others.[5] All this leads to the view that the device was first employed in central Asian art, where it underwent its subsequent development;

133. Fantastic monster tattooed on left arm of man in barrow 2 (c. $\frac{1}{2}$).

[1] Minns, B, p. 208, fig. 27; Tolstoy and Kondakov, A, vol. ii, p. 126, fig. 107; Bobrinsky, A, vol. ii, Pl. 21.

[2] Perrot and Chipiez, B, vol. ii, figs. 337, 412.

[3] Furtwängler, B, Pl. III, figs. 36, 38, 39; Pl. VIII, fig. 70.

[4] Dalton, B, p. 106, fig. 63.

[5] Rudenko, A, 1962, Pl. VIII, 7, 8; XII, 2; XIX, 1, 4–6; XXII, 13, 14.

134. Fantastic monster tattooed on left arm of man in barrow 2 ($\frac{1}{3}$).

in the form it took in Asia Minor its appearance could have been due to the ancient links between Hither Asia with Asia Minor, and the tribes of central Asia.

The last motif, fighting animals, or, more precisely, carnivores falling upon herbivores, predominantly ungulates, was well known in Hither Asia from the third millennium B.C. and became very widespread both in Hither Asia and Asia Minor, particularly among the Scyths and Altaian tribes, in the middle of the last millennium B.C. We meet it in Assyria [1] and in archaic Greece,[2] but nowhere does it seem to have been so popular in the last millennium B.C. as in the High Altai. Almost the whole composition of carnivores leaping on herbivores that occur in the Pazyryk barrows can be paralleled in the west and south, and, at a later date, to the east; examples of this, showing the carnivore attacking its victim from behind, are shown in fig. 135. The first example shows a lion attacking a bull (from Persepolis); B shows a leopard attacking an elk (from the Siberian collection); c shows a lion attacking a deer (from Kul-Oba); D shows a lion attacking a goat (from Kelermes in the Kuban); E shows a lion-griffin attacking an elk (from Seven Brothers' barrow); F shows a lion-griffin attacking an elk (from Pazyryk).

Although the earliest examples of the motif as yet known occurred in Mesopotamia, it reached its fullest development, it seems, in central Asia and southern Siberia, and then later spread far to the east. This motif is at all events a characteristic one in the Altai.

[1] Perrot and Chipiez, B, vol. ii, figs. 273, 443, 447.

[2] Furtwängler, B, Pl. III, figs. 2, 4; Pl. VI, figs. 44, 51, 52; Pl. XI, figs. 22–4.

135. Examples of predators springing on ungulates (see page 266).

From the point of view of representational art the tree-trunk coffin from Bash-Adar, barrow 2, has special interest.

This coffin (3·1 m. long, 0·56 m. high without the lid) has been hollowed out of a cedar trunk. Along its upper edge there is a line of nine evenly spaced bronze nails with large convex heads. Below the nails the outside of the coffin is covered by a row of four carved tigers, following one another from left to right (fig. 136). Below the tiger on the extreme left is incised the figure of an elk, or a young elk with forelegs thrown forwards and crupper twisted round, looking as if it is being attacked by the tiger.

Comparison with the drawing on the coffin lid, described below, suggests that ungulates were to have been drawn under each tiger's figure. The craftsman, however, never completed his carving and the general composition on the side of the coffin stayed unfinished.

The dimensions and shape of the lid, made from larch, precisely correspond to the dimensions and shape of the upper surface of the coffin, which it neatly fits. The hacking by the plunderers to open the coffin evidently damaged its original surface, but in spite of the loss of part of it, it is possible to restore the figures of the animals carved on it.

On the lid, as on the coffin itself, there was a row of four tigers, but going in the opposite direction to those on the coffin. Under the tigers were incised figures of two male or female elks, two boars and three mountain rams.

All eight tigers are of one type except for some differences of detail. One may notice the disproportionately large heads, the curved bellies, the strong clawed paws and the tails twisted at the end into a ring. In the tigers on the coffin the line marking the shoulder girdle is especially deeply incised, but those on the lid have no such line. The method of showing the texture of the fur and the stripes on the tigers by incised zigzag lines, looking like tongues of flame, is highly individual. Not only the bodies but also the tails of the tigers are covered by such lines, except the tail of one, which is covered by transverse lines.

Save for the front tiger on the lid, which has its tail squeezed between its legs,

136. Artistic carving on the side and lid (right) of the log coffin from Bash-Adar, barrow 2.

the tails of the rest hang freely. The differences between the heads are confined to minor details. In the open jaws the teeth and fangs are bared. The lips are usually indicated by a continuous convex line. In some of the tigers the upper, and sometimes the lower, lip is shown puckered. Eyes and nostrils are indicated by comma shapes, big for eyes, small for nostrils. Given the profile view of the head such a representation of the eyes and nostrils seems unnatural. A system of curls shows the creasing of the nose. The lower jaw was either left smooth or marked by a series of parallel lines with triangles at their bases. The ears are indicated by a combination of curls and in some cases the angle of the mandible with its rising arm. Two triangles were incised on the cheeks.

The tigers carved on the coffin have close analogies with representations of this animal in a series of gold buckle-plates in the Siberian Collection of Peter the Great.[1] Especially worthy of notice is the massive head, the same wavy rendering of the skin by lines drawn downwards and the strong clawed paws.

Two elks without antlers (or young elks) are shown on the lid, like the elk on the coffin, with head raised and turned back. One of them appears to have a twisted crupper, an attitude often found in Scythian and especially Altaian art, more particularly in scenes of a carnivore attacking an ungulate. The bent-snouted elk-heads are shown in strong profile, in a three-quarters turn from the body, with round eyes, marked nostrils, mouth slightly ajar and pointed ear on one side. Especially interesting is the way the divisions of the body are shown by two independent systems of curls. In one case the neck and under-mane are indicated by these curls. The second elk on the lid is shown recumbent, but as if alarmed; it might be getting up and looking over its shoulder. Stylistically it is executed like the other elks just described with its back half twisted round.

The mountain rams are shown in varying postures; two are peaceful animals at rest, but just startled with heads looking back, while one of the rams is running.

The attitude of a recumbent animal with drawn-up legs is well known by a whole series of representations of deer and other animals in the art of the Black Sea Scyths, where it came to form part of their tradition. However, the rendering of the animals at Bash-Adar and Tuekta barrows is quite different: the postures

[1] Rudenko, A, 1962b.

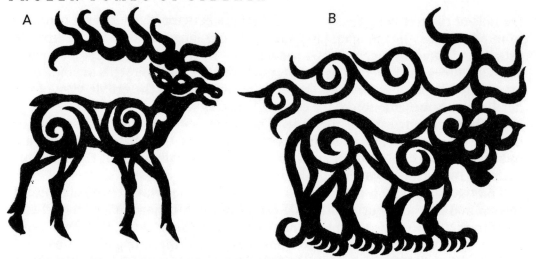

137A. Figure of a deer carved on coffin from Tuekta, barrow 2;
  B. Leather cut-out of tiger with antlers from Tuekta, barrow 1.

are more expressive. As the representation of the heads is schematic the ears are shown by a plain curl. The craftsman gave special attention to the horns, by the peculiarities of which it is possible to identify the species concerned. The rams' horns are indicated by overlapping 'scales', which are clearly carved on the bas-relief heads of mountain rams from barrow 2 at Bash-Adar. They are shown so long and curved back that they themselves conceal part of the head. Like the elk's, the ram's body is divided by different systems of curls with triangles between them; especially clearly marked are the shoulder and pelvic girdles, neck and under-mane.

Superbly expressive of emotion is the figure of the running ram with head raised and slightly thrown back and mouth ajar. The animal, as if it had lost heart while being pursued, is stumbling on its forelegs. Stylistically it resembles the figure described above. In this case, as in the representations of elks and recumbent mountain rams, the shape of the body is emphasized by lines, curls and triangles, as is also the structure of the legs of these fleet-footed creatures.

Of no less interest are the wild boars: one is shown statically, the other dynamically and very expressively.

The first boar stands on all four legs; its downcast head is realistically portrayed with large tusks and characteristic pig's snout; only the pointed pig's ear with traditional curl at the base is conventionally shown. The short body rendered with soft outlines is subdivided by the system of curls, with which we are familiar, into front and back halves. The structure of the thick legs with rear hoofs is emphasized by elongated lines with triangles on the end as in the elks

270

and rams. The bristles on the withers are exaggerated to look like a mane; the tiny short tail looks like a caricature.

The second boar is shown in the attitude of a strained, tensed, bristled-up animal about to spring into attack. The head of the first boar may have been somewhat exaggerated in size, but with the second it is so big that about a third of the figure is taken up by it. Powerful tusks protrude from the slightly open mouth, the pointed ear has the usual curl at the base and the tail is raised. The contracted body of this boar is not divided by curls into two or three parts, as with the other figures of ungulates, but formed by merely one system of curls.

This manner of subdividing the body by curls and similar shapes is characteristic not only of wood carving but was used on felt in saddle pendants, and cut out of leather in dress adornment from barrow 2 at Bash-Adar. The same style can be seen in the art of the Tuekta barrows which are contemporary with Bash-Adar. The representation of a tiger with antlers in leather on a saddle ornament from Tuekta, barrow 1 (fig. 137B) deserves mention, or one of the deer carved on the tree-trunk coffin from Tuekta, barrow 2 (fig. 137A). In the first instance the body of the tiger was divided into two shapes by an 'ox-horn', and in the second the convention employed in barrow 2, Bash-Adar, was repeated.

A few words may be said about the details of drawing, the so-called stops, commas and half-horseshoes, which are found mainly in the scenes of fighting animals but also occur on individual representations of animals. These conventions for indicating the principal muscles, ribs and other details prior to the Pazyryk discoveries had been known mainly in encrusted jewellery. Hence it had been assumed that they had reached the north, that is southern Siberia (several pieces in the collection of Peter the Great were the basis of the discussion), from the south in jewellery of inset precious stones or enamel. Yet this method of using certain shapes to emphasize details of the body structure can be seen in Urartian sculptures,[1] Assyrian bas-reliefs and coloured tiles.[2] However, it is only in the middle of the last millennium B.C., in the artistic creations of Achaemenid Persia, central Asia and farther north, including the Altai, that we encounter just this use of stops, commas and half-horseshoes. We may recall that we also find them in the Oxus treasure: on stone figures of goats, especially in scenes of the chase on a silver disk, in figures of deer and horned eagle-griffins.[3] The stops and half-horseshoes in the famous figures of a lion and a griffin in the polychrome tile frieze in the Achaemenid palace at Susa are widely familiar.[4] Some years ago I put forward the view that this device employed in

[1] Heuzey, B, bk viii, Pl. 1; Dalton, B, p. 27, fig. 17.

[2] Perrot and Chipiez, B, vol. ii, Pl. xv, figs. 114, 217, 268, 278.

[3] Dalton, B, Pl. vi, nos. 11, 12; Pl. vii, 18; Pl. ix, 24; Pl. xvi, 116.

[4] Dieulafoy, B, 1892, pt iii, Pls. iii, xi.

271

Persia had been borrowed from the figuring of animals on felt.[1] The discovery in barrow 5 of representations of lions with stops and half-horseshoes on cloth from Hither Asia has confirmed this suggestion (*Pl. 177A*).

Thus this conventional device for showing details of the body of an animal is not narrowly localized, but was used over an extensive area from the High Altai to Mesopotamia, with its centre it would seem in central Asia. It appeared relatively late, in all probability not earlier than the end of the sixth century B.C., and was never known to the Black Sea Scyths. In the Altai we meet it predominantly on lions and griffins, in scenes where they are fighting or falling upon herbivores. An especially noteworthy circumstance is that the convention was not employed to emphasize the body contours of leopards or tigers, nor do we see stops, commas and half-horseshoes on the monsters tattooed on the chieftain in barrow 2, or on the wooden plaque from Katanda.

In the final analysis it is possible to distinguish, in the Altaian art of the period being discussed, objects that are executed in the 'Scythian animal style', those revealing earlier cultural links with Hither Asia and, lastly, the latest objects appearing as a result of links with central Asia and Achaemenid Persia.

Although in round sculpture and in graphic silhouettes a craftsman was freer to give more realistic representations of animals, in decorations in certain pendants, where the motif had to be fitted into a fixed shape, conventions of one kind or another had to be devised. As we have seen, by altering the animal's posture the craftsman could easily fit it into any shape; besides this basic aim he had to render the most typical traits of the animal so as to carry maximum conviction. This he achieved mainly by exaggerating or intensifying just those elements which appeared to be the most characteristic; thus the animal's head was often disproportionately large in relation to its body.

Usually the body is rendered schematically and the whole attention is concentrated upon the head, so that when a deer or elk was represented quite commonly the dimensions of the antler would exceed those of the body. If a mountain ram was being depicted, then the horn was twisted as far as it could be, while the under-mane assumed such dimensions that it almost hid the body. In elk or saiga antelope the curved muzzle is always emphasized, while in carnivores of the feline family the toothed and fanged mouth with obligatory puckering of the upper lip is so big that quite often it reaches the ears. In representations of wolves the long, narrow muzzle is shown with bared teeth, and hence puckering on the upper lip and turned-up nose. In the griffins the eagle's beak is usually strongly hooked, while the ruff and the 'breeches' on the legs would be emphasized. In cocks exceptional attention was given to hypertrophy of the comb.

In all these respects the portrayal of the animals can be referred to that

[1] Rudenko, A, 1944.

specific style, usually known as the 'Scythian animal style'; it was characteristic of the art not only of the High Altai but of Black Sea Scythia.

The style caused the reproduction of animals to be done in certain ways. Thus, for example, the round eye, which we see in representations of birds and fish, is never found in carnivores, where it is always elongated and has a tear duct. The short, round ear is possessed only by cats; with other carnivores and ungulates it is long and pointed with a characteristic curl at the bottom and a lobe. The angle of the mandible is often shown as a curl, not uncommonly merging with the ear into one S-shape. Very characteristic also is the reproduction of the shoulder girdle, also in the form of a curl, turning into a spiral; fairly commonly the curl is repeated for the sake of symmetry on the crupper also.

All the peculiarities just enumerated are characteristic of the basic mass of representational art of the people of the High Altai, by which the style of their art at this time is defined. A predominance of representations of wild animals, executed in this special style, indicates that the art was formed in the period preceding the change to a stock-rearing way of life, when hunting, which had not lost its importance even in the period being considered, was still a basic occupation.

It remains briefly to touch on human representations, which occurred only in barrows 1 and 5. In the former a human head was used as a motif for decoration on saddlery, while from barrow 5 there is a monster with a human head and a scene with two human figures.

Representations of the human figure in the applied art of the pastoral tribes of this period are very rare; in the High Altai they were first found in barrow 5 at Pazyryk. Human heads engraved within a circle are usual in Scythian barrows, where they occur on gold plates sewn on to clothing, and on plaques or pendants decorating saddlery.

The human heads from barrow 1 are fairly realistic (*Pl. 92*), broad-faced with protruding ears and thick (possibly false) beards. They are not portraits but repeat motifs already well known in central Asian art. As an example a head of a devil may be cited on a round gold plate from the Oxus treasure, and on the front of a gold model wagon from the same collection.[1]

Even less of a portrait are the leather, silhouette saddle pendants with lotus crowns (*Pl. 138F*) or the horned human head with animal ears (*Pl. 138G*), both from barrow 1. The origin of these figures has become apparent since the find of remarkable half-lion, half-human figures in appliqué work on the felt wall-hanging from barrow 5 (*Pl. 173*). The creatures stand on their rear paws, hands raised up in the air. The twisted body is of blue colour, as if dressed in a

[1] Dalton, B, Pl. IV, 7; XI, 32.

costume, on to which are sewn red-brown rosettes. On the lion's paws are strong blue claws, but the human hands have fingers of a rosy, fleshy colour. The red-brown face is in profile and of Armenoid type with blunt, fleshy nose, projecting chin, black brows and black, twisted moustache. The eyes are black. The face is human, but the great projecting ear is clearly animal with characteristic curl below, rose-coloured like the hands but with zigzag yellow decoration within.

The head-dress is very fitting, blue in the upper part and brown in the lower, with diagonal yellow stripes running downwards and finishing in twists. There is a stylized deer antler of red and yellow colour on the head. The shape of the wing is remarkable, with long, raised wing feathers, red, yellow and blue and black at the end; the remaining polychrome wing feathers overlap one another and finish with twists. The highly individual tail, twisted and thrust forward between the legs, with a terminal like a stylized antler, is coloured red and yellow.

Representations of winged lions with human bodies (or just the head) appeared in Hither Asia not later than the beginning of the second millennium B.C. The motif occurs in sculpture and low relief in Hittite cities by the fourteenth century B.C. A similar motif occurs on ancient Babylonian and Chaldaean cylinders. This type of fantastic creature was a peculiarly Assyrian speciality and it is represented in bas-reliefs in the palace of Nimrud. A winged lion with human head is known from the costume of Ashurnasirpal, where the monster stands with its paw raised.[1] A creature depicted at Nimrud palace has a special significance for us, since it wears a head-dress somewhat recalling that on the Pazyryk sphinx, and the unusual treatment of the wings with feathers overlapping in rows is just like that on the wings of the monster in barrow 5. Wings are shown in just this way on Hittite sculptures.

In the monumental remains of Achaemenid Persia, in particular at Persepolis, representations of a sphinx are lacking, and in those exceptional cases where it occurs on seals its Assyrian origin is undoubted. This is a very important point, since it indicates that this motif could only have reached the Altai as a result of ancient pre-Achaemenian cultural links with Hither Asia not later than the seventh century B.C. Hence its individual local treatment in the form in which we found it, in barrow 5 at Pazyryk, can be understood.

Although in the native Altaian versions of lions and griffins, already studied in detail by us, we can detect not only borrowings of the motif but even of details in their execution (bearing in mind that representations of lions on cloth of actual Hither Asian origin occurred in barrow 5), the treatment of the Altaian sphinx is quite independent. Except for the peculiarities in the wings just mentioned, neither Assyrian nor, even less, Persian influence can be detected in it.

[1] Layard, B, 1849, Pl. 48; Perrot and Chipiez, B, vol. ii, p. 581, fig. 278 and p. 774, fig. 446; Ménant, B, pt ii, p. 37, fig. 21.

The lion's body, and especially the style of the paws, possibly show traces of influences from monumental Hither Asian lions, but the antlers in this case are deer's in a characteristic Altaian rendering. The ears are treated in a way familiar from the carnivores' ears, while the lion's tail, like the antler, is done in native style. The highly individual head-dress can to some extent be compared with the head-dress on an ancient Hittite bas-relief (where a winged lion with human body stands up like ours on its back feet) and also with a figure already mentioned at Nimrud.[1]

The Pazyryk sphinx is executed in polychrome felt appliqué, which made it difficult to render details and even more the expression on the face. All the same, by means of supplementary embroidery, an extremely expressive face with high forehead, massive 'assyroid' nose and projecting chin has been achieved. The eyes, with their large black brows, are finely done. These features, taken together with the twisted moustache, skilfully depict some kind of 'assyro-armenoid' type, who was evidently a native of the area where this motif first arose.

The rider seated before the goddess depicted on the great wall-hanging (*Pl. 154*) is of just the same type. The heads of both rider and goddess are disproportionately large. The rider's nose is large and snoutlike and he has a fine head of curly black hair; his black moustache is twisted. The face of the goddess is quite different; it is masculine and only the absence of a moustache and beard allow us to infer that she is female. A noteworthy feature is the absence of hair on the head; the head-dress appears to be worn over a shaven head. In this connection we may recall the head shaven around the crown of the woman in barrow 5, which is where this carpet was found. On the man's head the ear is rendered schematically, on the woman's it is shown reversed with the cavity facing backwards; this is not accidental since in all representations of this personage her ear is shown like this.

The costume of the goddess and rider in all probability was not the usual native dress. The narrow, waisted jacket with high collar, the fluttering short cloak, the narrow tight breeches are none of them normal male Altaian attire of that time. The goddess wears a long dress down to her ankles and a denticulated crownlike head-dress. The horse, however, in this scene is clearly a native thoroughbred, just the same trotter as the best horses buried with the tribal chiefs. The mane and tail have been trimmed, the tail plaited, the ear has an owner's nick, and the bridle and saddle are of typical Pazyryk kind as found in barrow 5. On his left side, as if prepared for war, the rider is wearing his bow-case (*gorytus*). The throne on which the goddess sits is also of local style with carved legs like those on the little dish-tables or like the balusters in the carriage from barrow 5. The very remarkable spray bearing buds and blossom held by the goddess is rendered in the native style.

[1] Pottier, B, fig. 31; Ménant, B, pt ii, fig. 21.

Thus in this scene as in the sphinx we see a hybrid of foreign and native motifs organically linked in a single idea.

The representations studied by us are important in another respect; they testify very clearly to the existence among the tribes concerned not only of a full range of the now familiar artistic decoration, but also to a monumental, if one can so express it, form of art used for adorning their dwellings. Furthermore, taken in combination with some coloured felt appliqué work from barrows 1 and 2, they offer some idea of the pictorial side of their art. From a modern point of view silhouette and sculptured wooden objects are rated much higher than the somewhat primitive pictorial representations, like that of the goddess and rider on his pink horse. If we are going to assess the polychrome felt appliqué work from the point of view of its decorative quality we must rate it high. We may recall the polychrome compositions of the lion-griffin falling upon a mountain goat or the eagle-griffin on a mountain goat from barrow 1 (*Pls. 169*A, *170*), the griffin's head from barrow 2 (*Pl. 167*B), the sphinx (*Pl. 173*) and even the unfinished bird from barrow 5 (*Pl. 149*A), the borders of some felt carpets, especially those with lotus ornament (*Pl. 148*B) from barrow 2 with their bright flowers. We have to recognize a quite high level for the period in the field of artistic skill.

One question remains: who exactly created these objects? Was it a case of specialist artists working at the headquarters of supreme or tribal chiefs, as some foreign archaeologists suppose,[1] or of a general popular creativity? That it was the latter is made evident by the complete air of daily use worn by the artistically designed articles; wholly utilitarian objects would hardly be thus specially designed. Accessibility of material in which the motifs were embodied favours this. The general use of the motifs, the methods of representation, the very style in which they were carried out, all proclaim that here we are dealing with a genuine folk art, and not with the work of foreign specialist artists at centres of a tribal nobility. On the other hand, naturally, there would be people more artistically gifted, although they were probably not occupied full time with the manufacture of fine articles. If we look at, say, the carved wooden decorations in barrows 1 and 2, then it is not difficult to notice that the majority have been executed by the same methods, in precisely the same way. The same can be said about similar articles from barrows 3, 4 or 5. The objects referred to in each barrow have their individual stamp, which, so it seems to me, can be regarded as individual qualities of the craftsman who made them, although the motifs and style of execution are the same. Furthermore it is obvious that different craftsmen specialized either in carving wood or bone, or in cutting out silhouettes and scenes and colouring them, or in patterns made with applied felt

[1] Andersson, B, p. 312.

and leather. The variety of treatment of the motifs justifies such an inference, done as they are in varied materials and using the different technical devices that occur within the range of finds of each barrow.

Prior to the Pazyryk excavations nothing was known about the music of the pastoral peoples we are studying. Classical writers tell us nothing about musical instruments and none had been found in barrow excavations.

In 1947 and 1948 the first stringed musical instrument came to light in barrow 2 at Pazyryk. It is illustrated in *Pl. 146* as restored by M. P. Gryaznov. The resonator, 83 cm. long, is hollowed out of a piece of solid wood and has four wooden stretchers along the top edge. The ends of the body are relatively wide (11–12 cm.), the middle part very narrow (up to 3–4 cm.). The lower face of the body is almost horizontal, but the centre concave, so that at its ends the instrument is 8·5–9 cm. high, but in the middle only 5 cm. The middle part of the body is covered by a wooden sounding board stuck on, 26 cm. long, with an X-shaped resonating aperture in the middle. Over the open part of the body were extended sounding membranes of thin, finely dressed leather, dyed red on the outside. In each membrane were three circular resonating holes, one near either end and one near the middle. The membranes were fixed to the body by thin wooden pegs. At the projecting ends of the body were lugs, perhaps for suspension of the instrument from the shoulder while playing. The string-holder, 24 cm. high, was fixed by a strap to a lug at one end of the broader part of the body, and at the other end fixed to a bow attached to another lug. To judge by what remained, the number of strings was not less than four. Thus the instrument in question was a kind of harp, analogous to one of the types of Assyrian harp that are represented in the bas-reliefs in the palaces of Khorsabad and Kuyunjik,[1] but in a distinct, essentially local, form.

A second musical instrument, a one-sided drum, consists of two halves of an ox-horn (fig. 138). Drums like this, almost complete, were found in the burial chambers of barrows 2 and 5, while there were further fragments in barrow 3. Their average height is 18 cm., and they are 10 cm. and 8 cm. wide in their broadest parts at the upper and lower ends and 6 cm. in the middle, narrowest, part. The body consisted, as mentioned, of two rounded plates of ox-horn, the edges of which overlap each other. They were attached by thread passed through a series of holes each about 1 mm. in diameter. The membrane was stretched on the upper, incurved end and fixed by stitching well down from the edge. On the drum from barrow 2 the seam was entirely covered by narrow gold platelets with twisted ornament. The membranes themselves did not survive, only the traces in the shape of a narrow white band. The workmanship of the drums is distinguished by exquisite care and attention. By their goblet shape,

---

[1] Layard, B, 1867a, Pl. xxx; Perrot and Chipiez, B, pt ii, p. 205.

and especially the method of attaching the membrane, the drums have close affinities to the one-sided drums of similar form and construction found formerly and today in Tibet, Afghanistan, Iran and Asia Minor.

The discovery of drums in all the barrows except No. 1 [1] (which had been thoroughly ransacked) testifies to their widespread use at that time, while the discovery of a multi-stringed musical instrument of harp type confirms the relatively high level (for its time) then attained by music-playing in the High Altai.

[1] [Translator's note. And barrow 4? M.W.T.]

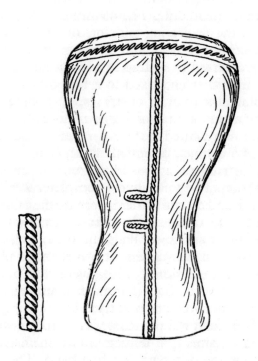

138. One-sided horn drum from barrow 2 (*c.* $\frac{1}{3}$).

10. RELIGIOUS BELIEFS AND RITUALS

THE FIRST SUBJECT related to the religion of the population of the Altai Mountains in the Scythian period is the burial rite, the primary source for the religious aspects of which is the barrows.

The Pazyryk barrows offer a clear picture of the burial rite of the ancient Altaians. The heads of the corpses were laid towards the east, facing towards the west. Hence it may be inferred that the next world was regarded as lying towards the west, where each day the sun sets.

The interment took place at a certain time of the year, at the beginning of summer or in the autumn. The custom of burying the dead in spring or autumn continued to survive among the ancient Turks of the sixth to eighth centuries A.D., although they did not bury their corpses and horses but burnt them. According to a Chinese chronicler, 'they bury those who die in spring or summer when the leaves on the trees and plants begin to yellow and fall; and he who dies in the autumn or winter they bury when the leaves begin to open'.[1]

The practice of burying only at certain seasons of the year (also probably due to the great expenditure of labour necessary in the construction of the huge barrows) was bound up with the custom of embalming a corpse to prevent its decomposition up to the moment of burial. Only the bodies of those of noble birth were embalmed, it would seem. With rare exceptions the skulls were also trepanned to remove the brain when the body was embalmed. Up to now not a single ordinary burial has been found where the skull had been trepanned; in the large barrows quite the contrary was the rule and all the skulls had been trepanned. We still do not know whether all burials took place at fixed seasons of the year or whether this was limited to the nobility.

All that has been said above allows us to infer that spring and autumn were the seasons generally favoured for interments. Future study of the ordinary graves (in which young animals rarely occur) may help to solve this.

Embalmment of the corpses was first recognized in Altaian burials after the

[1] Bichurin, A, pt i, p. 230.

279

excavations at Shibe in the Ursul valley.[1] Although the corpses of both the old and the young man had survived badly, nevertheless it was possible to establish that their entrails and musculature had been removed, and the brain extracted through a specially made hole cut out of the skull wall. The youth's eye-sockets had been sewn up, and thick sinew thread had been used to sew up all the slits in the body. The slits had been cut to a definite rule; those on the leg of the man in the Shibe barrow had been made in precisely the same way as on the legs of the man from barrow 5 at Pazyryk.

The skulls of the man and woman buried in barrow 2 had been trepanned in the area of the cervical bone, in exactly the same way as had that of the old man at Shibe. The skin over the left parietal bone of the woman in barrow 2 had been cut away and pulled back and then crude tools, chisel and mallet, had been used to knock out an irregular disk of bone (40 mm. by 55 mm.). After removal of the brain and filling of the cranium (with soil, pine needles and larch cones in the case of the man; the woman's cranium was not found) the plate of bone that had been struck out was put back in its former place and the skin secured with cord of twisted black horsehair.

For removal of the guts the stomach area of the man had been opened up; the slit started at the lower right edge of the thorax, running down 5–6 cm. from the navel to finish at the right front projection of the iliac bone. After extraction of the entrails this slit had been sewn up with sinew threads. On the inside of the right arm, starting at the armpit, running down to the ulnar cavity and beyond the articulating area of the ulnar bone, to within a few centimetres of the hand, a deep cut had been made in order to introduce some kind of fluid preservative into the muscles. On the left arm there was also a slit on the inner side extending from slightly below the head of the humerus through the armpit almost reaching the hand. The slits on the leg were also on the inside. On the right leg the slit began slightly above the inside of the ankle, ran between kneecap and back of knee, passed across the perineum on to the other leg, passed the back of the knee and inside of the shin and finished exactly 10 cm. above the ankle. After preservative matter had been inserted the slits on arms and legs as well as stomach had been sparsely stitched up with sinew thread.

Besides slits on the hands and legs there were numerous deep holes 1 cm. across on the buttocks, legs and arms at the shoulders, made evidently with the point of a knife, probably also with the object of introducing preservative matter within the sinews to prevent decomposition. What was used as a preservative we still do not know. Possibly it was common salt, a universal method, widely used in Egypt. It would not have been difficult to establish this if the preserved corpses treated in this way had been found in an undisturbed and unflooded grave; in barrow 2 the man's corpse had been thrown out by the looters and lay

[1] Gryaznov, A, 1928.

a long time in water, so it was impossible to establish the presence of salt in it.

The woman's body had been treated differently. The abdominal cavity also had been opened from the right side, starting at the sternum and going past the navel down to the iliac bone, but after removal of the guts it had been sewn up not with sinew threads but with black horsehair cord.

In removing the body from the burial chamber plant stalks or chopped-off roots of some kind were observed, which still have not been studied. The skin had been slit open behind at the waist on both buttocks, in the thighs and calves, and part of the muscles removed and replaced with grass of a sedge kind and then, as with the stomach, the slits had been sewn up with horsehair.

A rather different method of embalming had been employed in barrow 5. The man's skull had been trepanned through the left parietal bone. A slit 11 cm. long had been made in the skin and a piece of bone about 6 cm. in diameter chiselled out. The slit had been left unstitched. The skin on both sides of the chest had been slit open from the armpits down to the sixth rib and then sewn up with cord twisted from double plaits of horsehair. This kind of cord had been used to sew up nearly all the slits in the skin of both the man and the woman (exceptions will be specially mentioned). At 9 cm. below the bottom of the slit on the thorax the abdominal slit began and passed to the right of the navel down towards the left groin. A small slit had been made to the left of the navel, 2–3 cm. from it. On the arms the slits ran from the armpit area on the inside, slightly interrupted at the inside of the elbow, down to the hand and along its outside as far as the little finger. On the left arm there was a transverse slit on the outside above the wrist. Short slits in the skin (4–4·5 cm. long) had been made on the outer surface of the forearm near the hand. The middle finger of the man's right hand was bound at the nail with a woollen thread which was attached to the skin of the pubic area.

Behind, the skin had been slit from the occiput down the neck and spine finishing 3 cm. above the sacrum. This slit was intersected near the top by a transverse slit running from the outer upper edge of one shoulder to the other (Pl. 46). The longitudinal slit had been left unstitched for about 5 cm. on the neck, just above the transverse slit, and below it the skin was sewn up with a narrow thong. From the upper edge of the sacrum at 2–3 cm. from its inner corners slits ran downwards through the buttocks, thighs and calves to the feet, that were continuous except for gaps 3–4 cm. long behind the knees. On the soles of the feet were central slits running from ankle-bone to second toe.

Preparatory treatment of the woman's body for embalmment differed somewhat from that just described carried out on the man. The woman's skull had also been trepanned on the left side on the division between temporal and parietal bones, but the slit in the skin had in this case been sewn up (Pl. 45). In addition two slits 4–10 cm. long had been made in the occipital area. On the cheeks to right and left of the temples in front of the ears there were slits running downwards 9·5–10 cm. long which had been carefully stitched up with sinew thread. There was a semicircular slit on the neck to the right of the collar-bone. On the woman, as on the man, slits in the skin ran from the armpit area on both sides over the chest up to the teats; in removing the muscles the skin of the chest was attached by a sinew thread on the outside behind the teat to the skin of the body. On the right side from the lower edge of the thorax ran an ab-dominal slit passing the navel and the iliac bone, which finished in the groin between the pubis and the head of the femur. As on the man the slits on the arms ran from the armpits on the inner face down to the hand, interrupted only behind the elbow. Below this the seam was torn open and reached down the outside of the hand to the little finger.

On the woman's back the skin was slit above from shoulder to shoulder, just as on the man's body; there were two longitudinal slits, one on the neck and another on the back. The neck slit rose 10 cm. above the transverse slit; the back one ran from 6 cm. to 7 cm. below the same point parallel to the spine almost down to the sacrum. At this point the skin was torn away but, as in the man, below the sacrum and to left and right were slits that ran down the buttocks on to both legs as far as the back of the knees. After an interruption of 4–5 cm. the slits were renewed and reached the feet, and the left leg had an additional slit parallel to the main one on it. Both feet were slit twice, on the outside, down to the little toe (somewhat shorter on the right leg), and on the inside down to the big toe.

It is especially to be noticed that the skin at the elbow and knee joints had not been slit. Neither on the man nor on the woman had the skin at the perineum been stitched up. In order to preserve the natural shape at the neck and breast of the woman horse-hair padding had been inserted.

As is well known the practice of embalmment was widespread at the period of the construction of the Pazyryk barrows. Outside Egypt, where Herodotus described in detail the various methods of embalming bodies,[1] embalmment was practised in Assyria, Media and Persia in the middle of the last millennium B.C. Of the Black Sea Scyths Herodotus wrote: 'After the death of a king [*basileus*] they at once excavate a large square hole; in preparation the corpse is taken and covered with wax, but prior to this they slit open its stomach, clean it and fill it with chopped cypress, frankincense, seeds of parsley and anise, sew it up and bear it on a wagon.'[2] We now know that far to the north-east in the Altai Mountains there was just the same custom, but the full details of the embalm-ment are not known. It seems that in the various districts in the Altai the practice varied, although trepanation for removal of the brain and opening the stomach for removal of the guts were probably universally employed. Even in a

---

[1] Herodotus, A, bk ii, 86–8, 90.   [2] Ibid., bk iv, 71.

single barrow (No. 2 at Pazyryk) certain operations had been carried out on the man, but other somewhat different ones on the woman.

The custom of removing all the muscles from the corpse is noteworthy. Could not this be a survival of the ritual eating of the dead?

Herodotus related: 'They tell of the following custom among the Issedones: If someone's father dies all the relatives bring cattle to the son, they kill the animals, cut up the flesh of the corpse into pieces, mix up all the meat and arrange a feast.' [1] The Massagetae do the same thing: 'When someone grows old . . . they kill him and also a variety of animals, cook them up together and eat them.' [2] This practice was undoubtedly bound up with a belief in the possibility in this way of acquiring the supernatural powers which the dead man possessed.

Possibly this is the explanation for the extraction of the muscles from the embalmed bodies at Pazyryk, barrow 5, and possibly also in the Shibe barrow. A second question arises: why were the muscles left untouched in the corpses in barrow 2 and yet removed in barrow 5? As yet we cannot answer this question, but it prompts a number of suggestions. First, the Altaians, like the Egyptians, might simultaneously have practised various methods of embalmment depending on the social position of the dead person. Secondly, among different tribes the methods might have varied as well as the relationship between the dead persons. Among the Massagetae, for example, Herodotus reported that some of the corpses were eaten, some not: 'They do not eat the body of a man who has died of illness but bury it, lamenting that he did not reach the age to be killed.' [3] It is possible, furthermore, that the methods of embalmment altered in the course of time, but there is insufficient evidence to allow us to study such changes.

A willing move from this world into the next beyond the grave can sometimes be attributed to certain views about the continuation of life on the other side. Thus Herodotus wrote of the Massagetae: 'The normal boundaries of life are quite disregarded by them, and so when a person grows old all his relatives gather around him and kill him. . . . Among them such an end to life is regarded as the happiest possible.' [4]

Corresponding with this view about the continuation of life after its apparent end they continued to 'feed' a dead man up to his burial. Herodotus wrote: 'With regard to the other Scyths [i.e. not their kings] in the event of a death the corpse is placed on a cart by his closest relatives and carried amongst his friends, each one of whom offers the bearers a sumptuous feast and a portion of each regalement is reserved for the corpse.' [5] They placed the necessary dress for the

[1] Herodotus, A, bk iv, 26.
[2] Ibid., bk i, 216.
[3] Ibid., bk i, 216.
[4] Ibid., bk i, 216.
[5] Ibid., bk iv, 73.

dead man in the tomb, as well as objects of a domestic nature, weapons, a concubine, horses and saddlery.

The custom of burying a horse with its rider persisted for a very long time in the Altai. We meet it among Turks in the first millennium A.D. and in the eastern Altai among the Telesi up to the end of the nineteenth century. Among the Kazakhs and Kirgiz the burial rite has changed fundamentally, due without doubt to the influence of Islam, and burial with an accompanying horse is quite unknown. Nevertheless, in the middle of the last century as a kind of survival the following custom was observed: at the death of a rich Kazakh, on the seventh day following the people assembled and a great feast was offered to them. The saddle was put upside-down on the dead man's horse and his clothes hung over it with hat on top, and the horse was led in this manner to the dead man's tent, to which it was tethered by the lead rein. Then to the sounds of doleful singing the horse's tail was cropped. Such a horse was never ridden again and was called a widow. If a Kazakh died on a journey then his horse was led towards home with saddle inverted and only when it was near there did they crop the tail and trim the mane.[1]

Had the tribes we are studying purifying rituals and what were they precisely?

It is known from written sources that among pastoral tribes of the period the Scyths after the interment carried out a special purifying ritual. Herodotus described it thus: 'The burial completed, the Scyths cleanse themselves in the following manner. They soap their heads and wash their hair, and then to cleanse their bodies they do as follows: they set up three sticks leaning together which they cover over with woollen felts, and in the circular shelter created as best they can they put stones heated in a fire into a vessel set within this shelter. . . . In Scythia they grow hemp. . . . And then the Scyths take some of its seeds, creep under the felt and scatter the seeds over the hot stones, which gives off greater clouds of steam than in any Greek steam bath. The Scyths, delighted by the steam, are loudly exultant. This serves as a substitute for ablutions, for they never wash their bodies with water.'[2]

In the south-western corner of the burial chamber in barrow 2 at Pazyryk there was a cluster of six rods, below which rested a rectangular bronze vessel standing on four feet filled with pounded stone (*Pl. 35*). The length of these rods was 122·5 cm., their diameter about 2 cm. and the diameter of the lower, thickened ends about 3 cm. There was a perforation through each 2 cm. down

[1] Radloff, B, p. 449.

[2] Herodotus, A, bk iv, 73–5. I give a slightly different reading from that, for example, given by Mishchenko or Latyshev. There the Scythian fumigation is compared with a Greek bath, and the vessel in which the hot stones were put would have been a receptacle or even a bath. However, Herodotus wrote not of a bath or bathroom ($\dot{\alpha}\sigma\dot{\alpha}\mu\iota\nu\theta\sigma$) but of the steam room ($\dot{\eta}$ $\pi\nu\rho\iota\alpha$) or dry, usually round chambers heated by fires ($\pi\nu\rho\iota\alpha\tau\dot{\eta}\rho\iota\alpha$) for dry sweating.

284

from the top through which passed a thong that held them together. All the rods were bound round spirally with strips of birch bark.

Farther north in the western half of the chamber there was a second bronze vessel of the 'Scythian cauldron' shape, also filled with stones, under six sticks splayed out in the same way (partly broken and overturned by the looters) and covered over by a large leather hanging.

In each vessel besides the stones, as already mentioned above, there was a small quantity of seeds of hemp (*Cannabis sativa* L. of the variety *C. rideralus*, Janisch). Mention was also made of the hemp seeds in the leather flask attached to one of the sticks in the hexapod stand over the vessel of 'Scythian cauldron' shape. Burning hot stones had been placed in the censer and part of the hemp seeds had been charred. Furthermore the handle of the cauldron-censer had been bound round with birch bark, evidently because the heat of the stones was such that its handle had become too hot to hold in the bare hands (*Pl. 62*B).

Thus in barrow 2 two smoking sets were found: vessels containing stones that had been in the fire and hemp seeds; above them were shelters supported on six rods, in one case covered with a leather hanging and in the other case probably with a felt hanging, large pieces of which were found in the south-west corner of the tomb. Finally, there was a flask containing hemp seeds fixed to one of the legs of a hexapod stand. Consequently we have the full set of articles for carrying out the purification ritual, about which Herodotus wrote in such detail in his description of the Black Sea Scyths. There had been sets for smoking hemp in all the Pazyryk barrows; the sticks for the stand survived in each barrow although the censers and cloth covers had all been stolen except in barrow 2. Hemp smoking was practised evidently not only for purification but in ordinary life, as remarked in Chapter 4, by both men and women.

The habit of purifying by fire after burials (fumigation) described by Herodotus among the Scyths was evidently widely practised by tribes over an area that included the High Altai.

It seems there were customs of commemoration of the dead in the Altai; or at all events their neighbours, the Issedones, had such customs. Herodotus noted: 'Among the Issedones commemoration of the dead took place once a year, as with the Greeks when a son did honour to the memory of his father.' [1]

All the practices just described are connected with the rites of the dead, with the cult of ancestors, which, as has been noted, according to Chinese sources was general among the Huns, Wu-huan and other tribes living to the east of the High Altai. In this connection the following report in a Chinese chronicle is extremely interesting. The Huns held a Chinese general, Ershysky, as their prisoner. 'It happened that the mother of the shan-yu was ill. Vei Lyui [one

[1] Herodotus, A, bk iv, 26.

of the Hunnish leaders] ordered a magician through the inspiration of dead shan-yus to say that the Huns hitherto, when offering war sacrifices, always said that once Ershysky was captured he must be sacrificed. . . . Afterwards they impaled Ershysky so that he should be the sacrifice.'[1]

There is no doubt that graves were honoured by the pastoral tribes and preserved from interference by thieves. We know this as certainly about the Scyths as about the Huns.

In reply to the emissary of Darius asking why he avoided battle the Scythian king Idanthyrsus replied: 'I will explain why I do not hurry to do battle with you. We have no towns, no cultivated fields and no cause to fear that they will be reduced and razed, and so no motive to hurry into battle with you. If you consider it necessary to hasten a battle this is how to do it: we have the tombs of our ancestors; find them and try to destroy them; then you will find out whether we will join battle with you over these tombs or not.'[2]

From Chinese sources it is known that as a form of revenge against the Huns the Wu-huan dug up their graves.[3]

There are a series of finds in the Pazyryk barrows that shed much light on the religious beliefs of the ancient Altaians. Although, as we shall see below, religious beliefs had reached a relatively high degree of sophistication among these folk there must have been elements surviving that had been characteristic of earlier stages, and, amongst these, magic.

As amulets for protection against evil spirits or the evil eye cowrie shells (*Cypreae moneta*) resembling the female vulva were used, which were widely employed also in earlier and later periods not only in the High Altai but far beyond. Occurring singly, especially in barrow 6 at Pazyryk and barrow 1 of the ordinary Katanda barrows, they must be regarded as amulets, given the state of society.

In barrows 1 and 2 there were locks of hair sewn into pieces of leather and felt, and in addition in barrow 2 there were fingernails kept in a special leather pouch.

In the leather bag that was found at the head end of the coffin in barrow 2 amongst other objects was a rectangular leather pouch (*Pl. 145*A). It had been sewn up from a single piece of leather doubled over. The bottom edge had no seam and the sides were finely stitched with twisted sinew thread and the upper edge with a larger stitch. At the top corners long thin straps tied into a knot were threaded through. Within there proved to be a lock of black hair stitched in. Another lock of hair (*Pl. 145*B) stored in a triangular piece of dark brown, almost black, felt was found in the tomb where it had been thrown out with

[1] Bichurin, A, pt i, p. 76.   [3] Bichurin, A, pt i, p. 144.
[2] Herodotus, A, bk iv, 127.

other objects by the looters. In the felt along the long side near the obtuse angle a slit had been made in such a way that a small strip could be introduced into it. A lock of hair had been put in after which the slit edge was sewn up with twisted woollen thread. The same thread attached to one corner of the felt showed that it had probably originally been sewn on to something.

The human finger-nails were in the same tomb. Into the angle of a piece of thin but rigid leather (*Pl. 145c*) a small leather purse had been sewn (*Pl. 145D, E*), which contained nail clippings. It had been tied up with a narrow thong, rolled up and put in the piece of leather, after which this had been stitched through with thick, twisted woollen thread. This miniature purse was oval in shape and had been made from a single piece of finely dressed yellow leather, one long edge being left open and the other below stitched with fine sinew thread. A thin, narrow tying thong was sewn to the upper edge.

The presence of hair and nails in the tomb constitutes definite evidence of animism. At early stages of cultural development there was everywhere a belief not only that the body contained a life element (the soul) but also that its parts, including the hair and nails, had their distinct, partial souls. The hair and nails continue to grow and do not die or decompose and vanish after death. It was sufficient to possess the hair and nails of a person in order to gain control over his soul and influence his life. Hence it was a widely practised ancient custom to preserve the combed-out or trimmed hair and clipped nails in order to avoid the danger of their being used for magic or by evil spirits exercising their influences.

On the other hand, from a belief in continuity of life into the next world arose the necessity to preserve not only the body but its parts, the hair and nails. In central Asia and Persia the practice of putting the nails under the shroud has survived to the present day.[1]

The problem of animal worship is very involved, and even further elaborated in ingenious theories that seek to trace the origin of the so-called 'Scythian animal style'.

There is an interpretation very prevalent in the literature that the animals in the art of the pastoralists represent a kind of totemism, a view which is held by some foreign archaeologists, especially Andersson.[2] This view has been adopted by some of our own investigators under the influence of the pseudo-Marxist idealist concepts of N. Y. Marr; the 'totem' of these ideas has nothing to do with real ethnographic facts.

Neither the Greek historians nor the Chinese chroniclers make any reference to an animal cult among the Scyths and other pastoral tribes. With regard to the lion and griffin Lappo-Danilevsky made the suggestion that the lion was an attribute of the Scythian god Artimpasa and the griffin an attribute of the sun

[1] Andreev, A, issue 2, p. 27, note.　　　　　[2] Andersson, B, p. 315.

god Oetosyrus.[1] It is possible that the cock was sacred, for it heralded the dawn with its crowing and drove off the dark spirits of the night; we may recall the ritualistic role of this bird in Hither Asia from at least the seventh and sixth centuries B.C.

Although animals depicted on weapons and other utilitarian objects could be totemic, this would only have been the case in the earlier stages of economic and social development among hunting peoples and not among people at the social level of the Altaians. So if this or that animal was depicted on the riding equipment or other articles it can only be regarded as a survival of a long-vanished past and not as expressing the contemporary ideology of the time. In the art almost all the most conspicuous elements of the local fauna occur, so there is no justification for attributing some to totemic and some to non-totemic animals. Furthermore in sets of decoration from one outfit (that is, all worn by one horse) several different animals may be represented. This lends weight to our inference about the impossibility of the animals having a totemic significance. Finally, the Pazyryk barrows gave a fair number of representations of domestic animals, in particular the horse, and it can hardly be admitted that a domestic animal was also totemic.

Among a variety of suggestions not based on reliable data or on comparisons taken from the ethnographic literature, is one that regards the animals as mythological representations of bearers of different qualities: blood-thirstiness, remoteness, ferocity or sensitivity, and so on.[2]

The proper significance of the scenes of fighting animals, of predators leaping on herbivores, has been discussed more than once in the literature on the subject. They have been represented as a graphic portrayal of clashes that took place from time to time between the various tribes and clans in Pazyryk society.[3] Such an interpretation rests on no firm evidence and cannot stand up to any critical study.

The scenes of fighting or attack by one animal on another can be divided into two distinct categories following M. I. Artamanov: one of real carnivores attacking herbivores, the second of fantastic animals attacking just the same herbivores.[4] An original mythical idea behind the latter category, the monsters attacking herbivores, is probable if the cosmogony of ancient Hither Asia is borne in mind.

It was mentioned above that Hither Asian motifs had appeared in the art of the High Altai long before the time we are discussing. The dualism that was peculiar to the ancient religions of the Near East found its expression in scenes of struggling animals. It is possible that some of the dualistic ideas reached the Altai when the motif was adopted, but that by the time under discussion they

[1] Lappo-Danilevsky, A, p. 532.
[2] Gryaznov, A, 1950, pp. 80–2.
[3] Golmsten, A.
[4] Artamanov, A, 1948, p. 470.

had been considerably modified. Besides the attacks of griffins, eagle- and lion-griffins on deer, elk, mountain rams and goats, as well as fish seizing mountain rams we see also struggles between an eagle-griffin and a lion-griffin, between two griffins and between a lion-griffin and a tiger. These motifs are not used symbolically but as decoration, particularly on saddlery.

Certain forms peculiar to the Scyths of the Black Sea and High Altai occupy a special position. These are the creatures that combine in themselves traits of several species of animal: the body of a feline carnivore with deer's or elk's antlers with griffins' heads on the tips of the tines; deer with eagle's beak, feline tail with a griffin's-head terminal, or on antlers, or sometimes on the withers, and so on. A speciality of the Altai is the winged tiger, or leopard, again with a griffin's beak. They can probably be regarded as having a protective function; such objects do not occur in the saddlery. They constitute a basic motif of the tattooing on the chief's body in barrow 2; the same occur on plaques in the Katanda barrow and on several plaques in the Siberian Collection of Peter the Great.[1]

Similar, fantastic forms (complex in our eyes) are encountered in the horse accoutrements, but the crests, as opposed to the other decorations, including the frontal plates, were endowed with a special significance.

The last matter that need detain us is the figures on the great felt carpet from barrow 5. This is the wall-hanging where a rider stands before a goddess seated on a throne holding the sacred tree or a branch in blossom in her hand (*Pl. 154*). In order to identify this goddess we must turn our attention to the religion of the pastoral folk of this time.

From the information which can be derived from Chinese sources the tribes living to the east of the High Altai, the Huns and Wu-huan, worshipped the spirits and made sacrifice to Heaven, Earth, Sun, Moon, the stars and their ancestors.[2] Furthermore it is clear that the whole scene depicted on the carpet repeats the well-known scene on the rhyton from Merdzhany, where a mounted Scythian warrior stands before a goddess.

Let us now turn to Greek reports about the Scythian gods.

The deities worshipped by the Scyths were enumerated by Herodotus, who gave in each case the Greek equivalent. These gods were as follows: Tabiti (Hestia) who was reverenced above the rest, Papaeus (Zeus), Apia (Hera, the wife of Zeus), Oetosyrus (Apollo), Artimpasa (Aphrodite), Thamimasadas (Poseidon) (the latter only worshipped by the Royal Scyths according to Herodotus) and, finally, Ares.[3]

Tabiti was the goddess of the hearth, of family well-being, and her cult was

[1] Tolstoy and Kondakov, A, vol. iii, pp. 60–2, 64.

[2] Bichurin, A, pt i, pp. 49, 65, 76, 144.

[3] Herodotus, A, bk iv, 59.

289

linked to the worship of fire. An oath by the gods of the royal hearth, like the royal gods of the Persians, was regarded by the Scyths as the most sacred. As Lappo-Danilevsky suggested, this is the reason for the connection between the domestic hearth and the worship of ancestors.[1] This divinity held just such a primary position among the Persians.

Papaeus was god of the sky; equal with him was the female deity, Apia, goddess of the earth, linked to some extent with the nether regions, who was the goddess of fertility, equivalent to the Medo-Persian Anahita.

Oetosyrus was the god of the sun and was especially revered by the Massagetae. Both he and the goddess Artimpasa were worshipped by the ancient Iranians. The very Greek name used by Herodotus (Aphrodite of Uranus) shows that she was a secondary female deity of the Moon.

Thus in the carpet from barrow 5 we are looking at the masculine face of a goddess who, if we may rely on Scythian analogies, would be either Tabiti or Apia.

Hence it may be inferred that the religious beliefs which at that time were current among the pastoral tribes of eastern Europe and Asia, as also among the peoples of Hither Asia, were shared by the Altaian people. It is especially important to remember that this carpet is of local manufacture.

At all events, even from their gods just enumerated, it is clear that the Scyths worshipped the life-giving forces of nature which they spiritualized, and the personification of these forces was similar to that made by the religions of Hither Asia, especially Iran.

With regard to the rites practised in the Altai we know nothing. We do know, however, that the ancient pastoral folk of central Asia, like the Scyths, 'were not accustomed to worship idols'.[2] One of the principal rites would have been sacrificial offerings, although there were no priests or priestly caste either among the central Asian pastoralists or among the Scyths.

A Chinese chronicle recounts how as the Hunnish 'shan-yu and his elders ascended the Huns' Mountain on the eastern side of the River No-Shui they sacrificed a white horse'.[3] 'In the morning the shan-yu comes out of the camp and worships the rising sun and in the evening he worships the moon'.[4] In another place it was reported: 'The Huns had the custom of assembling three times a year in Moon ceremonies, when on the first, fifth and sixth moons, on a day which they call by this name, they make sacrifices to the spirit of the sky. . . . At these assemblies heads of the families discuss affairs of state and amuse themselves in horse jumping and camel racing.'[5]

---

[1] Lappo-Danilevsky, A, p. 525.
[2] Herodotus, A, bk iv, 59.
[3] Bichurin, A, pt i, p. 92.

[4] Ibid., A, pt i, p. 50.
[5] Ibid., pt i, p. 119.

The report of Herodotus about the Scythian rites of worship, according to which the method of sacrifice to each god was the same for all Scyths, is interesting in this connection.[1] The forelegs of the sacrificial animal were tied up and the performer of the sacrifice pulled the rope towards himself which threw the animal forward on to the ground. As it fell the sacrificer called upon the god to whom he was making the sacrifice and then quickly passed a loop over the neck of the animal which he twisted with a stick passed through it, and so throttled the beast. There was no pyre or preliminary rites or libations. Once he had strangled the animal and skinned it the sacrificer cast the pieces of meat and entrails dedicated to the god in front of him. For sacrificial purposes all the domestic animals were used, especially horses. 'The Massagetae sacrifice horses to the sun-god; the significance of this is that the swiftest of the gods should be offered the swiftest of animals.'[2]

Only the sacrifices to Ares were different from those made to the other gods. In a sacred place dedicated to him 'they set up an ancient iron sword which serves as an idol representing Ares'. In addition to cattle and horses as sacrifices they take every hundredth enemy male captive whom they kill, not in the same way as animals, but instead 'they pour a preliminary libation on his head, cut his throat over a vessel and collect the blood, which they pour over the sword'.[3]

In his analysis of this practice Lappo-Danilevsky compared the cult of the axe amongst the ancient Assyrians to that of the sword among the Scyths and Huns.[4]

The existence of a sword cult among the Huns, the neighbours of the Altaians, is clearly referred to in a Chinese source. It recorded that at the conclusion of a treaty of alliance between the Han and Hun rulers 'Chan, Myn, the shan-yu and the elders went up the Huns' Mountain by the east side of the River No-Shui, and impaled a white horse. The shan-yu took a costly sword and moistened its tip with wine; they drank the dedicated wine from the skull of a Yue-chi lord who had been killed by the Shan-yu Laoshan'.[5]

Herodotus' description of the burning of the bones of sacrificed animals, which was mentioned above, is of great interest. Special care of the bones of sacrificed animals, which could not be thrown away like others but had to be incinerated, is a very widespread custom. The practice of burning the bones of sacrificed animals existed among the Wu-sun, the Kalmyks and other steppe pastoralists, while tribes in the High Altai continued to deposit such bones on special wooden platforms up to the beginning of the present century. Undoubtedly the ancient Altaians had done just the same thing.

[1] Herodotus, A, bk iv, 60, 61.
[2] Ibid., bk i, 216.
[3] Ibid., bk iv, 62.

[4] Lappo-Danilevsky, A, p. 537.
[5] Bichurin, A, pt i, p. 92.

11. THE DATING AND CULTURAL-HISTORICAL PLACE OF THE FINDS FROM THE HIGH ALTAI

THE PAZYRYK barrows are not contemporary with one another; their absolute and relative chronology has been described in the Introduction. The differences are observable in the grave-goods, as well as in the external form and construction of the tombs.

Barrow 5, as we have seen (fig. 3), differs from the rest of the barrows in its attendant features. While the first four barrows had a row of upright stones running eastwards from the mound this was not present in barrow 5, but on the other hand barrow 5 was enclosed by a ring of upright stones from which radiated paved areas.

The construction of mound and orientation of the burials were identical in all the barrows. The burial chambers were broadly the same in construction, and the differences in detail do not constitute a criterion for chronological subdivision. The burial chambers of all the barrows were covered by layers of birch bark or sheets of it above which had been laid a layer of foliage of 'smoky tea', except in barrow 5 where the latter was absent.

The tomb shafts were filled with logs in barrows 1 and 2, but in barrows 3, 4 and 5 with logs and boulders.

The tree-trunk coffins were all of the same construction, only the gabled form of lid in barrow 5 differing somewhat from the rest. In barrows 1 and 2 figures of cocks and deer were fixed along the side, but the others were not decorated in that way.

The embalmed corpses survived only in barrows 2 and 5. In barrows 3 and 4, since the skulls were trepanned, it can be assumed that the bodies had been embalmed, but as the soft parts had decayed the details are uncertain. The methods of embalmment of the corpses differed in barrow 2, as we know from those used in barrow 5, where all the muscles had been removed from the bodies.

Who had been interred in barrow 1 we still do not know. In the remaining barrows, except no. 3, men with accompanying women had been buried, so that the custom of burying the chief with his concubine was a persistent one. In

293

barrows 2 and 5 the man and woman were laid together in the same coffin, but in barrow 4 in two separate ones.

Since the burial chambers had been robbed it was difficult to assess the content and character of the assemblage from the point of view of differences between the various barrows. One can only observe that in all the barrows there were the same tables with detachable tops, the same earthenware bottles with a narrow neck, the same apparatus for smoking hemp, the same one-sided horn drums and red woollen cloths of serge type. Imported woollen cloth of 'Gobelin' style and seeds of cultivated coriander were found in barrows 2 and 5. Furthermore silks were found in barrows 3 and 5 but not in barrow 2. On the other hand articles of leopards' fur were found only in the first two barrows.

Horse bodies had been deposited in all the barrows in the north side, either on the floor of the shaft or on the level of the ceiling of the chamber or, as in barrow 2, at the upper edge of the shaft. All the buried horses were geldings. The position of the horses in the tomb varied according to the number of animals and size of the area allocated to them. The heads faced predominantly eastwards, while at the eastern side of the shaft were buried the horses wearing crests and mane-covers.

The articles found in the horse burials, especially the saddlery, rather than the things from the burial chambers, have served as criteria for establishing the relative chronology of the barrows. Primarily it was noticed that in barrow 1, and it seems in barrow 2 also, the bridles were made from thin straps partially covered with fine leather. In barrows 3 and 5 the straps were as a rule doubled over and stitched through. In addition, in the majority of bridles from barrows 3 and 5, the noseband after being pleated with the side-straps became cheek-straps; this did not occur in barrow 1. Furthermore in barrow 1 the lead rein was held with a loop, but in barrows 3 and 4 with special slider blocks. In barrow 5 lead reins were not found.

The form of the saddles in barrows 1 and 2 differed essentially from that of those in the other three barrows. In both cases the saddle arches at front and back are low with narrow leather cut-out, open-work decoration and little narrow saddle bows on the arches. In the other three barrows the arches on the contrary are high with massive horn, wooden or leather decorations. In addition the saddles of the last three barrows had wooden spacers front and back between the cushions which did not exist in the first two barrows. A variety of pendants were fixed to the saddles in all possible combinations in barrows 1 and 2, but in the remainder of the barrows were in a definite position. Although in barrows 1 and 2 the majority of the wooden pendants decorating the bridle and chest-strap were fixed by a notch in their top edge, in the other barrows they were held with the help of perforated lugs or special perforations on the back. In the later barrows slides appear on the saddle-straps, in particular on the crupper, by means of which it could be lengthened or shortened depending on the size of the horse.

Thus the saddlery of the first two barrows differs essentially in construction of bridle and form of saddle and by details of fittings from the saddlery of the last three barrows, and in relation to the latter can be regarded as typologically earlier.

To judge by the sewn-on antler plates and pendant plaques, the saddles in the barrow at Karakol dug by Kiselev[1] and at Shibe[2] were just the same as in barrows 3–6 at Pazyryk.

Barrow 5 also differed from the others in the shabracks used with the saddles, absent in other cases.

The saddles of barrows 1 and 2 were also distinguished by their ornament; on the saddle covers there were figures of animals or scenes of fighting animals. In barrows 3 and 4 the covers were not decorated in this fashion, and in barrow 5 there was only one cover bearing the representation of an animal.

The material employed in the bits cannot form the basis of a chronological division, although there is no conflict with the sequence of construction noticed above. We may recall that in barrow 1 of ten bits one was bronze (more precisely copper), the remainder iron; in barrow 2 two out of seven were bronze; in barrow 3 of fourteen five were bronze; in barrows 4 and 5 all were iron.

Distinguishing features of barrow 5 were the absence of wickerwork shields intertwined with leather, and the unique carriage.

The carved wood and other decorations, which are especially numerous in the horse burials in all the barrows, cannot serve as a criterion of chronological sub-division either by motif or by technique of manufacture. The designs vary greatly of course, but in the cheek-pieces of barrows 1, 2, 3 and 5 the wooden forks are identical. In barrows 3 and 5 just the same representations of heads of saiga antelope occur, and in all the barrows there were circular frontal plaques. In distinction from the first two, barrows 3–5 more often had pendants of semi-lunate form and leather 'concertinas' on the cheek-straps at the cheek-pieces.

The same chronological sequence of the Pazyryk barrows emerges from the facts enumerated, as has been established by the methods of dendrochronology.[3]

Before the excavation of barrow 5 at Pazyryk I had dated the group of barrows to the fifth to fourth centuries B.C. by analogy with various articles found in Scythian barrows and with Persian remains of the Achaemenid period. Barrows

---

[1] Kiselev, A, 1935, p. 101, figs. 1–7.

[2] In the barrow at Shibe there were horn facings on the saddle arches and pendants just like those in barrows 3 and 4 at Pazyryk, but the wooden spacers are the same as in barrows 3 and 5.

[3] [Translator's note. Dendrochronology indicated the sequence was: nos. 1 and 2 in the same year, no. 4 a little later and 3 and 5 appreciably later. See p. xxix above. M.W.T.]

5 and 6 yielded additional material, for now we had not only artistic motifs but tangible imports to facilitate dating. These objects comprised woollen cloth decorated in Gobelin technique showing in one case women before a censer and in another lions; a pile carpet bearing figures of riders, deer and griffins; a Chinese mirror and Chinese silk with embroidered decoration.

The censer (or altar) before which the crowned women stand in attitudes of prayer has a typical high lamp-shield shape (fig. 139). Similar Assyrian censers or torches are known from representations on bas-reliefs at Kuyunjik and Khorsabad.[1] I am thinking of the scene of sacrifice in the camp of Sennacherib, where a flame burns on an altar with the sacred torch or censer beside it, and before them are two attendants facing the deity with arms raised. The same scene figures on a bas-relief at Khorsabad where two attendants stand with raised arms before the altar and censer. It seems that a sacrifice is being performed, since in their other hands the servants hold the traditional baskets containing the articles necessary to sacrifice.

At a later date we see the same censers on Persian cylinders and bas-reliefs at Persepolis,[2] where they are just the same as on our cloth, with a chain joining the hood to the foot of the censer. The latest representation of such a censer with a woman in a crown standing before it, which belongs to the first half of the fifth century B.C., occurs on a well-known cylinder in the Clerk Collection.[3] On this a goddess is shown seated on a throne, evidently the Persian Anahita, with a flower in her hand. Before her stands a female attendant who is offering her a bird. Next comes a censer ($\theta v\mu\iota\alpha\tau\dot\eta\rho\iota o\nu$) that is similar to ours holding the sacred fire before which a woman in a toothed crown and tunic performs a sacrifice. She holds a little basket containing the sacrificial equipment in her hands. On one of the Oxus treasure gold plates a woman is portrayed in a praying attitude similar to that on our cloth. She is represented in a toothed crown wearing a long cloak decorated with rows of disks, while her long hair hangs in a knot on her neck. Her right hand is in front of her face and her left hand holds a flower.[4] A similar woman with the same hair style but without a crown, wearing a long dress, in the same attitude of prayer, is depicted on one of the gold plates in the Oxus treasure.[5] Thus on the cloth being discussed in barrow 5 we would have a traditional scene of supplication, or more likely sacrifice to a deity, in which two crowned women stand before the sacred fire in an attitude of prayer with the right hand lifted. Their relatively small size emphasizes their humble social status. The towels held by each female attendant are noteworthy, being just like those carried by the female attendants in the Assyrian bas-relief at

[1] Layard, B, 1867a, pp. 30, 31; 1867b, pt 2, p. 354; Ménant, B, pt ii, pp. 69, 70, figs. 65 and 66.

[2] Layard, B, 1867a, p. 349; Herzfeld, B, Pl. 67.

[3] Ménant, B, pt. ii, Pl. 9, fig, 2; Dalton, B, p. 45, fig. 29.

[4] Dalton, B, Pl. xii, No. 38.

[5] Ibid., B, Pl. xiv, No. 89.

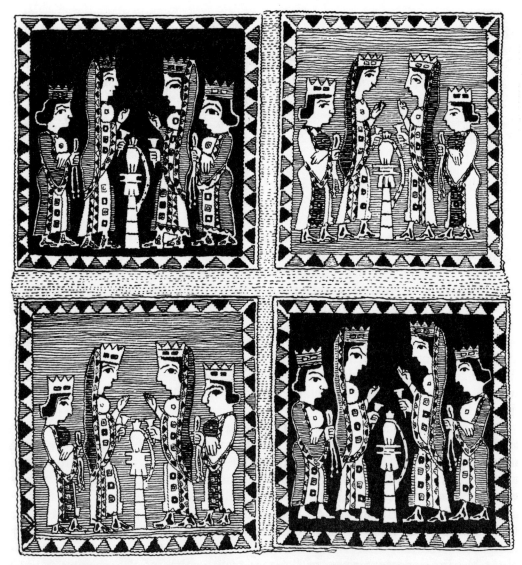

139. Cloth decorated with a design of women standing in front of a censer in an attitude of prayer, from barrow 5 (c. $\frac{2}{3}$).

Kuyunjik showing a feast of Ashurbanipal.[1] The women's costume in this scene is obviously Assyrian, but it has a series of traits in common with the costume on the plates of the Oxus treasure just mentioned. That this cloth originated from Hither Asia is not open to doubt, and there are no grounds for supposing it to be later than the fifth century B.C.

[1] Perrot and Chipiez, B, vol. iv, pp. 106, 107, figs. 27 and 28.

297

140. Cloth decorated with a design of a procession of lions, from barrow 5 ($\frac{1}{1}$).

Let us now examine the representations of lions (fig. 140) on the chest-piece of the same shabrack. On a strip of cloth worked in the Gobelin technique the lions are shown moving in even step with head and tail raised (the latter finishing in a brush). The material, technique of execution and detail of ornament (toothed line) testify to its being of the same period as that already studied and probably made by the same craftsman.

Similar lions are encountered in Assyrian bas-reliefs [1] and sculptures [2] and are especially numerous in Achaemenid Persia. It is sufficient to recall the lions following each other shown on the dress of Xerxes at Persepolis [3] or in the same way in relief on the tomb of Artaxerxes II [4] and finally in the famous coloured tiles at Susa.[5]

It is especially instructive to compare the lions of the Pazyryk cloth with those at Persepolis and Susa which are stylistically linked by the conventions used to indicate the fur in the mane, in the chest, on the thighs and the top of the tail. In Assyria the fur was rendered by separate dots, a fairly expressive convention,[6] and in Persia a similar convention was sometimes used (Susa), predominantly on relief zones or by special colouring of the relevant parts of the body and varying in position in the individual figures. In post-Achaemenian time such treatment of lions' figures is quite unknown. Consequently the chest-piece bearing representations of lions as well as that of the praying woman cannot be later than the fifth century B.C.

Let us now turn to the pile carpet. The discovery of a pile, smooth, sheared carpet obliges us to turn to the history of such textiles. For many centuries before our era fine carpets had been manufactured, according to ancient

[1] Perrot and Chipiez, B, vol. ii, p. 225, fig. 86.
[2] Ibid., p. 760, fig. 419.
[3] Herzfeld, B, Pl. 72.
[4] Ibid., Pl. 74.

[5] Dieulafoy, B, 1892, pt iii, Pl. III.
[6] Perrot and Chipiez, B, vol. ii, Pl. xv (lions in the coloured tiles at Khorsabad); Layard, B, 1867b, p. 311.

authorities, in Babylon, Assyria, Media and Persia. Since not a single example of this industry has survived we can only derive a picture of its products from other remains. In the painted alabaster reliefs at one time covering all parts of the palaces of Nineveh, Assyriologists regard a wide range of the decoration, including representations of fantastic monsters, as nothing more or less than imitations of the Gobelin work or embroidery used in Babylonian art. The style of these reliefs, the usual style of wall-hangings (rosettes, borders, etc.) makes the similarity even more impressive. Such reliefs, dating from not later than the eighth century B.C., constitute the oldest evidence of carpet manufacture.

There is no certain proof that the carpets just referred to were sheared smooth; more probably they had been made in the Gobelin technique, which could have reached a high degree of perfection by this time. The mats used to cover a horse in lieu of a saddle would in all probability have been pile made. At all events in Achaemenian Persia they produced sheared pile carpets; Xenophon reported that the city of Sard prided itself on its sheared carpets on which at the Persian court only the king had the right to tread.[1] The same author remarked that the Persians, becoming acquainted with fine array and luxury through the Medes, began to use carpets.[2] Later, in the time of Alexander the Great and his successors, in the palace they spread before the bed long-pile carpets of fine wool, dyed purple, which alternated with sheared carpets of Persian origin decorated with animals or other figures. The esteem in which these

141. A four-rayed star used to decorate the pile carpet from barrow 5 (c. $\frac{1}{3}$).

[1] See details in Müntz, B, p. 41.

[2] Xenophon, A, *Cyropaedia*, bk v, 5, 7; bk VIII, 8, 15, 16.

142. A griffin used to decorate the pile carpet from barrow 5 ($\frac{1}{4}$).

carpets (praised by Classical authors) were held can be reckoned by the purchase of a *triclinia babylonica* by Metellus Scipio for 800,000 sestercii (62,000 roubles) and by Nero at even greater cost, 4,000,000 sestercii (315,000 roubles).[1]

Like all sheared carpets the Pazyryk example is rectangular and slightly elongated, measuring 1·89 m. by 2 m. It has a complicated border framing a central field in which the same figures are repeated again and again (*Pl. 174*). They consist of a combination of four-rayed stars, with a cross-shaped ornament of four flowers with a square in the centre, all enclosed in a square frame (fig. 141). There are six such patterns in a row longitudinally and four transversely. The central field is enclosed by a row of repeated figures of a griffin with raised wing and turned back head (fig. 142). Beyond these is a series of browsing, spotted deer going in a clockwise direction (fig. 143).

The border following consists of rows of stars with a cross-shaped design of flowers, similar to that on the central field, but slightly altered and without the frame (fig. 144). A wide border figures hurrying riders following one another (fig. 145) in the opposite direction to the deer. The outside edge consists of the same griffins as enclose the central field, but rather larger and facing in the opposite direction. All five border friezes are enclosed in the same frames as that around the central field, rectangular strips between two lines.

This carpet, as the illustration (*Pl. 174*) shows, is polychrome with a preponderance of soft tones: dark red, light blue, greenish, bright yellow, orange and other shades.

In the weaving of the cords of this carpet the warp was given a steeper angle

[1] Müntz, B, p. 22.

143. A deer decorating the pile carpet from barrow 5 ($\frac{3}{5}$).

144. Stars decorating the pile carpet from barrow 5 ($\frac{4}{5}$).

145. A rider decorating the pile carpet from barrow 5 ($c.\ \frac{1}{2}$).

and the weft made more sloping. In making the knots the wool being knotted was only lightly twisted. In the final treatment of the warp under the carpet a taffeta weave was not used, as is normally the case in the most recent carpets, but the outer two threads of the warp were bound with woollen thread to form the knot lump. The number of threads per decimetre in the warp was about 120. The fixing weft passed three, or in places, four knots, after a row of knotting weft. The method of tying the knots on two warp threads is shown in fig. 146B. The number of knots in one square decimetre was 3,600, which gives a total of about 1,250,000 for the whole carpet. Reckoning that an experienced crafts-woman in central Asia or Asia Minor making a carpet as fine as ours would tie 2,000 or 3,000 knots a day, working alone she would have taken eighteen months to complete the carpet.[1]

In taking the carpet off the stand the threads of the warp were so cut that they left a fringe 1–1·5 cm. wide. When the pile had been sheared the carpet was barely 2 mm. thick.

A piece of another woollen pile carpet, only small tatters of which survived, had been used as a saddle-cover at Bash-Adar, barrow 2 (sixth century B.C.). Nevertheless it was possible to establish that this carpet was of exceptionally fine workmanship. In one square decimetre there were an average of 7,000 knots, almost double that in the pile carpet from Pazyryk, barrow 5. Another technique had been employed. Two rows of fixing weft were set in plain linen weave, so that ten to twelve threads of warp required fourteen of weft, and there were twenty-eight threads of weft in each centimetre square. The ends of the pile weft were not pulled tight as at Pazyryk (fig. 146B) but twisted into each other. In other words we are here dealing with a case of the so-called $1\frac{1}{2}$ knots (fig. 146A). The yarn of both warp and weft was double, strongly twisted in the former and weakly in the latter.

The Bash-Adar pile carpet was multicoloured and undoubtedly of central or Hither Asian origin.

In order to be able to assess the place of origin of the Pazyryk carpet let us consider its patterns. First to deserve our attention is the deer (*Pl. 175A*). At first impression it would seem to be an elk with typically palmating antlers, but its marked spottiness, the shape of the muzzle and the structure of the body indicate a fallow deer rather than elk. If we examine Hither Asian representa-tions of fallow deer (*Cervus dama*) then we notice that they are usually depicted as on the Pazyryk carpet with the same palmation of the antlers, although not carried so far.[2] Thus the whole appearance, including the relatively long tail, testify that Hither Asian male fallow deer with secondary sexual characteristics were intended. Another detail deserves mention: the comma and disk on the front leg (fig. 143) and the disk on the rear leg. In addition a wide strip pointed

[1] Shavrov, A.   [2] Herzfeld, B, figs. 419 and 420.

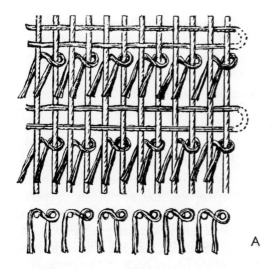
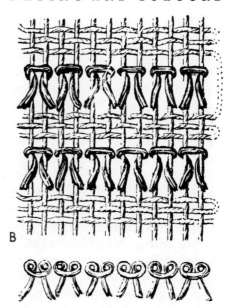

146. Carpet knots: Bash-Adar (A);
Pazyryk (B).

on top appears on the stomach beginning at the front disk. This detail as we have seen is peculiarly characteristic of Hither Asian representations of animals in Achaemenian times.

The eagle-griffins are just as indicative. It is difficult to decide whether they have a lion's or tiger's body. The turned-back, large-eared griffin's head, with tongue stuck out of a half-opened mouth, the raised wing and curled-up tail, are all just as characteristic. In this case there is a typical half-horseshoe on the griffin's crupper.

Entirely corresponding with the deer and griffins are the figures of cantering riders on stallions bearing not saddles but covers with chest-piece (*Pl. 175*B). The horses have their tails knotted and their manes trimmed.

The artistic treatment of all the covers is the same. The ornament of the central field has three variants (*Pl. 176*). The first is a conventionalized representation of a tree, and occurs in twos on the right and left side of the coverlet or singly in the transverse row. From this it may be concluded that the coverlets were all one piece. The second variant consists of a row of little squares and, finally, there are patterns of S-shapes with rosettes. Then there are coverlets with a plain undecorated field.

The central fields of the coverlets were framed by bands of squares, then of small squares and finally of clustered festoons. Even in the same type of saddle-cover there was a wide variation of colouring of the main field as well as of the details of ornament and clusters.

303

From this point of view of dating this carpet the most indicative features are the riders (*Pl. 175*B). The horse has a sharply bent neck, trimmed mane, forelock shaped into a plume and tail knotted into a bow. Instead of a saddle there is a carpet-like fringed shabrack with a broad chest-band. Such representations of war riding-horses, especially wearing carpet shabracks with chest-bands, are typical of Assyria.[1] Nevertheless a series of features, especially the method of tying the tail into a knot, are not Assyrian but later Persian. We can see such a knot and plumed forelock on bas-reliefs at Persepolis,[2] on the handle of the sword of Persian workmanship from the Chertomlyk barrow,[3] on numerous gems and coins of the Achaemenian period,[4] and, finally, in the hunting scene on the silver disk in the Oxus treasure, where we see, just as on our carpet, a representation of a carpet-like shabrack and broad chest-bands.[5] Comparison of these figures, where a pedestrian walks beside a horse, with the corresponding figures on the Persepolis reliefs is instructive.[6] In both cases the man walks on the left side of the horse with his right hand resting on its back at the neck. The rider wears a short jacket, breeches and a tight lower dress and an unusual head-dress resembling that worn by the riders on the Oxus disk.

Regardless of the workmanship, Median, Parthian or Persian, the date of the carpet, like that of the cloth discussed above, is in all probability fifth century B.C.

Let us now turn to the objects imported into the High Altai from the Far East, that is from China. Although the connections between the High Altai and Hither Asia extend right back to the eighth century B.C., the connections with China were formed only later, it would seem.

In the first two Pazyryk barrows there were no objects of indisputable Chinese origin, but against this in barrows 3 and 5 there were silks which can be justly considered as Chinese, and in barrow 6, contemporary with nos. 3 and 4, a Chinese mirror of the Tsin type was found (*Pl. 70*C; fig. 55).

The Tsin type is rare in the collections of Chinese mirrors studied thoroughly by Umehara[7] and subsequently by Swallow.[8] It is a pity also that, of the few known, even the provenance of the majority is uncertain and any precise dating is impossible. This is due to the fact that they have not been found in graves or amongst well-dated objects and, except for the latest examples, they do not bear inscriptions.

[1] Layard, B, 1867a, p. 167; Perrot and Chipiez, B, vol. ii, p. 47, fig. 5.

[2] Herzfeld, B, Pls. 77 and 79.

[3] Tolstoy and Kondakov, A, vol. ii, p. 145, fig. 122.

[4] Babelon, B, 1893, Pl. xxxvii, figs. 14–16; Dalton, B, p. 46, fig. 30; Furtwängler, B, Pl. xi, figs. 1–3, 8, 9, 13.

[5] Dalton, B, Pl. ix, No. 24.

[6] Herzfeld, B, Pl. 79.

[7] Umehara, B.

[8] Swallow, B.

The only criterion for arranging the mirrors in a chronological sequence, employed by Umehara, is based purely on the typology of the decoration. It has been observed that in the primary form of these mirrors the whole background of the decoration covering the back of the mirrors consists of stylized animals reduced to wings and feathers. It is noteworthy that this pattern had not been adapted especially for round mirrors, where it had to pass round a central lug. This method of decorating the whole mirror back with the same pattern continued endlessly over the full circular field and beyond shows that it had not been invented for mirrors but had been borrowed from other bronze objects, especially from vessels of the period of the warring princedoms (provinces).

In order to avoid monotony of squares (as on our mirror) around the central lug additional ornament in the shape of four heart-shaped leaves and leaning letter T's was applied. The latest mirrors of this type are distinguished from ours by finer ornament, consisting of spirals and zigzags, animals, dragons and, finally, inscriptions.

Menzies [1] refers bronze articles and mirrors of the type of Tsin to the period from 897 to 206 B.C., and Umehara limits the range of the group of mirrors that interests us to four to five centuries from the sixth to the second century B.C. The earliest (belonging to the sixth to the fifth centuries B.C.) he considers to be those bearing the T'ao-T'ieh mask and a background pattern limited to wings-and-feathers ornament, and by the same token those with T-shaped decoration could be dated, it would seem, to the fifth or at the very latest the beginning of the fourth century B.C.

We know nothing of ancient Chinese textiles from pre-Han times, for no comparative material exists. We may merely remark that the silks from the Pazyryk barrows differ essentially from the earliest surviving Chinese textiles.

The intricate pattern of rhombs which can be seen on the fragment of silk from barrow 3 (*Pl. 134*A) may be compared with the silks from the Noin-Ula barrows, but the simplicity of the motif precludes its use as a criterion for dating.

The Chinese silk used for covering one of the shabracks from barrow 5 (*Pl. 178*), like the cloth from the Middle East discussed above, probably had not been specially prepared for export to the barbarians. It is work of very high quality of fine design with an exquisite play of delicate colours in the embroidery. The basic motif is cock pheasants sitting on twigs, and hen pheasants in the spaces against the plain background, but the actual work is very varied (figs. 90, 91). At least five variants of cock and three of hen birds can be distinguished (fig. 92). The embroidery has been executed in chain stitch, just as on the Noin-Ula cloth.[2]

Such cloth, as V. M. Alekseev, who is thoroughly acquainted with our example, suggested, was made in China for very rich people, particularly for a

---

[1] Swallow, B, p. 39.   [2] Rudenko, A, 1962a.

princess at the time of her marriage. The subject of the embroidery, according to the commentary of Uzhu-Tszy, is connected with the age-old tale of the phoenixes, surprised amongst the magnificent wu t'ung (*Dryandra cardifolia*) trees, which symbolized the profusion of talents in the courts of an enlightened lord. In the personal opinion of Alekseev this subject is connected with the world of phoenixes who sing, like fire-birds, to the glory of their mistress and princess (for fêng is the bridegroom, and the huang his wife, the bride).

In Shih Ching, ode VIII, are the following lines (the translation being that of Prof. W. Watson [1]):

> *Phoenixes sing,*
> *on the high ridge;*
> *the wu t'ung trees grow dense, luxuriant,*
> *on the slope which faces the morning sun.*
> *The song harmonious, gentle.*

It is possible, as Alekseev suggested, that 'this motif and text known always to everyone' was referred to in the embroidery on the shabrack.

The lively reproduction of the phoenixes—and indeed the details—can surely be compared only with the phoenixes that occur on the early Tsin mirrors; consequently a date in about the fifth century B.C. is highly likely for the silk.

In spite of the appearance, in late barrows it is true, of imported Chinese articles, silks and mirrors, they should not be regarded as evidence of Far Eastern influences on the population of the High Altai at this time. Quite the contrary; the real connections, ancient and deep, were between this area and the south, central and Hither Asia.

As we have seen in the Altaian art, the motif of the griffin held a remarkable, although secondary, place. The oriental origin of this motif cannot be open to doubt. In the chapter on art it has been shown that a series of local, Altaian representations of griffins in barrows 1 and 2 can only be compared with neo-Assyrian griffins, since in Achaemenian times they were represented in a different way in Hither Asia. The struggling griffins on the copper gold-covered plates from barrow 2 especially are archaically conceived. They point back to even earlier examples of Sumerian art, and indicate undoubtedly pre-Achaemenian links between the Altaian tribes of Scythian times and Hither Asia. The same has already been observed in relation to the lions depicted in

[1] [Translator's note. The transliteration and translation have been freshly made from the original Chinese by William Watson, Professor of Chinese Art and Archaeology in London University, who has corrected several errors in the version in Rudenko. M.W.T.]

Shih Ching, Ta ya, Chüan a, v. 9.
Fêng huang ming i
yü pi kao kang
wu t'ung sheng i
yu pi chao yang
pêng pêng ch'i ch'i
yung yung chieh chieh

barrow 1, which find their prototype in neo-Assyrian art. On the other hand, with these there are remarkable examples of native work which display some inherently Achaemenian qualities. I am thinking of the eagle-griffins from barrows 1 and 2 and the lion-griffin from barrow 1 as portrayed on the saddle-covers. These things were not mere copies of foreign objects, but their appearance in Altaian art in Achaemenian times could only be as a result of earlier cultural links between the peoples of the two areas. (The same can be said of the lotus motif, represented by beautiful examples in the finds from barrow 2.)

In barrow 5 there were no lion- or eagle-griffins, or lotus ornament either. Nevertheless in the felt covers of native articles we again come across motifs known only in the ancient east. We are referring to the goddess sitting on a throne with a spray of flowers in her hand and a horseman in front of her (*Pl. 154*), and also to the winged lion with human body (*Pl. 173*). A winged lion with a human body was a very ancient motif in Hither Asia; we see it on the ancient cylinder seals, in Hittite sculpture, in Neo-Assyrian times,[1] but in Persia, even in the earliest Achaemenian remains, it does not occur. Comparison of the winged lion with human body and Assyroid face from Pazyryk with similar monumental neo-Assyrian figures makes it clear that only the latter could have served as models for the Altaian sphinx. In the Altai the motif underwent independent alteration through the native style, which caused not only the horns but even the tail to take the shape of deer antlers. Nevertheless the erect ears, the head-dress and the rosettes on the body closely follow neo-Assyrian examples.

The second subject, the goddess on a throne with a spray in her hand before whom stands a rider, has been studied closely in the chapter on art. Here I would only emphasize the community of this motif with the cultural world of Hither Asia.

Thus all that is known to us at the present time about the culture of the population of the High Altai, who have left behind them the large cairns, permits us to refer them to the Scythian period, and the Pazyryk group in particular to the fifth century B.C. This is supported by radiocarbon dating.

Archaeological remains of earlier date than those excavated by us occurred in the barrows dug in 1911 by A. V. Adrianov in the Maiemir steppe at the source of the Naryn, and also in the upper reaches of the River Bukhtarma, towards Solonechny Belok at the village of Chernovy. Subsequently a series of such barrows have been excavated by M. P. Gryaznov,[2] S. V. Kiselev and others. Gryaznov referred this group of barrows to a special cultural stage preceding that now being studied by us which he called the Maiemir stage, while Kiselev

[1] Layard, B, 1849, ser. 1, Pl. 48; Perrot and Chipiez, B, vol. ii, p. 774, fig. 446; Ménant, B, pt ii, p. 37, fig. 21.

[2] Gryaznov, A, 1947.

spoke of the 'Maiemir culture' and divided it into an early and late stage.[1] This is unfortunate because at present we have too little material to allow us to speak about a Maiemir culture or to regard it as a special stage in the development of the culture of the population of the Altai. We are still dealing, in fact, only with a certain chronological arrangement of remains that has specific typological peculiarities (special bronze mirrors, arrow-heads, bits, cheek-pieces, figures of carnivores twisted into a ring, analogous to those found in early Scythian burials of the seventh to sixth centuries B.C.)

Nevertheless remains of this type furnish interesting proof that already the folk of the Altai had links with the steppe folk of eastern Europe, including the Scyths. In addition they pose the problem as to the origin of those common cultural traits which our material has so clearly delineated.

The parallels in grave-goods and form of burial between the barrows of the Kuban valley, especially between the Seven Brothers, and those of the High Altai have been emphasized above. It is quite understandable that the population of the Kuban valley, like that of the High Altai, were more closely linked with the tribes of central and Hither Asia than, for example, the Scyths of the Dnieper area. There is a remarkable similarity between the material culture of the High Altai tribes and the people of the steppes of eastern Europe, and in ideology as evidenced by the existence of the same customs. Let us recall the practice of scalping slain enemies, embalmment of chiefs' corpses and burial with their concubines, identical custom of purification after burial, as described by Herodotus and as documented by the High Altai excavations. The latter proves that the numerous tribes of varied origin and speech, at this time inhabiting the huge expanses of the east European and Asian steppes and mountain fringes, who were living in basically the same way, that is by nomadic pastoralism, were drawn together by mutual links, common social structure and ideology, and differed only in slight local peculiarities. This deduction follows from study of the archaeological remains, but is confirmed by the reports of Chinese and Greek historians.

The same sources reveal not only inter-tribal relationships among the people we are studying, but connections with the peoples of the ancient states.

While in Asia ancient links with the Near East and China were maintained, the Black Sea tribes entered into contact with Greek culture. The High Altai region in the relevant times was linked directly, or indirectly through neighbouring tribes, with both China and central Asia, as the Pazyryk discoveries testify.

Hence one must not speak of an actual uniformity of origin of a group of tribes with a common language and entirely uniform material culture. There are no grounds for such an inference, no more than that the physical type was uniform. In time, when more positive archaeological data is available, it may be

[1] Kiselev, A, 1949, pp. 169, 170.

possible to go further, as has been partially done in the Black Sea area, and separate out in the Altai more or less distinct ethnic groups from the general mass.

The independent and quite distinct ancient culture of the folk of the High Altai did not vanish without trace; one way or another it entered into the basis of the future cultural development of the pastoral tribes and peoples of southern Siberia, and possibly central Asia, and notably of the modern Altaians, Kirgiz and Kazakhs. This circumstance confers upon the remains we have studied a special significance as a valuable source for the study of the past of a series of peoples of the U.S.S.R. The future investigation of these monuments constitutes an honourable and urgent task for Soviet archaeologists.

APPENDIX · INVENTORY OF ARTICLES FOUND IN THE PAZYRYK BARROWS [1]

BARROW 1

Structure

Site of barrow shown on plan in fig. 2, excavated in 1929 (*Pls. 1, 2*). Prior to the excavation the grave appeared as a cairn 47 m. in diameter and 2·2 m. high, at the centre of which was a crater caused by looting. A row of vertical stones ran eastward from the barrow. The burial shaft, 7·2 m. by 7·2 m. and 4 m. deep below original ground surface, lay at the centre of the barrow. After removal in a broad trench of the cairn and soil mound, at 0·7–1·4 m. below the buried ground surface the log filling of the shaft and the robbers' hole cut through it were observed (*Pl. 3*). On reaching the tomb's roof the looting had cut an oval aperture, 0·4 m. by 0·6 m., through it (*Pl. 4*).

The southern two-thirds of the shaft were occupied by the burial chamber, horses being buried in the northern part (section, fig. 4A). The chamber stood on a platform of crushed stone covering the bottom of the shaft. The tomb floor was made of thick planks, its outer box of unhewn, and inner box of hewn, logs. The void between the boxes was filled with crushed stone. The inner and outer ceilings were of undressed logs. The internal dimensions of the irregular quadrilateral tomb were on average 3·35 m. by 4·87 m. and 1·47 m. high. The chamber had been covered by several layers of birch bark above which was a layer of larch bark and above this a bed of foliage of the shrub 'smoky tea'. Over the chamber, supported on three pairs of vertical posts, were three beams (supporting numerous logs above), which had sagged under the weight of the superincumbent load of logs, soil and stones (*Pl. 4*).

On the southern side of the tomb stood the tree-trunk coffin with its lid removed by the looters (*Pl. 5*). In the northern inner wall a large window had been chopped through, in the outer wall only one log had been cut through. A cone of detritus had formed in the middle of the chamber below the robbers' trap (*Pl. 6*) and the void around it filled with laminated ice.

---

[1] Inserted into the cairns of all the Pazyryk barrows, except no. 7, there were secondary burials of the sixth to the eighteenth centuries A.D., but this inventory covers only the finds from the primary burials of Scythian times.

311

The horses had been buried, as mentioned, in the northern half of the shaft.

Finds

1. In the burial shaft above the chamber between the logs:
   Piece of a wooden shovel.
   Four broken wedges.
   Piece of a mallet for hammering wedges.
   Parts of trolleys (two yokes, two platforms, wedges, two sticks with sharpened ends, chopped-off rods, poles and so on).

2. In the burial chamber there were as follows:
   The tree-trunk coffin (*Pl. 37*c) with leather cut-out cocks decorating it (fig. 10).
   Three thick leather, cut-out, sculptural heads of mountain goats (*Pl. 137*c, d), part of a felt wall-hanging decorated with lions' heads (*Pl. 148*a) and feathers from it.
   Wooden and copper nails (with or without heads) which had secured the wall-hanging to the wall.
   Six (felt and straw) ring-supports for vessels.
   Piece of leather with hair sewn into it.
   Ram's sacral vertebrae.
   Carved wooden leg from little table (*Pl. 51*a).
   Solid wooden stool or pillow (*Pl. 53*a).
   Wooden handle of an axe (*Pl. 125*a, b).
   Rod from hexapod stand.
   Neck of clay bottle.
   Thongs, pieces of leather and woollen cord, gold-leaf.

3. In the horse burial there were as follows:

   Ten horse bodies disposed as shown in fig. 16a.

   First riding outfit consisting of bridle in *Pl. 79*a, the wooden pendants of which (as also cheek-pieces, *Pl. 77*) are decorated with palmettes. The saddle (*Pl. 79*b) is decorated with pendants in the form of human masks cut from leather (*Pl. 138*f). Scenes of an elk in the claws of a griffin (fig. 113) decorate the saddle-cover. A shield was attached to the right-hand side of the saddle (*Pl. 144*).

   Second riding outfit consisting of bridle (*Pl. 80*a) and saddle (*Pl. 135*). Bridle and chest-strap are decorated with double carved wooden palmettes (*Pl. 80*b, c) and opened-out elks. In the middle of the saddle-cover an eagle-griffin is depicted attacking a mountain goat (*Pl. 170*). The subject used on the saddle-pendants is the head of a ram between two horned lions' heads (*Pl. 171*). On the right side of the saddle was secured a shield made of sticks threaded through a piece of leather.

Third riding outfit consisting of bridle, saddle, head-dress, mane- and tail-covers. The bridle (*Pl. 81*A) has wooden cheek-pieces and straps decorated with leather sculptural goats' heads (*Pl. 81*D). The saddle-cover is decorated with a tiger falling upon an elk (fig. 108): the saddle-pendants are schematic representations of fish (*Pl. 167*D); leather goats' heads decorated the breast-strap (*Pl. 81*D) as well as leather griffins with extended wings and distended tails (fig. 119; *Pl. 81*B, C). The mane-cover is decorated with figures of cocks (*Pl. 123*A) and the head-dress with a crest in the form of a lion-griffin (*Pls. 120, 122*A). The leather tail-sheath is shown in *Pl. 124*A, and its ornament in fig. 98A.

Fourth riding outfit consisting of saddle and bridle. The latter (*Pl. 82*A) has wooden cheek-pieces in the form of a mountain ram (*Pl. 82*B), and is decorated by carved wooden heads of this animal (*Pl. 83*B, D) and palmettes. The saddle-cover decoration shows a tiger falling upon a deer (fig. 110). The breast-strap bears the same decoration as the bridle. A shield was attached to the right-hand side of the saddle (*Pl. 144*B).

Fifth riding outfit consisting of bridle, saddle, head-dress, mane- and tail-covers. The wooden cheek-pieces (*Pl. 84*A,B), have ram's head terminals (*Pl. 84*C) and the bridle-straps are decorated with facing mountain rams (*Pl. 83*E, F). The saddle (*Pl. 48*) bears figures of lions on the cover (fig. 114) and its pendants take the form of lions (*Pl. 172*). Amongst the decorations of the breast-strap, in addition to the rams' heads, there is a carved wooden figure of a ram's head in the jaws of a wolf.[1] The crest on the head-dress takes the form of deer's head with antlers (*Pl. 119*). The mane-cover is decorated with cocks (*Pl. 123*B). The decoration on the tail-sheath is shown in fig. 98B.

Sixth riding outfit consisting of bridle and saddle. The bridle (*Pl. 85*) with wooden cheek-pieces decorated with griffin's heads (*Pl. 86*C, D) has pendants in the form of a facing griffin (*Pl. 86*A, B) and also heads of a mountain ram in wolf's jaws (*Pl. 83*C). The saddle-cover is decorated with profile lions' heads (fig. 116), the pendants with a conventionalized fish seizing the throat of a mountain ram (*Pl. 47*). The breast-strap is decorated with carved wooden pendants in the form of palmettes and a facing griffin in the centre.

Seventh riding outfit consisting of bridle and saddle. The bridle (*Pl. 87*C) has

---

[1] [Translator's note. The plate reference given by the author (Pl. xxxv, 3 in Russian edition) is omitted since this is described as from the sixth set and the reference is repeated below. Perhaps this sentence is a slip and should be ignored. M.W.T.]

wooden cheek-pieces with carved griffin-head terminals (*Pl. 87*B) and wooden pendants at the strap junctions in the form of palmettes (*Pl. 83*A). A tiger attacking a mountain ram is depicted on the saddle-cover (fig. 112). The breast-strap bears just the same decoration as the bridle (*Pl. 87*A).

Eighth riding outfit consisting of bridle and saddle. The bridle (*Pl. 88*A) has wooden cheek-pieces carved to represent deer (*Pl. 88*B) and its straps are decorated with carved wooden elk or deer (*Pl. 89*B, C). Fighting eagle- and lion-griffins decorate the saddle-cover (fig. 115). The breast-strap bears the same decoration as the bridle (*Pl. 89*A).

Ninth riding outfit consisting of bridle and saddle. The cheek-piece terminals are carved as a leopard's head with a boar's tusk in its jaws (*Pl. 90*A), and the bridle-strap intersections bear a similar decoration (*Pl. 90*B, C). The saddle-cover is decorated with a lion-griffin attacking a mountain goat (*Pl. 169*A). The breast-strap bears the same decoration as the bridle.

Tenth riding outfit consisting of bridle and saddle. The bridle (*Pl. 91*) is decorated on the strap intersections and on the noseband with carved wooden human masks (*Pl. 92*A–D). The saddle-cover is adorned with heads of mountain rams (fig. 117) and the saddle-pendants are rams' heads (*Pl. 167*C). The breast-strap decorations are the same as on the bridle.

Of ten bits only one was bronze (*Pl. 85*), the rest iron.

Leather flask with fur top (*Pls. 59, 150*A).

Fur pouch (detail in *Pl. 132*D).

Whip (*Pl. 124*B).

Carved leather human head with horns and big ears (*Pl. 138*G).

Numerous pieces of gold-leaf covering carved wooden decorations.

BARROW 2

Structure

Site shown on plan of barrows in fig. 2, excavated in 1947 with broad trench (*Pl. 7*), work completed 1948. Cairn 36 m. in diameter and 3·75 m. high. Robbers' crater in middle of cairn. Row of vertical stones extended eastward from barrow. Rectangular burial shaft 7·1 m. by 7·8 m. reaching 4 m. below buried ground surface. Floor of the shaft covered with layer (10 cm. thick) of crushed stone and over this 5 cm. of soil. After removing the cairn and soil mound a dense filling of logs was found in the shaft at 0·4–0·5 m. below the old ground surface, through which the robbers had chopped a shaft measuring 1·45 m. by 2·3 m. (*Pl. 8*). This tapered as it passed through the logs, and the trap measured only 0·45 m. by 0·7 m. in the inner ceiling of the chamber (section, fig. 4B).

The burial chamber, floored with thick planks, occupied the southern two-thirds of the shaft. It consisted of an inner box of dressed, and an outer box of plain, logs with a double log roof. The void between the boxes was empty. The internal dimensions of the chamber were 3·65 m. by 4·92 m. and 1·53 m. high. The outer surface of the chamber had been covered by six layers of sheets of birch bark, then by larch bark and finally by a bed of 'smoky tea' (*Pl. 9*).

Along the northern and southern walls of the burial chamber were three upright posts (pressed back to the shaft wall on the north side by two logs) with trough-like hollows in their tops, which supported three transverse beams that had sagged under the superincumbent weight (*Pl. 9, 10*).

After the shaft had been filled with logs and soil almost to the top the horses had been buried on a platform of larch and juniper branches.

Against the southern wall of the ice-filled chamber stood the tree-trunk coffin. The burial shaft of barrow 2 is shown in section in fig. 5.

Finds (figs. 13, 14).

1. In the shaft over the burial chamber amongst the logs were found:
   Two broken shovels (*Pl. 36*B).
   Numerous (over 100) wedges (*Pl. 36*C).
   Three whole mallets (*Pl. 37*A) and fragments of several others.
   The wheel of a trolley (*Pl. 128*A).

2. In the burial chamber. The looting had taken place when the lower quarter of the chamber had already filled with ice (of the first phase). So some of the objects stood on the floor (fig. 14), but the great majority lay on the surface of the ice of the first phase, where they had been left by the robbers, in the chamber and tree-trunk coffin. Many articles and the corpses were found in the ice of the second phase formed after the chamber had filled with the water that had penetrated through the robbers' trap, and also in the cone of detritus and stones that fallen through the trap.
   Tree-trunk coffin with lid.
   Carved leather figures of deer decorating coffin (fig. 11).
   Body of woman, trunk, head (*Pl. 44*B, C), feet and calves, hand.
   Woman's pigtails (*Pl. 69*A–C).
   Double, twisted pigtail-cover (*Pl. 133*E, F).
   Iron hairpin (*Pl. 68*F).
   Body of man, trunk, head (*Pl. 44*A), left leg, right hand.
   Tattooing on body (figs. 51–4, 121, 123, 124, 126–34).
   Artificial beard (*Pl. 69*D, E).
   Black felt wall-covering of tomb.
   Wooden pegs (*Pl. 38*C).
   Copper nails with heads (*Pls. 34, 38*D) and without.
   Stone lamp (*Pls. 41, 52*A).

Four little wooden tables (one without top) with carved and turned legs. (*Pls. 50*A, B; *51*F–L).

Solid wooden stool or pillow (*Pl. 53*B).

Fur covering for above (*Pl. 58*; fig. 20).

Wooden vessel with long handle (*Pl. 54*A).

Wooden vessel on felt stand (*Pl. 54*C).

Horn handle from wooden vessel (*Pl. 54*B).

Corner of felt with felt ring-stand for bottle attached (fig. 21).

Felt rings.

Two earthenware bottles (*Pl. 55*B, C), one broken.

Cut-out leather figures of cocks decorating the bottles (fig. 22).

Cut-out leather lotus flower (fig. 120).

Leather saddle-bag (fig. 23) with animal-head terminals on the stick handle (*Pl. 136*C).

Leather pouch with fur flap (*Pl. 153*A; fig. 24) with copper figures of birds sewn to it (fig. 25).

Leather pouch with applied decoration (*Pl. 151*B).

Leather flask covered with applied decoration (*Pl. 152*B).

Leather purse with lid (*Pl. 61*A).

Leather pouch (*Pl. 61*B).

Square leather sheath.

Sable fur pouch (*Pl. 57*).

Flat leather flask decorated with a griffin grasping a black grouse (*Pl. 61*C).

Hemp seeds.

Seeds of cultivated coriander.

Seeds of hart's clover.

Tufts of yak's wool.

Cauldron-shaped copper censer (*Pls. 42*, *62*B) containing stones and hemp seeds.

Copper censer with four feet (*Pls. 35*B, *62*A), containing stones and hemp seeds.

Two hexapod stands (*Pl. 62*C).

Part of felt cover of hexapod stand.

Leather cover for hexapod stand (fig. 28).

Pieces of patterned borders of felt carpets (*Pl. 148*B, C).

Two man's shirts (fig. 29; *Pl. 63*), tatters only of one.

Back of man's caftan (*Pl. 151*A).

Corner of border of man's fur caftan (*Pl. 150*D).

Pieces of blue fur from man's caftan (*Pl. 150*E).

Sleeve of man's sable fur costume (*Pl. 155*A).

Man's felt stockings (fig. 31), one of which has coloured pattern on upper border (*Pl. 153*B).

316

Part of a man's pointed felt cap.

Woman's fur costume (figs. 32, 33) with applied leather cut-out decoration (*Pl. 152*A).

Fur apron (*Pl. 156*) with applied decoration (figs. 34–7) forming part of the above costume.

Woman's leather bootees bearing applied decoration (figs. 38, 39) and soles decorated with glass beads and pyrites crystals (*Pl. 64*A).

Woman's bootees with uppers of leopard's fur (*Pl. 155*D) with pattern on upper edge (*Pl. 64*B) and decorated soles (*Pl. 152*C).

Two woman's felt stockings (figs. 40, 41) with border decorated with felt festoons.

Woman's head-dress (reconstructed in *Pl. 65*C) made of black colt's fur with open-work leather rhombs sewn on it (*Pl. 155*C), with a 'diadem' of leather cocks (*Pl. 65*A, B) and mosaic pendants of coloured fur (*Pl. 150*C).

Four leather belts (*Pl. 67*A, F, G).

Silver plate from belt (*Pl. 67*B).

Silver pendants in the shape of horses (*Pl. 67*D, E).

Strap bearing figures of cocks (fig. 42).

Gold earrings (*Pl. 68*B).

Stamped copper figures of a lion-griffin, covered with gold-leaf (fig. 43A).

Fragment of a stamped copper plate decorated with a deer (fig. 43B).

Stamped copper pendant bearing rams' heads (fig. 44).

Stamped copper plates, covered with gold-leaf, bearing figures of mountain goats (fig. 45).

Stamped copper plates, covered with gold-leaf, showing 'clasping' eagle-griffins (fig. 46).

Torque with carved horn and wooden lion-griffins (fig. 50; *Pl. 68*D, E).

Horn comb (fig. 48A).

Silver mirror (*Pl. 70*A, B).

Bronze mirror (*Pl. 70*E) in leather and leopard's fur case (*Pl. 70*D).

Polychrome glass bead, glass beads, cylindrical marble beads (*Pl. 158*).

Iron knife with wooden sheath (fig. 101).

Broken wooden knife sheaths.

Mallet of maral antler (*Pl. 125*G).

Piece of hollowed-out goat's horn.

Pieces of kendyr cloth.

Pieces of coloured woollen cloth of linen weave (*Pl. 133*D).

Pieces of coloured woollen cloth of serge weave (*Pl. 133*C).

Strips of stiff woollen cloth of serge weave (*Pl. 133*B).

Strips of a woollen pile textile with whole loops (*Pl. 134*C).

As above but with loops cut away.

Strips and tatters of coloured woollen textile of 'Palas' type (*Pl. 157*A, B; fig. 104).

Cut-out leather feline head (fig. 125).

Carved wooden griffins' heads (*Pl. 136*H, I).

Carved wooden elk's head (*Pl. 136*G, J).

Carved wooden deer (*Pl. 137*G, H).

Carved wooden griffins (*Pl. 137*A, B).

Cut-out leather blackcock (*Pl. 137*F).

Cut-out leather elk (*Pl. 137*E).

Pieces of a cut-out leather composition, a mountain goat in the claws of a griffin (*Pl. 139*L).

Carved wooden figure of a deer's head in the beak of a griffin (*Pl. 142*D).

Carved wooden 'crest' representing a deer's head in a griffin's beak (*Pl. 141*A–D).

Two antler arrow-heads (*Pl. 143*B).

One-sided horn drum (fig. 138).

Musical instrument of harp type (*Pl. 146*).

Piece of leather with human hair stitched into it (*Pl. 145*A).

Piece of felt with human hair stitched into it (*Pl. 145*B).

Piece of leather with a little leather purse stitched into it containing human finger-nails (*Pl. 145*C–E).

Shreds of leather, felt and fur.

Gold-leaf.

3. In the horse burials there were found:

Seven horse skeletons (with slight traces of flesh and tails) arranged as shown in fig. 16B.

The bridles and saddles had survived badly and almost all the straps had disappeared.

Decorations of a bridle with iron bit and antler cheek-pieces (*Pl. 74*D), a horn frontal plate showing a pair of geese in the jaws of a carnivore (*Pl. 159*A) and horn plates with lotus ornament (*Pl. 159*B, C).

Decorations of a bridle with wooden cheek-pieces with terminals as feline heads (*Pl. 93*C), pendants in the form of sculptured figures of cats on pedestals (*Pl. 93*A, B) and a circular frontal plate (*Pl. 90*G).

Wooden cheek-pieces with goose-head terminals (*Pl. 94*B).

Wooden cheek-pieces with mountain ram's-head terminals (*Pl. 94*A).

Wooden bridle decorations: fragments of cheek-pieces with rams'-head terminals (*Pl. 93*E), frontal plate with cord ornament (*Pl. 90*H), pendants in the form of rams' heads (*Pl. 93*D), carved boards (*Pl. 90*F).

Carved leather fork from bifurcation of cheek-straps (fig. 74).

Leather bridle decorations: cheek-pieces with lions' heads (fig. 75B); lions' heads from cheek-straps (fig. 75A); deer's head in lion's jaws (fig. 75C).

Two bronze (*Pl. 74*C) and five iron bits.

Saddle with cover bearing decoration showing tiger leaping on mountain ram (figs. 67, 111).

Saddle with cover showing a tiger springing on an elk (fig. 109).

Saddle with figure of elk on the cover (*Pl. 168*A).

Saddle with eagle-griffin on the cover (*Pl. 168*B).

Saddle with cover showing carnivore attacking herbivore, partly surviving (*Pl. 169*B).

Two saddles with plain covers.

Saddle tassels (*Pl. 90*D, E).

Horn saddle pendants (*Pl. 94*C–E).

Girth buckle (*Pl. 94*F).

Part of breast-strap (fig. 76).

Horn saddle-strap runners (*Pl. 94*G).

Horse head-dress with crest (fig. 95; *Pl. 122*A).

Griffin's head from horse brow ornament (fig. 94; *Pl. 167*B).

Whip handle (*Pl. 165*B).

Piece of wood pasted with white sheepskin.

Leather bag, decorated with fur mosaic, which contained cheese (*Pl. 150*B).

Two shields made of sticks threaded through leather (the leather rotted away).

Gold-leaf.

BARROW 3

Structure

Site shown on plan in fig. 2, excavated in 1948. Prior to excavation it consisted of a low cairn 36 m. in diameter, 2·6 m. high with a hollow in the centre. A row of upright stones ran eastward from the barrow. After removing the cairn (*Pl. 11*) and earth mound with a broad trench (*Pl. 12*) the shape of the burial shaft measuring 6·5 m. by 7·8 m. was visible; it reached a depth of 5·2 m. below the buried ground surface (fig. 7A). In the topmost logs filling the shaft the robbers' passage, measuring 2·8 m. by 3·2 m., was visible (*Pl. 15*), which gradually reduced in size until in the inner ceiling of the chamber it measured only 0·37 m. by 0·48 m.

Under the upper logs of the shaft filling was a layer of large stones and boulders (*Pls. 13, 14*), which had sunk deeper. After removing the layers of logs and stones three sharply sagging beams came to light (*Pl. 16*), intended to keep the load off the burial chamber, resting on six upright posts.

319

The burial chamber occupied the southern part of the shaft and had a plank floor, double log walls and ceilings. The void between the walls was filled with crushed stone. The chamber was sealed by four layers of sheets of birch bark over which were a layer of larch bark and finally 'smoky tea'. When revealed the chamber was full of ice (*Pl. 17*). The internal dimensions of the chamber were 2·8 m. by 3·45 m. and 1·08 m. high.

The horses had been buried in the northern third of the shaft at a level with the lower ceiling of the chamber.

Finds

1. In the burial shaft over chamber and horse burials there were found:
   Wooden wedges, some long (*Pl. 36*c).
   Parts of trolleys, axles, platform, struts, wheels (*Pls. 126, 128*b).
   Sacral bone of a sheep.

2. In the chamber were found:
   Tree-trunk coffin.
   Man's skeleton (skull in *Pl. 43*A) thrown out of the coffin by the looters (*Pl. 18*).
   Two little tables (fig. 18; *Pl. 51*B, c).
   Solid wooden stool or pillow (*Pl. 53*c).
   Wooden spatula (fig. 27).
   Head-dress (*Pl. 155*B).
   Part of a second head-dress.
   Remains of sable fur.
   Woollen cord (*Pl. 66*B, *top*).
   Bunches of twisted woollen yarn (*Pl. 66*B, *below*).
   Piece of silk (*Pl. 134*A).
   Silk pouch (*Pl. 134*B).
   Pieces of woollens, linen weave, serge and looped material.
   24 arrow-shafts (*Pl. 143*c) bearing varied decoration (*Pls. 179, 180*).
   Remains of hexapod stands.
   Sacral bones of horse, cow and sheep.
   Flowers of *Scabiosa* and various mosses.

3. In the horse burial there were:
   14 horse skeletons disposed as shown in fig. 16c.
   Caftan of thin felt with hood (fig. 30).
   Three stick shields (fig. 107).
   Set of horn bridle decorations, antler cheek-pieces and slider blocks (*Pl. 95*A–C).

Set of horn saddle decorations with 'antlers' as the theme of decoration (*Pls. 95F–I, 96E*); saddle arch facings decorated with elk heads (*Pl. 96A*); girth-strap facings bearing feline heads (*Pl. 96B*); slides (*Pl. 95D, E*); runners (*Pl. 96C, D, F*) and horn buckle (*Pl. 96G*).

Bridle (fig. 65) with bronze bit and carved wooden decoration.

Parts of a bridle with wooden cheek-pieces (*Pl. 97B*), frontal plate (*Pl. 98B*), runner and slider block (*Pl. 98F, G*).

Set of decorations for bridle with iron bit, the theme of which is rosettes (*Pls. 97C, 98D*).

Bridle with bronze bit and decoration the motif of which is a carved wooden swan (*Pls. 40, 97A*; fig. 64).

Bridle with bronze bit (fig. 57) and decoration the motif of which is a carved wooden stylized 'bird's head' (*Pl. 98H, I*).

Bridle with bronze bit (*Pl. 99A*) and decorative motif (as also on breast-strap) provided by carved wooden mountain rams and balls (*Pls. 98A, E; 99C, D*); fork at cheek-strap in the shape of opened-out wolf's head (fig. 63); runner (*Pl. 99B*).

Set of bridle decorations the motif of which is a carved wooden elk's head (*Pls. 78, 100A–C*), and triangular frontal plate (*Pl. 100D*).

Set of saddle decorations from same outfit with elk's head, antlers, hares and 'lion cub' serving as motifs (*Pl. 101A–D; 102A–C, E–J*).

Set of decorations from bridle with bronze bit (*Pl. 103E*), the basic motif provided by carved wooden heads of saiga antelope (*Pl. 103B–D*), and horse-shoe-shaped frontal plate (*Pl. 103A*).

Set of bridle and saddle decorations the basic motif of which is a horned and big-eared lion's head carved of wood (*Pl. 104A–D, F, G*), with slider block (*Pl. 104E*) and forks on cheek-straps (*Pl. 104H*).

Frontal plate (*Pl. 105D*).

Of 14 bits 5 were bronze, the rest iron.

Remains of saddle with arch facings (figs. 72H, 77), saddle- and girth-straps (figs. 78, 79) with pendant plates decorated with stylized antlers (*Pls. 102D; 105C, F*).

Remains of saddle with decorations from front arch (*Pl. 163A*), girth-strap (fig. 80) and carved wooden plates (*Pl. 105B, G*).

Set of wooden saddle pendants (*Pl. 105A, E*).

Remains of saddle with arch decoration (*Pl. 163F*).

Remains of saddle with arch decoration (*Pl. 163D*).

Remains of saddle with cut-out gold-leaf decoration on arch (figs. 81–3)

Remains of saddle with arch decoration (*Pl. 163B*).

Remains of saddle with arch decoration (*Pl. 163C*).

Remains of saddle with arch decoration (*Pl. 163E*).

Fragments of saddle cushions.

Wooden saddle spacers (*Pl. 76*A).

Horn arch facings from two saddles (*Pl. 106*A–D).

Horn saddle pendants, facings, runners and slides (*Pl. 107*A–N).

Carved wooden head of fantastic bird, a horse crest (*Pl. 121*A).

Carved wooden head of horned and fanged fantastic bird, a horse crest (*Pl. 121*B).

Carved leather pieces of bridle and crest decorations (figs. 96, 97).

Carved wooden figure of bird (*Pl. 49*).

Saddle rod with a feline head fixed to one end (*Pl. 136*E).

Numerous pieces of gold-leaf and lacquer that had covered the carved wooden decorations and saddle arches.

BARROW 4

Structure

Shown in the plan in fig. 2, dug in 1948. The cairn was 24 m. in diameter and 1·5 m. high with a hollow in the centre. A row of vertical stones ran eastward from the mound. After removing the cairn and earth mound in a broad excavation the shape of the burial shaft was observed, measuring 5·3 m. by 5·6 m. and reaching 4·1 m. below the old ground surface (fig. 7B). The logs in the shaft had decayed away. The stones and debris fallen into the shaft indicated the robbers' passage. The burial chamber occupied the south part of the shaft and consisted of plank floor, box of dressed and plain logs (very decayed) in the roof. Remains of birch bark and foliage of the shrub 'smoky tea' were found covering the chamber. Its internal dimensions were 2·14 m. by 3·75 m. and 1·2 m. high.

The voids between the walls of the chamber and the sides of the shaft (except on north side) were filled with crushed stone.

The horses had been buried in the northern part of the shaft and covered by four layers of logs, the upper one of which passed over the roof of the chamber.

The lower shaft was filled with logs passing over both burial chamber and horses and filled in above with boulders and soil, under the weight of which the roof of the chamber had sagged and its walls had been distorted.

Finds

1. In the shaft, in its north-east corner, steps made out of a log were found (*Pl. 38*A).

In the debris that had fallen through the robbers' hole were found:

Large rim-sherd of earthenware bottle.

Cut-out leather griffin's head with large ears and antler (*Pl. 142*A).

Solid antler chisel (*Pl. 125*H).

Two wooden legs of a little table.

2. In the ice-filled burial chamber were found:

Two tree-trunk coffins with skeletons lying in them of a man (skull in *Pl. 43*B) and a woman (*Pl. 19*).

A little table (fig. 19, *Pl. 51*D).

Legs from another (*Pl. 51*E).

Solid wooden stool or pillow (*Pl. 52*B).

Rods from two hexapod stands.

White cylindrical beads.

A wooden peg in the nasal area of the man's skull.

3. In the horse burials were found:

Fourteen horse skeletons arranged as shown in fig. 16D.

Only the decorations of the bridles and saddles survived. The bits had been exclusively of iron, to judge by the ferric oxide staining the cheek-pieces, and no bronze bits were found.

Set of horn bridle accessories and their decorations (*Pl. 108*A, B, D, E, L).

Set of horn bridle accessories and their decorations (*Pl. 108*C, F–I).

Antler slider blocks from reins (*Pl. 108*J, K).

Two sets of horn facings from saddle arches, horn saddle pendants, girth-strap facings, runners and slides, girth buckle (*Pl. 108*M, *109*A–M).

Wooden cheek-pieces and set of bridle decorations of which the motif is a wolf (*Pl. 110*A, B).

Wooden cheek-pieces bearing figures of wolf and set of bridle pendants decorated with roebuck in the jaws of a wolf (*Pl. 110* C–G).

Set of wooden bridle decorations of which the motif is a cat (*Pl. 111*A, C, E, G; fig. 84).

Wooden cheek-pieces and set of decorations of which the motif is a horned cat's head (*Pl. 111*B, D, F).

Wooden cheek-pieces and set of bridle decorations of which the motifs are a big-eared bird's head and fantastic birds (*Pl. 112*E, G, H).

Wooden cheek-pieces and set of bridle decorations of which the motifs are a fantastic boar's head (*Pl. 112*A, I), carved leather monsters (fig. 85), and a crest taking the shape of the horned head of a boar (*Pl. 113*B, C).

Parts of wooden cheek-pieces (*Pl. 112*B–D, F).

Whip handle (fig. 99).

Remains of stick shields.

Gold-leaf.

BARROW 5

Structure

Site shown on plan in fig. 2, dug in 1949 (*Pls. 20, 21*). Cairn 42 m. in diameter,

3·75 m. high with a deep hollow in the middle. Surrounding the cairn at 2·5–3 m. from its edge was a circle of upright stones, spaced fairly widely apart. Around the barrow and adjoining it were radial areas of paving (fig. 3).

The removal of the cairn (*Pl. 22*) and earthen mound in a broad excavation revealed the outline of the burial shaft, which measured 6·65 m. by 8·25 m. and was found to be 4 m. deep beneath the buried ground surface. Below the topmost layer of logs filling the shaft was a layer of large stones and boulders weighing up to 3 tons (*Pl. 23*), and beneath them a treble layer of logs (*Pl. 24*). The robbers' passage measured 1·45 m. by 1·90 m. and was distinctly visible in the lower layer of logs just mentioned (*Pl. 25*). On removing the log filling the birch-bark sheets (*Pl. 33*) covering the top of the chamber were exposed (*Pl. 26*) with the robbers' hole (0·89 m. by 0·93 m.) chopped through it (*Pls. 26, 27*). In the inner ceiling the hole measured 0·43 m. by 0·9 m.

On removing the two ceilings it became evident that the chamber was filled with ice (*Pl. 28*). The tomb's floor of thick planks rested directly on the shaft bottom and both boxes and ceilings were of undressed logs. The intervening space had been left empty. The internal dimensions of the tomb were 2·3 m. by 5·2 m. and 1·4 m. high.

In contrast to the other large barrows at Pazyryk there was no layer of foliage of 'smoky tea' covering the birch-bark roofing over the tomb.

The superincumbent load of stones and boulders and layers of logs was carried by three horizontal beams supported over the chamber by three pairs of vertical posts set by its southern and northern walls (*Pl. 25*; beams removed).

The horses had been buried in the northern third of the shaft, where also some grave goods had been deposited. Other articles had been put between the south wall of the shaft and the chamber.

A section through the burial shaft of barrow 5 is shown in fig. 6.

Finds (figs. 6, 15, 17)

1. In the shaft amongst the logs were platforms from trolleys.
   By the west wall of the pit:
   Shaft of a sled or drag (*Pl. 130*).
   Parts of the carriage and a large quantity of thin sticks.
   In the robbers' passage on inner ceiling of tomb, a solid wooden stool or pillow
      (*Pl. 52c*).

2. In the burial chamber were found:
   A tree-trunk coffin pressed shut by a special log 'wedge' projecting from the
      south wall of the chamber (*Pl. 29*).
   Man's corpse (*Pls. 30, 44D, 46*).
   Woman's corpse (*Pl. 45*).

Remains of a felt wall-hanging decorated with a sphinx (*Pl. 173*), a bird (*Pl. 149*A) and a patterned border (*Pl. 149*B).

Pegs that had secured wall-hanging to chamber walls (*Pl. 38*B).

Legs of three little tables (*Pl. 52*D) and part of the top of one.

Felt cushion stuffed with deer hair (*Pl. 58*).

Horn with little wooden spoon (*Pl. 60*).

Female head-dress and pigtail (*Pl. 66*A).

Part of a felt stocking.

A fleece.

A goat's skin.

Rods of hexapod stands.

Carefully dressed rectangular boards with tie-on straps.

One-sided horn drum.

Remains of cheese.

Six-sided turquoise bead (*Pl. 158*).

Sherd of an earthenware bottle.

Seeds of cultivated coriander.

3. In the horses' burial and against the south wall of the shaft there were buried:
Nine horse bodies (fig. 17).

First riding outfit consisting of bridle, saddle and shabrack. The bridle is decorated with carved wooden figures of 'burrs' (*Pl. 113*A; fig. 62). The saddle bears plain scutiform pendants (figs. 68A, 69B, 70B). Felt shabrack covered by fine woollen Hither Asian cloth (*Pl. 177*B) with chest-piece covered by Hither Asian cloth decorated with lions (*Pl. 177*A; fig. 140).

Second riding outfit consisting of bridle, saddle and shabrack. The bridle is decorated with carved wooden disks (*Pl. 114*) and the plain saddle is adorned with carved wooden scutiform pendants decorated with stylized 'antlers' (*Pl. 118*D, E). The felt shabrack bears an applied pattern (*Pl. 160*).

Third riding outfit consisting of bridle, saddle and shabrack. The bridle bears carved wooden decorations the motif in which is a feline head (*Pl. 117*A, B), wooden cheek forks in the shape of a wolf's head (*Pl. 117*A). The plain saddle is covered at the arches with red lacquer. The felt shabrack bears an applied pattern (*Pl. 161*).

Fourth riding outfit consisting of bridle, saddle and shabrack. The bridle is decorated with carved wooden saiga antelope heads and grooved runners (fig. 58; *Pl. 115*A, B). The saddle is adorned with carved wooden and leather saiga antelope heads, with leather facings on the saddle arches bearing horses' heads and with wooden pendants and facings on the crupper-strap carved to represent horned feline heads (fig. 66, 68B; *Pls. 164*A–D, *115*C–E). The felt shabrack bears an applied pattern (*Pl. 162*).

Fifth riding outfit consisting of bridle, saddle, shabrack, head-dress and mane-cover. The cheek-pieces have griffins' heads on the upper terminals and the bridle-straps are decorated with carved wooden feline heads, with deer at the strap intersections (fig. 87; *Pls. 116*A, B; *117*D, E), while the cheek forks take the form of a wolf (*Pl. 117*C). The saddle (fig. 88) has a cover decorated with stylized elks' heads and crosses cut out from a silky fabric (*Pl. 167*A), while the arches are decorated with cut-out leather elks (*Pl. 165*A). The motif employed in the carved wooden saddle decorations was cats and cats' heads (*Pls. 116*C–F; *117*D, E). The felt shabrack is covered by a white silk embroidered with polychrome silk (figs. 89–92; *Pl. 178*). The horse head-dress with crest consists of a carved wooden deer's head (*Pls. 118*F; *121*C, D) and the leather mane-cover with the horse's hair is painted red.

Four identical bridles from draught horses decorated with carved wooden hemispherical plaques (*Pl. 118*A, C). All the bits were of iron.

Parts of trolleys on thick axles with solid wheels (*Pl. 127*).

Four-wheeled wagon or carriage with draught-pole and harness for four horses, wooden forks at the yoke and traces (*Pl. 129*).

Canopy of carriage of twigs and felt. Sculptural felt figures of swans adorning canopy (*Pl. 166*).

Numerous thin rods.

Log steps.

Part of the dome of a portable dwelling with stretchers and parts of sides.

Large felt carpet or wall-hanging bearing figure of seated goddess and rider standing before her (*Pls. 147, 154*).

Pile carpet from Hither Asia (*Pls. 174, 175*; figs. 141–5).

Maral antler.

Much gold-leaf covering carved wooden decorations.

BARROW 6

Structure

Site shown on plan in fig. 2, dug in 1949. Cairn diameter 14–15 m., 0·7 m. high above buried surface with robbers' crater in middle. The dimensions of the shaft were 3·4 m. by 3·4 m. and 2·2 m. deep. Log chamber (2·2 m. by 2·3 m.) occupied southern part of shaft, standing three members or 0·5 m. high.

Finds (fig. 8)

Skeletons of an adult (probably a woman) and a young girl.

Skeletons of three horses.

Chinese mirror (fig. 55; *Pl. 70*C).

Large quantity of white (marble) cylindrical beads, and glass and cornelian beads.

Cowrie shells (*Pls. 68*c, *158*).
Red lacquer plates.
Gold runner beads.
Two earthenware bottles (*Pl. 55*A).
Horn saddle facings and pendants (fig. 93).
Iron knife.
Piece of an iron rod.
Gold-leaf.

BARROW 7

Structure

Site shown in plan in fig. 2, dug in 1949. Only distinguishable by slight hollow left by robbers' digging. A trench measuring 4 m. by 4 m. was made in the central part of the barrow. The burial shaft measured 2 m. by 2 m. and was 1·9 m. deep below the buried ground surface. Remains of a box two members high were found on the south side, floored with boards and roofed with planks.

Finds

Leg bones and skull of an infant.
Fragment of an apron (*Pl. 157*c).
Pieces of fur clothing (*Pl. 157*D).
Remains of decorated costume and gold plates of varying form.
An antler tine.

BARROW 8

Structure

Site of barrow shown in plan in fig. 2, dug in 1949. Diameter of cairn 14 m. and height above buried surface 0·65 m., with hollow in middle. Burial shaft measured 3·2 m. by 3·6 m. and about 3 m. deep. At 2·65 m. below the buried surface remains of a box tomb 3 members high.

Finds

Skeleton of a woman.
Bones of one horse.
Antler pick (*Pl. 37*B).
Stamped square copper plates (fig. 47B).
Copper bead covered with gold.
Gold-leaf.

PRINCIPAL WORKS REFERRED TO AND FURTHER READING

Translator's Note. This section is divided into three parts, *A*, *B* and *C*. *A* consists of Russian or Classical works in Russian editions, and *B* of works in French, German and English; they correspond to the list given by the author in his corrected copy of the 1953 edition, to which no additions have been made. *C* is a short guide proposed by the translator for the reader who wishes to pursue the subject further, using mainly English works.

A

AMMIANUS MARCELLINUS. *Rerum Gestarum Libri* XXXI.

ANDREEV, M. S. 1923. Prophetic Dreams, some Tokens and the Child's Game 'Magpie-Crow' among several Peoples, particularly in Central Asia. *News of the Chief Central Asian Museum* (Tashkent), vol. ii.

ANTIQUITIES OF THE CIMMERIAN BOSPHORUS. 1854. *Antiquities of the Cimmerian Bosphorus preserved in the Imperial Hermitage* (St Petersburg).

ARTAMANOV, M. I. 1947. Social Structure of the Scyths. *Herald of Leningrad University*, No. 9.
1948. Ramen, barrow 3, at Kostromskaya. *Soviet Archaeology*, vol. x.
1950. *Origin of the Slavs.*

BERNSHTAM, A. N. 1947. A Buckle from Bekkarrinsk. *Short Reports of IIMK, AN, SSSR*, vol. xvii.

BICHURIN, N. Y. 1950. *Collected References to Peoples Inhabiting Central Asia in Antiquity* (Moscow-Leningrad). (First published in 3 parts in 1851.)

BOBRINSKY, A. 1887–1901. *Barrows and Chance Archaeological Finds near the Hamlet of Smela*, 3 vols. (St Petersburg).

CTESIAS 1844. Fragments from Ctesias collected by Müller for his Edition of Herodotus.

DEBETS, G. F. 1948. *Palaeoanthropology of the U.S.S.R.* (works of the Institute of Ethnography, AN, SSSR).

DIODORUS SICULUS. *The Library.*

GOLMSTEN, V. V. 1933. *The Cults of Ancient Siberia* (Leningrad).

GRIGORIEV, V. V. 1871. *About a Scythian People, the Sacae* (St Petersburg).

GRUM-GRZHIMAILO, E. G. 1926. *Western Mongolia and the Uryankhaisk District* (Leningrad).

GRYAZNOV, M. P. 1928. Excavations in a Prince's Grave in the Altai. *Chelovek*, 2–4.
1947. Remains of the Maiemir Stage of the Early Nomads of the Altai, *Short Reports of IIMK, AN, SSSR*, vol. xviii.
1950. *Pazyryk, Barrow 1* (Leningrad).

HERODOTUS. *History in Nine Books.*

HESYCHIUS OF ALEXANDRIA. *Lexicon.*

HIPPOCRATES. *On Air, Waters and Places.*

KISELEV, S. V. 1935. Report on the Altaian Expedition of the State Historical Museum in 1934. *Soviet Archaeology*, vol. i.
1947. The Altai in the Scythian Period. *Journal of Ancient History*, vol. ii.

1949. Ancient History of Southern Siberia. *Materials and Researches on the Archaeology of the U.S.S.R.*, vol. ix.

LAPPO-DANILEVSKY, A. 1887. Scythian Antiquities. *Notes of the Section for Russian and Slav Archaeology of the Imperial Russian Archaeological Society*, vol. iv (St Petersburg).

MARX, K. 1940. *The Forms preceding Capitalist Society* (Politizdat).

MARX, K. and ENGELS, F. 1937. *Collected Works*, vol. xiv, pt i.

1937. *Collected Works*, vol. xvi, pt i.

MÜLLER, C. *See* CTESIAS.

NICHOLAS OF DAMASCUS. *World History.*

PALLAS, P. S. 1788. *Journeys through Various Provinces of the Russian State* (St Petersburg).

PLINY THE ELDER. *Natural History.*

POMPONIUS MELA. *De Situ Orbis.*

POTAPOV, L. P. 1948. *Outline History of the Altaians* (Novosibirsk).

PRIDIK, E. 1911. Melgunov's Treasure. *Materials for the Archaeology of Russia*, vol. xxxi.

ROSTOVTSEV, M. I. 1914. The Silver Vessel from Voronezh. *Materials for the Archaeology of Russia*, vol. xxxiv.

RUDENKO, S. I. 1929. Graphic Art of the Ostyaks and Voguls. *Materials for Ethnography*, vol. iv.

1930. Contribution to the Palaeoanthropology of the Southern Altai. Collection called *Kazakhs* (Leningrad).

1931. A Scythian Burial in the Eastern Altai. *Reports of GAIMK*, vol. ii.

1944. The Scythian Problem and the Altaian Finds. *News of the Academy of Sciences of the U.S.S.R.* (Sec. Hist. Phil.), vol. vi.

1948. *Pazyryk, Barrow 2* (Leningrad).

1949a. Ancient Scythian Tattooing. *Soviet Ethnography*, vol. iii.

1949b. The Culture in the Altai at the Time of the Erection of the Pazyryk Barrows. *Short Reports of IIMK, AN, SSSR*, vol. xxvi.

1949c. Preliminary Report on Excavations in the Ulagan valley in 1947. *Soviet Archaeology*, vol. xi.

1949d. Tattooing among the Asiatic Eskimos, *Soviet Ethnography*, vol. i.

1950. Excavations on the Pazyryk Group of Barrows. *Short Reports of IIMK, AN, SSSR*, vol. xxxi.

1951. Pazyryk, Barrow 5. *Short Reports of IIMK, AN, SSSR*, vol. xxxvii.

1952. *The Discoveries in the High Altai and the Scyths* (Moscow-Leningrad).

1960. *The Culture of the Population of the Central Altai in Scythian Times* (Moscow-Leningrad).

1962a. *The Culture of the Huns and the Noin-Ula Barrows* (Moscow-Leningrad).

1962b. *The Siberian Collection of Peter I* (Moscow-Leningrad).

RUDENKO, S. I. *and* N. M. 1949. *Art of the Scyths in the Altai* (Moscow).

SHAVROV, N. M. 1902. *Carpet Production in Asia Minor* (Tiflis).

SMIRNOV, Y. I. 1909. *Oriental Silver, An Atlas of Ancient Silver and Gold Vessels of Oriental Origin found mainly in the Russian Empire* (St Petersburg).

SOROKIN, N. 1873. Journey to the Voguls. *Proceedings of the Natural History Society of Kazan University*, vol. iii, pt. 4.

STALIN, I. 1947. *Collected Works*, vol. v.

1950. *Concerning Marxism and Linguistics* (Gospolitizdat).

STRABO. *Geography.*

TEVYASHOV, E. E. 1910. *On the Purpose of the Side Openings in the Sockets of Scythian Bronze Arrowheads* (St Petersburg).

TOLSTOY, I. *and* KONDAKOV, N. 1889–90. *Russian Antiquities in Artistic Remains*, issues 2 and 3 (St Petersburg).

TURAEV, B. 1911. *Scythia in the Hieroglyphs.*

VIDONOVA, E. C. 1938. The Katanda Robe. Collected Articles in the Archaeology of the U.S.S.R. *Proceedings GIM*, vol. viii.

VITT, V. O. 1952. Horses from the Pazyryk Barrows. *Soviet Archaeology*, vol. xvi.

XENOPHON. *Anabasis.*
Cyropaedia.

ZAMYATNIN, S. N. 1946. The Scythian Cemetery 'Many Barrows' near Voronezh. *Soviet Archaeology*, vol. viii.

B

ANDERSSON, J. G. 1932. Hunting Magic in the Animal Style. *Bulletin of the Museum of Far Eastern Antiquities*, vol. iv.

BABELON, E. 1888. *Manuel d'Archéologie orientale* (Paris).

1893. *Les Perses Achéménides, les satrapes et les dynastes tributaires de leur empire en Chypre et Phénicie* (Paris).

CONTENAU, G. 1927–47. *Manuel d'Archéologie orientale. Depuis les origines jusqu'à l'époque d'Alexandre* (Paris) vols. i–iv.

DALTON, O. M. 1905. *The Treasure of the Oxus with other Objects from Ancient Persia and India* (London).

DIEULAFOY, M. 1885. *L'Art antique de la Perse, Achéménides, Parthes, Sassanides* (Paris) vols. i–iii.

1892. *L'Acropole de Suse d'après les fouilles exécutées en 1884, 1885, 1886 sous les auspices du Musée du Louvre* (Paris).

DUSSAUD, R. 1938–9. The Bronzes of Luristan. Types and History. *A Survey of Persian Art* (London), vols. i and iv.

FURTWÄNGLER, A. 1900. Die Antiken Gemmes. *Geschichte der Steinschneiderkunst im Klassischen Altertum* (Berlin).

GRIAZNOV, M. P. *and* GOLOMSHTOK, E. A. 1933. The Pazirik Burial in the Altai. *American Journal of Archaeology*, vol. xxxvii.

HERZFELD, E. E. 1941. *Iran in the Ancient East* (London, New York).

HEUZEY, L. 1900. *Monuments Piot.*

LAYARD, A. H. 1849. *The Monuments of Nineveh*, ser. 1 (London).

1867a. *Nineveh and Babylon* (London).

1867b. *Nineveh and its Remains* (London).

MÉNANT, J. 1886. *Recherches sur la glyptique orientale. Cylindres de l'Assyrie* (Paris).

MINNS, E. H. 1913. *Scythians and Greeks, a survey of ancient history and archaeology on the north coast of the Euxine from the Danube to the Caucasus* (Cambridge).

MORGAN, J. de. 1905. Délégations en Perse. *Recherches archéologiques*, viii, ser. 3 (Paris).

MÜNTZ, E. *La Tapisserie* (Paris).

PERROT, G. *and* CHIPIEZ, CH. 1884–90. *Histoire de l'art dans l'antiquité* (Paris), vols. ii–v.

POTTIER, E. 1926. *L'Art Hittite* (Paris).

RADLOFF, W. 1893. *Aus Sibirien. Löse Blätter aus meinem Tagebuche* (Leipzig).

ROSTOVTZEFF, M. 1922. *Iranians and Greeks in South Russia* (Oxford).

1929. *The Animal Style in South Russia and China* (Leipzig-London).

SALMONY, A. 1933. *Sino-Siberian Art in the Collection of C. T. Loo* (Paris).

SCHWEINFURTH, G. A. 1883. Neue Beiträge zur Flora des alten Aegypten. *Berichte des deutschen botanischen Gesellschaft*, vol. i.

SWALLOW, R. W. 1937. *Ancient Chinese Bronze Mirrors* (Peiping).

UMEHARA, S. 1935. *L'Étude sur le miroir antérieur à la dynastie des 'Han'* (Kyoto).

WARD, W. H. 1920. *Cylinders and other Ancient Oriental Seals* (London).

WEBER, O. *Assyrische Kunst* (Berlin).

C

This guide to further reading has been prepared by the translator to assist the English reader who may wish to pursue the subject and its many ramifications further. The list consists mainly of works in English, but also includes some in German and French. The reader will not be able to follow the subject very far unless he is prepared to read these languages. The list is confined to books, but in some of these references will be found to the extensive periodical literature on the subject.

INTRODUCTORY. K. Jettman, *Art of the Steppes* (trans. from the German), (London, 1967); T. T. Rice, *The Scythians* (3rd ed., London, 1961); E. D. Phillips, *The Royal Hordes, Nomad Peoples of the Steppes* (these two lavishly illustrated, popular books both contain extensive bibliographies); A. L. Mongait, *Archaeology in the U.S.S.R.* (London, 1961); S. I. Rudenko, *The Most Ancient Artistic Carpets and Textiles in the World* (in Russian with summaries and figure captions in English, French and German) ('Iskusstvo', Moscow, 1968); M. Gryaznov, *The Ancient Civilization of South Siberia* (London, 1969).

GENERAL ORIENTATION. Herodotus, *The History* (Rawlinson's translation); E. H. Parker, *A Thousand Years of the Tartars* (2nd ed., London, 1924); W. Radloff, *Aus Sibirien, Löse Blätter aus dem Tagebuche eines reisenden Linguisten* (editions of 1883, 1893, Leipzig); R. Grousset, *L'Empire des Steppes* (Paris, 1939). Radloff was stationed at Barnaul, 250 miles north-west of Pazyryk, from 1859 to 1870. The title of the work is misleading, for it contains the classic accounts of the modern Altaians and Kazakhs, describes the climate and geography of the Altai, the Chinese sources, the Russian colonization of Siberia and Radloff's own excavations; O. Lattimore, *Studies in Frontier History, Collected Papers 1928-58* (London, 1962); W. Watson, *Inner Asia and China in the Pre-Han Period* (London, 1969).

SCYTHIANS. E. H. Minns, *Scythian and Greeks* (Cambridge, 1913); M. Rostovtzev, *Iranians and Greeks in South Russia* (Oxford, 1922), and *The Animal Style in South Russia and China* (Princeton, 1929). Since the main discoveries in the Black Sea area were made between about 1850 and 1918 these older works are still valid, but the classification of the art by Rostovtzev is to some extent obsolete; M. I. Artamanov, *Treasures from Scythian Tombs* (London, 1969).

PERSIA. A. T. Olmstead, *A History of the Persian Empire (Achaemenid Period)* (Chicago, 1948); R. Ghirshman, *Iran from the Earliest Times to the Islamic Conquest* (London, 1954); A. U. Pope (ed.), *A Survey of Persian Art* (Oxford, 1938) vols. i and iv; O. M. Dalton, *The Treasure of the Oxus* (2nd edition, London, 1926). The affinities of the remains at Pazyryk are with Achaemenid Persia.

EARLY USE OF HORSES. J. Wiesner, *Fahren und Reiten im Alt Europa und im Alten Orient (Der Alte Orient*, XXXVIII, heft 2–4, 1939); J. A. H. Potratz, Die Pferdetrensen des Alten Orient (*Analecta Orientalia*, XLI), (Rome, 1966). The latter is an authoritative, up-to-date account of what is known about early bridles. F. Hančar. *Das Pferd in der Vor- und Frühgeschichte* (Vienna, 1956).

RELATED SUBJECTS. W. Watson, *China before the Han Dynasty* (London, 1961) (contains extensive bibliography); F. Altheim, *Geschichte der Hunnen*, vol. i, *von den Anfangen bis zum Einbruch in Europa* (Berlin, 1959); W. W. Tarn, *The Greeks in Bactria and India* (2nd edition, Cambridge, 1951); A. K. Nahrain, *The Indo-Greeks* (Oxford, 1957); S. I. Rudenko, *Die Sibirische Sammlung Peters I* (German translation).

1 and 2 General view of Pazyryk group of barrows, and excavation of barrow 1.

Excavation of barrow 1

3 Robbers' forced entry through log filling being revealed.

4 The transverse beams that supported the log filling exposed with aperture made by robbers through chamber roof below.

5 Inside of burial chamber with log coffin against south wall and its displaced lid above it, with upright post in foreground showing hollow in which transverse beam rested.
6 View of northern side of burial chamber showing cone of debris fallen through robbers' trap in foreground and 'window' chopped out of inner box wall on east side filled with ice.

Excavation of barrow 2.

◁ 7 The cairn being
removed.

◁ 8 The rotted logs at the
top of shaft and the
robbers' forced access.

9 South-west corner
of burial shaft showing
a transverse beam
bowed under weight of
filling above, below it
foliage of 'smoky tea'
and finally the birch
bark covering the
chamber.

10 Double log ceiling
of chamber.

Excavation of barrow 3.

11 Removal of cairn.

12 Taking rock filling out of the shaft.

13 Log layer over upper part of shaft filling of stones. ▷

14 Removal of boulders from the shaft. ▷

Excavation of barrow 3.

15 Robbers' forced entry visible in lower layers of log filling.

16 The bowed beams above the chamber and twigs of 'smoky tea' below.

17 The chamber filled with ice.

18 Inside the burial chamber showing in the foreground edge of log coffin, skeleton of man in the ice, upturned table tops on the right, and in the background outside the chamber the large upright posts and horse bones.

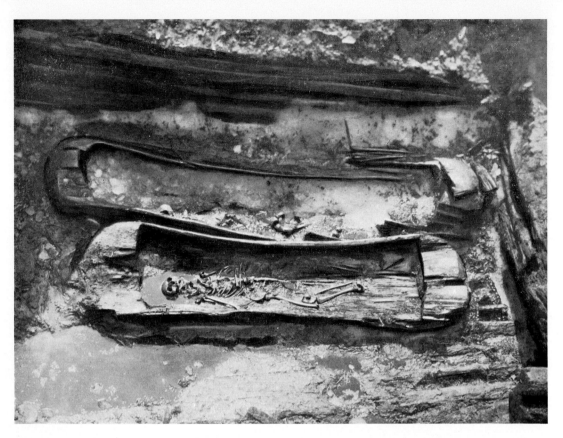

Excavation of barrow 5.
23 Top layer of rocks in the burial shaft.
24 Log filling in shaft above chamber.

25 Robbers' forced access visible in log filling.

26 Top layer of outer chamber with birch-bark removed with inner chamber top visible through robbers' trap, and at back behind the upright posts parts of the carriage.

Excavation of barrow 5.   *27* Extricating logs from the burial shaft.
28 Inner and outer ceilings removed and the double chamber revealed filled with ice, while at the
back above the horse burials the wheels of the carriage can be seen.

29 Inside the chamber with the bodies of the man and woman in the tree-trunk coffin.
30 Man's body in the coffin with wedge of logs above knocked into south wall of chamber.

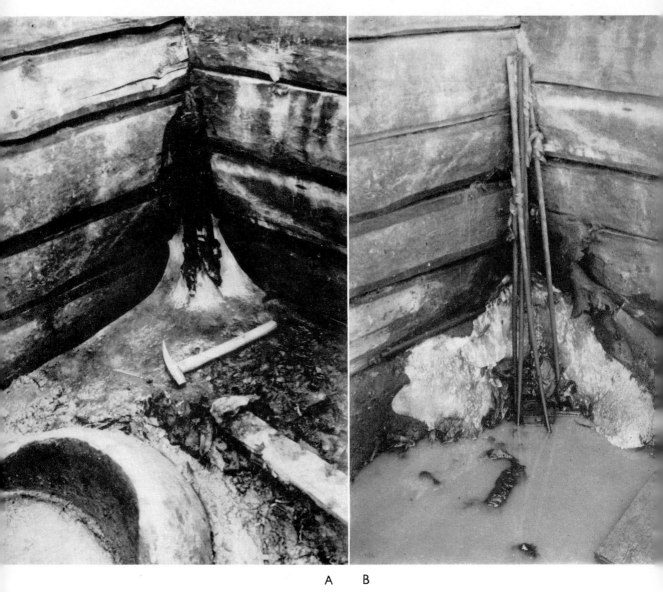

A   B

35 Chamber of barrow 2.

A, legs of hexapod in ice;
B, legs of hexapod and censer with feet.

36 A, stake from barrow 3; B, shovels from barrow 2
(1/8); C, wedges from various barrows (1/7).

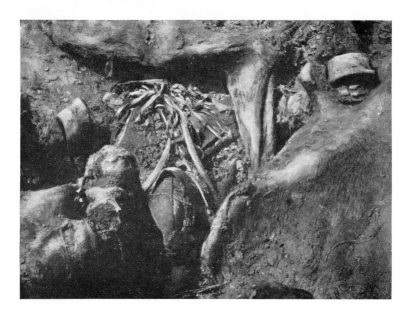

39 Saddles in horse burial of barrow 1; *top right :* a horse hoof.

40 Bridle in horse burial of barrow 3.

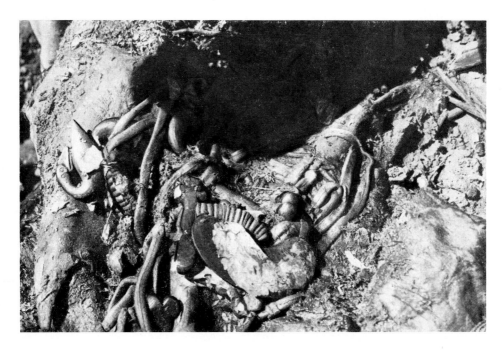

41 Lamp lodged in the
on the floor of the tomb
in barrow 2.

42 Censer lodged in the
ice of barrow 2.

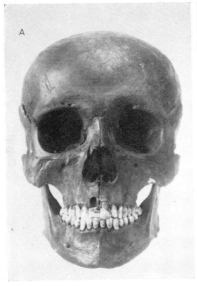
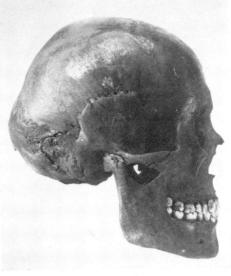

43 Male skulls. A, from barrow 3 facing and in profile; B, from barrow 4 facing and in profile; C, from Shibe barrow.

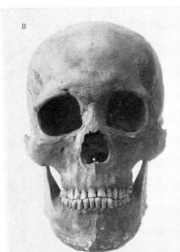
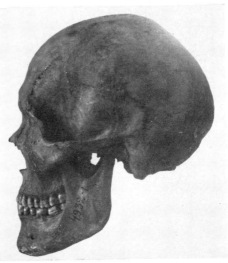

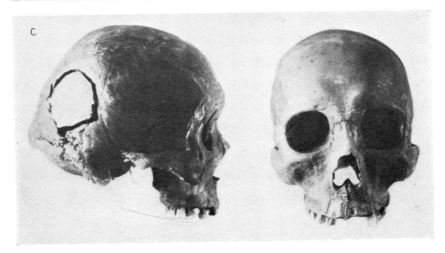

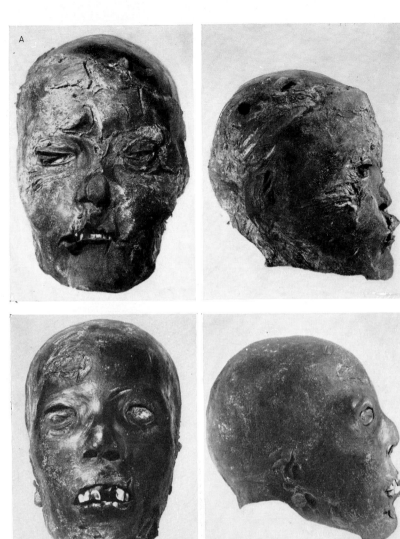

44 Mummified heads.
A, Man's head from barrow 2, facing and in profile, showing aperture made by blow from a battle-axe.
B, Woman's head from barrow 2, facing and in profile.
C, Trepanned woman's skull from barrow 2.
D, Man's head from barrow 5, in profile.

A

B

C

D

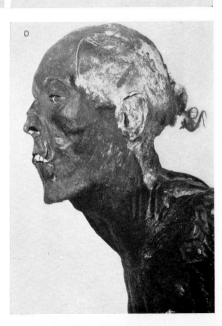

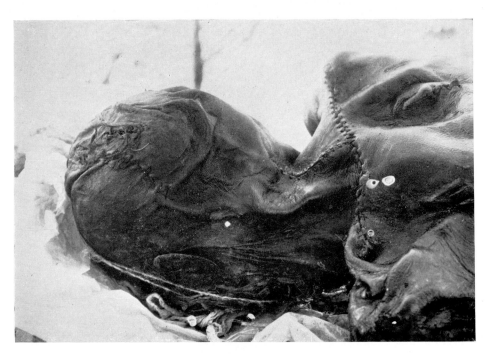

45 Head and back of embalmed female corpse from barrow 5.

46 Head and back of embalmed male corpse from barrow 5.

47 Saddle pendant from barrow 1; a ram's head seized by a fish (*c.* 1/5).

48 Saddle from barrow 1.

49 Figure of a bird from barrow 3 (1/2).

50 A, little table from barrow 2 (1/5); B, table leg (foreshortened view).

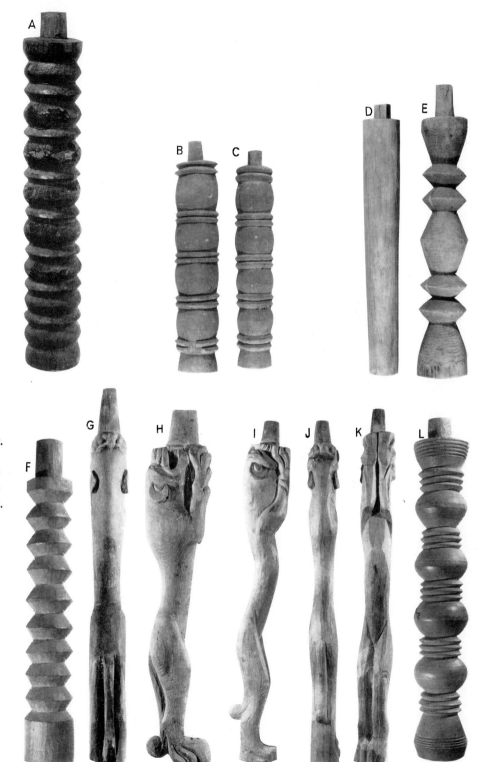

51 Table legs.
A, from barrow 1
B, C, from barrow 3
D, E, from barrow 4
F–L, from barrow 2.

52 A, lamp from barrow 2 (1/4); B, C, wooden stools or pillows from barrow 4 (B, 1/4) and barrow 5 (C, 1/5); D, table legs from barrow 5 (1/4).

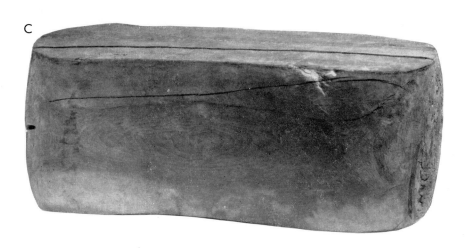

53 A, B, wooden
stools or pillows from
barrow 1 (A, 1/4),
barrow 2 (B, 1/3),
and barrow 3 (C, 1/4).

A

B

C

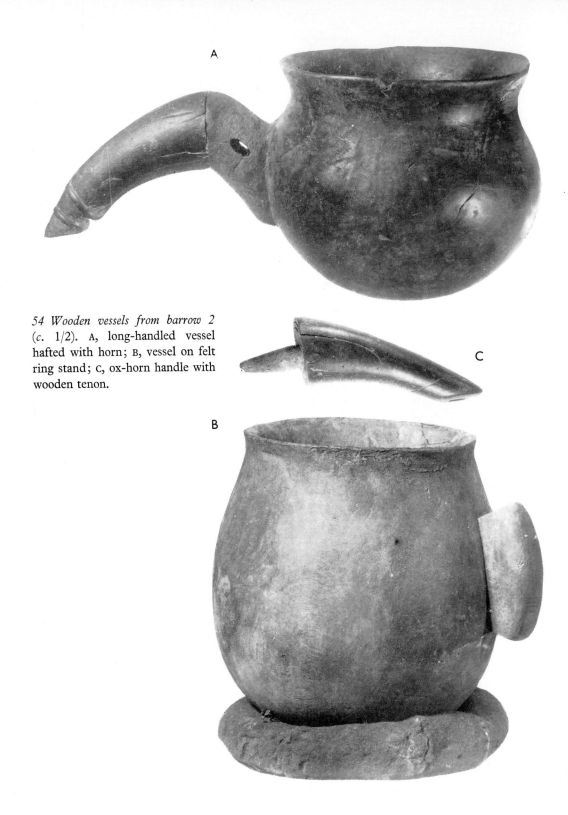

54 Wooden vessels from barrow 2 (c. 1/2). A, long-handled vessel hafted with horn; B, vessel on felt ring stand; C, ox-horn handle with wooden tenon.

55 Earthenware bottles. A, bottle from barrow 6 (1/3); B, C, large bottle from barrow 2, shown in B with its cut-out applied leather cocks affixed.

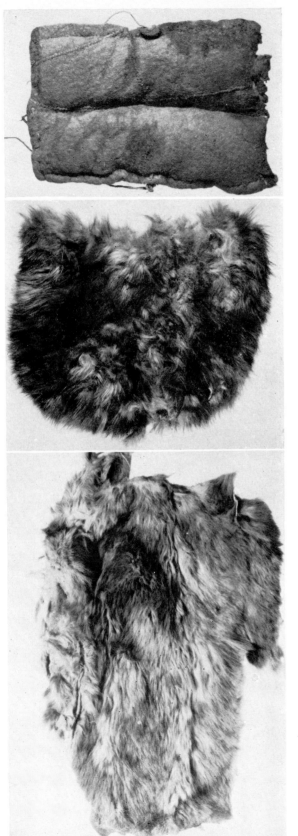

56 Felt cushion stuffed with deer hair from barrow 5 (*c.* 1/4).

57 Pouch of sable fur from barrow 2.

58 Stool-cover or pillowcase of steppe cat fur from barrow 2.

A

59 A, B, leather flask
covered with fur, from
barrow 1 (*c.* 1/4).

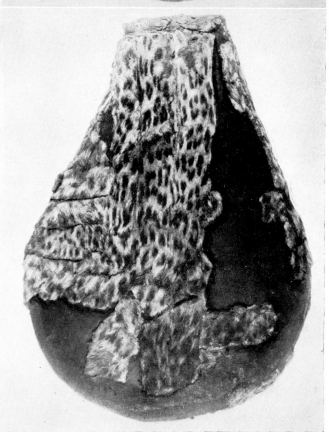

B

61 *Leather vessels from barrow 2* (1/2). A, small purse with flap lid; B, little bag-like pouch; C, flask with applied patterns.

60 Horn (*above*) and wooden spoon (*left*) from barrow 5 (3/4).

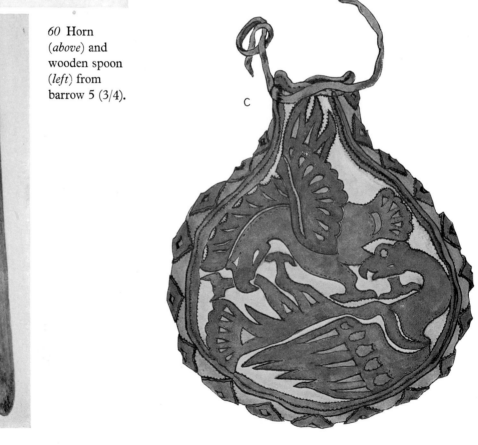

62 Apparatus for burning hemp, from barrow 2. A, copper censer on feet; B, copper censer with pedestal (1/3); C, rods of hexapod cover-stand.

63 Man's shirt, from barrow 2.

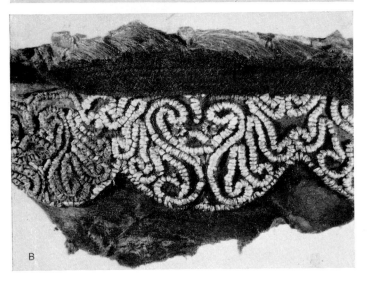

64 A, sole of woman's bootee decorated with glass beads and pyrites crystals, from barrow 2; B, decoration on top of upper of woman's bootee from barrow 2 (3/4).

65 Woman's head-dress. A, 'diadem' decoration of head-dress from barrow 2; B, leather cut-out cock decorating 'diadem', from barrow 2; C, fur head-dress, reconstructed.

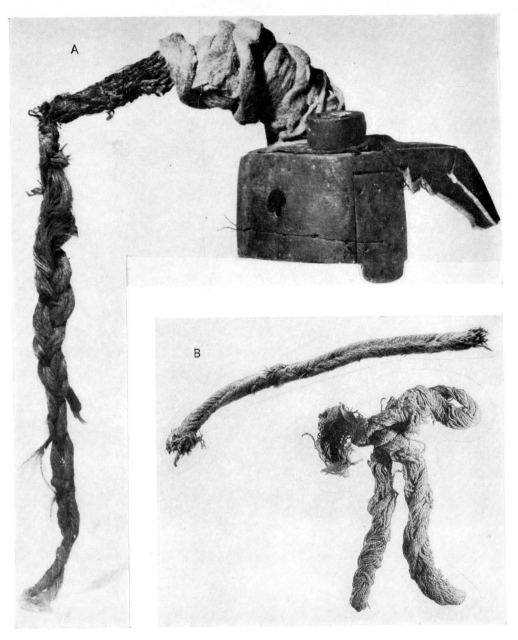

66 A, wooden head-dress with pigtail from barrow 5; B, girdles from dress in barrow 3: (*top*) woollen cord; (*below*) caftan girdle.

67 Accessories of dress and adornment (c. 3/4). ▷
A, belt with silver plates, from barrow 2; B, silver plate from the same belt; C, bronze belt plate-clip from barrow near Biysk; D, E, silver belt pendants in the form of little horses, from barrow 2; F, G, belt-ends from barrow 2; H, copper belt-end from Aragol barrow.

68 A, gold earring from Aragol barrow; B, gold earring from barrow 2; C, shell from barrow 6; D, E, carved wooden lion-griffins that formed part of a neck torque from barrow 2 (D with heads removed); F, iron hairpin from barrow 2.

69 A, a woman's pigtails from barrow 2; B, C, parts of hair curls from same; D, E, false beard of man in barrow 2.

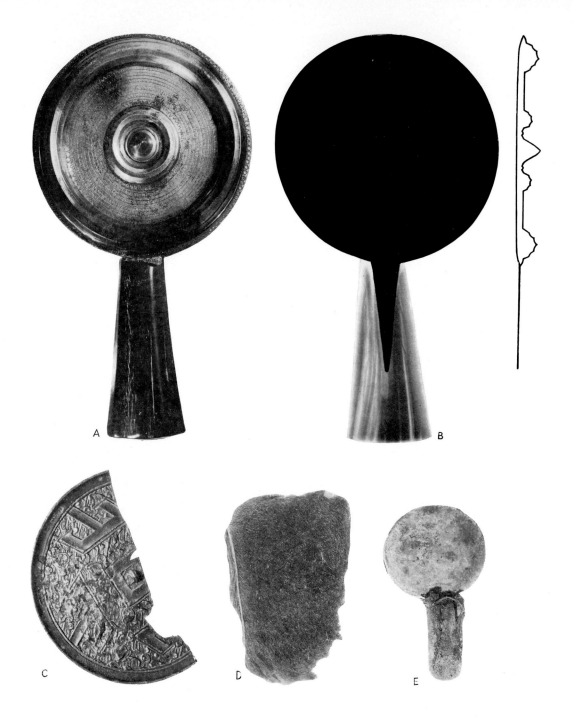

70 A, silver mirror from barrow 2; B, X-ray photograph showing silver mirror from barrow 2 in section (2/5); C, Chinese mirror from barrow 6; D, fur case of bronze mirror from barrow 2; E, bronze mirror from barrow 2.

71 A, B, horse tails from barrows 2 and 3.

72 Horse tail tied into a knot, from barrow 1.

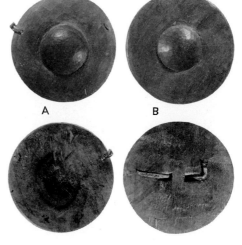

73 A, B, circular frontal plates from barrow 1 (1/2).

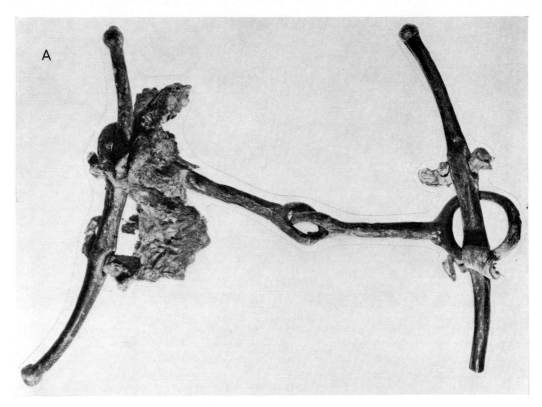

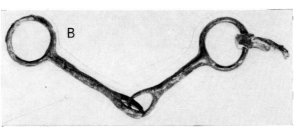

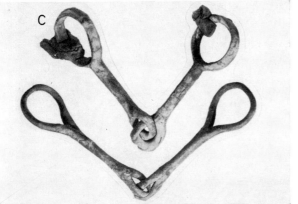

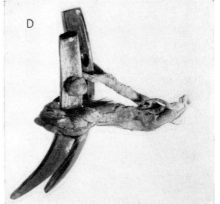

74 Horse bits. A, B, from Aragol barrows; C, D, from Pazyryk barrow 2.

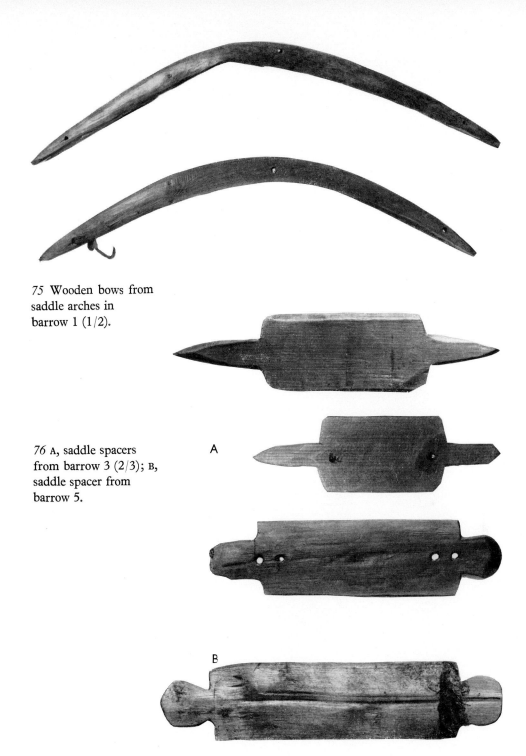

75 Wooden bows from
saddle arches in
barrow 1 (1/2).

76 A, saddle spacers
from barrow 3 (2/3); B,
saddle spacer from
barrow 5.

A

B

77 Cheek-piece from barrow 1 (*c.* 1/2).

78 Elk heads decorating bridles in barrow 3 (2/3).

79 *First riding outfit*
from barrow 1.
A, bridle; B, saddle.

*80. Second riding outfit
from barrow 1.* A, bridle;
B, C, wooden enrichments
of the same.

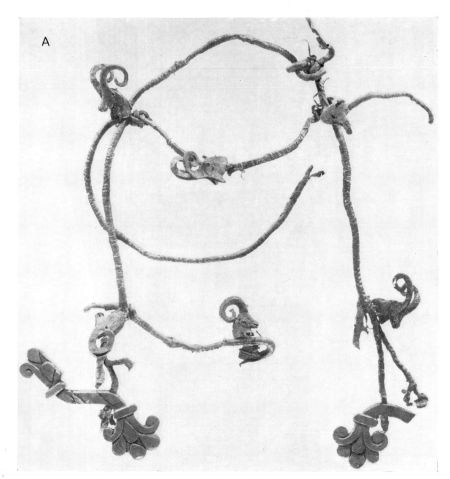

*81 Third riding outfit
from barrow 1.* A, bridle;
B, leather cut-out of head
of griffin from decoration
on breast-strap; C,
leather cut-out griffin
from centre of breast-
strap; D, leather cut-out
of head of goat from
bridle; (B, C, and D *c.* 1/2).

82 Fourth riding outfit from barrow 1. A, bridle; B, cheek-piece from A.

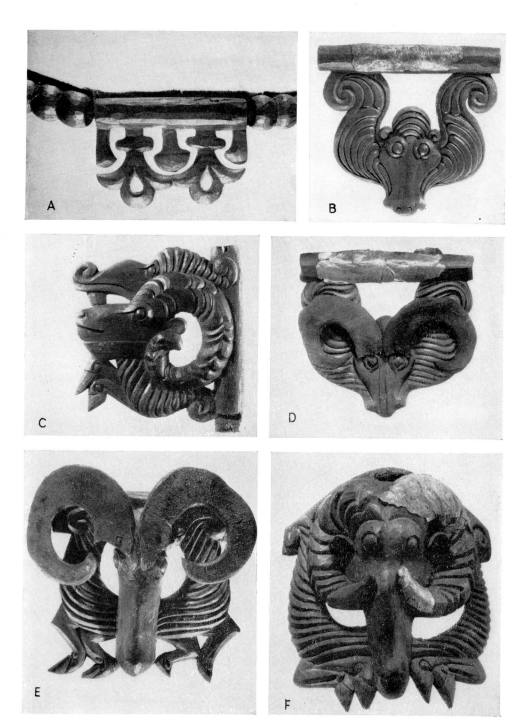

83 Wooden enrichments of riding gear from barrow 1 (1/2). A, pendant in the form of palmettes (outfit 7); B, D, pendants in the form of mountain rams' heads (outfit 4); C, pendant in the form of a mountain ram in the jaws of a wolf (outfit 6); E, F, pendants in the form of facing mountain rams (outfit 5).

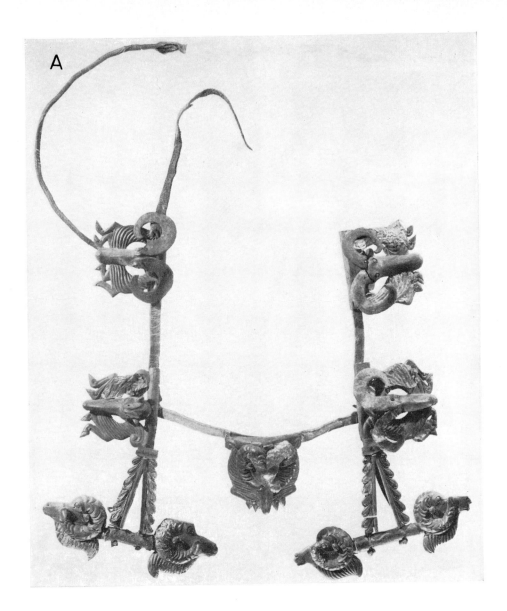

A

B

84 Fifth riding outfit from barrow 1. A, bridle; B, fork of cheek-strap from same; C (*opposite*), cheek-piece of same.

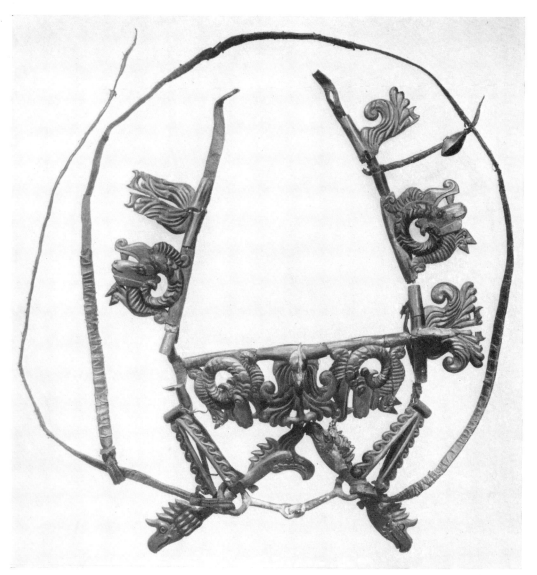

85 Bridle of sixth riding outfit from barrow 1.

C

86 *Carved wooden decorations of bridle in Pl. 85 (c. 1/2).* A, B, griffins; C, D, cheek-pieces with griffin-head terminals.

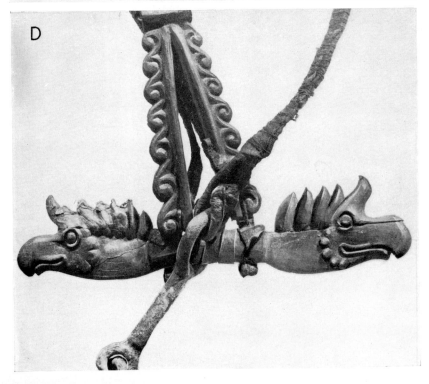

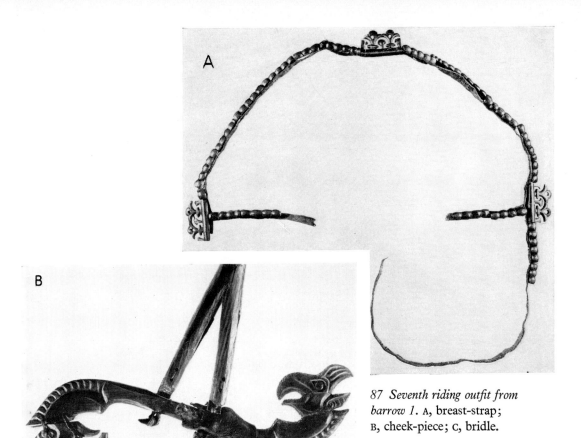

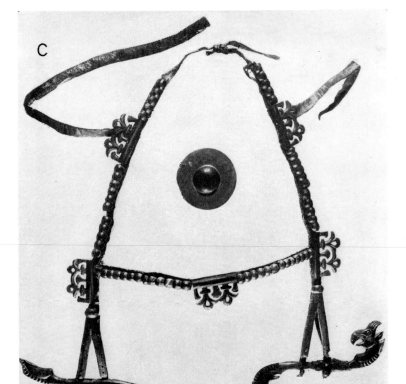

87 *Seventh riding outfit from*
barrow 1. A, breast-strap;
B, cheek-piece; C, bridle.

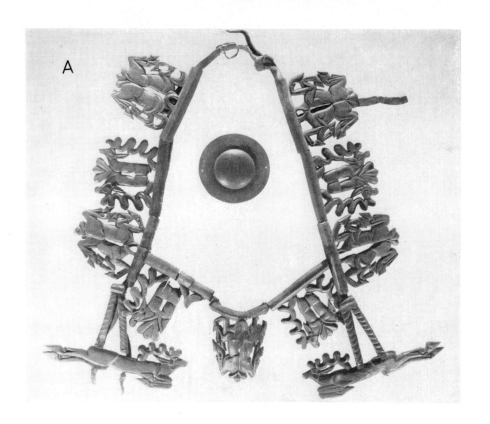

88 Eighth riding outfit from barrow 1. A, bridle; B, cheek-piece.

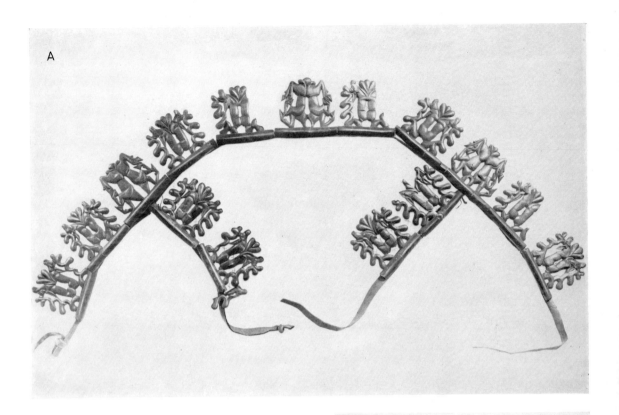

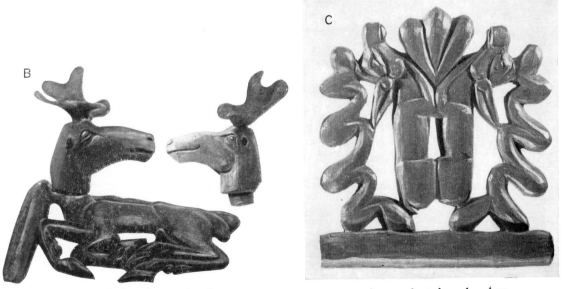

89 Eighth riding outfit from barrow 1. A, breast-strap ornament; B, wooden pendant shaped as deer, and deer head; C, wooden pendant shaped like two deer pressed chest to chest.

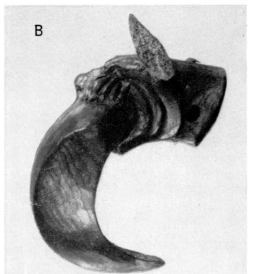

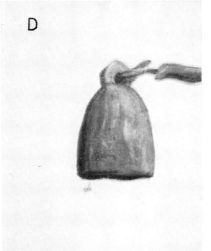

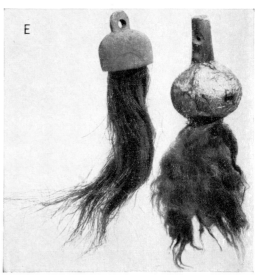

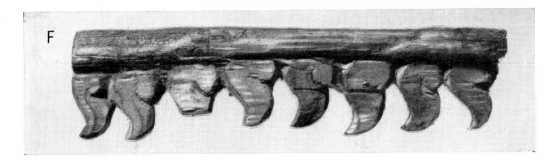

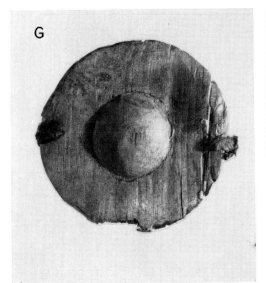

90 Saddlery decorations from ninth riding outfit of barrow 1 and from barrow 2. A, cheek-piece (barrow 1); B, C, carved wooden pendants in the form of a leopard's head with a boar's tusk in its jaws (barrow 1); D, E, saddle tassels from barrow 2; F, bridle decoration from barrow 2; G, H, bridle frontal plates from barrow 2; I, J, saddle tassels from barrow 1.

91 Bridle of tenth riding outfit from barrow 1.

92 Enrichments of bridle in Pl. 91 (3/5). A–D, wooden cut-outs in the form of human heads (*c.* 7/8). ▷

A

B

C

D

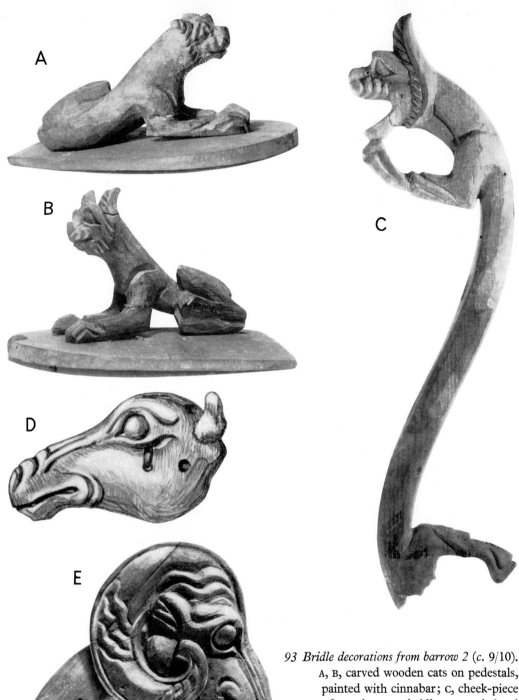

93 Bridle decorations from barrow 2 (c. 9/10).
A, B, carved wooden cats on pedestals,
painted with cinnabar; C, cheek-piece
from the same bridle; D, ram's head
from bridle decoration; E, ram's head
carved on end of wooden cheek-piece.

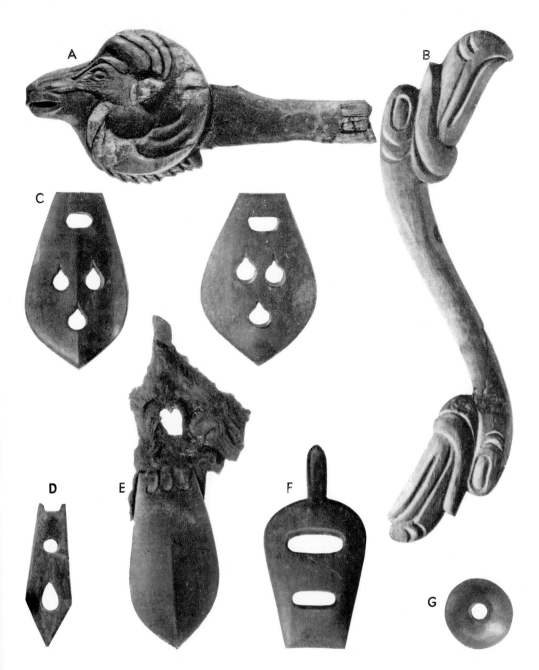

*94 Saddlery equipment and decoration from barrow
2 (c. 3/4).* A, ram's head carved on end of wooden
cheek-piece; B, cheek-piece with goose-head
terminals; C–E, horn saddle pendants; F, horn
buckle from girth-strap; G, horn saddle-strap
runner.

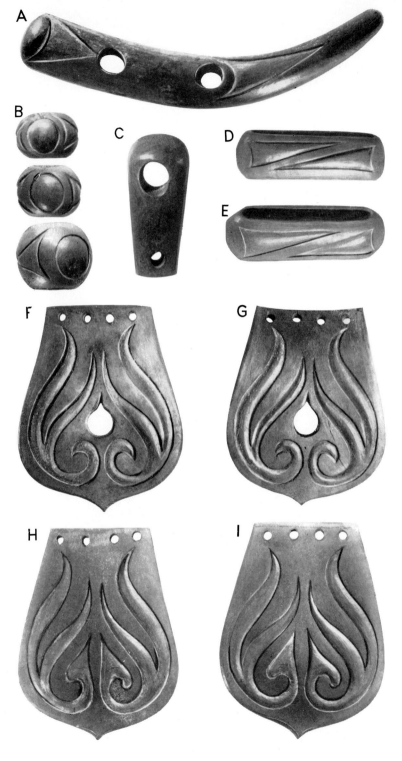

95 Collection of horn and antler saddlery accessories from barrow 3 (the incisions painted with red lacquer).
A, antler cheek-piece;
B, spheroidal runners;
C, reins slider block;
D, E, saddle-strap slides; F–I, saddle pendants (3/4).

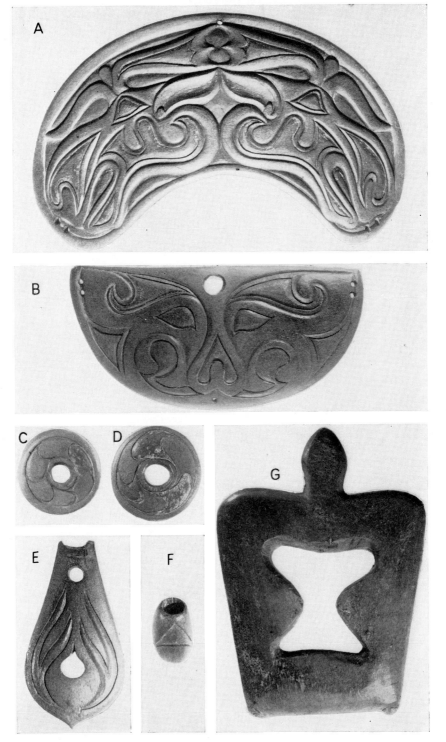

96 Collection of horn saddlery accessories from barrow 3 (incisions filled with red lacquer) (c. 3/4). A, facing of saddle arch showing elks' heads; B, semicircular plates on upper girth-strap showing a cat's head; C, D, saddle runners; E, saddle pendant; F, runner from throat-lash of bridle; G, girth-strap buckle.

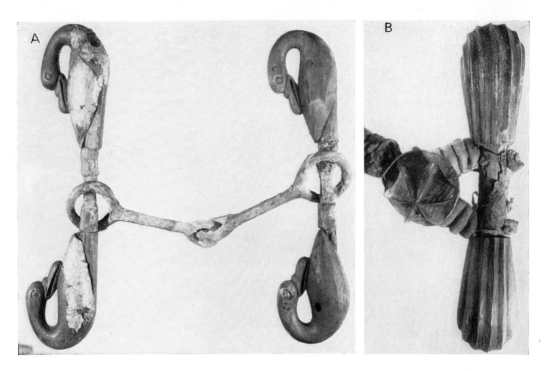

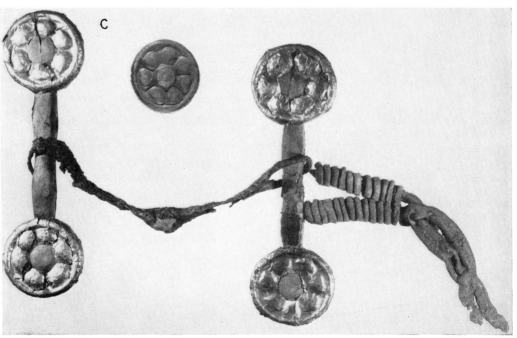

97 Bridles from barrow 3 (c. 1/2). A, bronze bit and cheek-pieces with swan terminals; B, wooden cheek-piece with carved 'paw' terminals; C, iron bit and cheek-pieces with rosette terminals.

98 Carved wooden saddlery decoration from barrow 3 (3/4). A, saddle pendant; B, frontal plate; C, toggle of buckle; D, rosette from bridle; E, mountain ram decorating bridle; F, runner shaped like horse's hoof; G, reins slider block; H, I, bridle pendants.

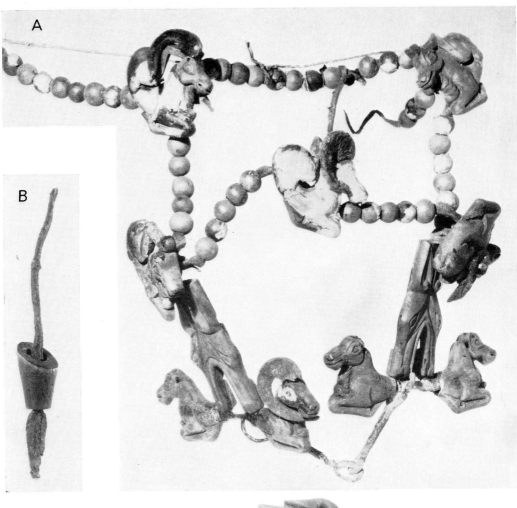

99 Bridle and decoration from barrow 3. A, bridle; B, runner from throat-lash; C, carved wooden mountain ram as bridle pendant; D, cheek-piece.

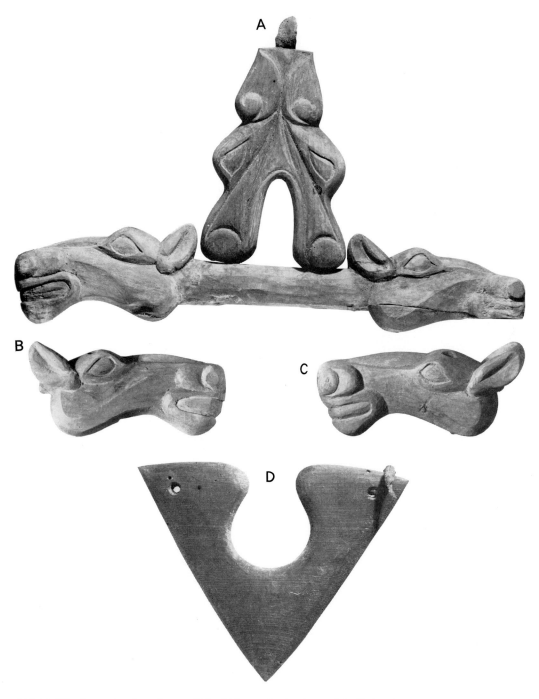

100 Bridle decoration from barrow 3 (c. 3/4). A, cheek-piece with elk-head terminals; B, C, elk-head pendants; D, frontal plate.

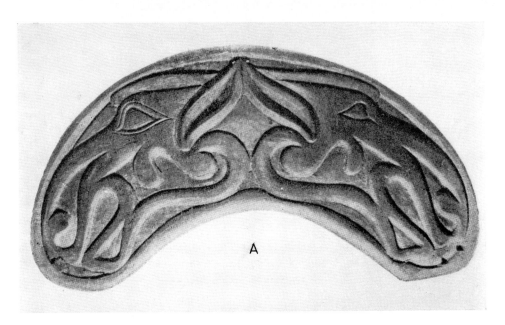

101 Excised wooden saddle decorations (cavities painted with cinnabar) from barrow 3 (3/4). A, saddle arch facing with elk heads; B, C, semicircular plaques with deer antlers; D, runner beads decorating breast- and crupper-straps.

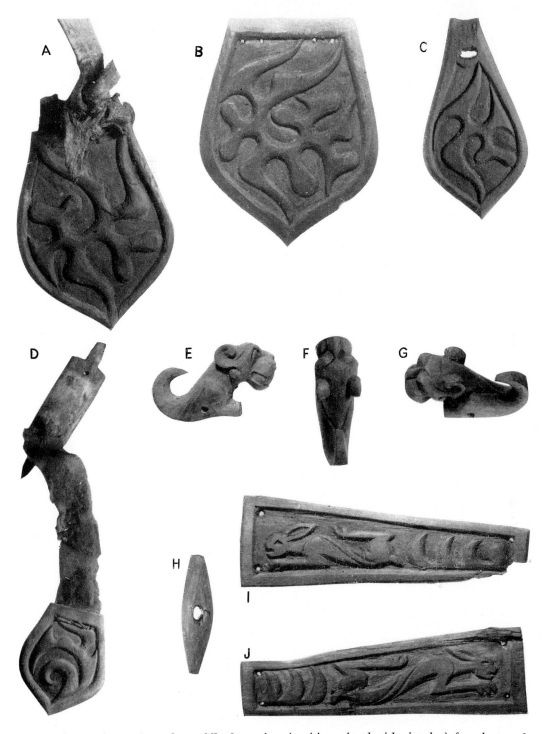

102 Excised and carved wooden saddle decorations (cavities painted with cinnabar) from barrow 3 (2/3 except D, 1/2). A–C, pendants with deer antlers; D, Saddle-strap pendant with deer antlers; E–G, carved 'lion cubs'; H, toggle from buckle; I, J, facing from crupper-strap with hares.

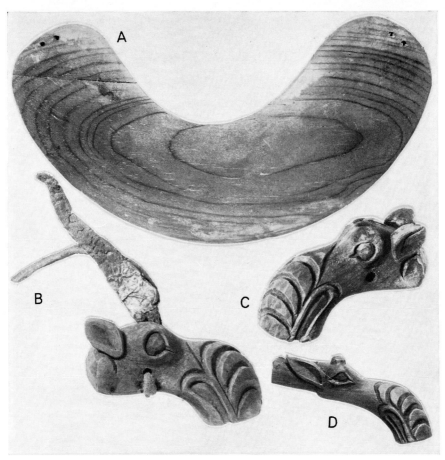

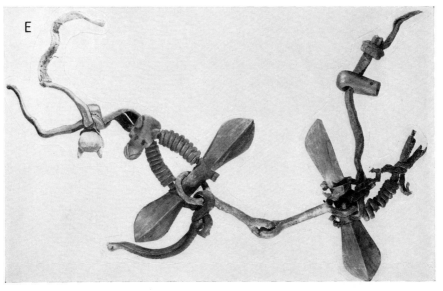

103 Wooden bridle
decoration from
barrow 3 (motif : head
of saiga antelope)
(A–D 3/4). A, frontal
plate; B, C, saiga
pendants; D, runner
in shape of saiga
head; E, lower part
of bridle.

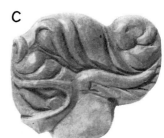

104 Set of carved wooden bridle and saddle decorations from barrow 3 (motif: horned lion's head) (3/4). A, cheek-piece with carved lion and griffin-head terminals; B, C, profile lion heads as bridle pendants; D, F, lion head, facing, as saddle pendants; E, rein slider; G, lion head, facing, as bridle pendant; H, wooden fork for bridle cheek-straps.

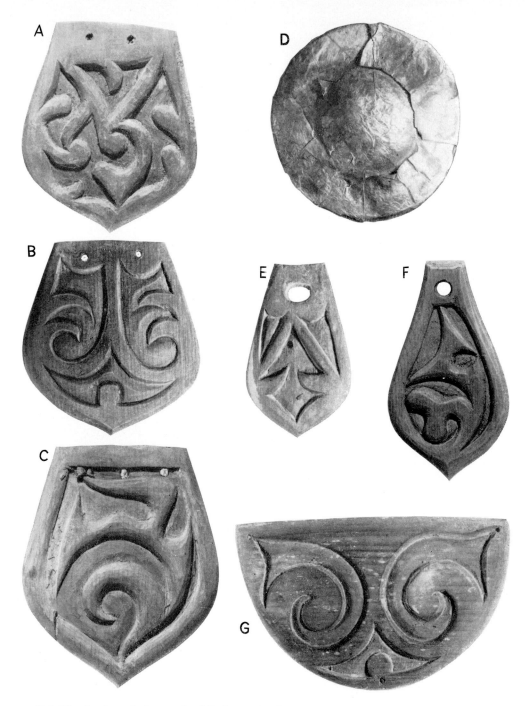

105 Wooden frontal plate and saddle decoration from barrow 3 (3/4). A–C, pendant plates to saddle-strap; D, frontal plate, gold plated; E, F, pendant plates from front saddle arches; G, semicircular plate from upper girth-strap.

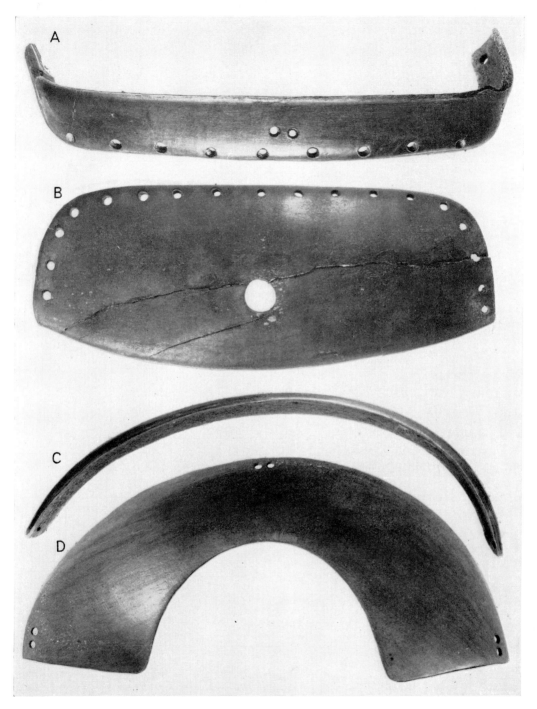

106 Horn facing with bows from saddle arches from barrow 3 (c. 2/3). A, B, bow and facing of trapezoidal shape; C, D, bow and facing of curved shape.

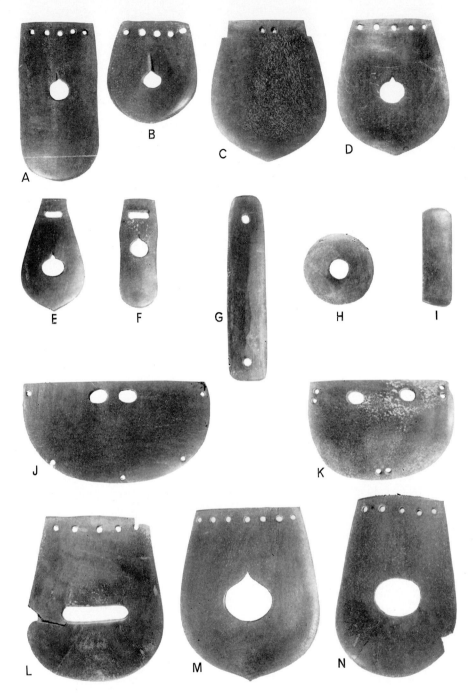

107 Horn saddle equipment and decoration from barrow 3 (1/2). A–D, terminal pendants of saddle-straps; E, F, pendants from front arch; G, saddle spacer (?); H, low conical runner; I, slide; J, K, semicircular facings from upper girth-strap; L–N, girth-strap pendants.

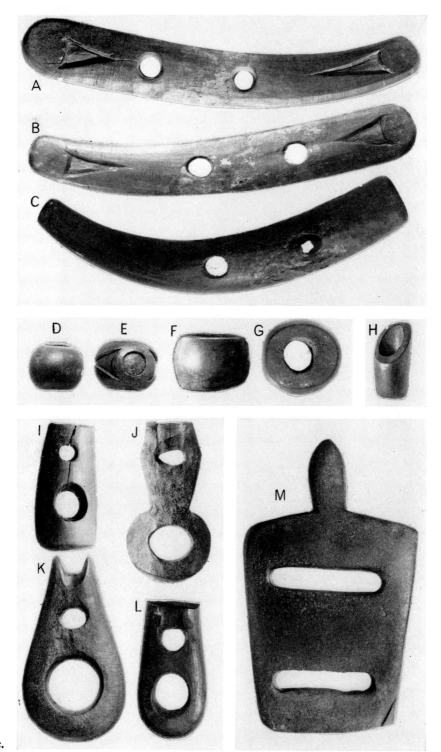

108 Horn saddlery accessories from barrow 4 (3/4). A–C, cheek-pieces; D–G, bridle-strap runners of spherical shape; H, runner from throat-lash; I–L, reins sliders; M, girth buckle.

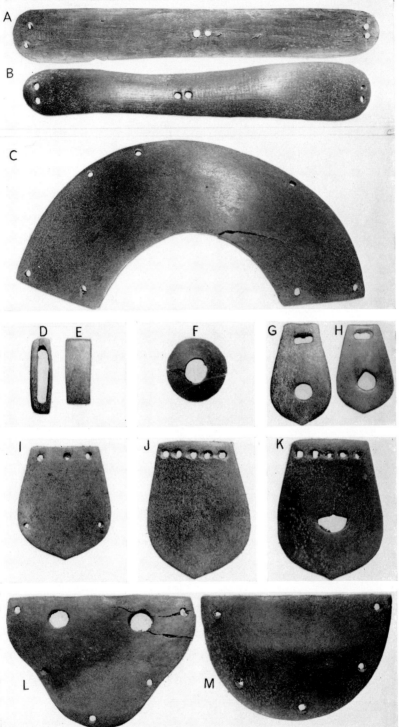

109 Horn saddle accessories from barrow 4 (2/3).
A, B, saddle arch cover bars
C, bow-shaped facing from saddle arch
D, E, slides
F, low conical runner
G, H, pendants to front saddle arch
I, J, K, saddle-strap terminal pendants
L–M, semicircular facings from upper girth-straps.

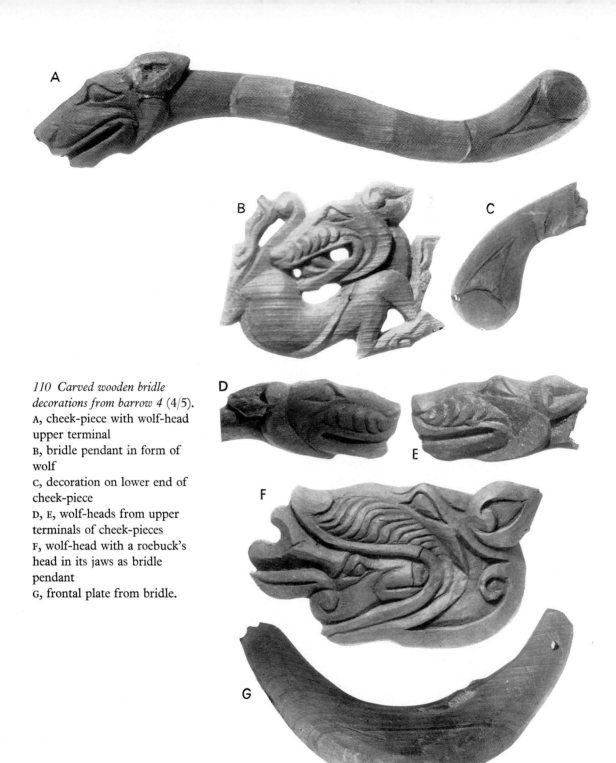

110 *Carved wooden bridle decorations from barrow 4 (4/5).*
A, cheek-piece with wolf-head upper terminal
B, bridle pendant in form of wolf
C, decoration on lower end of cheek-piece
D, E, wolf-heads from upper terminals of cheek-pieces
F, wolf-head with a roebuck's head in its jaws as bridle pendant
G, frontal plate from bridle.

111 Carved wooden bridle decoration from barrow 4 (7/8). A, triangle engraved on lower terminal of cheek-piece; B, cheek-piece with horned cat's-head upper terminal; C, feline head, upper terminal of cheek-piece; D, F, horned feline heads, facing, in medallion bridle-plates; E, G, cats as bridle plates.

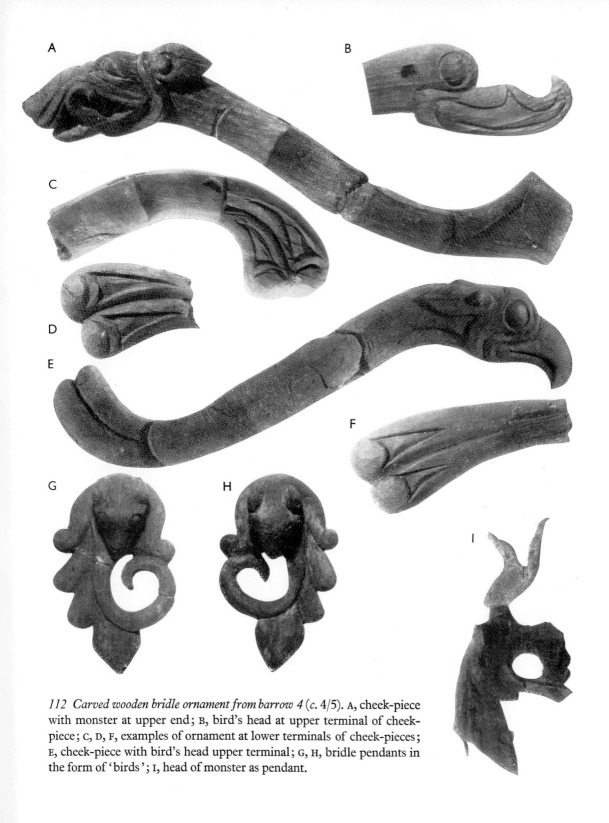

112 Carved wooden bridle ornament from barrow 4 (c. 4/5). A, cheek-piece with monster at upper end; B, bird's head at upper terminal of cheek-piece; C, D, F, examples of ornament at lower terminals of cheek-pieces; E, cheek-piece with bird's head upper terminal; G, H, bridle pendants in the form of 'birds'; I, head of monster as pendant.

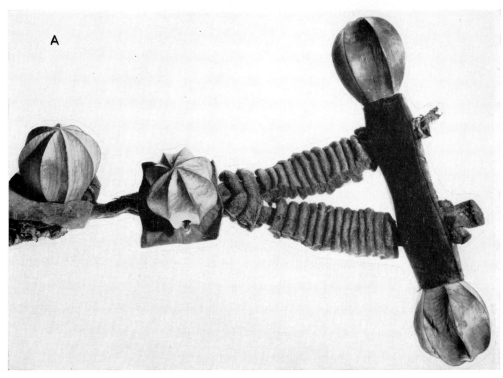

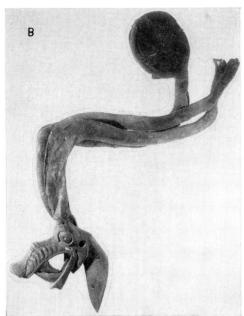

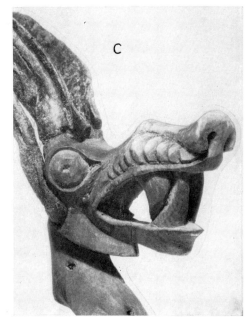

113 A, cheek-piece with cheek-strap from barrow 5 (*c.* 2/3); B, C, horse finial from barrow 4 (B, *c.* 1/2).

114 Bridle of second riding outfit from barrow 5.

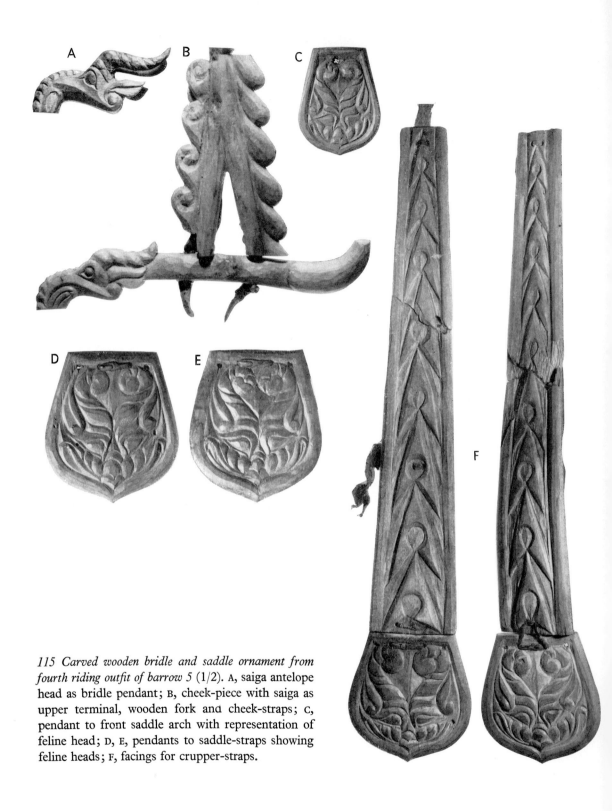

115 Carved wooden bridle and saddle ornament from fourth riding outfit of barrow 5 (1/2). A, saiga antelope head as bridle pendant; B, cheek-piece with saiga as upper terminal, wooden fork and cheek-straps; C, pendant to front saddle arch with representation of feline head; D, E, pendants to saddle-straps showing feline heads; F, facings for crupper-straps.

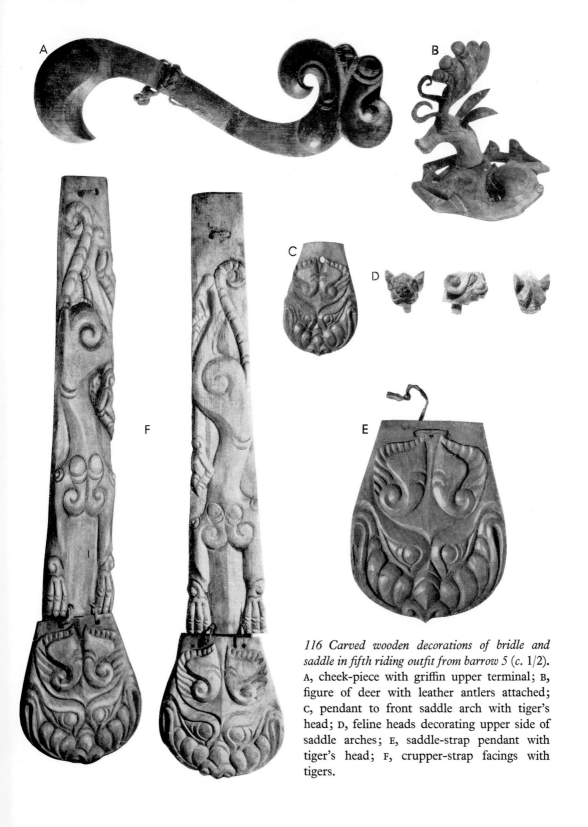

116 Carved wooden decorations of bridle and saddle in fifth riding outfit from barrow 5 (c. 1/2). A, cheek-piece with griffin upper terminal; B, figure of deer with leather antlers attached; C, pendant to front saddle arch with tiger's head; D, feline heads decorating upper side of saddle arches; E, saddle-strap pendant with tiger's head; F, crupper-strap facings with tigers.

A

D

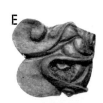

E

B

C

117 Carved wooden saddlery decoration from barrow 5 (2/3). A, cheek-piece with feline head as upper terminal and fork for cheek-straps in form of wolf's head; B, feline heads as bridle pendants, from third outfit; C, fork for cheek-straps in form of wolf's head, from fifth outfit; D, E, feline heads from straps of fifth outfit.

A

C

D

E

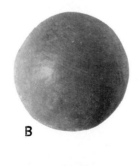

B

F

118 Harness decoration and saddlery from barrow 5 (2/3). A, carved wooden cheek-piece for draught horse; B, hemispherical wooden ornaments at terminal of cheek-piece for draught horse; C, wooden fork for cheek-straps from bridle for draught horse; D, wooden pendant to front arch of saddle; E, wooden pendant to girth-strap; F, one of the tines of a leather antler shaped as a bird's head.

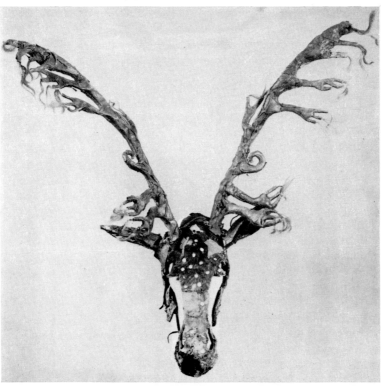

Horse masks from barrow 1.

119 Head-dress with finials in form of deer antlers.

120 Head-dress with crest in the
form of a horned lion-griffin head.

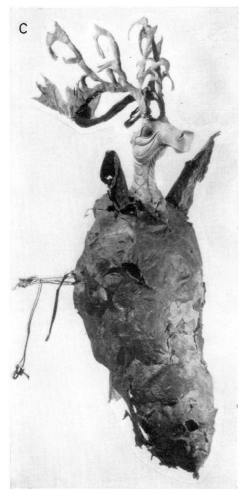

121 Horse head-dress. A, wooden head of fantastic bird, finial from barrow 3; B, carved wooden head of monstrous horned, fanged bird; crest from barrow 3; C, head mask from barrow 5 with deer's head finial shown in D; D, wooden deer's head with attached leather antlers.

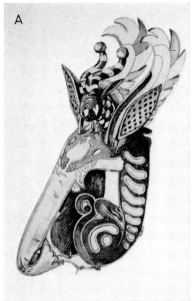

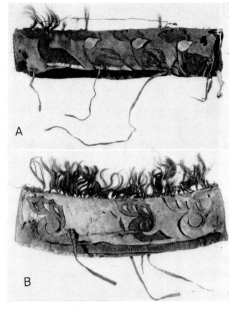

123 Mane-covers from barrow 1.

122 Horse head-dress. A, with crest, from barrow 1 (reconstructed). B, from barrow 2, with crest in the form of a mountain goat's or a ram's head with a bird sitting on its neck.

124 Leather sheath on a horse tail (A) and a whip (B) from barrow 1.

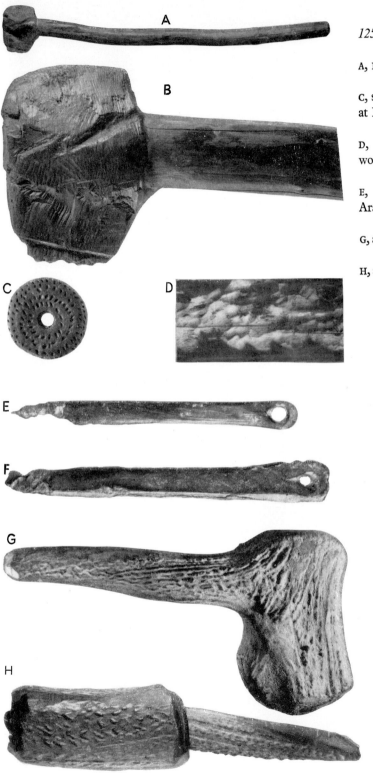

125 Various tools.

A, B, axe haft from barrow 1

C, spindle whorl from barrow at Biysk

D, plank face showing adze-work, from barrow 2

E, F, bronze knives from Aragol barrow

G, antler mallet from barrow 2

H, antler chisel from barrow 4.

126 Trolley wheels in barrow 3.

127 Wheel on its axle in barrow 5.

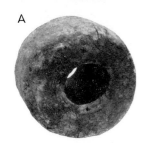
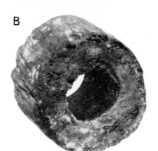

128 Trolley wheels: (A) barrow 2 (1/16); (B) barrow 3 (1/12).

129 Wheels of the carriage in barrow 5.

130 Primitive sled in barrow 5

131 Reconstruction of the carriage in barrow 5.

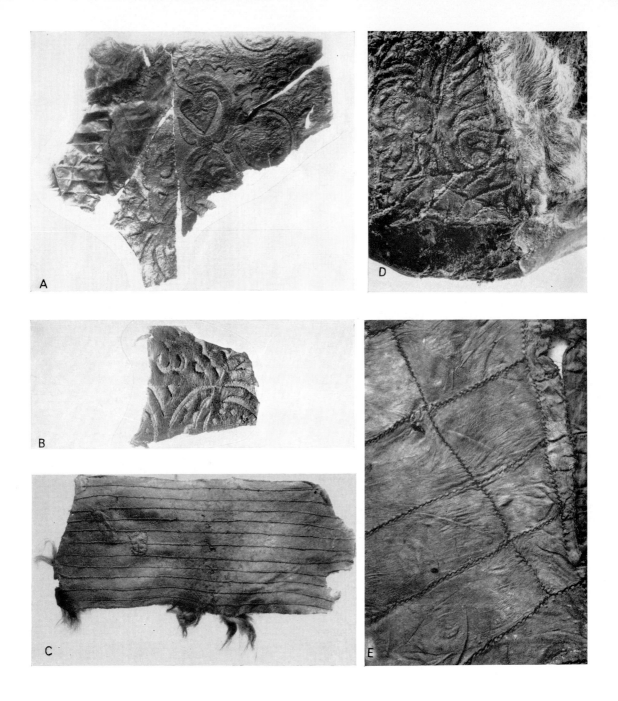

132 Examples of sewn leather decoration (3/5).
A–C, pieces of fur clothing from barrow 2; D, ornament on pouch from barrow 1; E, piece of fur clothing from Shibe barrow.

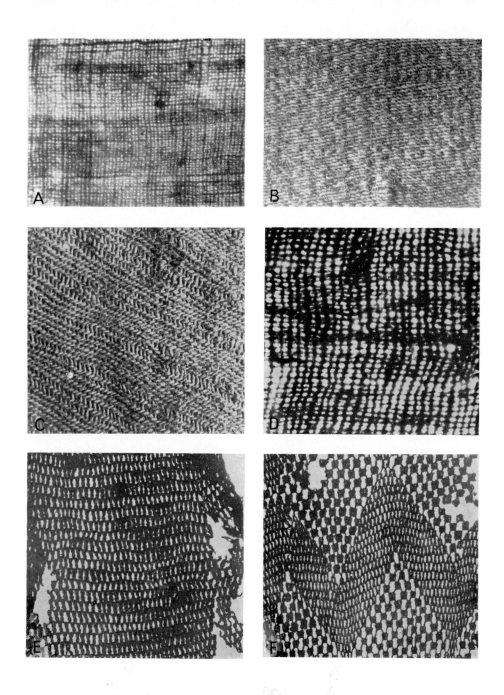

133 Examples of cloth from barrow 2 (× 2).
A, kendyr cloth of linen weave; B, C, woollen cloth of serge weave; D, woollen cloth of linen weave; E, woollen cloth of lace weave from inner cover of pigtail; F, woollen cloth of lace weave from outer cover of pigtail.

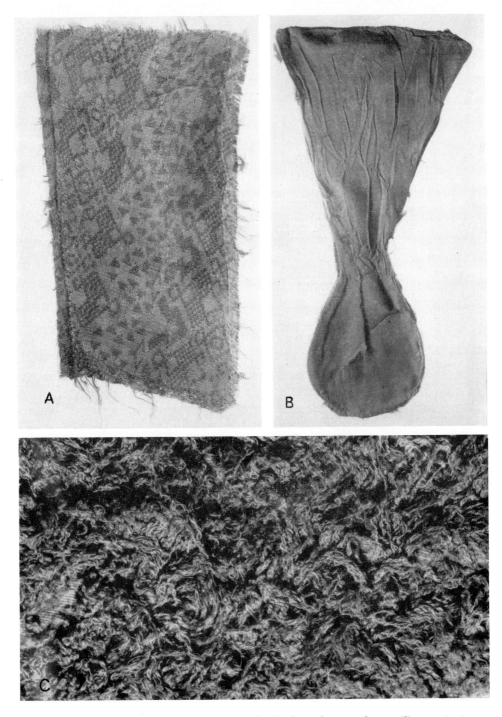

134 Examples of cloth. A, piece of patterned silk from barrow 3; B, silk pouch from barrow 3; C, piece of woollen cloth with whole pile loops, from barrow 2.

135 Saddle from second riding outfit in barrow 1.
A, extended view of top; B, side view.

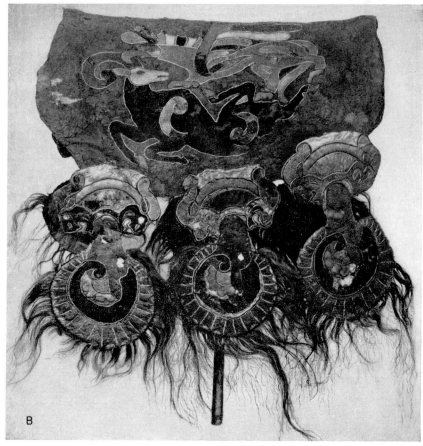

136 *Articles sculptured or carved in low relief (c. 3/4 except G).* A, lion's-head runner of antler from small Katanda barrow; B, bronze open-work belt buckle, deer seized by winged lion-griffin, from barrow near Biysk; C, wooden feline heads on terminals of bag handle from barrow 2; D, tiger's head of antler, runner from barrow at Biysk; E, F, saddle rods with feline head terminals, E from barrow 3, F from fifth riding outfit in barrow 5; G, wooden elk head with leather antlers, pendant from barrow 2; H, I, wooden griffin heads, H with leather ears; pendants from barrow 2; J, as G, without antlers.

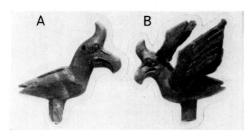

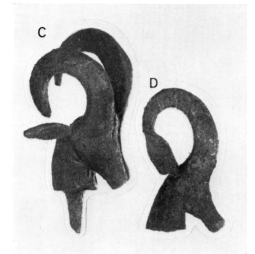

137 Wood and leather articles sculptured or carved in low relief (c. 2/3). A, B, wooden griffins from barrow 2, B with attached leather ears and wings; C, D, sculptured leather mountain goats' heads from barrow 1; E, cut-out leather elk from barrow 2; F, cut-out leather blackcock from barrow 2; G, H, carved wooden deer with attached leather antlers from barrow 2.

138 *Saddlery adornments* (3/5). A, feline head cut in a wooden medallion from the Frolov collection. B, wolf head from same collection; C, wolf head from the Pogodin collection; D, E, feline heads from the Frolov collection; F, G, cut-out leather human heads from barrow 1.

139 *Saddlery adornments.* ▷
A, horn bow of saddle arch from Shibe barrow (1/2); B–D, horn saddle adornments from Shibe barrow; E, part of a horn saddle arch facing from the Frolov collection; F, carved wooden head of feline from the Frolov collection; G, wooden tassel from Shibe barrow; H, I, saddle pendants from the Frolov collection; J, carved wooden medallion with cat's head from Shibe barrow; K, wooden facing of saddle arch from the Frolov collection; L, fragments of a leather cut-out composition (mountain goat in the claws of a griffin) from Pazyryk barrow 2.

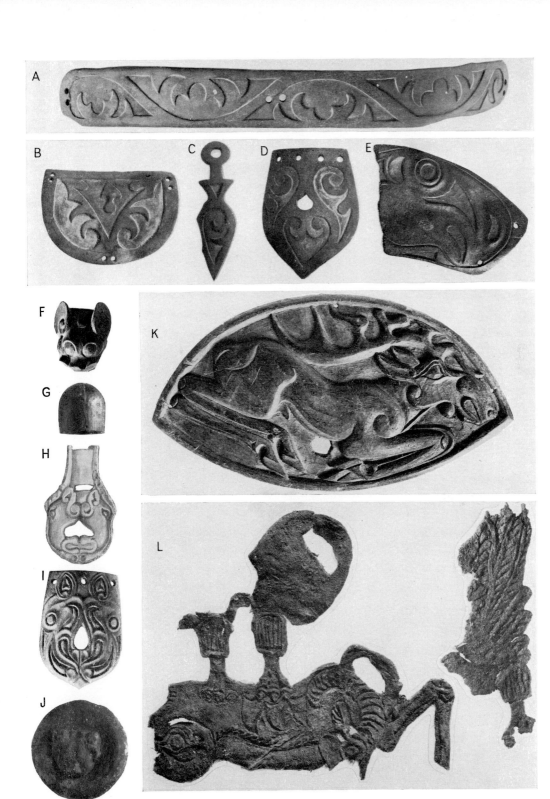

140 *Miscellaneous decoration* (1/2). A, horn saddle bow from the Uvarov collection; B, excised wooden belt-plate from Katanda barrow; C, carved wooden wolf's head from Katanda barrow; D, carved wooden goose from the Pogodin collection; E, excised wooden belt-plate from Katanda barrow showing struggling beasts; F, carved wooden monster from Katanda barrow; G, hemispherical wooden adornment from Katanda barrow showing struggling beasts; H, wooden disk with excised swans from the Pogodin collection.

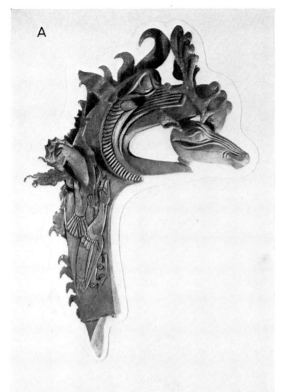

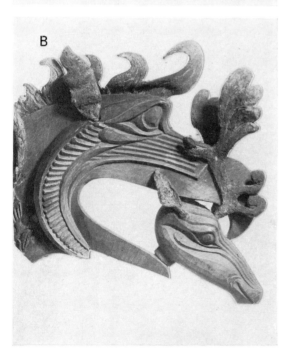

*141 Carved wooden crest from
barrow 2.* A, crest with deer's head
in griffin's beak; on the flat sides,
goose in a griffin's claws (1/3); B,
detail of a deer's head in griffin's
beak; C, detail of inserted griffin's
head at side; D, detail of incised
goose in griffin's claws.

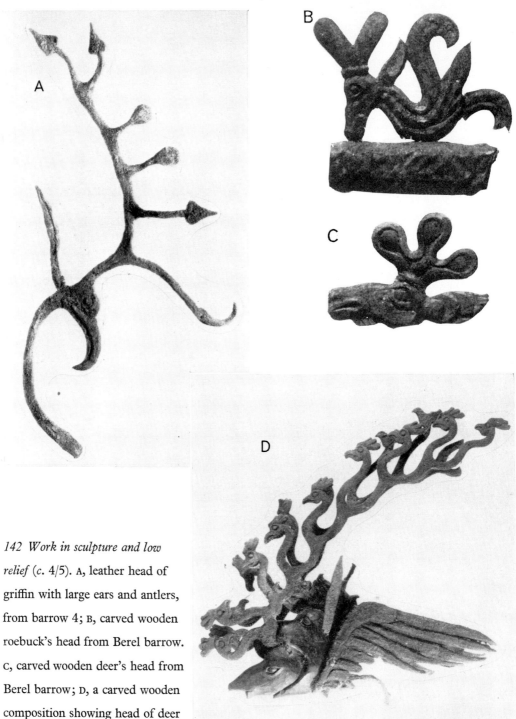

142 Work in sculpture and low relief (c. 4/5). A, leather head of griffin with large ears and antlers, from barrow 4; B, carved wooden roebuck's head from Berel barrow. C, carved wooden deer's head from Berel barrow; D, a carved wooden composition showing head of deer in beak of griffin, from barrow 2.

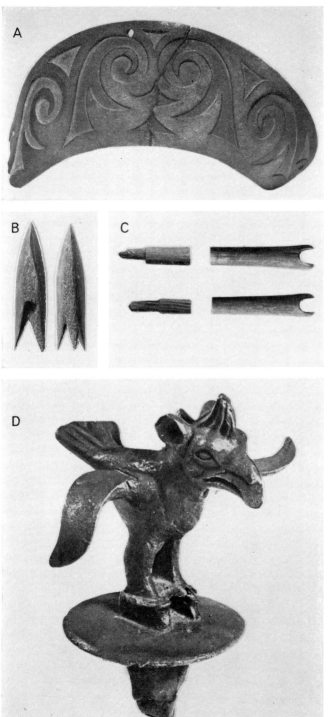

143 (2/3). A, excised horn facing for saddle arch from the Pogodin collection; B, antler arrow-heads from barrow 2; C, nocks on arrow shafts from barrow 3; D, cast copper griffin from Berel barrow; E, griffins on a frontal plate from Tuekta, barrow 1.

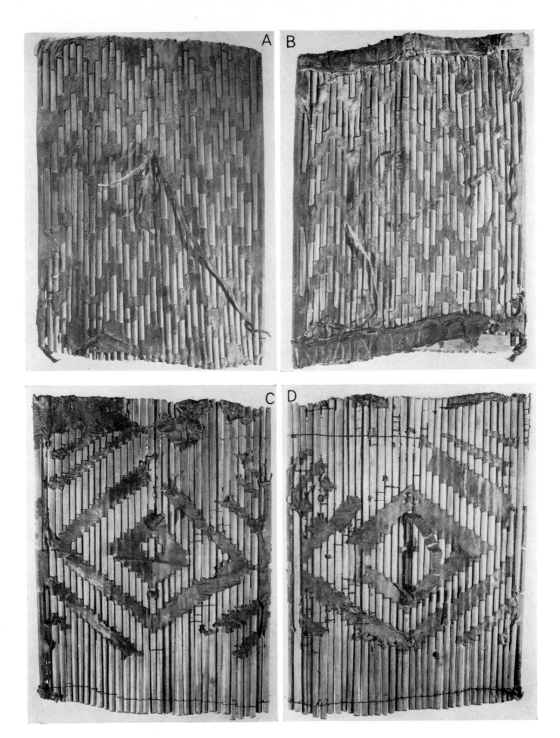

144 *Shields from barrow 1* (1/4).

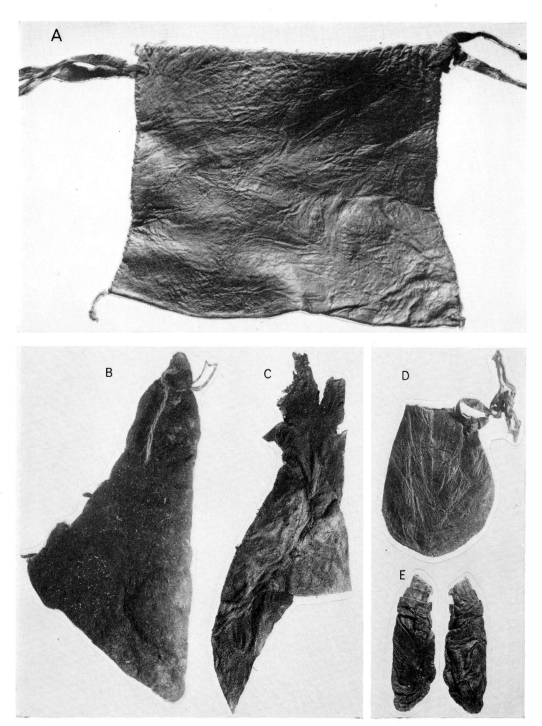

145 Amulets from barrow 2 (A, 1/1; B–E, 3/5). A, a rectangular piece of leather with human hairs sewn into it; B, piece of felt with human hairs sewn into it; C, triangular piece of leather into which has been sewn a purse containing human finger-nails; D, leather purse in which human finger-nails were found; E, the same prior to restoration.

146 Musical instrument from barrow 2; a kind of harp (1/6).

147 Large felt carpet or wall-hanging (4·5 × 6·5 m.) from barrow 5.

148 Decoration applied to felt carpets or wall-hangings. A, felt wall-hanging from barrow 1; B, border of felt carpet with lotus pattern from barrow 2; C, border of felt carpet from barrow 2.

149 Decoration applied to felt carpets or wall-hangings.
A, representation of a bird from piece of felt wall-hanging from barrow 5; B, border of felt wall-hanging from barrow 5.

150 (opposite) Examples of decoration of fur and leather.
A, leather flask covered by mosaic pattern, from barrow 1 B, pattern of fur and leather on a leather bag which contained cheese, from barrow 2 C, polychrome pattern in fur decorating woman's head-dress from barrow 2 D, corner of the border of man's caftan from barrow 2 E, blue fur with gold disks, probably from man's caftan, in barrow 2.

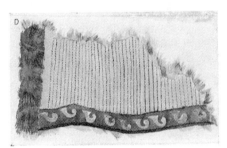

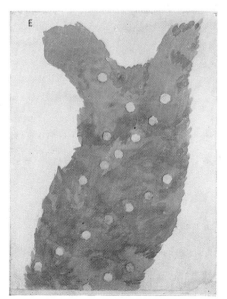

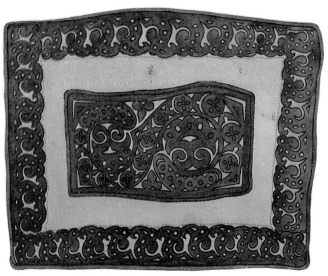

151 Examples of applied patterns.
A, back of man's caftan from
barrow 2; B, leather pouch the
outside of which is covered by
applied work, from barrow 2.

152 Examples of patterns. A, applied leather pattern on woman's dress from barrow 2;
B, leather flask covered with applied decoration, from barrow 2; C, cut-out decoration on
sole of woman's bootee in barrow 2.

153 *Examples of decoration.*
A, leather pouch with fur flap from barrow 2 (reconstructed)
B, applied felt pattern on upper border of man's stocking from barrow 2.

154 *Scene showing rider before a goddess seated on throne holding a branch in blossom; applied decoration on felt wall-hanging from barrow 5.*

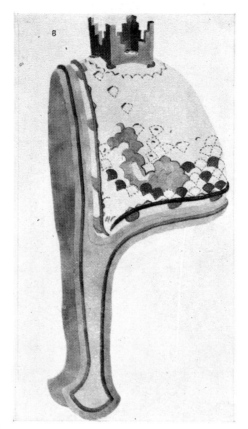

155 *Examples of dress.*
A, sleeve of man's
sable costume from
barrow 2
B, man's head-dress
from barrow 3
C, part of woman's
head-dress from
barrow 2 decorated
with rhomb pattern
of cut-out leather
against a background
of black colt's fur
D, woman's bootee
from barrow 2
(reconstructed).

*156 Outside of woman's apron covered with
applied leather patterns.*

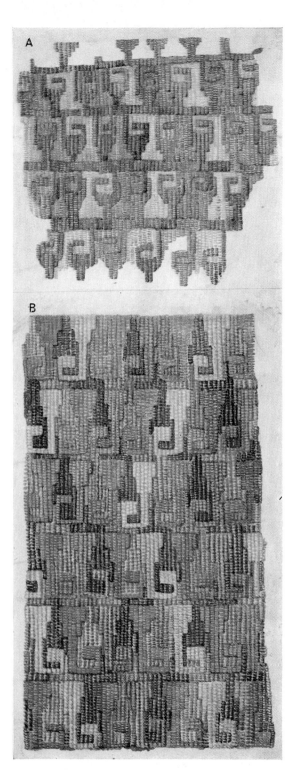

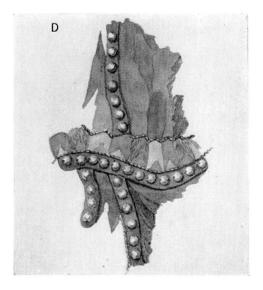

157 *Examples of cloth and fragments of dress*. A, B, examples of cloth of 'Palas' (Kilim) type from barrow 2; C, fragment of child's apron decorated with applied leather and gold, and gold saiga heads, from barrow 7; D, fragment of the same garment as in C.

158 Examples of beads and shells.

159 Horn bridle decoration from barrow 2. A, frontal plate; B, C, plates with lotus patterns.

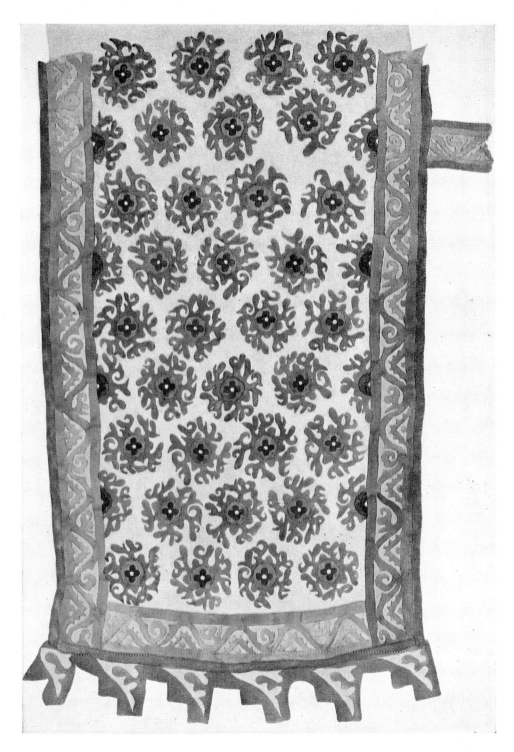

160 Decorated felt shabrack from barrow 5.

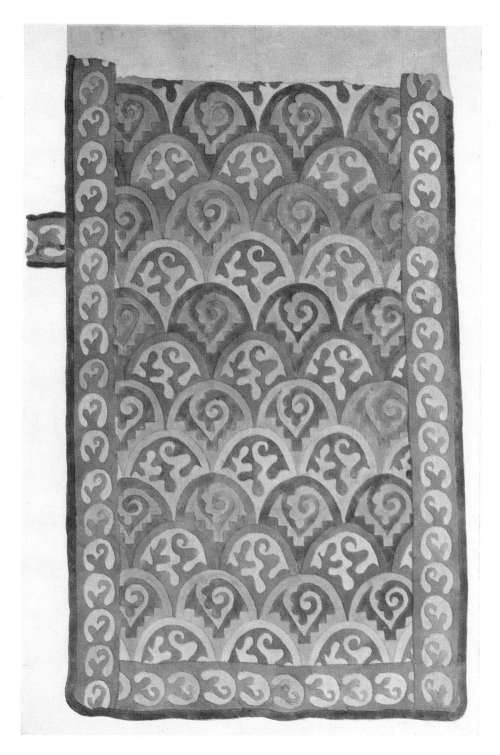

161 Decorated felt shabrack from barrow 5.

162 *Decorated felt shabrack from barrow 5.*

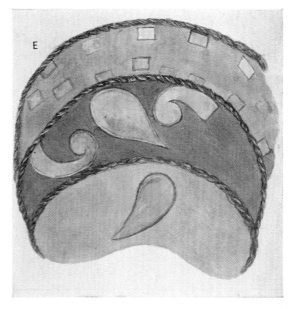

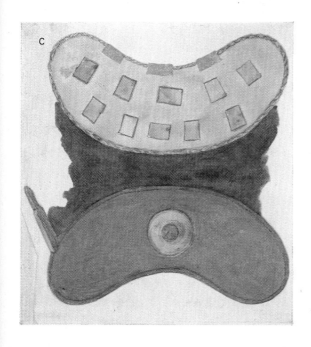

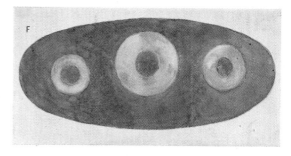

163 Decoration on saddle arches from barrow 3.

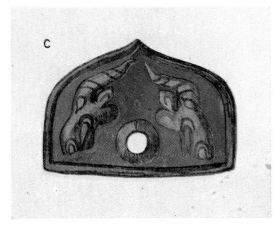

164 Leather cut-out decoration from a saddle in barrow 5. A, facing from upper edge of saddle arch;
B, facing from outside face of saddle arch; C, facing on upper girth-strap at point of attachment to
breast-strap; D, facing on lower end of upper girth-strap.

165 Decoration of saddle arches and whip handle. A, facing on outer surface of saddle arches from barrow 5; B, front and back ends of whip handle from barrow 2.

166 Sculptural figures of swans made from felt, decorating the
canopy cover of the carriage in barrow 5.

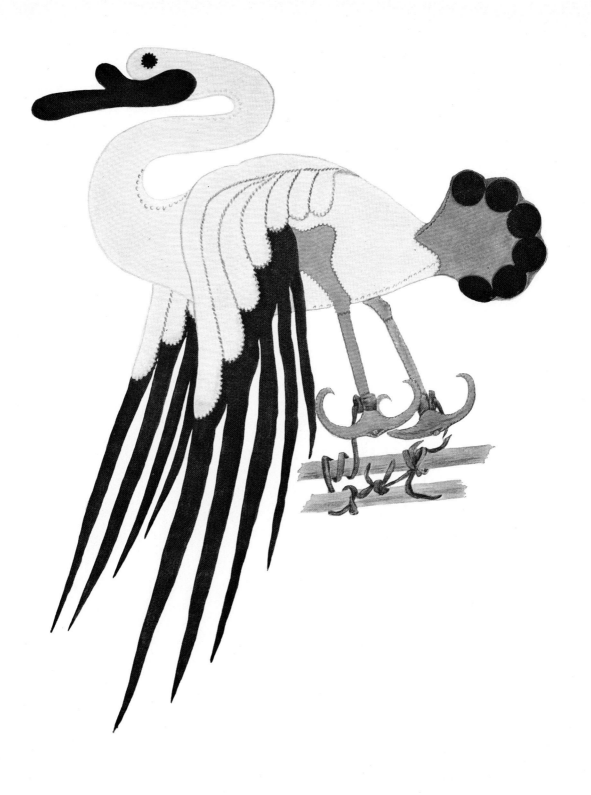

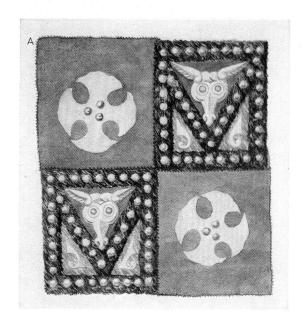

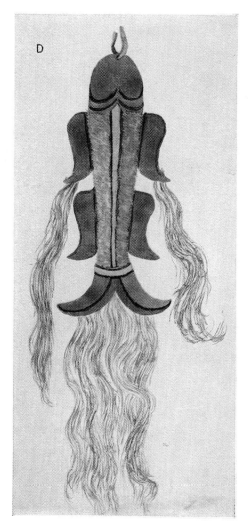

167 Decoration on saddlery. A, part of saddle-cover from barrow 5; B, griffin's head from horse crest in barrow 2; C, ram's head saddle-pendant from barrow 1; D, fish as a saddle-pendant from barrow 1.

168 Decoration from saddle-covers in barrow 2. A, elk in applied felt; B, eagle-griffin in applied felt.

170 Scene depicting eagle-griffin seizing a mountain goat; applied felt on saddle-cover in barrow 1.

169 (opposite) Decoration from saddle-covers.
A Scene of lion-griffin seizing a mountain goat; applied
felt on saddle-cover in barrow 1.
B Piece of applied felt from saddle-cover in barrow 2.

171 Ram's head between two horned lions' heads, saddle-pendant from barrow 1.

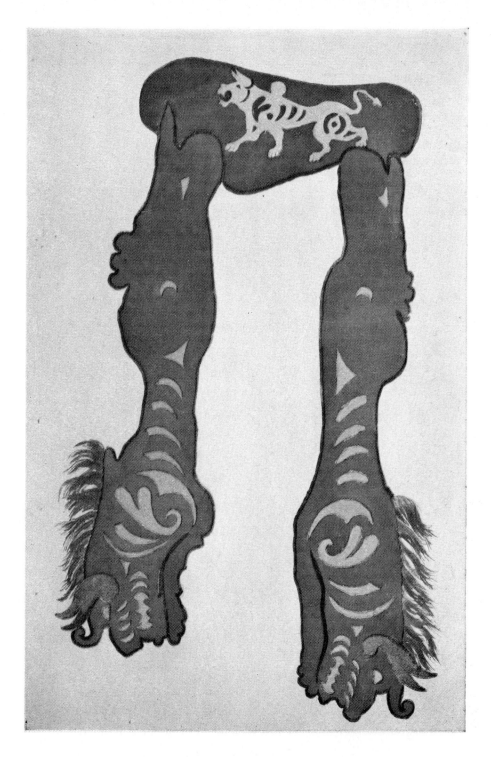

172 Representations of lions on saddle-pendants from barrow 1.

174 Pile woollen carpet from barrow 5.

*173 (opposite) A sphinx, a winged and antlered half-lion, half-human figure,
in applied felt on the felt wall-hanging
from barrow 5.*

175 Details of carpet in Pl. 174. A, Deer; B, Riders.

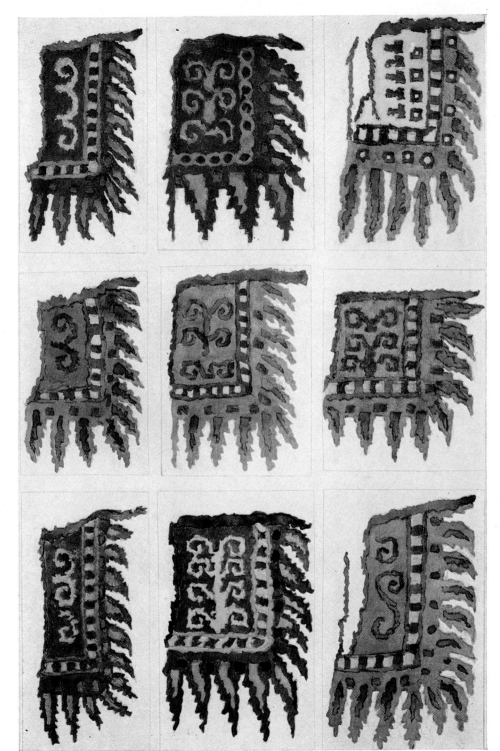

176 Rugs or shabracks depicted on the horses on the pile carpet from barrow 5 (here shown with the front at top).

177 *Examples of woollens from barrow 5.* A, part of a cloth band covering chest-piece of shabrack bearing figures of lions B, sample of cloth used for covering shabrack C, part of border of cloth shabrack showing women at prayer.

178 Example of embroidery on silk (tussore) material that covered a shabrack in barrow 5.

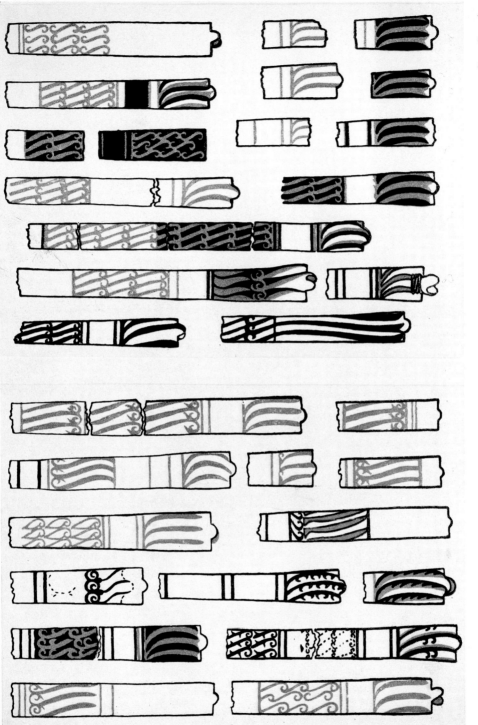

179 Decoration on arrow-shafts from barrow 3.

180 Decoration on arrow-shafts from barrow 3.